Coordinating the Internet

Coordinating the Internet

edited by Brian Kahin and James H. Keller

A Publication of the Harvard Information Infrastructure Project

The MIT Press, Cambridge, Massachusetts, and London, England

997 The President and Fellows of Harvard College

This book was printed and bound in the United States of America.

Library of Congress Cataloging-in-Publication Data

Coordinating the Internet / edited by Brian Kahin and James H. Keller.
      p.   cm. — (A Publication of the Harvard Information
Infrastructure Project)
    Includes index.
    ISBN 0-262-11230-2 (hc : alk. paper). — ISBN 0-262.61136-8 (pbk :
alk. paper)
    1. Internet (Computer network)   2. Telecommunication policy.
    3. Internet   (Computer network)—Management.   I. Kahin, Brian.
    II. Keller, James H.   III. Series.
TK5105.875.I57C666   1997
    384.33—dc21   97-13176
                                                                 CIP

Contents

Preface

The transition of the Internet from a U.S. government-funded project to commercial infrastructure has been incremental, but perceptions have changed dramatically. For years, the world saw the Internet as a creature of the U.S. Department of Defense. Now there are claims that the Internet is a self-governing organism controlled by no one and needing no oversight. For years, Americans thought that the Internet was free, paid for by the National Science Foundation (NSF) and other government research agencies. Now it is understood that the Internet is not free, but it is inexpensive and is typically paid for (at both institutional and individual levels) on a fixed-rate basis.

The U.S. government role in the global Internet *is* greatly diminished. Yet, through the Federal Networking Council, the NSF and the Defense Advanced Research Projects Agency continue to support and oversee critical administrative and coordinating functions, such as the allocation and assignment of network numbers. The management of the generic Top Level Domains—*.com*, *.org*, *.net*—still proceeds under a cooperative agreement between the National Science Foundation and Network Solutions, Inc., although it is supported by user fees.

Nonetheless, the Internet is remarkably decentralized and uninstitutionalized. Its future is not tied to any particular organization, although a number of different organizations play critical roles. As it grows in scope, bandwidth, and functionality, the Internet will require greater coordination, but it is not clear what kind of coordinating mechanisms and institutions will evolve. The goal of this volume is to try to clarify the needs, issues, and possible solutions related to these challenges.

Some coordination problems, such as settlements, may be addressed through bilateral agreements negotiated in the open market. Other problems, like network number and domain name management, seem to require a level of universal agreement— although it may still be possible to leave much of the allocation of numbers and names to the marketplace. The remarkable success of the Internet Engineering Task Force in developing consensual standards suggests that new, agile institutions may be needed.

Within the Internet community there is great skepticism that traditional international organizations are suited to the task. Indeed, it is doubtful that any one organization could span the range of issues that are in need of some degree of coordination. The questions addressed in this book range from intra-industry issues such as settlements and statistics collection to the sprawling problem of domain names, which affects the commercial interests of millions of companies around the world. Broader issues raise public policy questions that seem to demand at least the blessing of an international organization—such as the International Telecommunication Union (ITU) or the World Intellectual Property Organization (WIPO)—that represents national governments. The Internet Society, which is probably as representative of the Internet community as any organization can claim to be, has taken the lead on the domain name problem by involving the ITU and WIPO (and others) in setting up the International Ad Hoc Committee (IAHC).

If the domain name issues can be resolved, then anything is doable. Perhaps the IAHC is the harbinger of the sort of light and agile regulatory regime that might be right for the volatile and dynamic Internet. On the other hand, conventional needs, such as the collection of statistics, might be managed within a trade group like the Commercial Internet eXchange Association (CIX). The CIX was originally established to operate a settlement-free exchange facility. This fact seems to be an accident of history, as it now appears that Internet providers will establish financial settlements for interconnection and traffic exchange as a private matter in a competitive market.

Whether undertaken through an association or an ad hoc process, collective action faces some unique obstacles in the Internet environment:

• the U.S. government has played a stabilizing role in key coordinating functions, which has historically diminished the need for collective action;
• as in other new industries, stakeholders are focused on proprietary exploitation of new opportunities; and
• Internet providers face a host of extrinsic issues such as liability for copyright infringement and the threat of regulation that exert great demands on their collective attention.

Statistics and quality of service standards look like good ideas but pale beside these larger policy issues.

As noted above, the "largest" policy issue tackled in this book is the allocation and management of the Top Level Domain name space, and even that is dealt with from the limited perspective of short-term needs and tensions. Remarkably, despite the enormous value attributed to domain names, and increasing analogies to the problems of spectrum allocation, we found no economists tackling the issue.

In this project, we carefully avoided dealing with the many extrinsic issues facing the Internet industry around the world: content regulation, service regulation, taxation, liability for acts of users, jurisdictional problems, etc. These are tough, complicated issues that the Internet industry and community need to confront, preferably in a concerted manner. They are also on the agenda of the Harvard Information Infrastructure Project. However, we have sought to focus here on what we see as the first-order priority of establishing a stable, internationally based, legal and institutional foundation for the Internet upon which solutions to these higher-level problems can follow.

The issues addressed in this book arise from functions historically within the purview of U.S. federal research programs. Ironically, the subsidy and oversight provided by the U.S. government research agencies helped the open infrastructure of the Internet to grow unburdened by coordination costs and relatively free of the jockeying for control that is common for other technologies and platforms. They set the precedent and pattern of nonproprietary standards and open interconnection that still drive the growth of the Internet today. Yet all this happened outside the reach of U.S. policy development and regulatory agencies.

With the push to internationalize and partially privatize these functions, there is clearly a strong desire to maintain the balance of cooperation and competition that has worked so well for the Internet. It was in this spirit that Harvard, the Internet Society, the CIX, the ITU, and the National Science Foundation planned the project that has resulted in this volume. A workshop held at Harvard in September 1996 brought together key individuals and organizations within and beyond the Internet community. We hope that this book, which includes many papers prepared for the workshop, helps broaden understanding of the issues and move this agenda beyond the United States to the many other countries that now share a similar stake in the future of the Internet.

Like Internet technology, Internet administration and governance are now moving fast, and this book offers a snapshot taken at the end of 1996. We have also established a Web site at <http://ksgwww.harvard.edu/iip/cai/cisupp.html> as a living adjunct to the book, as well a link to supplementary materials, such as RFCs, available on the Internet. As part of our goal of fostering cooperation among diverse Internet interests, we solicit everyone's help in maintaining the Web site as a comprehensive virtual archive. We invite readers to provide feedback and suggestions to *iip@harvard.edu.*

Brian Kahin and James Keller
Information Infrastructure Project
Cambridge, Massachusetts
January 1997

Acknowledgments

To many who grew up with a libertarian view of the Internet, "Internet governance" may seem an oxymoron. Yet it has become evident that as the Internet has flowered as a core service in the global information infrastructure, competitive commercial interests, national sovereignty concerns, and differing institutional traditions for managing information assets around the world require some degree of consensus on the policies and institutional mechanisms that may be required to preserve the values traditional to it. The organizations and individuals who came together to create this book have initiated an important discussion on how that consensus might be reached and what its objectives should be.

This volume is the product of a collaboration among a number of institutions: the National Science Foundation (NSF), the Internet Society (ISOC), the Commercial Internet eXchange (CIX), the International Telecommunication Union (ITU), and the Information Infrastructure Project (IIP) at Harvard University. Each of these organizations has a substantial stake in the future of the Internet and its governance. The National Science Foundation is, along with the Defense Advanced Research Projects Agency (DARPA), the government agency most responsible for the Internet's creation and flowering. NSF also provided funding for the editing of this volume and for the September 1996 workshop in which the papers were debated. The membership of the Internet Society represents the broadest constituency internationally of the Internet. The CIX represents a cross section of enterprises that make the Internet available to U.S. users, and the ITU is the international institution most frequently cited as possibly playing a formal role in resolving transnational issues concerning Internet governance.

The work that led to this publication was guided by a Steering Committee comprised of Scott Bradner (Harvard University and ISOC), Kim Claffy (San Diego Supercomputer Center), Barbara Dooley (CIX), Don Heath (ISOC), Brian Kahin (Harvard), James Keller (Harvard), Mark Luker (NSF), Jeffrey Ritter (Ohio Supercomputer Center), and Bob Shaw (ITU).

For support of this and other work of the Harvard Science, Technology and Public Policy Program's Information Infrastructure Project, we are grateful to Hughes Telecommunication Corporation, Bellcore, ATT, and IBM, as well as the firms supporting the extension of this program to the international arena—Advanced Network and Services Corp., NYNEX, Motorola, and EDS.

We are especially indebted to Mary Albon for the copyediting, to Nora O'Neil who, faced with an aggressive publication schedule, kept this effort on track, and to Carrie Miller who assisted in a number of critical capacities, including management of our Web activities. Finally, our thanks are owed to the many practitioners and scholars who participated in the workshop and in other ways contributed to the policy debate whose outcome is so vitally important to the future health of the Internet in all its manifestations.

Lewis M. Branscomb
Aetna Professor in Public Policy
and Corporate Management, Emeritus

Glossary of Acronyms

ACM	Association for Computing Machinery
ACTA	America's Carrier Telecommunication Association
ALE	Address Lifetime Expectancy
APNG	Asia-Pacific Networking Group
APOPS	Asia-Pacific Operations SIG
ARPA	Advanced Research Projects Agency
AS	Autonomous System
ASCII	American Standard Character Information Interchange
ATM	Asynchronous Transfer Mode
AUP	Acceptable Use Policy
BGP	Border Gateway Protocol
BGP4	Border Gateway Protocol version 4
BMWG	Benchmarking Methodology Working Group
BOC	Bell Operating Company
BOF	Birds of a feather
CAIP	Canadian Association of Internet Providers
CCIRN	Coordinating Committee for Intercontinental Research Networking
CCITT	International Consultative Committee on Telegraph and Telephone
CCLC	Common Carrier Line Charge
CIDR	Classless Inter-Domain Routing
CIX	Commercial Internet eXchange
CMIP	Common Management Information Protocol

CNRI	Corporation for National Research Initiatives
CSU/DSU	Channel Service Unit/Data Service Unit
DARPA	Defense Advanced Research Projects Agency
DEC	Digital Equipment Corporation
DDD	Direct distance dialing
DNS	Domain Name System
DOD	Department of Defense (U.S.)
EC	European Community
ECJ	European Court of Justice
EGP	External Gateway Protocol
EOF	European Operators Forum
ETSI	European Telecommunications Standards Institute
EU	European Union
FARNET	Federation of American Research Networks
FDDI	Fiber Data Distributed Interface
FIX	Federal Internet Exchange
FNC	Federal Networking Council
GIX	Global Internet Exchange
GSMP	General Switched Management Protocol
HPCA	High-Performance Computing Act
HKIX	Hong Kong Internet Exchange
HTML	Hyper Text Markup Language
HTTP	Hyper Text Transport Protocol
IAB	Internet Architecture Board
IANA	Internet Assigned Numbers Authority
ICMP	Internet Control Message Protocol
IDDD	International direct distance dialing
IDNB	Internet Domain Names Board
IEEE	Institute of Electrical and Electronics Engineers
IESG	Internet Engineering Steering Group
IEFT	Internet Engineering Task Force
IFMP	Ipsilon Flow Management Protocol
IFRB	International Frequency Registration Board
INTA	International Trademark Association
IP	Internet Protocol
IPng	Next-generation Internet Protocol
IPPM	Internet Protocol Provider Metrics
IPv4	Internet Protocol version 4

IPv6	Internet Protocol version 6
IRR	Internet Routing Registry
ISDN	Integrated Services Digital Network
ISO	International Standards Organization
ISOC	Internet Society
ISP	Internet Service Provider
iTLD	international Top Level Domain
ITU	International Telecommunications Union
ITU-T	ITU Telecommunications Standardization Sector
IX	Internet Exchange
IXC	Inter-exchange Carrier
LAN	Local Area Network
LATA	Local Access and Transport Area
LEC	Local Exchange Carrier
LINX	London Internet Exchange
MAE	Metropolitan Area Ethernet
MAN	Metropolitan Area Network
MFS	Modification of Final Judgment
MIB	Management Information Base
MIX	Metropolitan Exchange Point
NANC	North American Numbering Council
NANOG	North American Network Operations Group
NANP	North American Numbering Plan
NANPA	North American Numbering Plan Administrator
NAP	Network Access Point
NASC	Number Administration Service Center
NAT	Network Address Translator
NIC	Network Information Center
NLANR	National Laboratory for Applied Network Research
NNTP	Network News Transport Protocol
NOI	Notice of Inquiry
NPA	Numbering plan area
NREN	National Research and Educational Network
NSF	National Science Foundation
NSI	Network Solutions, Inc.
NSP	Network Service Provider
NTIA	National Telecommunications and Information Agency

OECD	Organisation for Economic Co-operation and Development
OSI	Open Systems Interconnection
PBX	Private Branch Exchange
POP	Point of Presence
PICS	Platform for Internet Content Selection
PVC	Permanent Virtual Circuit
RBOC	Regional Bell Operating Company
RFC	Request for Comment
RIP	Routing Information Protocol
RIPE	Reseaux IP Europeens
RIR	Regional Internet Registry
RSVP	Resource Reservation Protocol
SAIC	Science Applications International Corporation
SCP	Service Control Point
SITA	Société Internationale de Télécommunications Aeronautiques - France
SMDS	Switched Multimegabit Data Source
SMS-800	Service Management System-800
SNA	Systems Network Architecture
SNMP	Simple Mail Transfer Protocol
SONET	Synchronous Optical Network
SVC	Switched Virtual Circuit
TCP/IP	Transmission Control Protocol/Internet Protocol
TIRCS	Trunk Inventory Routing Control System
TLD	Top Level Domain
TTL	Time to live
UNESCO	United Nations Educational, Scientific and Cultural Organisation
UPU	Universal Postal Union
URL	Universal Resource Location
USPTO	U.S. Patent and Trademark Office
VAN	Value Added Network
WAN	Wide Area Network
WATS	Wide Area Transmission Service
WIPO	World Intellectual Property Organization
WWW	World Wide Web
XIWT	Cross Industry Working Team

The Problem of Internet Governance

—

The Self-Governing Internet: Coordination by Design

Sharon Eisner Gillett and Mitchell Kapor

Introduction

If the Internet were an organization, how would we describe its management?

To answer this question, we first distinguish two extremes of management style: centralized and decentralized. In the centralized extreme, managers make their presence essential to most day-to-day functioning. Without their involvement, little information would be exchanged and few decisions would be made. Managers have lots of power, but they can never take a vacation.

In contrast, in the decentralized organization, managers create systems that allow their organizations to run without them most of the time. All routine events, constituting 99 percent of organizational life, are handled by members of the organization empowered by the system. The manager's roles are to set up the initial system, to integrate new activities into it as they emerge, and to deal with the one percent of truly exceptional events.

Contrary to its popular portrayal as total anarchy, the Internet is actually managed. It runs like a decentralized organization, but without a single person or organization filling the manager's role. The system that allows 99 percent of day-to-day operations to be coordinated without a central authority is embedded in the technical design of the Internet. The manager's job—handling the exceptional one percent—is performed by not one but several organizations.

As the size, international scope, and financial importance of the Internet continue to grow, Internet management is perceived to be coming under increasing pressure. Internet technology is called on to coordinate a system of unprecedented scale and complexity. The organizations that fill the Internet's managerial role today do so mostly as an accident of history, and the legitimacy of these arrangements is increasingly questioned. The intent of this volume is to identify the organizational and technical pressures in the coordination of today's Internet and discuss what changes may best relieve them.

Informed discussion of potential changes requires, however, that the decentralized organizational model of the Internet first be properly understood. It can be especially difficult to understand which coordination issues are handled by the 99 percent system, and which fall into the one percent category that truly requires managerial intervention. Without this understanding, there is a dangerous temptation to apply big hammers to coordination problems that are properly viewed as small nails. This risk is especially great for the many people who, because of the realities of exponential growth, have not grown up with the Internet (so to speak) but will help to chart its future. Although the Internet looks quite different from traditional communications infrastructures (such as the telephone system, and the mass media of print, radio, and television), there is a natural tendency to apply the better understood, more centralized mindset associated with these systems to the Internet's coordination problems.

The aim of this chapter is to provide context for the rest of the volume by giving participants a deeper understanding of the Internet's current coordination system. It begins by describing the decentralized nature of the Internet: how the 99 percent looks different from more traditional infrastructures, and the design of the underlying technical and cultural system for coordination. This system relies much more heavily on automation and loosely unified heterogeneity than on institutions and centrally dictated uniformity. By demonstrating the link between this approach and the Internet's success, we hope to give newcomers a gut-level trust in the power of the Internet's unusual organizational model. For old-timers, we offer a new, more socially oriented interpretation of what is already familiar technically.

Next the chapter lays out the one percent category, describing what the exceptional functions are, how they are managed today, and where the stresses lie in the current system.

Instead of proposing specific changes (a difficult job that we leave to those more directly involved in the process), the chapter concludes with a list of questions to ask about proposed changes. These questions are intended to determine how well each proposal enhances, or at least does not detract from, the Internet's distinguishing social, economic, and political properties—its highly valued openness, diversity, and dynamism.

Coordination of the 99 Percent: The Decentralized Nature of the Internet

The Internet is more decentralized than any of the communications systems that have come before it, including print, telephony, television, and the original model of an on-line information service. This decentralization is reflected both in the choices presented to users, and in the underlying structure that creates those choices. We first examine the user's view, then turn our attention to the scaffolding underneath.

The User's View

The closest approximation to the Internet's organizational model is the on-line service—America OnLine (AOL), CompuServe, Microsoft Network, and so on. Under pressure from the World Wide Web, these services have evolved considerably. Looking at the major changes to their business model helps bring out what is different about the Internet, as Table 1 illustrates.

The first difference is the most important: Who decides what content is made available? In the original on-line service, this choice is made by the service operator, who takes on the role of information "gatekeeper"—just like newspaper editors who decide which stories to run, publishing houses that decide which books to print, radio and TV executives who decide which programs to air, and cable TV operators who decide which channels to carry. The gatekeeper model contrasts with the decentralized World Wide Web, in which users themselves decide what information to make available—and correspondingly, what information to look at. Since users can, they do put their content on the Web. This decentralized decision-making has led both to the greater volume[1] of content available on the Web, and to its diverse span—for example, from amateur undergraduate home pages to professional content providers such as *The New York Times.*

The second difference is the choice of user interface. Using the original AOL service meant using AOL's software, period. Using the Internet, in contrast, leaves the user free to choose not only which software vendor, but which type of application to use.[2] As new services are invented (e.g., Internet telephony), the user is free to adopt them (or not). This open user choice is essential to the rapidly flowing stream of competitive innovations that have become so familiar in Internet software, from basic browser capabilities, to third-party plug-ins that add new media formats, to entirely new types of services.

The final difference in user choice concerns network plumbing. On-line services bundle information and communication services together, in contrast to the Internet's specialized, largely independent content and connectivity providers. On-line service customers miss out on the price and service competition that comes with the Internet's diverse array of access providers.

Why don't other communications systems offer as much user choice as the Internet? The reasons are both technical and social. Technical, because it is not easy to guarantee universal compatibility if each user is allowed to choose his or her own type of computer, communications software, and connectivity operator. Social, because the flip side of choice for the user is lack of control for the system operator. Had the Internet been designed as a for-profit system, such lack of control might not have been tolerated. Consider, for example, that as the business model has shifted from the original on-line service to the Web, control over the process of making content available has shifted from the on-line service operator to the content owner. This shift has not exactly been welcomed by on-line service providers, since it has put pressure on the revenues they receive from content owners.

Technically, what the Internet achieves sounds almost oxymoronic: decentralized interoperation. The Web emerged with many different organizations developing client (browser) and

Table 1 Web vs. Original On-line Service Model

Original on-line service model	Web-influenced on-line service model	Web model
Central information choice ("gatekeeper")	Personal Web pages Central choice of (professional) content providers	Anyone can provide content
Closed user interface (proprietary software)	Pre-selected third-party software, sometimes customized	Any Internet-compatible software
Connectivity bundled with content	Connectivity bundled with content	Anyone can provide connectivity, separately from content

server software, yet any browser can display any server's page.[3] A Macintosh user can exchange e-mail with a PC user, with neither user aware of the difference in machines. There are multitudes of Internet connectivity providers, and they simultaneously compete and exchange each other's traffic, using a wide variety of arrangements for physical interconnection and exchange of payments.[4] At the core of these unusual juxtapositions lies the Internet's design for interoperability—the defining principle that creates a unified Internet out of a collection of disparate networks and services. Interoperability is the system that allows 99 percent of the Internet to run without a manager. We now turn our attention to how this interoperability is achieved, looking first at protocols in general as a coordination tool, then at the open Internet protocols in particular.

Protocols: A Coordination Tool

In its ruling on the initial challenge to the Communications Decency Act, the U.S. District Court for the Eastern District of Pennsylvania included this explanation of the decentralized nature of the Internet:

No single entity—academic, corporate, governmental, or non-profit—administers the Internet. It exists and functions as a result of the fact that hundreds of thousands of separate operators of computers and computer networks independently decided to use common data transfer protocols to exchange communications and information with other computers (which in turn exchange communications and information with still other computers). There is no centralized storage location, control point, or communications channel for the Internet. . . .[5]

A *communications protocol* is a set of rules governing how computers exchange information with each other. The rules spell out how the data to be exchanged must be formatted and in what sequence any exchange of information must take place. For example, the interoperability of Web clients and servers that we remarked on above relies directly on two protocols: the Hypertext Markup Language (HTML), which specifies the format of documents to be exchanged, and the Hypertext Transfer Protocol (HTTP), which governs the order of conversations between browsers and servers. Indirectly, the Web's interoperability also stems from a number of other protocols, including the Internet Protocol and Transmission Control Protocol (together known as TCP/IP), that HTTP relies on for interoperable lower-level services.[6]

Protocols by their very nature constitute a coordination tool— exactly the kind of system that can automate the routine 99 percent of computer-to-computer interactions. But there is a catch. Protocols automate interoperability only if all computer operators agree to use the same ones. How can such uniformity be achieved without a central authority mandating the adoption of particular protocols?

The Internet Protocols: Open Standards

The Internet protocols became widely accepted standards in an unconventional way. Unlike the Open Systems Interconnect (OSI) protocols developed by the International Standards Organization (ISO), TCP/IP did not have the official imprimatur of an internationally recognized standards authority. Unlike commercial networking protocols developed contemporaneously, such as IBM's SNA, Digital's DECNET, and Xerox's XNS, they did not have the marketing resources of a large company behind them, nor was their design oriented toward any particular vendor's hardware. Instead, they were developed by researchers funded by the U.S.

government, and consequently made freely available to anyone who wanted to use them—in other words, they became *open standards*. They were developed in an iterative fashion and improved over time in a process that was not controlled by financial interest, leading to a free, quality product that people wanted to adopt. The seemingly ironic outcome of this process is that the free choices of millions of individuals led to much more universal adoption of the common Internet protocols than any of the other more centrally mandated alternatives.

Those who have recruited volunteers or raised funds will intuitively understand why this outcome is not really so ironic. People are most willing to contribute toward a collective goal or system when they do not feel coerced, when their participation is perceived to be in their individual interest, and when the requests made of them are small. Given that TCP/IP was free, solved real-world, cross-platform communication problems, and was readily available without needing to get anyone's permission, the decision to adopt it satisfied all of these criteria.[7]

Open standards are key to the Internet's juxtaposition of interoperability with distributed power and control. For example, anyone who wants to create a Web site can freely use the relevant document and network protocol formats (HTML and HTTP), secure in the knowledge that anyone who wants to look at their Web site will expect the same format. An open standard serves as a common intermediate language—a simplifying approach to the complex coordination problem of allowing anyone to communicate successfully with anyone else.

The common intermediate language approach is embedded in the fundamental design of the Internet. The researchers working on the Advanced Research Project Agency's internetworking program in the early 1970s faced a basic design decision: should they follow the model of the telephone system and tightly integrate multiple networks into a centrally managed system, or build a loose confederation of independently managed networks? The confederation approach they adopted met several needs. First, it recognized diversity: a network constructed out of noisy mobile radios has different technology and management needs than a fixed network of high-quality circuits.[8] Second, it recognized practical reality: existing networks represent administrative boundaries of control that are easier to respect than to cross. Finally, it avoided single points of failure to create a robust, survivable network.

Confederation is accomplished through the Internet Protocol (IP), an open standard designed to layer between the protocols (such as HTTP) that are specific to particular applications, and the technologies (such as Ethernet) that are specific to particular physical networks.[9] A small amount of Internet Protocol information is added to each network message, and used to deliver the message to destinations beyond the local network. The necessary processing is accomplished by special-purpose computers placed at the logical "edges" of networks and referred to as gateways or routers (labeled as "R" in Figure 1).

The separate router box represents the cost of confederation. Compared to integrating the functions of this box directly into a physical networking technology, a separate box is an inefficient approach.[10] Especially as computing price-performance has continually increased over the long term, however, the technical inefficiency of this design has turned out to be more than counterbalanced by its social benefits—for example, that it can be adopted without requiring users to replace their existing networks. We now look at these benefits. In the language of design, we are examining the *affordances* and *constraints* of IP. By affordances, we mean the characteristics of an object's use that are readily promoted by its design; by constraints, we mean the uses that the design makes difficult, if not impossible.[11]

Affordances of the Internet's Design

Re-use of Investment
Confederation means that if you already have a network connecting your internal computers, you do not have to replace it to connect to external computers. You just have to add a gateway and run IP on top of what you already have. Because the IP approach affords reuse of existing networks, existing investments are protected—leading, of course, to greater adoption.

Easy Change
The modular design of the Internet affords the evolution and adaptability that have been so critical to its long-term survival. This

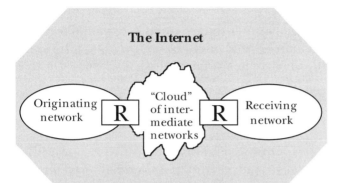

The Internet

Originating network

R

"Cloud" of inter-mediate networks

R

Receiving network

Figure 1   The Internet's Confederation Approach.

change is evident throughout all layers of the Internet. We start with physical layer examples and work our way up to applications.

Because IP is minimal and general-purpose, it has proven able to ride on top of an enormous diversity of networking technologies. Local Area Networks (LANs), for example, were not yet in use when IP was designed, yet IP worked over the very different types of physical networks that emerged as LANs became commonplace. As network technologies continue to evolve (e.g., Asynchronous Transfer Mode, or ATM), network engineers continue to adapt IP to them. The design of IP does not constrain the deployment of newer, faster, better, or cheaper physical networks. Without this property, the Internet could not have supported the growth rate that it has.

The Internet's modularity has even permitted IP itself to change (although not without the pain associated with changing something that has now been widely deployed). The layering built in to Internet protocols allows not just IP (and friends) but also other protocol stacks, such as ISO's OSI, to be used in the Internet. The same mechanisms that afford such multiprotocol support are being pressed into service to allow a transition to a new version of IP, needed to cope with the Internet's successful growth.

Finally, IP's generality affords the emergence of new applications. The Internet's designers did not really know what the network would be used for. Their best guess, that people would use it to access computing resources located elsewhere (i.e., remote login), was supplanted by the popularity of applications, such as electronic mail, that allow people to communicate with each other. Had they oriented the network toward remote login applications, the Internet would have turned out to be an interesting historical footnote. Instead, they created a general-purpose platform that enabled the emergence, nearly two decades later, of the graphical World Wide Web, catapulting the Internet into prime time.

Minimally Coercive Decision-making

IP's confederation approach achieves a collective system with a minimum of coercion. All the benefits of universal intercommunication can be had with only one decision forced on users: they must use the freely available IP somewhere in their protocol stack. All other choices are left to users.

Among these local choices are many that we are not used to seeing so widely distributed. Newcomers to the Internet are usually surprised to learn that no central body decides what applications or content will be developed, or assumes overall responsibility for the functioning of the Internet's constituent networks. We now look in more detail at each of these aspects of the Internet's decentralized decision-making. We start with the role choice that lets any user be an information or service provider, and move on to the operational choice that allows the Internet to function as a network of independently managed networks.

IP does not make any distinction between the users and providers of the Internet. If a computer runs IP, it can run any service that layers on top of IP. Higher-level protocols may distinguish—for example, a Web browser is a different software package from a Web server—but at the universal protocol layer, there is no distinction. Anyone whose computer runs IP can run either a Web browser or a Web server. In other words, anyone who is part of the Internet can function as either a user or a provider of Web services.

IP's egalitarian design affords choice to users over what role to play on the Internet. Do they want only to be a user, or do they want to provide networking, application, or content services to others? If they choose to provide new applications or content, which kind?

Putting these choices in the hands of individual users—instead of corporate or governmental gatekeepers—radically distinguishes the Internet from other communications media. It is much harder to imagine ordinary people creating their own cable TV programs than their own Web pages. Few companies have created new on-screen TV guides, but many have been able to create their own on-line search or indexing pages for the Web. Large telephone companies, fearing cannibalization of their existing businesses, were unlikely to develop Internet telephony products, but no such concerns hindered the startups that originated them instead.

More than any other affordance of the Internet's design, individual role choice has given the Internet its characteristic information abundance and diversity, as well as its entrepreneurial dynamism. Not surprisingly, it is also the aspect of the Internet's design that most threatens organizations accustomed to controlling the flow of information or the pace of innovation.

Individual choice also applies to the operators of Internet connectivity services. IP is deceptively simple: it defines a delivery service, known as datagrams or packets, and an identification scheme, known as IP addresses. What it does not define is just as important. One of the Internet's design goals was to create a system with no single points of total failure—components that, if disabled, would also disable the rest of the system. Making one network of the confederation into a special or privileged network would run counter to this principle. By not including features that would enable or force one network to control or manage another, IP embodies the assumption that networks will relate as peers. Thus, IP's design constrains the emergence of "chief" networks.[12]

Peer networking contrasts with the norm in more centrally oriented systems, such as the U.S. telephone network before full-fledged long-distance competition. AT&T's network was the king: if a caller wanted to use a different long-distance service, s/he was forced to dial extra digits. The dominant network was also the control network, and this assumption was so built in to the design of the system that leveling the competitive playing field required technical changes to remove the implicit default.

No such control network or implicit routing default is built into today's Internet. In fact, Internet routing is only one of many operational details that is controlled in a decentralized fashion by thousands of independent connectivity providers. For example, each provider independently decides:

- whether to enter the business in the first place;
- which other providers to interconnect with, whether bilaterally or through a multilateral exchange point;
- whether, on what basis, and how much to (try to) charge for any exchange of traffic (such charging is referrred to as "settlements");
- how much capacity to provide today and in the future;
- which user segments to target with what pricing scheme;
- what level of service quality to provide; and so on.

The result is a decentralized mesh of interconnection, with a wide variety of institutional arrangements and consumer choice in Internet access, and a dynamism that makes the industry exciting and innovative as well as bewildering.

Because they are selling the ability to communicate across a network, providers depend on each other for interconnectivity. In all other respects, however, they compete with each other just like providers of other services, from barbers to bankers. There is a tension inherent in this so-called "co-opetition." As in any industry, Internet connectivity operators vary not only in size, but in how well they execute different aspects of their business. The interdependence forced by interconnectivity means that lower-quality operators may detract from the service provided by higher-quality operators, while higher-quality operators may end up providing a free ride to others.

Looking at such tensions from a centralized mindset directs people to the conclusion that the connectivity industry will eventually consolidate into a centrally managed system.[13] The economies of scale that lead to consolidation, however, should not be confused with a need for centralized control. While the number of providers will likely decline, IP's constraint against "king" networks suggests that quality control may remain decentralized—for example, by providers agreeing to adhere to a common set of service quality standards. In other words, Internet connectivity might one day resemble the accounting industry, in which competing companies follow the same set of accounting rules, more than the telephone system in the days of Ma Bell. How such standards can be developed, especially given the challenges of today's commercial, international Internet, is discussed later in this volume.

An Open, Layered Platform

As the common intermediate language of the Internet, IP hides the details of the networks it confederates from the applications that run on top of them. From the application developer's perspective, IP replaces the real-world heterogeneity of networks with a virtual universal *platform*.

IP is a basic building block, intended to be supplemented by higher-level protocols more oriented toward the needs of particular applications. Application developers do not interface directly to IP, but to the layers above it. The higher the layer, the more specific the purpose of the protocol. For example, IP delivers packets with no reliability guarantees, and all Internet traffic uses it. TCP, which layers directly on top of IP, reliably delivers ordered streams of data; most, but not all, Internet traffic uses TCP. HTTP, which layers on top of TCP, delivers Web pages; all traffic between Web browsers and servers uses HTTP, but none of the traffic for non-Web services does. All of these protocols—IP, TCP, HTTP—are freely available, openly published standards, enabling any application developer not only to build on top of them, but to give away the resulting programs if they so choose.

The open, layered platform architecture means that a software engineer trying to develop an interoperable Web browser does not have to think about whether the software will run on Ethernet or ATM networks; s/he only needs to make sure it runs over IP and interoperates with the Web client at the other end. As a practical matter, the platform architecture greatly simplifies—and therefore expedites—the development of interoperable Internet applications.

By creating a business environment with unusually low barriers to entry, the platform architecture affords the specialization and rapid innovation that are so characteristic of the Internet. The general-purpose nature of IP means that many different applications—including those not yet invented—can layer on top of it. This layering leaves application developers free to concentrate on their portion of the problem, such as publishing documents (e.g., the Web) or managing messages (e.g., e-mail and news). Lower layers—with interfaces that are openly specified and freely available to all—take care of the rest. Since an entrepreneur with a new application idea does not have to first build a network to deliver it, more entrepreneurs can build more applications, creating more value from the network.[14] The open, layered platform thus affords faster, broader, and more competitive value creation than more conventional, vertically integrated communications systems.

The Culture of Interoperability

We have discussed how the Internet's technology affords its decentralized operation. But technology is only part of the picture. The other part is people. All the clever design in the world cannot create an interoperable system unless enough people hold interoperability as a shared goal. Interoperability is like Tinkerbell: it only works if everyone believes in it.

Where technology ends, cultural values begin as coordination mechanisms. Two deeply held cultural values make the collective Internet work. The first is that interoperability is sacrosanct—it is the defining characteristic of the Internet. The second is that to achieve interoperability, protocol implementations must be conservative in what they send and liberal in what they receive.[15]

The liberal/conservative rule is needed to deal with imperfection, incompetence and malice. Protocol specifications contain unintentional ambiguities, and their implementations may contain mistakes. By receiving liberally, implementations automatically become tolerant of the errors that are bound to occur in the open environment of the Internet. Instead of depending on centralized quality control or licensing of service providers to guarantee compatibility, errors are simply expected and, to the extent possible, gracefully dealt with.

This approach has worked in the Internet because so far errors have not been overly costly. As people and businesses come to depend on the Internet as critical infrastructure, the limits of this approach will certainly be tested.[16] This is one aspect of the Internet's decentralized organizational structure that we would not expect to be emulated in an environment in which mistakes could be extremely expensive or life-threatening. A malformed protocol header can be ignored, usually without grave consequences; a malformed voltage on a communications circuit, on the other hand, could end up sending 10,000 volts through a telephone repair person.

Liberal reception is also a way to deal with people who try to subvert interoperability. Because of interoperability, an application may be stuck with what it considers to be lowest-common-denominator services. A vendor may choose to unilaterally enhance some services, potentially sacrificing interoperability. But if receiving protocol implementations gracefully ignore new features that they cannot understand, interoperability can still be maintained. To illustrate with a hypothetical example: if vendors of Web servers each choose their own nonstandard ways of marking "all-singing, all-dancing" text in HTML, then a Web browser that ignores this format and simply displays plain text will still interoperate, while one that rejects the entire page will not.

Summary: Principles of the 99 Percent

In summary, day-to-day coordination of the Internet is informed by the following principles:

• *Value interoperability.* The success of the Internet depends on a shared belief in the importance of interoperability. Erosion of this belief could be the single biggest threat to the Internet's future. More widespread understanding of the importance of this shared value is therefore critical.

• *Automate coordination.* Use protocols whenever possible to automate interactions. Automate conformance monitoring and error handling as well.

• *Distribute power, control, initiative, and authority—but still interoperate.* The philosophy of IP is that minimally coercive collective systems work best. The art of IP is designing the right interface so that standardized interaction and local control can comfortably coexist.

• *Expect change.* Adapting to change is the norm. Build systems that will be flexible in the face of change, even though this approach has short-term costs.

Coordination of the 1 Percent: Internet Administration Today

The previous section explained how open standard protocols and the culture of interoperability automate the coordination of 99 percent of the Internet. Now we turn our attention to the exceptional one percent. Exceptions arise when protocols are not mature enough to fully automate what needs to be done, when reaching common agreement is part of the coordination process, and when resources have to be unique. In this section we first list the specific exceptions, then explain in more detail how each is managed today and where the stresses lie in the current system.

Routing. Each connectivity provider operates routing tables that direct traffic within the Internet. The data in these tables are based partly on the computations made by distributed routing algorithms, and partly on manually specified configurations. Errors in one provider's manual configurations can cause problems for traffic from other networks. The coordination problem is figuring out ways to either prevent or contain the damage from misconfiguration.

Service Quality Standards. As discussed above, these do not currently exist for the Internet. If they did, individual providers could characterize the level of service offered to users. To be useful, such standards would have to be commonly agreed to by all providers. Processes to secure such agreement lie outside the realm of automated coordination by protocol.

Protocol Standards. Similarly, protocol standards only work if they are universally agreed on. The processes by which Internet protocols are developed and standardized lie outside the day-to-day Internet coordination mechanisms.

Unique Identifiers. All communications systems need some way to uniquely identify their communicating entities. The telephone system uses telephone numbers. The postal system uses addresses. Each of these, when fully formed with country codes or names, uniquely differentiates every communicating entity in the world.

The Internet has two forms of unique identification for the computers connected to it. The first is the computer's IP address, a numeric identifier generally meaningful only to other computers. The second is its domain name, intended to be meaningful to people. The domain name *flowers.com*, for example, is much more memorable than 192.18.13.1, just as 1-800-FLOWERS is more memorable than 1-800-356-9377.

Because these identifying names and numbers have to be unique, their assignment has to be coordinated in some fashion. How that coordination should take place in the future is one of the key questions discussed in this volume.

Like addresses and names, protocol parameters have to be unique. Unlike addresses and names, though, these identifiers are purely internal to Internet technology (i.e., completely invisible to users). They include numbers that indicate which version of a protocol is in use, which higher-level protocol's data is being sent in an IP packet (e.g., the Transmission Control Protocol or the User Datagram Protocol), which type of program should process that packet on the receiving host (e.g., a file transfer server or a Web server), etc.

Now that we know what the different types of exceptions are, we are ready to examine in more detail how each is coordinated today, and what is perceived as wrong with the current system, if anything.

Routing

Controversy surrounds the question of whether routing configuration information is subject to sufficient quality control today. Each provider implements its own filtering and sanity check mechanisms. Developing a scalable, dynamic mechanism for performing quality control on routing configuration information is an open research problem. Further consideration of this issue is beyond the scope of this volume.

Service Quality Standards

These are not coordinated today, but would need to be developed by common agreement. When IP was commonly agreed to, the number of networks was very small. The challenge for quality metrics is to reach agreement in an environment with large numbers of commercial providers with vested financial interests in how quality gets defined. Since the provider base is international, enforcement of standards could also become an issue if it cannot be automated.

Protocol Standards

In the canon of Internet mythology, Internet protocols are developed by the Internet Engineering Task Force (IETF). This statement is true, but it is far from the whole story.

Certainly, the IETF plays a major role. It develops Internet protocols as well as standardizing what has already been developed elsewhere. But it would be wrong to think that the IETF has any kind of monopoly on the development of Internet standards. If a protocol is useful and made widely (usually freely) available, it can easily become a de facto Internet standard before being touched by the IETF—as the Web's protocols did. And nothing stops companies from inventing their own protocols and attempting to turn them into universal standards through marketing genius, instead of through the IETF (at least initially). This dynamic has been observed many times, for example in Sun's development of NFS and Netscape's enhancements to HTML.

Standards that affect the Internet are also developed in other fora, such as the ATM Forum, the World Wide Web Consortium, and so on. The IETF focuses less on physical communication and application-level standards, and more on the interoperability that sits in between: IP, the routing protocols that work with it, the domain naming utilities that translate names into IP addresses, the mappings between IP and different physical infrastructures (e.g., how to run IP over ATM, mobile networks, or dial-up lines), etc.

Nothing needs fixing about what we have described so far. To be sure, de facto standards setting is a less-than-perfect process. Internet telephony is a case in point: the first vendors kept their protocols proprietary and failed to make their software ubiquitous through some sort of give-away strategy. The predictable result: non-interoperable Internet telephony applications, inhibiting growth. This outcome is not stable, however, since the initial experiment proved the value of Internet telephony. Bigger players, such as Netscape, will add telephony functionality to their software, and better interoperability will emerge.

The bottom line is that even with de facto standards, the drive toward ubiquity is strong enough to keep interoperability a business requirement.[17] The alternative—of no de facto standards—is neither practical nor desirable. Much of the innovation and dynamism of the Internet results from just these kinds of experiments.

What is perceived as needing change is a small piece of this bigger picture. The IETF originated in the nonprofit, government-funded research community. Even as commercial interests have come to play much larger roles, the IETF still receives on the order of $0.5–1.5 million per year from the National Science Foundation (NSF) of the U.S. government.[18] This funding pays for the secretariat function—the staff and equipment needed to administer the IETF mailing lists, Web server, meeting arrangements, and so on—and keeps the meeting attendance fees to a nominal level. The open question, then, is how should this function be paid for if the U.S. government wants to get out of the Internet coordination business?

The amount of money involved is quite small by corporate standards, especially compared to the indirect corporate support for employee's time and travel that already goes into much IETF work. Even $1.5 million spread across the thousand or so people who attend each of the three IETF meetings per year comes out to only about $500 per meeting attendance. The IETF process has managed to preserve its highly valued open process even as indirect corporate support for its activities has increased. Presumably, the remaining expense is small enough that it too could be distributed in some fashion across attendees while still maintaining that openness.[19]

Protocol Parameters

From standards, we now turn our attention to numbers. We start with the numbers that are not controversial—the numeric identifiers internal to Internet protocols. These protocol parameter values are currently assigned by the Internet Assigned Numbers Authority (IANA). IANA is a virtual name that currently refers to a group of people who work at the University of Southern California's Information Sciences Institute (USC ISI) under the direction of Jon Postel. Their main function is networking research, and their existence is predominantly funded by U.S. government research grants. Their performance of this function is a product of history, not design. Postel picked up the role of number coordinator because it needed to be done when he was a graduate student involved in the birth of the ARPANET, and he never quit doing it.[20]

There is no current movement for this system to change as far as protocol parameters are concerned, and it is instructive to understand why not. First, protocol parameters are not perceived as scarce, so there are no political pressures involved. Second, they are an extremely low-volume operation. Assigning them takes more effort to discuss than to do, so tacking them on to network research is not unreasonable.

These characteristics are not expected to change for protocol parameters. IP addresses and domain names, though, are a different story. If they shared these characteristics with protocol parameters today, there would have been little impetus for this volume.

We treat addresses and names separately, since they have some very different attributes. IP addresses are meaningful to connectivity providers and have strong technical (i.e., routing) implications; domain names, on the other hand, are meaningful to users and have strong trademark (i.e., legal) implications. Since there are orders of magnitude more users than providers, domain names are potentially the more difficult issue.

IP Addresses

A user who wants to add a network to the Internet today experiences the following process for obtaining a guaranteed-unique IP address:

1. The user applies to his/her Internet connectivity provider for address space. Typically, the provider has a block of addresses from which it can make an assignment to fulfill the request.

2. These address blocks are allocated to providers by Regional Internet Registries (RIRs). Providers located in Europe apply to RIPE NCC; in the Asia-Pacific Region, APNIC; anywhere else in the world, the InterNIC. RIPE NCC and APNIC are service organizations operated and funded by a consortium of Internet connectivity providers in their respective regions. InterNIC is older than the

other two and, as an artifact of history, does things differently. It is operated by a private company currently known as SAIC Network Solutions. The InterNIC receives funding both from the U.S. government and from user fees that it assesses on commercial (*.com*) domain names, which it also manages.[21] To maintain reasonably consistent policies, the three regional registries coordinate intensively with each other, mostly on an ad hoc basis using e-mail.

3. Infrequently (every few months), IANA allocates large chunks of address space to the regional registries, to suballocate to providers as they see fit.[22]

What is potentially wrong with this picture? A few things:

• *Current Internet Protocol (version 4) addresses are perceived as scarce.* Based on extrapolation of past growth rates, the registries feel compelled to allocate remaining IPv4 address space conservatively. In addition, in an effort to simplify the Internet routing system, registries prefer to allocate larger contiguous blocks of addresses, which are of course less plentiful than smaller blocks. These policies together contribute to a perception of address space scarcity. Whether such conservation is actually creating hardship for providers and users does not appear to have been authoritatively researched; it should be. Clearly, though, the conservation policy puts the registries—organizations whose origins lie in the research community—into the unfamiliar and uncomfortable position of having to weigh competing commercial claims. As David Randy Conrad describes the situation:

The current mechanisms by which addresses are allocated fundamentally [rely] on trust. The allocation authorities must trust the requesters to provide an accurate and honest assessment of their requirements in order for appropriate amounts of address space to be allocated and the requesters must trust the allocation authorities to be fair and even handed. In the past, this trust-based model was both efficient and effective as, by and large, there were no particular constraints on the amount of address space which might be allocated and the community requesting the space was more academically oriented than commercially reliant on obtaining those resources. However, with the rapid ascendancy of commercial networks on the Internet, the trust model for resource allocation is under severe pressure.[23]

It is also unclear how much conservation is truly necessary. Only a small fraction of the already allocated space is actually utilized.[24] A new version of the Internet Protocol, IPv6, has been standardized with a much larger address space, although of course no one can predict when (if ever) it will become widely deployed. In addition, several technologies are emerging to make more efficient use of IP address space, whether version 4 or version 6.[25] The bottom line is that uncertainty in the future growth rate combines with uncertain user adoption of technical changes to make it impossible to predict whether there are enough IPv4 addresses to satisfy demand.

• *The ultimate authority, and therefore chain of appeal, is not clear.* If a user or provider is not happy with the allocation received, to whom should s/he appeal? Conrad describes three possible answers to the question of who has ultimate authority for IP address allocation, and different communities that view different answers as correct. His three models beautifully illustrate the problem with IANA's historical authority: it may not survive challenges to its legitimacy. After considering whether IANA's authority derives from the U.S. government, the Internet Society, or Internet connectivity providers, he writes of the latter option:

This model works as long as the ISPs [Internet Service Providers] and the IANA/RIRs [Regional Internet Registries] can cooperate. Should the historical cooperation between these two sets of organizations break down, the ISPs, again working in concert, could conceivably create an 'Anti-NIC' allocating new addresses from the unused pool without regard to IANA/RIR policies.[26]

In other words, IANA's authority depends on how close Jon Postel comes to performing this role with the wisdom of King Solomon.

• *The U.S. government is still funding the InterNIC.* This creates two problems. First, the National Science Foundation would like to get out of the Internet coordination business. Second, long-term government funding is well known to have a "sugar daddy" effect on efficiency incentives for its recipients; why strive for greater efficiency when that might make next year's funding levels go down? The incentives look better in the provider consortium funding models of RIPE NCC and APNIC, since the providers can always create a new consortium to take their business elsewhere if enough of them are not happy with the registry's performance. The provider consortium model appears to work well for these regions. Before rushing to adopt it for the InterNIC, however, we note two observations. First, RIPE NCC and APNIC have been well represented and heard from at the various workshops convened to discussed Internet coordination, but less has been heard from their customers, whose perspective might be different. (We are not trying to say that it is, only that it might be, and that this possibility should be checked.) Second, RIPE NCC and APNIC currently deal with fewer providers than InterNIC; what works for 20 or 200 might not necessarily work for 2,000, or when the disparities in scale among the provider population are quite large. The latter factor could make a provider consortium into a playing field that is anything but level. A consortium may turn out to be the best solution, but we should at least be aware of its potential problems.

• *Address allocation is technically nontrivial.* The continued exponential growth of the Internet puts intense pressures on the routing and addressing systems. There are now many constraints on which addresses can be allocated and still be universally routable.[27] Providers that operate across multiple regions complicate the picture further. The bottom line is that successful address allocation requires administrators with strong technical skills, not just political or legal expertise.

Domain Names

Naming is technically simpler than addressing, but it is much more visible and meaningful to users, creating even more stresses on the current system of name assignment.

From the user's perspective, getting a domain name looks much like getting an IP address: most users apply through their Internet connectivity provider. Beyond that, though, domain names look different. Unlike IP addresses, domain names are not part of a finite space, and providers do not have a chunk of them to allocate. Instead, users request names that are meaningful to them, and providers forward their requests to the appropriate Internet naming registry.[28]

There are many such registries, each with responsibility for different Top Level Domains (TLDs). The TLD is the name after the last dot; it may be national (such as *.au*, for Australia) or international in scope (an iTLD), such as *.com*, *.edu*, *.net*, and *.org*. The appropriate registry to apply to depends on which of these TLDs the user wants a name in.

National domains are administered specifically to each country, for example by a university, a national telephone company, or a branch of the government. According to Jon Postel, he is the person who approves or denies the infrequent requests from organizations wishing to manage a country's name space. Generally, he grants the request to whoever applies first.[29] He uses the ISO country code list to determine what is a country, sparing him from entering the realm of international geopolitics.

Each registry sets its own policies. For example, in Australia an entity has to be a registered corporation to get a name in *.com.au*. The InterNIC, which administers the iTLDs *.com*, *.edu*, *.net*, and *.org* for the whole world, imposes no such restriction on the *.com* domain. (RIPE NCC and APNIC do not administer any TLDs, although they do forward requests to the appropriate registries. They also run backup name servers for their regions.)

Fortunately for the InterNIC, the Domain Name System (DNS) is hierarchical. Once a TLD is given out (e.g., *mit.edu*), it is up to the recipient to manage it further. Since most of the changes to the name space happen at these lower levels, most of DNS is effectively self-administered.

Still, the runaway growth of the *.com* domain has put intense pressure on the InterNIC. In the fall of 1995, the InterNIC began charging an annual fee of $50 to maintain *.com* registrations, in order to supplement NSF funding that had been allocated based on a much smaller Internet. This action sparked much protest in the Internet community. Ignoring the inevitable complaints from people accustomed to receiving free service as a guest of Uncle Sam, the gist of the protest was that the InterNIC was in a monopoly position with respect to commercial domain name assignments, and was perceived as acting like a monopolist by providing poor service for excessive fees.

Since monopolies are generally considered to be bad things, especially by the Internet community, we have found it instructive to ask why the InterNIC ended up in this position. The answer is partly technical and partly historical. DNS is implemented as a distributed and replicated database, logically organized in a hierarchical fashion. Translating the name *foo.mit.edu* into an IP address may involve as many as three name servers: a root (or ".") server, a TLD server for *.edu* and an MIT-operated server containing the address of *foo* in *mit.edu*. Each name server gets its data from a "zone" file, which is maintained centrally but replicated to all the servers at the same level in the hierarchy. Thus the InterNIC's monopoly on commercial name registrations arises from it being the only organization that makes changes to the *.com* zone file, and from the implicit agreement among lower-level server operators to point only to servers supplied by this file.

Today's technology could, however, allow multiple organizations to cooperatively maintain a single file if they want to, or to create more commercial TLDs beyond *.com*. But *.com* is contentious for reasons that go beyond the InterNIC's monopoly, and these have slowed the process of change by engendering a broader debate about what changes to make.

• *Domain name space is flatter than real-world identifiers.* This problem is often stated as "the good names are all taken." For example, in the physical world, there can be multiple entities named Acme—Acme Research, Acme Computer, Acme Explosives, Ltd., and Acme Explosives, Inc. But on the Internet there can only be one *acme.com*. When Acme Explosives, Inc., finds that Acme Computer got there first, it can sue for trademark infringement, try to buy out the name, or become *acme-explosives.com*—assuming, of course, that Acme Explosives, Ltd., did not get that one first, in which case it could sue, buy out, or pick something yet longer . . . and so on. Since shorter names are easier to guess, remember, type, and fit on a business card, being forced to lengthen your name is not perceived as a good thing.

• *Domain names conflict with trademarks.* Some names are trademarked, and the trademark owners expect the legal protections they experience in the physical world to extend to the electronic world. To these users, who got a domain name first is irrelevant if the use of that name is perceived as violating a trademark that they wish to protect.

- *As with IP address allocation, the ultimate authority for domain name assignment, and therefore the chain of appeal, is murky.* The authority of registries to decide who gets which name was not conferred in the ways people usually think of as legitimate, such as through legislation or treaties. When authority arises as an accident of history, and its exercise has financial implications, lawsuits are bound to occur. When they do, there is significant uncertainty about whom to sue and in what venue. This problem is especially acute for disputes involving iTLDs. If, for example, the parties disputing the name and/or the InterNIC are in separate countries, redress may be hampered by the very real limits of the international legal system.

Evaluating Proposals for Change

Having described how the Internet is coordinated today, we now propose a series of questions to ask about suggested changes. These questions are based on our analysis of the factors that have made the Internet's unconventional organizational model perform well in some ways but poorly in others. Internet old-timers may find that the factors are familiar, but that in some cases we offer a different interpretation of their application to the current situation.

Does the Proposed Change Create Abundance, Instead of Just Managing Scarcity?

Scarcity is a key characteristic that distinguishes administrative from political processes. If there is enough pie to go around, people focus on whether the process for giving out pieces is efficient. If there is not enough pie, then they ask whether the allocation process is fair. For example, it is a political process to decide who can attend MIT, but an administrative one to hand out an identification card to each person who ends up attending. Plenty of groups will challenge the former process, but few will challenge the latter.

Before we undertake the design of political processes or institutions to manage scarce resources, we should first ask ourselves whether the resources really have to be scarce. If they do not, a less controversial technical or administrative solution may be much easier to design and implement.

We base this question on our observation of events surrounding the NSFNET transition, when the Internet went from having a default backbone network managed by the U.S. National Science Foundation (NSFNET) to a mesh of networks with no default. Around the time of this transition (spring 1995), economists predicted that for the Internet to remain usable once the government subsidy was removed, long-haul Internet bandwidth would have to be allocated more efficiently.[30] Bandwidth allocation has not changed, however, and although the Internet certainly has points of congestion today, long-haul bandwidth is rarely among them.[31] Instead, more bandwidth has become available to meet the demand. Long-distance telecommunications is now a competitive industry, at least in the United States. As long as no fundamental limits are being hit, capacity tends to emerge in response to revenue opportunities such as new Internet traffic. A similar dynamic is currently under way in the construction of new interconnection points.

For this dynamic to apply to other Internet coordination problems, the relevant resources must not be hitting fundamental limits. Domain names clearly fall into this category: serious barriers to expansion of the name space are social, not technical. The IETF process has produced many proposals for change, but few (if any) have been implemented because of the perceived need for consensus, which is highly valued but notoriously slow to achieve. After circulating for close to a year, Internet Drafts in this debate appear to be gradually heading toward a consensus for the creation of new TLDs, a step in the right direction.

A recent development that deserves mention is an experimental effort, in the spirit of the Internet's "anyone can" philosophy, to simply add a new TLD, *.biz*, to an extended root nameserver, and try to get connectivity providers to point their DNS servers at it.[32] This bottom-up approach can create problems: if your network provider does not point to the extended database, you will not be able to send e-mail to *foo@bar.biz*.[33] But if this approach catches on, it has the positive potential to broaden the name space rapidly.

As discussed above, it is less clear how close we are to reaching fundamental limits to the IP address space. We should be cautious about introducing new allocation mechanisms predicated on a scarcity that is more a matter of debate than fact. If more than anecdotal research reveals that current allocation mechanisms are truly harming providers and users, then we should at least be careful to make any new allocation mechanisms as temporary and narrowly limited in scope as possible, while we focus energy on using new technologies to extend the address space. The worst outcome would be to institutionalize an allocation process that stays in use long after the rationale for it has disappeared.

Are Functionality and Authority Distributed?

Technically, the history of Internet coordination is a story of increasing decentralization, afforded by the development of distributed algorithms robust enough to work on a large scale under hostile, real-world conditions, and their modular insertion into the operational Internet. For example, the Domain Name System was introduced in 1983 as follows:

Currently hosts in the ARPA Internet are registered with the Network Information Center (NIC) and listed in a global table (available as the file <NETINFO>HOSTS.TXT on the SRI-NIC host). The size of this table, and especially the frequency of updates to the table are near the limit of manageability. What is needed is a distributed database that performs the same function, and hence avoids the problems caused by a centralized database.[34]

DNS has come a long way since 1983, but it has not yet hit the limits of decentralization.

The ultimate in decentralization is to put users in control. On the Web, for example, users decide what content to make available. What if they could also participate in a distributed database that would let them decide their domain name in an automated fashion, instead of having to register it through a centralized authority?

Control that is fully distributed to users is not always practical or desirable, as in the case of Internet routing.[35] But what is practical changes over time, and it is better to consider and reject the possibility of user control for a good reason than not to think of it at all.

Adopting a decentralized mindset may also bring out intermediate scenarios that would otherwise not come to mind. For example, what if there were multiple name registries? The ad hoc, e-mail based coordination of the InterNIC, RIPE NCC, and APNIC on IP address allocation policies demonstrates that multiple organizations can successfully share authority. We need not always seek a single institution in which to vest authority. In fact, given the international nature of the Internet, authority is more likely to be workably legitimate if it is distributed. For example, allocations of country-based domain names, which are administered by locally selected authorities according to locally determined policies, have been much less controversial than allocation of names in the international domains.

We should also avoid the temptation to seek a single authority for both naming and addressing. They are different problems, and may be best taken care of by different organizational and technical approaches.

At the CIX/ISOC Internet Infrastructure Workshop held in February 1996, one of the participants argued that operation of DNS registries is fundamentally different from Internet connectivity: it needs a chartering (read: licensing) process and cannot be done by just "anyone with a PC and three modems." This statement may be true, but before accepting it, we would first ask, "Why not?" Operating Internet routing appears much more complex than registering domain names, and it is fully distributed among connectivity providers.[36] If tighter control is seen as essential to DNS reliability, then at the least the gain in reliability should be weighed against the creativity and innovation lost by not widely distributing power.

How Well Does the Proposed Change Afford Technical Evolution?

Ever since journalists began to notice the Internet, they have been reporting the fatal flaws that are going to stop its growth. The list of flaws keeps changing, however. The Internet has survived as long as it has by adapting, and there is no reason to expect this evolution to stop. The Internet's modular architecture allows it to embrace technical change one component at a time. If anything, the pace of change has accelerated as the Internet has become attractive to venture capitalists.

Proposed solutions to Internet coordination problems should leave room for change. For example, some of the pressure for "good" domain names comes from people's need to guess email and Web addresses. Internet search and indexing systems have made tremendous progress over the past two years, although they are still not as good as we would like them to be. If a really good, commonly used directory service were to emerge, it would remove a lot of today's pressure on domain names, and we would not then want to be stuck with a big institutional hammer for what has become a small nail.

Institutional solutions that might be appropriate for today's technology could turn out to be burdensome for tomorrow's; at their worst, they might even delay the development of tomorrow's technology. The Internet experience to date suggests that technical evolution should always be considered as a possible solution to coordination problems, ahead of institutionally based arrangements.

Will All Stakeholders Perceive Authority as Legitimate?

Authority can only be readily exercised if it is perceived as legitimate by all stakeholders. IANA derived its authority from the Internet community's shared history and trust in Jon Postel. It would be naïve to expect such authority to remain unchallenged as the community grows to encompass large numbers of stakeholders who share neither of those.

This question has different implications for addressing and naming. Addresses are meaningful to the provider community, so it makes sense to propose that authority for addressing end up in organizations that overlap with that community (for example, IANA, and provider consortia such as the CIX, RIPE NCC, and APNIC). But it is fantasy to suggest that authority for the domain name appeals process will be perceived as legitimate if it is assigned to IANA in its present incarnation, the Internet Society (ISOC), or the Internet Architecture Board (IAB). The stakeholder community for domain name assignments is the whole world, and none of these organizations comes close to being representative.

The usual solution when everyone is a stakeholder is to let governments represent them; but governments are notoriously bad at handling highly technical, rapidly changing issues, and intergovernmental organizations are even worse. Practically speaking, the appeals process for Internet coordination disputes is now the same as the appeals process for anything else in the world: the courts. As we have already noted, the courts are less than ideal for resolving international disputes. But in this world of increasingly global business, the Internet is hardly alone with that problem—it is just out in front.

Courts are also less than ideal for resolving disputes of any technical complexity—a realm in which the authority of organizations like the IAB may be perceived as more legitimate. Perhaps an intermediate solution can be found in which Internet technology organizations play a technical advisory role to standard legal proceedings.

Summary and Conclusion

In this chapter we have shown how the fundamental Internet Protocol is designed to create a minimally coercive system, in which everyone benefits from collective interaction while retaining as much local choice as possible. We have described the technical and cultural coordination mechanisms used to achieve interoperability, and discussed their organizational affordances—the broadly decentralized decision-making that gives 99 percent of the Internet its characteristic openness, diversity, and bottom-up dynamism. We have put into context the major controversies surrounding the remaining one percent of Internet coordination, having to do with the allocation of IPv4 address space and assignment of domain names. Finally, we have suggested four questions to ask about proposed changes to Internet coordination, and discussed how they apply to some of the current problem cases.

We hope that reading this chapter has caused you to critically examine the mindset you bring to the questions raised in this volume. Since many of the functions under discussion have historically been performed under the funding and direction of the U.S. government, it is not surprising that we tend to focus on institutions of various sorts as their eventual home. But this instinct can lead us astray when dealing with a system that is as fundamentally decentralized as the Internet. It would not surprise us if changes to the current system end up taking place in a bottom-up, "anyone can" manner, or if authority ends up scattered across many different organizations, not concentrated into a single institution. In other words, it would not surprise us if coordination of domain name assignment and IP address allocation eventually looked a lot more like coordination of the rest of the Internet.

Notes

1. On January 13, 1997, for example, the AltaVista Web search site reported that it had indexed "31 million pages found on 476,000 servers." See <http://altavista.digital.com/>.

2. Such choice is not always considered an advantage. Users without much time, or technical sophistication or interest, may prefer to let someone else package a fully integrated service for them. This is the niche that the on-line service providers are currently filling with respect to the Internet. They are moving away from the old model, in which they were tied to their own versions of each component, toward being able to select what they consider to be the best competitive alternative for each piece on the user's behalf.

3. If this is ever not true, it is considered a bug in the software—the browser, the server, or both.

4. Internet connectivity provision is a highly dynamic industry; estimates at the time of this writing put the total number of commercial providers in the United States in the 2–3,000 range, with approximately six to ten of these having achieved national scope. See the Maloff Company's *1995–1996 Internet Service Provider Marketplace Analysis* for more quantitative information about this industry (more information about this report is available at <http://www.trinet.com/maloff/>).

5. U.S. District Court for the Eastern District of Pennsylvania (1996), paragraph 11.

6. As a practical matter, Internet protocols are organized into levels of functionality, or layers. Lower-layer protocols such as IP provide general-purpose services such as interconnecting networks and exchanging bits, while higher-layer protocols like HTTP provide specialized services such as exchanging documents. Multiple higher-layer protocols, each with its own specialized purpose, can take advantage of the same lower-level services. Layered organization is seen often in computing. Consider, for example, a personal computer which runs a lower-layer, general-purpose program—the operating system—to support multiple, task-specialized higher-layer programs—applications such as spreadsheets and word processors. Instead of each application having to include code to drive, say, the computer's printer, the operating system incorporates this function and provides it as a service to the applications. Layering is also evident in the physical

world. For example, many types of delivery services, including documents (e.g., Federal Express), pizza (e.g., Domino's), and furniture (e.g., United Van Lines) layer on top of roads—a common, general-purpose infrastructure for transporting material goods. See Hafner and Lyon (1996), pp. 146–147 for a historical look at the development of Internet layering.

7. See Segal (1995) for an inside look at the TCP/IP adoption process.

8. These descriptions refer, respectively, to the packet radio network and the terrestrial ARPANET, two of the original networks ARPA wished to interconnect. The needs described here are adapted from Clark (1988) and from an interview with David Clark, October 24, 1995.

9. See Clark (1996) and Computer Science and Telecommunications Board of the National Research Council (1994) for more in-depth discussion of the layering issues in IP's design.

10. Interview with Robert Kahn, April 26, 1996.

11. Norman (1989), p. 9, defines affordances as "the perceived and actual properties of the thing, primarily those fundamental properties that determine just how the thing could possibly be used . . . . A chair affords ('is for') support and, therefore, affords sitting." We are not claiming that the uses of technologies are completely predetermined by their technical properties, only that those properties make certain uses easier or harder and therefore more or less likely.

12. Clark (1996).

13. See Resnick (1994) for a discussion of the centralized mindset that leads people to make erroneous assumptions, such as that a flock of geese must have a leader.

14. The entrepreneurs who succeed may find it worthwhile to vertically integrate later, but this step does not have to happen at the beginning when money and credibility are in shorter supply.

15. Partridge and Kastenholz (1996), p. 176.

16. The several large routing brownouts reported over the past year can be considered a grand experiment in this regard. See, for example, Nash and Wallace (1995). Routing management is currently performed in a decentralized, ad hoc manner by the network engineers employed by Internet connectivity providers. Providers who perform more manual configuration are generally at greater risk of failure. Keeping routing working properly on a day-to-day basis could well be the most labor-intensive component of Internet coordination today (interview with Jon Postel, May 2, 1996)—dwarfing the forms of coordination that have institutional components (i.e., naming and addressing)..

17. For a discussion of the tension between making software ubiquitous and restricting it to a single platform (i.e., making it non-interoperable), see Red Herring Editors (1996).

18. Interview with Robert Kahn, May 26, 1996; interview with Tony Rutkowski, November 6, 1995.

19. Unlike the other standards fora mentioned above, the IETF is not a membership organization. Anyone can attend IETF meetings or participate in e-mail discussions. Decisions are made by consensus instead of by vote, and attendees are treated as individuals, not representatives of organizations. The results of the process—draft and final Request for Comment (RFC) documents—are freely available to anyone over the Internet.

20. Interview with Jon Postel, May 2, 1996. Postel's official title at ISI is Associate Director for Networking. The name IANA is intended to refer to a role, not an institution or person. People often blur this distinction, however, since the person behind the role has always been Jon Postel.

21. The U.S. government funding comes from NSF because Network Solutions started doing the Internet registry job in the NSFNET days.

22. This description is based on an interview with Jon Postel, May 2, 1996. See Conrad (1996) for a more in-depth discussion of IP address allocation. See also the Web pages for RIPE NCC <www.ripe.net>, APNIC <www.apnic.org>, and InterNIC <rs.internic.net> for more details on each organization's historical origins and evolution, as well as <www.isi.edu/div7/iana> for more information about IANA.

23. Conrad (1996).

24. Personal communication with Randy Conrad of APNIC, September 1996.

25. These technologies include: address translation, which would allow large networks to be represented by a small number of external addresses; and automated network renumbering, which would make it more reasonable for registries to allocate smaller blocks of addresses.

26. Conrad (1996).

27. See Mockapetris (1983) and Rekhter and Li (1996) as starting points to gain a deeper appreciation of the linkage between routing and addressing. Renumbering of existing networks may also be required to contain routing table explosion.

28. Users can also apply directly to registries if they know to whom to apply. The necessarily brief description in this section is mainly based on an interview with Jon Postel, May 2, 1996. Among the many RFCs with more information about the domain naming system, good places to start are Postel (1994) and Kane (1996).

29. This job is not without its humorous moments. Postel relates that he once got letters from two different branches of one country's government, each proclaiming a different entity to be the authority. He handled it by exchanging the letters between them and telling them to "get back to me when you decide."

30. See the notes from MIT's workshop on Internet Economics, held in March 1995 and available at <http://rpcp.mit.edu/Workshops/iew-notes.txt>. Fundamentally different assumptions regarding scarcity, and the differences in outlook to which they lead, were quite evident in discussions between economists and technologists at the workshop. Economic education often involves studying

the optimal allocation of scarce resources. The Internet confounds the resulting economic worldview by suboptimally allocating abundant resources and still working well enough. Papers from the workshop are available at <http://www.press.umich.edu:80/jep/econTOC.htm>.

31. Servers and local access infrastructure are much more likely to be at fault. See also "Internet Meltdown!: Imminent or Unlikely?" by Stuart Feldman of IBM Research, available at <http://www.alphaWorks.ibm.com/>.

32. See Kane (1996) and <http://www.alternic.net>. This effort is independent of IANA and the InterNIC, illustrating the practical limits to their authority imposed by the Internet's architecture. One could get the impression from reading RFCs and Internet Drafts that some constellation of the IETF, Internet Architecture Board (IAB), and/or Internet Society (ISOC) has the authority to decide what will happen to the domain name space. AlterNIC's initiative demonstrates the more bottom-up reality of the change process.

33. This problem is similar to what employees experience when their organizations' internal telephone systems have not yet been updated with new area codes: they cannot place calls to certain telephone numbers.

34. Mockapetris (1983), p.1.

35. See Clark (1988).

36. Some would reverse this argument to claim that routing brownouts over the past year point to the need for licensing connectivity providers. We have heard this argument from some existing providers, who certainly understand the technical issues involved better than we do, but who would also clearly benefit from higher entry barriers.

References

Clark, David D. 1988. The Design Philosophy of the DARPA Internet Protocols. In *1988 Sigcomm Symposium.* (Stanford, CA: ACM Press). 106–114.

Clark, David D. 1996. Interoperation, Open Interfaces, and Protocol Architecture. In *White Papers: The Unpredictable Certainty: Information Infrastructure Through 2000,* ed. Computer Science and Telecommunications Board of the National Research Council. Washington, D.C.: National Academy Press.

Computer Science and Telecommunications Board of the National Research Council. 1994. *Realizing the Information Future: The Internet and Beyond.* Washington, D.C.: National Academy Press.

Conrad, David Randy. 1996. *Administrative Infrastructure for IP Address Allocation.* CIX/ISOC Internet Infrastructure Workshop http://www.aldea.com/cix/randy.html.

Hafner, Katie and Matthew Lyon. 1996. *Where Wizards Stay Up Late: The Origins of the Internet.* New York: Simon & Schuster.

Kane, Margaret. 1996. What's in a Name? Lots, If It's a Domain. *PC Week Online* (July 31): http://www.pcweek.com/news/0729/31edom.html.

Mockapetris, P. 1983. *Domain Names—Concepts and Facilities.* Network Working Group Request for Comments 882.

Nash, Kim S. and Bob Wallace. 1995. Internet Hiccup. *Computerworld* (September 11): 1, 16.

Norman, Donald A. 1989. *The Design of Everyday Things.* New York: Doubleday.

Partridge, Craig and Frank Kastenholz. 1996. Technical Criteria for Choosing IP the Next Generation (IPng). In *IPng: Internet Protocol Next Generation,* ed. Scott O. Bradner and Allison Mankin. Reading, Mass.: Addison-Wesley.

Postel, Jon. 1994. *Domain Name System Structure and Delegation.* Network Working Group Request for Comments 1591.

Red Herring Editors. 1996. Letter to Bill Gates: ActiveX vs. Java. *The Red Herring* (August 1996): 34–36.

Rekhter, Y. and T. Li. 1996. *Implications of Various Address Allocation Policies for Internet Routing.* Network Working Group Request for Comments 2008.

Resnick, Mitchel. 1994. *Turtles, Termites, and Traffic Jams: Explorations in Massively Parallel Microworlds.* Cambridge, Mass.: MIT Press.

Segal, Ben M. 1995. *A Short History of Internet Protocols at CERN.* CERN PDP-NS http://wwwcn.cern.ch/pdp/ns/ben/TCPHIST.html.

U.S. District Court for the Eastern District of Pennsylvania. 1996. *Adjudication on Motions for Preliminary Injunction in ACLU v. Reno, ALA v. U.S. Department of Justice.* http://www.eff.org/pub/Censorship/Internet_censorship_bills/HTML/960612_aclu_v_reno_decision.html.

Governance of the Internet: A UK Perspective

Mark Gould

Introduction

The Internet is probably the largest of the open networks which now form a supraterritorial and diffuse global entity. The notion of physical territory is necessarily alien to the technical norms governing the Internet—instead, the standards and protocols of Internet communication have developed in such a way as to transcend the limits of geography and politics. However, it is not the case that the network is entirely otherworldly. Some aspects of the real world cannot be ignored. At the very least, the cables which carry Internet traffic have a physical presence. Likewise, the users of the system, whether they be human or corporate, have legal personalities which create for them rights and responsibilities which are determined by the societies in which they are established. Nobody exists solely on the Internet—rather, activities which involve the network may be constrained by the norms of the real world. In the same way, although the network itself has an existence apart from the real world, that world still exerts pressures on it. One of those pressures is for regulation of various aspects of the network itself. This chapter explores some of the ways in which the Internet may satisfy that need by adhering to certain "constitutional" principles in its organization and governance while maintaining its unique status. In particular it is argued that the Internet institutions form the basis for a type of constitutional governance which, when enhanced, might stave off most calls for external regulation.

Independence of the core Internet institutions from national government funding requires that some attention be paid to the ways in which the functions essential to the operation of the network, such as Internet Protocol (IP) number allocation and domain registration, are provided. There are two reasons for this. The first is that as the commercial and private use of the Internet has boomed, great strains have been placed on these core services. While under such strain, it is increasingly likely that some users may become displeased with the level or nature of the service they receive. Likewise, those who are not yet participants in the Internet at any level may legitimately believe that their interests are not being properly considered. It is important that there are mechanisms in place to resolve such grievances, either by the application of legal norms in the ordinary courts, or by the provision of efficient, certain, open, and fair procedures for the allocation of potentially disputed or scarce resources. The second reason is that, even though disputes may have arisen in the past, their resolution may have been facilitated by the legitimacy conferred upon the core institutions by their financial connection with the United States government. Once that connection is severed, and the institutions are effectively privatized, the institutions will have to create their own authority in such a way as to satisfy at least three major groups: (1) the users, or clients of the core services (and, through them, all Internet users); (2) national governments (which may wish to impose their own regulatory frameworks); and (3) current nonusers (who might, for example, want to protect their intellectual property rights). The coincidence of the need to have legitimate authority over the core Internet functions (which may have a public character that is apparent beyond the network) and the need to respond to legitimate grievances about the way that those functions are carried out create a strong pressure for some sort of Internet "constitution."

Internet Governance as a Type of International Organization

Unfortunately, the Internet does not lend itself well to a constitution in the normal sense of the word. Unlike a nation-state, the Internet has no identifiable territory. Its citizens, on which a democracy might be based, are not easily identified. It does not have the same concerns as a nation-state. However, some of its features may be used as the basis for a set of principles which might be termed "constitutional." Given the global nature of the Internet, it would appear to be appropriate for it to be governed at an international level. There are a variety of models which could be adopted, but none is likely to be completely adequate for the task. International governance is, however, a useful starting point.[1]

It is a commonplace to note that in a complex world it is no longer possible for individual nation-states to act independently of all others. Whether because of the increasingly global nature of the economy, or because of a desire to avoid armed conflict, nations find themselves drawn to each other for various purposes. These purposes range from the eradication of various diseases, which is at the heart of the work of the World Health Organization, to the creation of standards for the rules governing international exchange of mail items, which is one of the primary responsibilities of the Universal Postal Union (UPU). Beyond these international organizations which exist for a narrow primary reason, there are groupings of nations which have a wider economic or political purpose. Most common among these are the free-trade organizations, such as the European Free Trade Association and the North American Free Trade Association. Finally, there are a very small number of supranational organizations, of which the European Union (EU) is probably the most developed, within which the interests of member-states are in some areas secondary to the interests of the organization itself. Countries which belong to international or supranational organizations are constrained to some degree from acting freely. A member of the Universal Postal Union undertakes to abide by the rules emanating from that body, and is therefore in breach of its obligations in international law if it fails, for example, to honor its duty to accept UPU-compliant postal packets from another UPU member. The effects of that breach, however, may depend in part on the international and domestic political system and in part on the extent to which the domestic legal system accepts the pronouncements of international tribunals. The same comments would apply to the free-trade organizations, although there a greater loss may be suffered by a member-state which fails to fulfill its obligations, as the other members may justifiably exercise their market power to sanction the dissenting state. At the far extreme, a supranational organization is likely to have formal mechanisms which effectively prevent member-states from dissenting from properly promulgated supranational norms. It has been noted that the traditional model of international organization may not be entirely appropriate for the governance of the Internet. I would go further than this, and suggest that any externally imposed organization may be inferior to a form of governance derived from common Internet practice. However, international organizations may offer clues to the issues which might be of concern to an Internet "constitution."

Given the supraterritorial nature of the Internet, it might seem appropriate to examine the forms of governance of supranational organizations. It is particularly instructive to see the ways in which power and authority are exercised in such organizations. Supranational organizations, such as the European Union, differ from nation-states in their status, but their constitutions and legitimacy are generally derived from the nation-states of which they are comprised. In the case of the EU, this principle is partly clear from the founding treaties, but is extended in the jurisprudence of the European Court of Justice (ECJ), which is the judicial organ of the Union and its constituent communities.[2] In two cases, which are equivalent in EU constitutional law to the United States Supreme Court's decision in *Marbury* v. *Madison*,[3] the ECJ created the doctrine of direct effect and established the primacy of European Community (EC) law. The language used in these decisions is telling. In *Van Gend en Loos* v. *Nederlandse Administratie der Belastingen*, the court had to consider whether individual importers were permitted to rely on the provisions of the Treaty of Rome in an action against the Dutch tax authorities. It held that this would be possible since the nature of the provision (Article 12) was such as to create clear obligations on the member-states. This was justified in the following passage:

The Community constitutes a new legal order of international law for the benefit of which the states have limited their sovereign rights, albeit within limited fields, and the subjects of which comprise not only

Member States but also their nationals. Independently of the legislation of Member States, Community law therefore not only imposes obligations on individuals but is also intended to confer upon them rights which become part of their legal heritage. These rights arise not only where they are expressly granted by the Treaty, but also by reason of obligations which the Treaty imposes in a clearly defined way upon individuals as well as upon the Member States and upon the institutions of the Community.[4]

The view of the court, then, is that member-states have no authority to ignore the clear provisions of the treaties. In later cases, the principle of direct effect was extended to include some types of secondary legislation,[5] and to allow individuals to enforce treaty provisions against other individuals.[6] Despite some criticism of the court's action in creating the doctrine,[7] it is important in asserting the Community's right to act, and to prevent the member-states from acting, in specific areas of responsibility. This right would have no value if the member-states could treat Community law as coequal with, or inferior to, their own domestic law. In most countries that is the position as regards ordinary international law. However, the European Court has asserted the supranational nature of EC law to prevent member-states from acting contrary to the treaties or secondary legislation. In *Costa v. ENEL*, the court had to decide whether an Italian court could be obliged to apply national law rather than being permitted to ask the European Court for a decision as to the meaning of certain treaty provisions. In holding that the national court was so permitted, the ECJ noted that:

• The executive force of Community law cannot vary from one State to another in deference to subsequent domestic laws, without jeopardizing the attainment of the objectives of the Treaty....

• The obligations undertaken under the Treaty establishing the Community could not be unconditional, but merely contingent, if they could be called in question by subsequent legislative acts of the signatories....

• The precedence of Community law is confirmed by Article 189, whereby a regulation 'shall be binding' and 'directly applicable in all Member States'. This provision which is subject to no reservation would be quite meaningless if a State could unilaterally nullify its effects by means of a legislative measure which could prevail over Community law.

- It follows from all these observations that the law stemming from the Treaty, an independent source of law, could not, because of its special and original nature, be overridden by domestic legal provisions, however framed, without being deprived of its character as Community law and without the legal basis of the Community itself being called into question.

- The transfer by the States from their domestic legal system of the rights and obligations arising under the Treaty carries with it a permanent limitation of their sovereign rights, against which a subsequent unilateral act incompatible with the concept of the Community cannot prevail.[8]

This permanent limitation was held in later cases to preclude national courts from applying fundamental constitutional rights in preference to Community law,[9] and to prohibit member-states from requiring that lower courts defer to national constitutional courts when considering the validity of domestic norms.[10]

The doctrine of primacy of EC law is still disputed, either politically (particularly in the United Kingdom, where it clashes with the constitutional doctrine of parliamentary sovereignty[11]) or legally (especially in Germany, where the Federal Constitutional Court has reserved its right to uphold the German Constitution in preference to EC rules[12]). On the whole, however, the member-states accept that the twin doctrines of direct effect and primacy are legitimate and justified in order to bring about the objectives for which the European Community and now the European Union were established. This acceptance is founded in part at least on a recognition that these objectives are incapable of being achieved effectively by individual states, that the court's own authority is bounded by adherence to the law, and that the Community's legislative body is made up of member-state representatives. The first notion is a political one, and is contingent on an acceptance of the principles on which the Union is based, which must be assumed for a state to have signed and ratified the founding treaties. There is no guarantee, however, that this assumption will remain true for all time. The latter two points of view are interesting, and could have ramifications for this model of Internet governance. Article 164 of the EC Treaty requires the Court of Justice to "ensure that in the interpretation and application of this Treaty the law is observed." This provision has been interpreted by the court to mean not just that the rule of law is thereby imported into the EC "constitution," but that principles common to the constitutions of the member-states should be relied upon in assessing the legality of Community legislation.[13] In addition, the court tends to interpret secondary legislation teleologically, with a view to its purpose. This tendency may be enlarged to suggest that the court views the Community (and thus the Union) as a form of teleocracy.[14] That is, the organization exists solely for the purpose of European integration within the bounds set by the member-states, and all legislation must serve that purpose and not be used for general purposes. Such a suggestion would certainly be approved by the more Euroskeptic member-states, and should not be unacceptable to the others. Ideas of legality, then, are more complex in the EU than in most national constitutions. The democratic ideal, conversely, is less apparent in EU governance. A system in which the only directly elected body has little real power in the legislative process, and where legislation is the responsibility of member-state governments acting collectively may justifiably be said to have a democratic deficit. If one accepts that the EU constitution is a teleocratic one, then one might be less concerned about that deficit since one of the functions of democratic control is to limit the excesses of government, and those excesses are limited by the constitution itself, which prohibits any action which is not intended to promote the goal of integration.

In many respects the nature of the Internet causes problems for national legal orders which are similar to the problems created by supranational and international political and legal organizations. Membership in an international standards-setting organization means that a country may not be able to enact its own rules in that area unless they fit the norms already promulgated by the organization. Likewise, a member of a free-trade association will not be able to regulate its trade with fellow members. Simple statements such as these ignore the fact that it may not be straightforward to delineate the borders of responsibility between nation and organization. It is often necessary for these borders to be disputed before they can be drawn clearly. Indeed, such disputes may be an effective way of arriving at a division of responsibilities which can be respected by all concerned. Even when a matter (such as standards harmonization) falls squarely within the competence of an international organization, the process of determining the content of the rules may be a laborious process, owing to the expression of national prejudices, or of commercial or industrial interests (which may themselves be tainted by nationalism). In a like manner, matters such as the use of mnemonic domain names for Internet hosts may raise legal issues which cannot easily be settled before an agreement is reached about the proper jurisdiction in which they should be settled, and the adoption of network standards (whether technical or social) may equally be fraught with potential for conflict between national desires and the needs of the network itself. While the Internet institutions may currently ignore interests other than the smooth operation of the network, national governments may perceive some political advantage in attempting to pursue their own interests in controlling the nature or content of the network. The nub of the problem, then, is to determine when matters are strictly a matter for Internet governance and when they might be better left for resolution at a national level.

Crucially, the Internet derives neither its organizational forms nor its practical legitimacy from the states in which it was founded or from the states within which it now finds its real-world expression. More important, most of those states made no choice at a governmental level to allow Internet access. All the examples of international organizations considered thus far require a country to decide whether or not to join the organization and (often a separate decision) whether to accept the rulings of its adjudicative organs, if any. The suggestion that Internet institutions treat themselves as legitimate authorities to make binding decisions founders on the rocks of enforcement. No state will enforce the rules of a body that it does not recognize. This means that an alternative source of authority for Internet institutions needs to be found. One possibility might be to set a teleocratic limit on the powers of those institutions. Thus, the legitimacy and forms of organization of the Internet should be based on the (primarily technical) needs of the network itself. Any new development in the governance of the Internet would place the needs of the network above the interests of any one state. If this principle were accepted, it would be unlikely that a simple international organization on the model of the UPU or even a free-trade association would suffice to guarantee wide international acceptance of rules and decisions made by Internet institutions. In order for Internet governance to work, it would need to have the same degree of power that the European Court of Justice has acquired on behalf of the EC. The jurisprudence of that court makes it clear that the EU constitution depends on agreement by the member-states to limit their sovereign rights and authority in limited areas. Could the Internet cope without such a limitation by the states in which there was a network presence? Alternatively, could it manage if some states agreed not to exercise their jurisdiction in Internet-related matters, whereas other states did not?

One hope might be to persuade national courts that the Internet does not impinge on the work of the state. Such a division of responsibilities might be similar to the division between the spiritual jurisdiction of early canon law, as opposed to the temporal justice of kings and nobles.[15] Unfortunately, the relative strengths of the institutions of Internet governance and national government are completely mismatched, which was not the case when the Church competed with secular authorities. The analogy between the Internet and supranational organizations such as the Church or the EU is deficient in important respects, but it is still useful as an analytical model, especially when the difficult question of accommodating both national and network interests is considered. A more important issue than organizational style is to determine what type of "constitutional" principles should be applied to the Internet, and which "governmental" functions Internet governing bodies ought to fulfill.

What Should an Internet "Constitution" Include?

Having considered briefly the models of international governance which are available, we need to consider what form Internet decision-making and dispute resolution mechanisms might take.

What is it that the institutions do, and how should they carry out these tasks? Should all the institutions follow similar processes, or are there "local" issues which imply that a different approach may be needed for some types of work? Are these the only functions that are required for the governance of the Internet?

Consideration of these issues necessarily leads to an assessment of the proper nature of the rules governing the Internet. When thinking about constitutional law, most of the world probably starts from a written document containing a set of rules which define to a greater or lesser extent the responsibilities of governmental organs, their relationships with each other and with individual citizens. This is not true in the United Kingdom, where there is no defining text and the constitution is derived from history, the ordinary law of the land, and the political habits of the participants in government. While this is not altogether satisfactory, especially insofar as it reduces the certainty available in the constitution, it may be an appropriate model for a system which has not yet settled on its essential functions and institutions. One might wish that the Internet had a settled system of governance that could be enshrined in some constitutional document, but it is probably unwise to forgo consideration of the essential structures within that system until it is settled.

The basic functions required by Internet governance are similar to those encountered in the real world. A rule-making power is needed, and currently exists in the Internet Engineering Task Force (IETF), for the creation of the standards by which the Internet is constituted, governed, and administered. Within the framework of Requests for Comment (RFCs) adopted by the IETF and promulgated by the Internet Society (ISOC) there is a decision-making (or administrative) function which is currently devolved between various institutions. For example, the Internet Assigned Numbers Authority (IANA) makes decisions about number assignments and delegation of national domains; Network Solutions, Inc. (NSI), makes decisions (on behalf of Internic) about the allocation of international Top Level Domains (iTLDs), and the regional registries allocate IP number blocks. Each of these decisions may have consequences that are felt beyond the parties involved.[16] The third central function of a state is the judicial one.

At present this is not mirrored in the system of Internet governance,[17] and the creation of such a compulsory and coercive dispute resolution function raises difficult issues.

It has been assumed up to this point that some form of Internet governance is necessary. Is this a valid assumption? It is not unreasonable to suggest that the resources administered at the core of the Internet are merely examples of private largesse, and therefore need not be regulated in their distribution. If queries arise about infringement of third-party rights and interests, they could be resolved in the law courts between the third party and the recipient of largesse—why involve the distributing institution? Such an approach, which is typified by the operation of a "first come, first served" domain registration policy by NSI, is potentially risky. Even if the risk is minimal and can therefore be ignored, the process itself only takes into account the interests of a few. If one takes the view that these resources have a public character, then even though they are administered by a private commercial enterprise they should be regulated in order to ensure that the community at large can be sure that they are being administered in the best way possible, and especially by taking into account interests which are not necessarily particularly powerful. Are these resources, then, public in nature? Following the immense growth in the Internet as a means of communication, I would argue that the core functions should be treated as public. In its early years, the Internet was more akin to a private system, but its growth into a major infrastructure means that the market-type allocation of resources of those early years is now inappropriate. As an infrastructure, decisions about the network are likely to be felt outside the circle of network users. These externalities may be positive (such as the ease of access to information which may reduce costs for governments or commercial organizations) or negative (such as the impact on trademarks by domain registration), and their effects need to be considered in the processes of governance. Additionally, there is a risk that the exercise of monopoly power in the distribution of network resources may result in the exploitation of consumers. Further, as the Internet becomes more commercialized (especially with the creation of a competitive Domain Name Service (DNS), as has been proposed by IANA[18]), it is going to be essential for certain functions to be underwritten in the event of failure of a provider of a core Internet function.[19]

Appropriate Constitutional Principles

Once it is decided that some form of constitutional regulation is desirable, it is necessary to determine the principles on which that constitution should be based. Even if the model used is that of a supranational organization, there are still some features which are similar to those found in nation-state constitutions. These features may not be readily applicable in a regulatory system for the Internet. A constitution that is concerned with the regulation of a state and its people has different concerns from one that is purely directed toward the efficient and fair operation of an international network of computers. Conversely, some aspects may be similar. More important, the foundations of a national constitution are very different from those of the Internet. So whereas democracy is an important feature of most constitutions in the world—providing the most valuable form of legitimacy for a system which may impose sanctions on those whom it governs—it would be extremely difficult to apply in the governance of the Internet. The first problem here would be to define the electorate. One might merely include those who use the Internet's core services directly. This would exclude those who buy services from those core users, and who might have an equally valid claim to representation. Even if we include this latter group (and there are logistical problems inherent in enfranchising such a large and disparate number of people), those who are not yet participants in the Internet but who might have an interest in the allocation would be excluded. If we could find a satisfactory way of defining the electorate, there would remain the problem of representation. Is it right that all types of user should have an equal say? Should the views of nonusers be given equal weight to the opinions of those who have actually invested in the system? It might be possible to adapt the principle of democracy to the particular constraints within which the Internet works. A system could be posited which would take into account the interests and desires of particular groups, such as consumers, providers, and third parties. While this may go some way toward assuaging the critics of a nondemocratic system, it would remain difficult to ascertain with certainty what those interests or desires are. It may also be the case that within an apparently homogeneous grouping there may be different and potentially conflicting goals and aspirations.

It would appear, then, that any attempt to ensure legitimacy substantively, by referring to the desires of a particular group, would likely prove so cumbersome and controversial as to be impractical. We might turn instead to formal forms of legitimacy. In traditional constitutional models, these forms include adherence to the rule of law, and principles derived therefrom, including a (possibly notional) separation of powers and principles of natural justice or due process. These are worthy objectives for any system of Internet governance. Additionally, following the supranational constitution of the European Union, a teleocratic principle might be applied, so that the objectives for which the institutions operate (the good functioning and development of the network, for example) might take precedence in cases of dispute.

The Rule-making and Decision-making Processes

The rule-making process, especially the work of the IETF, is already well developed, and should provide a useful starting point for the other aspects of the work of Internet institutions. Implicitly, the IETF does take a teleological view of its work, since the primary function of the "legislative" RFCs that it adopts is to ensure the efficient working and development of the network. Indeed, the standards-track RFCs may fairly be considered to be constitutional in the sense that they provide the rules by which the technical aspects of the Internet are governed. The way in which the IETF works also confers legitimacy on the rules it creates. The fact that the "legislative" process is, in principle, open to all, renders it more democratic in some respects than some apparently democratic national legislatures, which may in fact be dominated by historical, political, or commercial considerations.[20] However, some of the success of the IETF may also be attributed to the field in which it works. It is reasonably straightforward to create firm, binding technical standards since failure to comply with those standards will mean that the network fails to work (and that failure will be felt most keenly by those who ignore the standards). When rule-making encroaches on areas that do not involve the clear-cut issues raised by technical governance, it is more than likely that those rules will be controversial unless they are legitimated in some other way.

Legitimacy may also be derived from the form of the decision-making process. If we take the allocation of domain names as an example, one might point to participation, impartiality, openness, and certainty as being valuable legitimating factors. Participation is notably absent from the present process, probably on the ground that it would lead to a cumbersome and time-consuming consideration of objections to proposed allocations of domains. While this efficiency might have been a valid consideration when the Internet was relatively small and uncommercialized, it now has to compete with the need to reduce litigation over decisions already made, and therefore contribute to the certainty of those decisions. While it is probably impossible to eradicate litigation, it might be reduced where proper consultation has been made before the allocation of Internet resources.[21] Participation in the domain registration process might only require that applicants indicate to the world at large that they intend to apply for their proposed domain names. If no objections were received within a specified time, the domain could be allocated. If there were objections, then the naming authority would have to decide on the merits of the objections and allocate the domain or not. (At this stage the need for an Internet-related dispute resolution mechanism should become apparent.)

Acceptance of the principle of participation necessarily leads to a demand for that participation to be conducted in conditions of fairness. Decisions of the Internet institutions should be made after due process, or in conditions imposed by natural justice. This would require that all sides of an argument be heard before making a decision,[22] and that the decision-maker be impartial.[23] As far as I know, no allegations have been made that the current processes breach these principles, except insofar as they exclude those who are not a party to the decision (which only leads to those people exercising their right to dispute the decision outside the decision-making process—i.e., in the courts). Because it is likely that those outside the Internet may be interested in decisions made by the institutions, it is more appropriate that they use formal techniques derived from the real world, rather than mirroring the rule-making processes of the IETF, which do not, on the whole, need to take external pressures into account.

The requirements of openness and certainty are fairly clear. The process of deciding on an allocation of resources needs to be transparent so as to show that it is just. A closed and secretive process is likely to be tainted by criticisms of bias or partiality.[24] Certainty is a principle which is currently lacking in some aspects of the decision-making process of Internet institutions. For example, NSI's current rules on domain allocation enable it to withdraw domain names on little notice, thereby suggesting that the allocation is of a transient nature.[25] Not only is there a positive benefit in certainty for its own sake (as exemplified by the development of legitimate expectation as a ground for judicial review of administrative action in English law[26]), but the Internet itself would presumably function more efficiently when some decisions could be changed as little as possible.[27]

A similar critique may be made of the IANA proposal for extension of the iTLDs. Setting aside the very real concerns raised by Robert Shaw in his chapter in this volume about the absence of proper authority for this proposal, another cause for concern is that the allocation process for new registries provides no independent means of binding dispute resolution for disappointed bidders.[28] The proposal does outline an appeals process for use in the event of disputes arising out of a registry's domain allocation policy (albeit one which is essentially administrative rather than judicial),[29] but nothing is said about the more controversial process of deciding which bidders should be given the power to administer domain registries. In other respects the proposal is more satisfactory. The ad hoc group that is intended to decide on the new registries is expected to create its rules in an open fashion,[30] and the process of evaluation of the bids should also be "neutral, impartial, and open."[31] The only "constitutional" lacuna occurs when the final decisions have to be made.[32] Here there is no reference to the resolution of disputes arising out of the ad hoc committee's decisions, nor to any way in which the "unbiased and fair" nature of the committee's method might be tested. Given the disputes that have arisen over the allocation of domains by NSI, this omission is surprising.

Dispute Resolution

Whichever "constitutional" principles are thought to be relevant to Internet governance, it is necessary to consider how they (and the legitimacy they confer on the institutions) may be accommodated with the right of sovereign nations to coerce their own citizens and with real-world constitutional or legal principles. This need becomes most pressing when considering whether a dispute resolution function is necessary or appropriate within the structure of Internet governance.

The major problem here is defining the proper ambit of Internet dispute resolution. Some matters may fall entirely within the purview of the Internet authorities (e.g., misuse of resources allocated by IANA), while others are exclusively matters for national legal or governmental authorities (such as publication of unlawful material using the Internet). There may be, however, a number of disputes which might be equally well resolved in either context and over which there may be competition between the network authorities and national governments (the use of cryptography might be a good example here). This problem mirrors the problems encountered by federal states and by supranational organizations in defining the responsibilities and competences of the federation or organization and its component parts. In the EU, for example, as we have seen, the European Court of Justice has resolved the problem by creating the doctrines of direct effect and primacy of Community law. Neither of these developments would have been possible had the member-states not chosen in the founding treaties to provide a mechanism by which domestic courts could request rulings on matters of Community law from the ECJ. This process provides two useful outcomes. In the first place, it ensures even application of the principles of Community law in all the member-states. Second, and on a more practical level, it provides a means of ensuring that the rules of Community law are enforced since it passes that burden to domestic courts rather than leaving it to the ECJ. A more important problem is raised by the need to impose sanctions. If it is considered to be necessary for Internet institutions to impose sanctions in order to carry out their dispute-resolution function effectively, it has to be decided which sanctions are permissible, or even possible. The obvious (and perhaps only) choice is to allow denial of service, although in many instances this penalty might well be disproportionate.

An alternative to the model of internal regulation of Internet functions would be to allow all disputes to be resolved in the real-world dispute resolution systems—whether courts of law or alternative dispute resolution. Even if this is proscribed by an internal system of governance, it is possible that those affected by Internet decisions might wish to invoke a real-world solution. In a national context, regulators are bound by the law and by judicial rules. In the context of Internet governance there is no judiciary and no law beyond that created by the process of constituting the network and by the practices of the administrators of the Internet and the rules by which they choose to be bound. One way of resolving both of these problems would be to insist that all disputes relating to administration of Internet functions are resolved in one particular jurisdiction.[33] This is straightforward enough where there is a contract between the administrator and the offended party. It is less obviously resolved where there is no such contract and the locus of a dispute is not clear owing to the supraterritorial nature of the Internet. Even if a jurisdiction can be chosen, on what basis should it be chosen? At present, the U.S. courts (especially those in Virginia) have de facto jurisdiction over the work of the Internet administrators. Why should this remain true? Should someone from Russia or Japan who wishes to challenge the allocation of an international Top Level Domain by NSI be subjected to the costs incurred in pursuing a claim in a foreign court whereas a U.S. plaintiff would not be so disadvantaged? The alternative might be to decide that, in actions against the Internet administrators, plaintiffs would be allowed to bring suit in their own jurisdictions. This would be fairer to plaintiffs, and would mean that no nationality would have an advantage over any other, but it would inevitably cost the institutions considerably more. There would also remain a problem which was envisaged by the founders of the European

Communities and which was resolved by the creation of the European Court of Justice.

Where plaintiffs are allowed to bring suit in their own countries, it is more than likely that a situation will develop that will only lead to greater inequity, and potential chaos. This is the problem of disparate application of law, which has two facets. The first is that, whatever the principles on which Internet decision-making is based (such as the efficient development of the network), it is difficult to imagine a real-world court giving those principles appropriate force—instead they are likely to take into account only established legal doctrine. In the Treaty of Rome, this was avoided by allowing national courts to make interlocutory references to the European Court of Justice, which was the only body competent to rule on the "interpretation and application of the Treaty."[34] This is reinforced by *requiring* courts from which there is no appeal to make such references in cases where the reference would be conclusive. The second facet follows from the first, and is that the established legal doctrines applied in different states are likely to differ considerably from state to state, and thereby create disparities between states, which some plaintiffs may use to their advantage by "forum shopping."

The "obvious" answer, which is to create an arbitral or judicial organ within the system of Internet governance whose jurisdiction ousts all others, carries with it a heavy responsibility. Such an institution must command the respect of all national courts and legal systems and also that of individual users. The problem here is that the member-states of the EU are willing to accept the dominant jurisdiction of the ECJ because there are other benefits which accrue from membership in the Union, and because the risks inherent in not allowing the ECJ to have primacy are double-edged: a state may feel hard done by as a result of the way in which a particular aspect of the court's jurisprudence has developed, but it may be compensated by an equivalent benefit accruing from other developments. If the ECJ had not asserted the doctrines of direct effect and supremacy, it is likely that the EU could not have developed in the way that it has—and most member-states are satisfied with that development. An Internet "court" would not be able to claim similar respect automatically. In the first place, it would have nothing to offer countries that were willing to be bound by its decisions. In fact, quite the opposite is true. If a country failed to respect the decisions of the court, and instead reserved the right to allow its domestic courts to decide legal issues relating to Internet matters, those courts might find themselves in great demand for Internet-related dispute resolution. This is an example of the free market in rule sets to which David Post has drawn attention.[35] However vital this might be in creating choice in interpersonal disputes and in determining choices between networks, such a free market is more likely to stultify development of an efficient and effective system of governance within a particular network.[36] Since a number of international agreements allow enforcement of judgments in other jurisdictions, even countries that had accepted the right of the Internet to regulate its own affairs might find that their courts were bound to enforce decisions of courts in third countries that had not. One way of avoiding this problem might be to offer a system of decision-making and dispute resolution that was so fair, just, and clear that no complainant would wish to bring a case outside the Internet institutions. It is difficult to imagine what such a system would look like since in almost any court or tribunal aspects of procedure or jurisprudence would be contested or contestable. The battle for the "hearts and minds" of potential litigants is likely to be a hard one.

Toward a Model of Internet Governance

There is already a valuable model for Internet governance provided in the IETF. Unlike other international standards bodies the IETF is not subjected to undue pressure exerted by national or industrial interest groups. Instead, the process by which RFCs are created is dominated by consideration of the needs of the network itself.[37] The principles of cooperation and collaboration followed by the IETF are part of the social ethos of the Internet, and should be carried forward into the wider regulation of Internet goods. However, we also need to recognize that some real-world principles of administrative decision-making would be valuable when transposed into Internet institutions.

Apart from the principles already outlined above, a concern might reasonably be expressed about the diffuse nature of Internet organization. Without the common authority imposed by U.S.

government funding, there is a risk that each of the institutions may go its own way in pursuit of a particular set of objectives. It is already the case that national registries make their own rules for administration of their name space; it may be that this is thought inappropriate. The IETF, by contrast, is organizationally bound to the Internet Architecture Board (IAB) and ISOC. Such a relationship is not necessarily suitable for the administrative bodies such as Internic. Instead, it may be useful to borrow the regulatory model common in the United States and used by the British government to ensure that the privatized public utilities carry on their commercial functions within guidelines set at arm's length from government—but after consideration of government, consumer, and commercial interests.[38] An Internet regulator (perhaps responsible to the Internet Society) would be able to insist that the otherwise independent entities allocating Internet resources should do so in accordance with a variety of considerations. These might include: the objectives laid down by the Internet Society and the IAB; the framework of standards created by the IETF; legal principles derived from the real-world concerns of users and third parties; the desires of consumers; and the interests of commercial participants in the Internet.

In conclusion, then, it is unlikely that a fixed system of governance for the Internet can be put in place since the principles governing such a system are not yet agreed. Likewise, it is not clear that the institutions that might exist within such a system are decided.[39] However, in the same way that the UK constitution is constantly in a state of flux yet manages to exist nonetheless, it is possible to posit a working model of governance that should suit the preoccupations of the Internet. Such a model would borrow the notion of teleocracy from the European Union, and use it to ensure that the principle of network development and efficiency remains at the heart of the Internet. That same notion would underpin the creation of a compulsory and coercive dispute resolution forum within which as many Internet-related disputes as possible would be decided (even if this only resulted in interinstitutional disputes being referred, it might be an improvement over the existing state of affairs). Likewise, the institutions themselves would recognize the principle of network efficiency and use it in their rule- or decision-making processes. Finally, where there is no current regulation, some consideration might be given to ensuring via the imposition of a network-aware regulator that all the processes that administer Internet resources comply as far as possible with the interests of those who are affected by them.

Acknowledgment

My thanks are due to Aileen McHarg and Keith Gymer, who commented on an earlier draft of this chapter, and to the participants in the workshop on Coordination and Administration of the Internet at the Kennedy School of Government, 8–10 September 1996, (especially Fred Baker, Ken Fockler, David Johnson, and Tony Rutkowski), from whom I learned a great deal.

Notes

1. In keeping with the traditional use of the term "international organization," I am only concerned here with organizations that consist predominantly or entirely of nation-states. I accept that there may be other models of global organization, but few of these currently exist, and in a sense the Internet is already such an organization.

2. The European Union is at present a political organization. Within the EU, there are three other organizations which have law-making powers. The most important of these is the European Community (EC), which was formerly known as the European Economic Community. Principles of EC law may be applied *mutatis mutandis* to the other organizations.

3. Cranch (5 US) 137 (1803).

4. Case 26/62, *Van Gend en Loos v. Nederlandse Administratie der Belastingen,* European Court Reports 1 at p. 12 (1963).

5. Case 41/74, *Van Duyn v. Home Office,* European Court Reports, 1337 (1974).

6. Case 152/84, *Marshall v. Southampton and South-West Hampshire Area Health Authority (Teaching),* European Court Reports, 723 (1986).

7. See, for example, P. Pescatore, "The Doctrine of 'Direct Effect': An Infant Disease of Community Law," *European Law Review* 8 (1983): 155–177.

8. The European Court of Justice in Case 6/64, *Costa v. ENEL,* European Court Reports, 585 at p. 594 (1964).

9. Case 11/70, *Internationale Handelsgesellschaft mbH v. Einfuhr- und Vorratsstelle für Getreide und Futtermittel,* European Court Reports, 1125 (1970).

10. Case 106/77, *Amministrazione delle Finanze dello Stato v. Simmenthal SpA,* European Court Reports, 629 (1978).

11. A matter which was only judicially resolved by the House of Lords in *Factortame Ltd. v. Secretary of State for Transport*, Appeal Cases, 85 (1990).

12. See *Re Wünsche Handelsgesellschaft*, 3 Common Market Law Reports, 225 (1987) (the *Solange II* case).

13. Case 29/69, *Stauder v. City of Ulm*, European Court Reports, 419 (1969); the *Internationale Handelsgesellschaft* case; Case 4/73, *Nold v. Commission*, European Court Reports, 491 (1974); Case 44/79, *Hauer v. Land Rheinland-Pfalz*, European Court Reports, 3727 (1979).

14. By analogy with democracy and aristocracy, a teleocracy would be a system of government based on a particular objective or goal (from the Greek *telos, teleos*: end, and *kratos*: strength, power).

15. See J.H. Baker, *An Introduction to English Legal History* (London: Butterworths, 1990), chapter 8.

16. Many of the contributions to this volume show how these consequences might be felt, but the chapters by Hoffman and Claffy and Rekhter et al. on IP address allocation, as well as the many differing views on the Domain Name System, are particularly telling.

17. In RFC 1591, the Internet Domain Names Board (IDNB) is given the task of "act[ing] as a review panel for cases in which the parties [in the allocation of new Top Level Domains] can not reach agreement among themselves." Similarly, RFC 1602 gives an arbitral function to the Internet Architecture Board (IAB). These both appear to be more administrative than judicial procedures.

18. See J. Postel, "New Registries and the Delegation of International Top Level Domains"<URL:ftp://ftp.isi.edu/in-notes/iana/administration/new-registries> (accessed 7 October 1996, copy on file with author).

19. The necessity, for example, of reliable interconnections for commercial use of the Internet was pointed out to me by Erik Bataller of CommerceNet.

20. See, for example, Yves Mény, *Government and Politics in Western Europe* (Oxford: Oxford University Press, 1990), passim.

21. As IANA already does before the delegation of responsibility for national domains in disputed areas. See RFC 1591.

22. In English law this requirement may be mitigated by consideration of the circumstances in which a decision is taken: *Re H.K. (an infant)*, 2 Queen's Bench Reports, 617 (1967).

23. See, for example, *Dimes v. Grand Junction Canal Co. Proprietors*, 3 House of Lords Cases, 759 (1852) and *R. v. Gough*, 2 Weekly Law Reports, 883 (1993).

24. It is axiomatic that "justice must not only be done but be seen to be done."

25. See <URL:ftp://rs.internic.net/policy/internic/internic-domain-6.txt> (accessed 7 October 1996, copy on file with the author).

26. The doctrine is commonly said to originate in the decision of the Court of Appeal in *Schmidt v. Secretary of State for Home Affairs*, 2 Chancery Reports, 149 (1969).

27. Which decisions should be unchangeable is a matter that needs careful consideration.

28. See the IANA proposal, note 18 above.

29. Ibid., section 9.

30. Ibid., section 5.7.

31. Ibid., section 6.3.

32. Ibid., section 6.7.

33. This is implicit in NSI's rules for domain registration, in section 4 of which it is stated that domains may be revoked on receipt of a court order from a U.S. federal or state court: <URL:ftp://rs.internic.net/policy/internic/internic-do-main-6.txt>. At the workshop where this chapter was originally presented, Grant Clark of NSI suggested that NSI would respond to courts in any appropriate jurisdiction. This is at odds with the wording of NSI's published policy, which refers rather confusingly to "a federal or state court in the United States appearing to have jurisdiction" (in sec. 4 and sec. 6(f)) and to "any court of competent jurisdiction in the United States" (in sec. 7(a) and (b)).

34. Article 177 EC.

35. David G. Post, "Anarchy, State, and the Internet: An Essay on Law Making in Cyberspace," *Journal of Online Law* (1995).

36. Johnson and Post's chapter in this volume suggests that competition is also possible at the constitutional level. It is likely that there are technical objections to such competition.

37. The original credo of the IETF, as expressed by Dave Clark in 1992—"We reject kings, presidents and voting. We believe in rough consensus and running code"—has been transformed into a more thorough statement of objectives in RFC 1958, *Architectural Principles of the Internet.*

38. See Tony Prosser, "Regulation, Markets and Legitimacy," in Jeffrey Jowell and Dawn Oliver, eds., *The Changing Constitution* (3rd edition) (Oxford: Clarendon Press, 1994), for an introduction to and overview of the regulatory process as applied in the United Kingdom.

39. Even more important, but beyond the scope of this chapter, there is a problem with the funding of a coherent system of governance.

And How Shall the Net Be Governed?: A Meditation on the Relative Virtues of Decentralized, Emergent Law

David R. Johnson and David G. Post

Introduction

Now that lots of people use (or plan to use) the Internet, many governments, businesses, techies, individual users, and system operators (the "sysops" who control ID issuance and the servers that hold files) are asking how we will be able to (1) establish and enforce baseline rules of conduct that facilitate reliable communications and trustworthy commerce, and (2) define, punish, and prevent wrongful actions that trash the electronic commons or impose harm on others.

In other words, how will cyberspace be governed, and by what right?

By creating a new global space that disregards national borders and that cannot readily be controlled by any existing sovereign,[1] the net weakens many of the institutions that we have come to rely on to resolve the basic problems of collective action—the selection of means by which individuals coordinate and order their interactions so as to achieve what they believe is a greater good. Thus, the very nature and growing importance of the Internet calls for a fundamental reexamination of the institutional structure within which rule-making—at least as applicable to activities conducted solely on the net—takes place. As more fully discussed below, that reexamination might lead us to conclude that the Internet allows the problem of collective action to be solved by a new, decentralized process that does not closely resemble those we have used in the past to pass laws and enforce behavioral norms.

Questions about whether and how the Internet shall be governed are now arising most pointedly in connection with the issuance of domain names (like *ibm.com*). Domain names are translated by means of lookup tables distributed across the Internet into the Internet Protocol (IP) addresses (e.g., 123.45.67.89) that determine how messages are routed over the net. Because domain names are easier to remember than long strings of numbers, and because Top Level Domains (TDLs) are often used in e-mail addresses (e.g., *fred@ibm.com*), they have become a particularly valuable form of "virtual real estate." Yet despite their value and importance, it is far from clear who (if anyone) has the authority to determine who may use any particular domain name (and on what terms and conditions may they do so), or to establish the basic structure of the Domain Name System (DNS)—the combination of technical standards and trade practices pursuant to which domain names are registered and the associated lookup tables are distributed across the Internet.

As described in Request for Comment (RFC) 1591,[2] the Internet Assigned Numbers Authority (IANA)

is responsible for the overall coordination and management of the Domain Name System (DNS), and especially the delegation of portions of the name space called top-level domains. Most of these top-level domains are two-letter country codes taken from the ISO standard 3166. A central Internet Registry (IR) has been selected and designated to handled the bulk of the day-to-day administration of the Domain Name System. Applications for new top-level domains (for example, country code domains) are handled by the IR in consultation with the IANA. The central IR is INTERNIC.NET. Second level domains in COM, EDU, ORG, NET, and GOV are registered by the Internet Registry at the InterNIC....Currently, the RIPE NCC is the regional registry for Europe and the APNIC is the regional registry for the Asia-Pacific region, while the INTERNIC administers the North American region, and all the as yet undelegated regions.

Although both IANA and InterNIC (which has delegated DNS administration to Network Solutions, Inc. [NSI], a private company) receive U.S. government funds for their operation, no contract, constitution, or treaty gives either of these bodies or the U.S. government the right to set policy regarding domain names on the global network. Nor do these bodies have any obviously valid claim to the exclusive delegation of registration duties. The financial support provided by the U.S. government has not given it ownership of any intellectual property or physical asset essential (other than in the very short term) to the operation of a Domain Name System. To the contrary, domain name lookup tables function because local hosts point their domain name servers at these tables; a form of custom, not law, dictates the particular root servers to which local hosts point for this information.

The current uncertainty regarding governance of the Domain Name System extends to much more than the technical standards governing domain name registration and selection of root servers. Basic economic and policy questions remain unanswered at present, NSI (with the National Science Foundation's blessing) demands payment for registration of domain names. But again, no statute or international convention—or even universal acceptance of trade practice—clearly legitimizes NSI's right to charge that fee (or justifies any particular amount that might be charged). Nor is there any obvious source of guidance regarding what other conditions (such as a promise to abide by particular laws, to resolve disputes in a specified manner, or to waive certain claims) may be imposed as a prerequisite to domain name registration. Thus no one can now say that any given condition must, may, or may not be imposed as a minimum requirement for this particular passport to "netizenship." Nor do any of the many different private and governmental organizations that are currently discussing a range of questions in this area—e.g., how many Top Level Domains should be permitted, whether multiple registries should be allowed to compete, and what duties might reasonably be imposed on those who operate registries—have an uncontested or clearly legitimate claim to the authority to decide these matters unilaterally.

These questions are of crucial strategic importance, because only through an IP address and an association of that address with a locatable reference, whether through a domain name or a directory, can an individual meaningfully enter cyberspace in the first instance. To become a sysop offering access to the Internet one must obtain an IP address block and a domain name. Domain name-based e-mail addresses are the essence of on-line identity for individual users. Dispensers of these virtual addresses thus stand at the border checkpoint between the virtual and the nonvirtual world, and the contract pursuant to which one receives a domain name or other on-line ID can potentially serve as the means—perhaps the most effective means—by which the most basic rights and obligations of all cyberspace participants can be specified.

Thus, although the current domain name policy debate appears to apply primarily to ministerial duties performed by a registry, merely for the purpose of avoiding duplicative names, the contracts entered into with such a registry (and any associated subsidiary contracts through which individual users contract with the domain name/address holder to obtain access to the Internet) could prove of primary importance in determining both the degree of freedom and the level of order on the Internet.

Why Must the Net Be "Governed" at All?

Some may ask why the Internet must be "governed" at all. Even the three-judge federal court in Philadelphia that threw out the Communications Decency Act on First Amendment grounds seemed thrilled by the "chaotic" and seemingly ungovernable character of the Internet.[3] And the Internet now prospers precisely because of its decentralized architecture and the absence of centralized rule-making authority. Everyone who can buy a computer and has access to the global telephone network is free to establish a node on the Internet. Everyone is free to create editorial value by pointing to others' creations. New users connect by agreement with any nearby node or by getting an e-mail address from any commercial or noncommercial supplier. Lots of systems have lots of different rules governing the behavior of users, and users—at least in most countries—are free to leave any system whose rules they find oppressive. Some systems demand full identification from users; some allow or even encourage anonymity. Some impose editorial controls to create "kid-friendly" or "lawyer-friendly" environments; others act more like common carriers that accept all comers. Some require and enforce promises to abide by traditional copyright laws; others require all participants to waive claims that interfere with redistribution of the materials users post on-line. And access by sysops to domain names and IP addresses that make it possible to settle new territory in cyberspace has not been conditioned on any required promises to comply with (or to require users to comply with) specific laws or behavioral standards. That has, certainly, left sysops free to impose their own rules on end-users. But the diversity of differing venues on the Internet, and the ability of users to decide where to visit (and where *not* to visit) and with whom to communicate, have both tended to keep sysop tyranny in check and to limit the adverse impact of wrongdoing by individual users.

This decentralized decision-making has helped to make it possible for large numbers of people with different goals to get interconnected. But the problem of collective action remains and, indeed, grows more urgent as the Internet becomes larger and more complex. Anarchy, after all, has costs. For example, it just will not do for packets to be systematically misrouted. People will not trust their important commercial and private dealings to a network in which a domain name might be translated to a different IP address depending on where the message happens to originate. Nor indeed will large numbers of users visit on-line spaces if they encounter systematic fraud or vandalism or other activities that they view as harmful or antisocial. There are activities that, when permitted even in only a few on-line venues, impose costs on all others, and against which individuals will want to protect themselves. Spamming—the distribution of large numbers of unsolicited email—is a form of wrongdoing that may be beyond the capacity (or desire) of a particular local sysop to control, but it can make lots of users of lots of other systems miserable. The same could be said of launching destructive code. Some Web pages may invade your privacy on contact. Some parts of the electronic forest path may even be conducive to highway robbery. As the global village transforms itself into a complex electronic city, crime cannot be far behind. If the natural result of decentralized activities on the Internet were the development of unpredictable technical environments and unsafe social spaces, then calls for top-down, centralized forms of collective action would become louder and more persuasive. Thus, even with respect to activities that take place solely on the Internet, we face the questions of whether and how to generate and enforce rules to control antisocial users and the sysops that tolerate them.

Moreover, the Internet can be used to facilitate communications among individuals whose on-line actions impose harm even on those who only frequent the nonvirtual world. Most real world communities will want to be assured that the Internet will not be used systematically to undercut their security. On-line tax havens could harm the physical infrastructure of local communities that lose tax revenues. On-line conspiracies to commit violence in the real world would surely draw a response from the potential victims. Accordingly, both users of the Internet and all of those affected by their actions will likely demand some form of governance or order that prevents wrongdoing. The key question now posed in connection with the Domain Name System, and derivatively with respect to every other aspect of on-line interaction, is whether that governance must take the traditional form of centralized, top-down lawmaking, or whether instead the nature of the Internet allows for the decentralized creation of another very different form of public order.

Competing Models

There are four basic competing models for the governance of the global Internet.

• Existing territorial sovereigns can simply seek to extend their jurisdiction, and to amend their laws as necessary, to attempt to govern all actions on the Internet that have substantial impacts on their own citizenry.

• Sovereigns can enter into multilateral international agreements to establish new and uniform rules specifically applicable to conduct on the Internet.

• New international organizations can attempt to establish new rules—and new means of enforcing those rules and holding those who make the rules accountable to appropriate constituencies.

• De facto rules may emerge as a result of the complex interplay of individual decisions by domain name and IP address registries (regarding the conditions to impose on possession of an on-line address), by sysops (about which local rules to adopt, which filters to install, which users to allow to sign on, and with which other systems to connect), and by users (regarding which personal filters to install and which systems to patronize).

We believe that, in part because of serious problems with the first three traditional models, and in part because of the surprising ability of decentralized action to address serious problems that might previously have been thought to require top-down centralized lawmaking by a sovereign with a monopoly on the authorized use of force, the Internet may well be capable of being "governed" primarily by the fourth method—a mechanism that Tom Bell (following Hayek) calls "polycentric law,"[4] and that we will call "decentralized, emergent law."

The decentralized, emergent form of collective action involves voluntary acceptance of standards (or, as the Internet Engineering Task Force motto would have it: "rough consensus and working code" Despite the fears of those who cannot conceive of order arising from anything other than top-down, hierarchical control, this is *not* a process that *necessarily* leads to chaos and anarchy. To the contrary, the technical protocols of the Internet have in effect created a complex adaptive system that produces a type of order that does not rely on lawyers, court decisions, statutes, or votes. We will argue that the same decentralized decision-making process that created the Internet at a technical level may be able to create a workable and, indeed, empowering and just form of order even at the highest level of the protocol stack—the realm of rules applicable to the collective social evaluation and governance of human behavior.

Because decentralized action may well be capable of generating responsible self-regulation of the Internet, proponents of other forms of collective action might be best advised to hold off any efforts to achieve top-down control—lest they prematurely preempt the growth of what might be the most efficient and empowering form of Internet governance. Existing sovereigns need not waive their ultimate power to take action to protect the well-being of their citizens, of course. But they should sensibly defer action to see whether the collective actions of domain name registries, sysops, and users produce a set of operational rules that provides reasonable security for the vital interests they are charged to protect. If the Internet is allowed to develop a responsible self-regulatory structure via decentralized, emergent lawmaking, and if this new mechanism proves up to the task of building a productive and nonpredatory order, then all concerned will have saved the large resources that might otherwise have been spent trying, perhaps without similar success, to impose rules from a centralized source.

The Problems with Traditional Models for Centralized, Top-Down Governance, as Applied to the Net

Geographically Based Law

The nongeographic character of the Internet makes it very difficult to apply current, territorially based rules to activities online.[5] Local sovereigns may have a monopoly on the lawful use of physical force, but they cannot control on-line actions for which physical location is irrelevant or cannot even be established.

To be sure, any local sovereign can seek to control the persons within its geographic jurisdiction. Thus, it has not escaped the attention of current governments that system operators collectively hold the effective monopoly on the "lawful use of electronic force" with regard to actions on the Internet—at least with respect to the admission of users and messages into their own on-line areas. Moreover, because sysops must have physical hard disks that are present within particular territorial areas, they are clearly subject to the jurisdiction of the countries where they conduct their operations. The United States could pass a law threatening to shut down the operations of all sysops within its reach that do not abide by specific rules, and substantial compliance by U.S.-based systems would surely follow.

But overly aggressive regulation only drives disfavored activities "offshore"—what Michael Froomkin and others have described as "regulatory arbitrage"—and disconnect the local territory from the new and valuable global trade. And any legal doctrine that would give the right of regulation of the Internet to one country (or state, county, or city) would have to give that right to all sovereigns which would result in conflicts that would render the system internally contradictory and totally unworkable. The United States will surely resist assertions of jurisdiction by other countries over servers within its own territory. And other countries would just as surely reject any effort to impose U.S. law on the rest of the world.

The problem with using existing territorial governments as the source of rules for activity on the Internet is not merely that such rules are unlikely to have universal, long-term impact; rather, it is that no existing sovereign possesses the legitimate authority to make such rules. This traditional model of governance represents, in effect, an extraterritorial power grab when transposed to the Internet, a form of colonialism long rejected (and rightly so) in the nonvirtual context. Not only are the political institutions of established sovereigns poorly suited to creating wise rules for the Internet because any sovereign's rules for on-line conduct, even if arrived at democratically, do not take into account the interests of all of those they would affect if they were implemented in the on-line world, but also no country's efforts to "plant its flag" on the Internet and in effect declare sovereignty over the Internet are more clearly grounded in legitimacy than any other's, and would—and should—be met with fierce resistance.

International Treaties

The problems raised by conflicts between national laws, as well as the ability of users and sysops to flee (virtually) across physical borders, might be addressed by creating a uniform law of the Internet by treaty. But this second model for governance also has many problems. The treaty process is agonizingly slow, especially in contrast to the extremely rapid development of new technologies, new behaviors, and new governance issues on the Internet. Moreover, it is not clear that any treaty process could obtain agreement from all nations—and, again, the opportunities for regulatory arbitrage in such contexts, and the negative externalities created by actions sanctioned in countries that do not agree with the majority, are likely to be substantial. It is one thing to live with the fact that some few countries sanction fraud (or, for example, gambling of a type banned locally) when those countries are far away and hard to reach. It is quite another thing to have every tax haven or money-laundering-friendly sovereign electronically right next door. No treaty regime would be likely to succeed in imposing uniform rules on the Internet unless every sovereign whose citizens connect to the Internet were to join in the agreement. The very difficulty of that task—and the increasing rewards to those who disagree with the majority view and invite widely condemned activities under their protective sovereign umbrella—suggests that the treaty route to Internet governance is unlikely to be very successful.

Even if some core principles for the governance of the Internet could be agreed upon by treaty, such an agreement would almost certainly take the form of a high-level document written with a fair degree of generality. But the devil is in the details. The Internet continually presents novel questions that test our prior under-standings of law—and many of those questions need rapid resolu-tion if the potential for development of new forms of business and community on the Internet is to be realized. For example, a new treaty might declare that copyright law is applicable to the Internet (or, if the United States has its way, might even amend that law in various ways). But such a treaty would not likely resolve the ques-tion of whether caching a Web page is permitted by an implied license under certain conditions. Such a treaty would not likely make clear how U.S.-based First Amendment doctrines and copy-right principles are to be reconciled as applied to material originat-ing on Web sites outside the United States. Such a treaty would not likely provide for sufficient, low-cost, easily accessible dispute resolution procedures to give meaningful guidance to those argu-ing about whether some posting represents "fair use." The bottle-neck characteristics of any centralized lawmaking machinery, and the natural frailties of lawmaking processes based on writing authoritative texts—make centralized systems unsuitable for tack-ling a diverse, rapidly changing, large-scale set of problems—like that posed by the Internet.

International Organizations

Suppose we created a new international organization, not linked (directly or by treaty) to the sovereign power of any territorial government, whose mission was merely to establish and enforce the most basic rules for the Internet (such as the key conditions associated with establishing a domain name registry or holding a domain name and IP address). This third model could avoid some of the problems identified above, because it would not be tied to a particular territory and would not need to obtain, as a condition of addressing any particular issue, the agreement of all interested governments. But it would create new problems of its own. While some territorial governments might be content to defer to such a self-regulatory regime, how could such a nongovernmental organization impose its rules on the Internet as a whole? Even if it somehow controlled the current Domain Name System, how could it prevent the creation of a new one? And by what right would any such organization "govern"?

The problems with any top-down governance of the Internet, even by an institution specially created for that purpose, become apparent if we try to apply democratic values—as surely we would, and should—in this new environment. To prevent domination of some global governance body by any single group, the "legislative" arm would have to be held accountable by means of some form of election of representatives. But who would be represented, given a world in which the notion of separate "individuals" is virtually meaningless? Should we have an upper house elected by current domain name holders and a lower house representing those who merely have e-mail addresses? How could we prevent—or even define—vote fraud in an environment in which identity on the Internet need not trace back to unique, singular identity in the real world? Should we allow for representation by constituencies who are importantly affected by on-line activities but are not themselves on-line? We intuitively believe that a top-down governance mechanism for the Internet should be made accountable to relevant constituencies. However, once we abandon as unworkable the current system of national sovereignties as the source of such accountability, it is not easy to find an acceptable alternative.

More fundamentally, what would keep such a governance mechanism from being captured by factions? The right to set the rules for the global network would be too valuable not to become the focus of intense factional strife or, worse, to be bought. This is especially troubling in light of the ability of oppressive majorities to use the Internet itself to marshal support for their cause. As Phil Agre has pointed out to us, Madison's optimism in Federalist Paper 10 about the ability of a large geographic territory to damp down the influence of factions is seriously undermined by the use of global communications. At a minimum, the risk of corruption would be heightened by the absence in this context of intermediary social institutions of the type that can contend for influence and generally prevent extremism and oppression. Thus, even if we could create an apparently satisfactory method for making a new international governance mechanism "accountable," any such mechanism might all too rapidly be captured, by one means or another, by special interests.

Moreover, even if we could devise some sort of centralized governance mechanism that would be consistently and appropriately politically responsive to on-line constituencies, it is far from clear how we could protect the most basic rights of unpopular minorities or of those whose property the majority might prefer to take. Without a judiciary and a bill of rights, any such institution would find it all too easy to pick on the weakest sysops and users. It is not easy to set up an appropriate balance of powers within a new organization with quasi-governmental powers when the participants and constituents come from geographic places that have widely divergent views regarding democratic institutions, centralized authority and even "fairness" itself. And, even if we could write a bill of rights for the Internet and create a judiciary capable of interpreting it, such mechanisms would deal only with the most fundamental problems—hardly supplying an appropriate source for the myriad decisions that must be made, somehow, every day regarding whether some particular on-line behavior is or is not permitted in the context in which it occurs.

Can Net Policies and Rules Be Made and Enforced without Centralized Decision-Making?

We certainly do not mean to suggest that the governance models sketched out above will or should have no impact on the Internet. Merely to suggest that there are "problems" with implementation of any or all of these models is not to prove that they are inadequate for any of the tasks at hand; after all, proponents of representative democracy are fond of saying that while it is a terrible system, it is better than any known alternative. The fundamental question is whether, at least for the global electronic communications network, the fourth governance model of decentralized and emergent lawmaking might have significant advantages over the alternative models and should be looked at as the presumptive primary source of on-line order.

Consider what makes the Internet work. The Internet itself solves an immensely difficult collective action problem: how to get large numbers of individual computer networks, running diverse operating systems, to communicate with one another for the common good. The Internet is really nothing more than a set of voluntary standards regarding message transmission, routing, and reception. There is not now and never was a central governing body that decreed or voted to adopt a law stating that TCP/IP is required to be used by those wishing to communicate electronically on a global scale, or that HTTP is required to communicate over a particular portion of the global network (the World Wide Web). If you connect to a neighboring host and send out packets of data that conform to the protocol, your messages can be heard by others who have adopted the protocol. All are free to decline to follow the standard and to obey some other protocol, and they will communicate only to those who, literally, speak their language. Many people and groups have, in fact, seceded from (or declined to join) the global net, forming local area, or proprietary wide area, networks.

The rule-making process for baseline protocols of the Internet had none of the vices of centralized, top-down, bureaucratic or political governance. The rules instead evolved from the decentralized decisions by individuals to adopt a promising standard because it served their own interests. To be sure, successful rules were created by individuals and small groups, and they spread more quickly as a result of government-funded innovations and communications. But they did not stem from or rely in any way on the law of a geographically defined territory. They did not require any agreement among representatives of sovereign nations. And they did not necessitate the creation of a new policymaking apparatus that required an international bureaucracy or that faced questions about the accountability of decision-makers to particular constituencies. Minorities are protected by their right to propose inconsistent rules and, indeed, to follow those alternative rules if they believe the benefits of doing so outweigh the costs. Enforcement of a predominant rule set stems naturally from uncoordinated, decentralized decisions.

Can this same decentralized process, used to choose technical protocols, also successfully govern the behavior of users and sysops and domain name registries—and allow the effective and just pursuit of the public good on the Internet? A number of objections might be raised.

Objection 1

Any system of rules governing human behavior must have mechanisms to define, identify, and punish wrongdoing. The rules heretofore adopted in regard to transmission protocols can do so unambiguously because a packet either has TCP/IP headers or it doesn't, a document either complies with HTML standards or it doesn't, and violators are automatically detected and "punished" by becoming effectively dysfunctional and invisible to the system as a whole. How can rules regarding fraud or infringement emerge from a similar decentralized process of voluntary sysop adherence, when those actions cannot be so identified by the automatic interaction of software protocols?

Clearly, the preservation of civilized interaction on the Internet will require something other than mere "working software code." But sysops already can and do define, using words, the kinds of behavior that they consider wrongful in the context of their own systems. The contracts they offer to their subscribers describe minimally acceptable behavior, and sysops can and do banish users who violate their rules. Moreover, both users and sysops can and do interpret the rules they set for themselves to decide which messages they wish to accept and from whom. Thus, human intervention—wetware code—substitutes for the software code that enforces the rules at lower levels in the protocol stack. The resulting programs may not operate with flawless consistency. But they can "work"—in the sense of producing relatively predictable results. Thus, the mere fact that any decentralized, emergent law would involve subjective judgments does not mean that it could not have the same virtues that have been demonstrated for such decentralized mechanisms as a source of the "rough consensus and working code" that makes the Internet possible.

Objection 2

At present, virtually anyone can obtain a domain name and IP address from some source and set up a system. What prevents the rise of "data havens" that harbor a new type of pirate ship? Or, given pervasive interconnections, what prevents someone from moving rapidly from one system to another, perpetrating harm in each, but escaping before being caught?

These are substantial objections, to be sure. It may be that the best answer is that system operators and their users possess an entire arsenal of means by which wrongdoers may be excluded and repelled. Sysops could point their domain name servers only to registries that condition access to domain names on agreement to abide by whatever minimum standards of conduct they deem appropriate. Sysops can themselves deny access to anyone who does not act responsibly, as they define that term. Insofar as particular IP addresses are associated with "wrongdoing" (however one may choose to define that term), sysops and users can establish software filters that exclude messages from those addresses—a form of electronic confederation of local communities. Insofar as domain names and IP addresses underlie the links on the World Wide Web, sysops that host and users who create Web pages can decide to whom to point—and can point to other Web sites only if satisfied with the policy choices made by those other parties. Those who are especially concerned about potential harm from outside sources could, at the extreme, install software filters that would preclude receipt of any message that did not originate from a known location or that had not been rated by a trusted source.

Although it would certainly seem an overreaction to screen out all communications from anyone who had not passed some "good netizenship" test, the many different kinds of filters available to sysops and users serve to demonstrate that the real power to create a responsible public order on the Internet lies with the participants themselves. Sovereigns cannot compel agreement by rogue countries to accept a new global law. Outlaws cannot be isolated and "punished" based on their physical location—because the Internet cannot readily recognize the geographical location from which online activities take place. But it is relatively easy—or, at least, easier—for sysops to isolate and shun wrongdoers on the basis of their *virtual* location. And it is relatively easy for domain name registries and sysops to use the ID-issuance process to establish minimum standards of behavior applicable inside particular domains.

The problem posed by the ability of individuals to perpetrate harm, suffer banishment from particular communities, and reappear in new electronic guises to perpetrate further harm can be "solved" by the use of registries tying issuance of electronic identities to identifiable individuals (and the use of stable authentication devices). This, it need hardly be said, is a controversial suggestion, replete with deep consequences for personal privacy and control over one's personal identity. *But that proves our point:* rather than attempt to achieve a worldwide consensus on the "right" answer to this question in order to decide in some quasi-legislative fashion whether or not to implement such registries, we can allow individual users to decide for themselves whether the benefits of such systems in terms of personal security outweigh the costs to their personal privacy or other values they may hold dear.

Objection 3

How can we know whether a decentralized, emergent form of lawmaking for the Internet will produce a definition of the public good with which we agree? How can the nations of the world defer to this semichaotic process of private decision-making without knowing how far the net result will diverge from whatever set of rules existing sovereigns would have adopted if they had undertaken to deal with the problems of the Internet by traditional means?

This objection can be turned on its head. As suggested above, ultimately the best case for decentralized, emergent law stems from the lack of any objective criteria by which to measure whether any particular set of rules is optimal. Should we have one uniform set of rules on any particular topic, such as the application of copyright law to on-line postings, or should we allow every "local" on-line area to set its own rules? That question, obviously, must be answered by both local and global constituencies—and there is a strong argument that decentralized decisionmaking is the most cost-effective and accurate means of reflecting the real preferences of participants on the Internet with regard to the structure of electronic federalism. Insofar as we want a form of collective action that is relatively certain to reflect the views of participants on the Internet, and that attains this accuracy at minimal cost, we probably cannot find a better mechanism. The interaction between rule-making by sysops and navigational decisions of users produces a very close fit between the overall desires of the on-line public and the actual experiences of these participants. The option and burden of identifying connections to avoid, or users to banish, or specific messages to filter, can be spread across the entire base of Internet users, as sysops and users decide unilaterally whether or not to rely on the recommendations of others. This new form of "Internet leverage" makes policing the boundaries of one's personal portion of cyberspace light work indeed, as compared with the task of projecting one's views onto some centralized global policymaking process.

The central problem for the regulation of the Internet is not how to enforce widely agreed upon rules, but how to define what we mean by wrongdoing. What is infringement? Defamation? Invasion of privacy? Unacceptably obscene? The Internet creates many different phenomena requiring the development of new rules. Is it wrong to send large volumes of unsolicited commercial e-mail? What notice should be given before a host system writes a cookie file to my hard disk? Under what circumstances is it wrong to cache a Web page? The great virtue of the Internet is that it allows multiple, incompatible resolutions of such policy questions by giving those who disagree with the resolution of any particular question the means to avoid contact with one another. If many people disagree on applicable standards, then the remedy is to allow each set to migrate to different areas of the Internet (and to filter out messages from uncongenial areas). If almost all agree on certain basic standards, then that agreement itself solves the problem, because outliers can be banished and their negative externalities filtered into irrelevancy. There will always be "outlaws" on the Internet, but the power of digital filtering is such that they can be kept safely away from the mainstream, and vice versa, most of the time.

Objection 4

How can a decentralized, private system of this type produce anything we could call "law"? Consensual adoption of standards of behavior is simply a matter of ethics or custom. Protection against wrongdoers has always required something stronger than that—the ability to deploy physical force in the real world, to put people in real jails. And justice has always meant treating like cases alike, giving everyone equal rights.

Because the decentralized system creates a different sets of rules for people who visit different on-line spaces, those who conceive of law as a single, consistent set of timeless, top-down authoritative texts will be unconvinced—or unhappy. A decentralized, emergent rule-evolving system does destroy traditional notions of equality before the law. Even thinking about the idea that applicable rules may be different for every single user, depending on where the user goes on the Internet, and how that user's electronic agents negotiate with incoming messages, makes a lawyer's head ache. But the best answer to this objection is that the basic purpose of law is to maximize individual rational choice, and to minimize the role of power or force enjoyed by the few, in determining outcomes. Because the Internet allows easy movement among differing spaces, as well as easy (on-line) separation of people who do not agree on basic ground rules, it can afford *not* to be consistent. Its inconsistency gives all users an equal right to create or select the rule sets they find most empowering. This emergent law of the Internet can thus maximize individual, well-informed choice without failing to give clear, prospective guidance regarding applicable rules for any particular on-line space.

The more daunting part of this objection is the suggestion that, ultimately, the only way to subdue a determined wrongdoer is by physical force. We certainly cannot allow private parties to deploy physical force in a decentralized way. But the objection that on-line rules are not truly "law" until backed up by physical force is, at most, a semantic challenge because the underlying premise of decentralized Internet governance is that the nations of the world would agree to enforce the rules established by sysop and user interactions, just as they now enforce contracts entered into by private parties. Contracts represent more than mere ethics. They can and do guide behavior. They get enforced. And their mandatory terms constrain options available to those who would rent a car, or a hotel room, just as clearly as would a local ordinance (indeed, usually more clearly and flexibly, because the sources for contractual rules are more dispersed, more market driven and more flexible than any legislature or bureaucracy). Thus, the prospect of governing the Internet via decentralized, emergent decision-making does not imply that the use of force by governments would be irrelevant, but only that it would be deployed in the service of rules made predominantly by private actors.

Objection 5

Even if nation-states were to agree to defer, in general, to the results produced by decentralized, emergent rule-making of the type described here, surely they would feel the need to intervene to outlaw actions that threatened important interests of their constituencies. And, given the degree of disagreement, worldwide, on any given issue, wouldn't those exceptional interventions gobble up the general rule, leading us back to governance by territorially based sovereigns, international treaties, and maybe some transnational organizations gingerly establishing noncontroversial rules?

There is no doubt that every country—and state, county, and city—will feel a strong urge to intervene, to try to regulate the Internet, in some instances. But there is an existing international law doctrine of "comity" that strongly suggests that no local jurisdiction should have the right to impose its own law in preference to that of a foreign jurisdiction that has a stronger interest in the appropriate resolution of the dispute in question. How often and how strongly local sovereigns will seek to intervene to regulate the Internet will depend, in turn, on how strong a case can be made by

Internet participants that they, collectively, have the greatest interest in being allowed to make the rules. This will turn in part on
whether the Internet in fact engages in responsible self-regulation
or instead becomes a haven for activities that large numbers of local
authorities define as serious wrongdoing. In short, decentralized,
emergent law can work to create some form of order—but whether
that order will face a determined onslaught of local regulation
depends on whether the self-regulatory order is sufficiently "responsible" from the perspective of the territorial powers that be.

Objection 6

The law that emerges from this decentralized process is not predictable. It may not be stable. It might not produce results we would,
from our current perspectives, consider wise.

It is true that complex adaptive systems can behave in ways that
are difficult, or even impossible, to predict. But the top-down
lawmaking process is itself unpredictable and can produce results
many think are unwise. Moreover, decentralized systems can behave in a much more stable fashion than those driven by centralized decision-making. The failure (or success) of a particular
domain name registry, or a specific set of policies imposed on a
subset of users, will be far less disruptive than the failure (or
mistake) of a single centralized policy body. If a user leaves an on-
line system because she disagrees with the local rules, or a particular system fails because many users share such a view, merely
normal marketplace disruptions result. Finally, the beauty of complex adaptive systems is that they conduct very efficient searches. By
allowing the "initiative" of individual components to find a wide
range of alternative starting points, and then relying on the uphill
march of imitation and the copying facilitated by on-line communications of the reputations of various on-line venues, the decentralized, emergent lawmaking system will quite likely find the high
ground in policy space.

The Internet Needs a Good Foreign Policy

The strongest apparent objection to a decentralized, emergent law
of the Internet is that actions on the Internet can have unaccept-

able real-world impacts on people who have not agreed to abide by the rules of the on-line space from which those negative externalities arise. It is one thing to say that a person cruising the net can steer clear of a known "den of thieves" (and, indeed, much more readily than ever before find out whom to avoid). It is quite another thing to suggest that no centralized or territorially based law should govern the use of the Internet by a den of real-world thieves to track your physical movements and to plot to burgle your house! Even activities conducted *solely* on-line may have significant real-world effects. The unauthorized use of logos and domain names might (conceivably) cause confusion with or dilute the real-world trademarks attached to physical goods. Havens for on-line copyright infringement might detract from an author's ability to sell a physical copy of a book. And, perhaps, an obscene file might warp the mind of a pervert who lives down the street, placing your children at risk of harm.

But the argument that all on-line activities must be governed by traditional, top-down, real-world legal standards, just because they might have an important impact on the real world, goes too far. The very same thing could be said about forms of interaction among all self-regulatory groups, including churches, clubs, stock exchanges, businesses and nongovernmental organizations. We want, in general, to empower individuals and groups to regulate their own affairs. The mere possibility of negative externalities cannot itself, in the abstract, answer the question of Internet governance.

More important, even with respect to those on-line activities that do have demonstrable negative impacts on the real world, the claim that rules must be imposed from above depends ultimately on the right of the persons who wish to impose those rules to govern the conduct of people who, by definition, have decided to adopt a different set of rules. If the offending on-line activity is conducted by people who live in a different country from those who are offended, the "wrongdoers" may have a legal right (under the law of their local state) to engage in the activity in question. No matter how strongly the residents of Tennessee feel about an obscene Web page based in Amsterdam, there may be no basis in current law on which to control that activity by means of traditional top-down legal rules.

Nevertheless, one might postulate some on-line activities that would threaten most real-world citizens and would not be tolerated or protected by any geographic state. Imagine, for example, a host computer based in international waters, using wireless technology to broadcast messages that enable terrorist groups to make chemical weapons and coordinate an attack. In such a case, the small Internet "community" that patronized that on-line venue would be, in effect, at war not only with the remainder of the on-line world but also with the authorities and citizens of the real world. Any scheme for responsible self-regulation of the Internet must deal, conceptually, with this kind of hard case. The decentralized, emergent form of order deals with this type of case by conceding that, at this extreme, the national sovereigns may exercise force to defend their interests—just as sysops and users may use their own electronic form of force (their prerogatives to banish users or to leave a particular system) to set boundaries on others' otherwise uncontrollable wrongdoing.

Because the Internet does have real impacts on the real world, it can best hope to preserve its decentralized, emergent character if it "renders unto Caesar what is Caesar's." If on-line commercial transactions radically undermine the tax system needed to build the physical infrastructure, territorial governments may be entitled to defend that core interest by shutting down host sites specially designed to facilitate such transactions. Perhaps the sysops that facilitate on-line transactions should anticipate this problem and create a centralized means for on-line commerce to pay a fair tax, to a single collector, to discourage more disruptive and potentially duplicative enforcement proceedings by local authorities. In the face of such responsible action by the Internet itself, local authorities would be more likely to recognize that they do not possess a writ that automatically runs to all areas of the Internet, and that they should not seek to set the rules governing on-line interactions that do not have a serious negative impact on the tangible world they govern.

It bears remembering that the users of the Internet and the "real world" policymakers most affected by on-line activities are, to a first approximation, the same people. As a group, netizens will not want to support activities that threaten core values they share as real-world citizens. There are lots of novel issues that arise from the ability of electronic messages to cross territorial borders—but they will be resolved in part by the ability of every user and system to filter out unwanted messages, and, in part, by the ability of such crossborder communications to bring the world into close agreement about core values.

Notwithstanding the overlap between real world policymakers and participants on the Internet, there is reason to fear that the communications process by which various constituencies come to understand their own interests—and as a result of which the various sources of authoritative decision-making will decide to proceed or to defer to others better situated to make and enforce applicable rules—needs to be enhanced. Rule-setting on the Internet has traditionally been done by a small group of engineers who have had an aversion to discussion of softer policy matters. Those who make national laws have not generally understood the special policy issues posed by the Internet or been aware that the Internet is capable of producing responsible self-regulation. If either group has been concerned that rules made by the other would impinge to an unacceptable degree on the vital interest of a particular geographic or on-line territory, there has been little opportunity to communicate that concern effectively to the other.

The need for workable, accepted rules to govern the new trade in ideas and services that takes place on line can be largely satisfied without any massive new legislative agenda or rule-making spree by the established authorities of the tangible world. But what may be needed is an enhanced communications process by means of which territorially based communities can make known to the Internet community when on-line actions threaten their vital interests. And of course there is a need for methods by which the on-line community can more effectively communicate to the governments and citizens of the real world when the actions and policies of these traditional venues impinge strongly on on-line values or freedoms.

Domain Name Policy as a Key First Problem for Collective Action—Revisited

To determine whether the combination of decentralized decision-making and better communications between real-world authorities and virtual communities could lead to a workable form of governance for the Internet, let us examine more closely the current core hard case: the policies governing creation of new Top Level Domains. If there is any issue that at first glance appears to call for strong centralized rule, it is the question of how domain names are issued and how they are translated into IP numbers. The Domain Name System (DNS) determines where data packets are sent. If two separate registries both issued a "right" to use *ibm.com,* and mapped this domain name to different IP addresses, and if half of the Internet derived its DNS lookup tables from one regime and half from the other, massive confusion would ensue. If different registries impose differing conditions on access to Internet real estate or on-line identity, then there can be no single definition of "netizenship"—and wrongdoers (by someone's definition) will seek out the most tolerant regimes. Because of their mnemonic character, certain domain names and domain name uses are already being challenged as infringing on trademark rights deemed vital by companies that sell branded products. And there is an increasing number of other questions that implicate the potentially intense and conflicting interests of particular communities. For example, can a registry charge for the use of a domain name? If so, how much? And what decision-making process governs the expenditure of the money? May "indecent" domain names be registered? Must those who use domain names agree to resolve their disputes by arbitration? Agree to abide by copyright laws? Issue e-mail addresses only to identifiable users? The Domain Name System thus already poses stark questions regarding the relationship between any self-regulatory system for the Internet and the powers of existing legislatures and courts.

There is reason to believe that even these challenging and contentious issues can be resolved by decentralized, emergent decision-making. For example, even the apparently fatal conflict between inconsistent domain name registration systems seems likely to be avoided without top-down controls. Most users and sysops are interested in accurate routing of messages, and thus they will want to connect to the DNS sources that most other people use. The confusing dual and inconsistent system hypothesized above is unstable (or, rather, could never arise in the first place) because the most widely used of the two systems would soon attract virtually all of the traffic (or all of the connections from downstream systems). Thus, the successful deployment of two incompatible versions of a Top Level Domain, or two widely distributed yet incompatible sets of lookup tables, is about as likely as the simultaneous growth in one country of two languages that have the same words mapped onto different meanings. Because people look to reliable sources for their information, good data drives out bad. Network economies, and the creation of order from positive returns to information structure, save the day. Thus, while it is physically possible and currently lawful for system operators to create a mess by pointing their domain name resolving software at multiple incompatible sources, that nightmare scenario probably will not occur and need not be prohibited by legislation of any kind.

Similarly, there is good reason to believe that some combination of domain name registries and domain name holders will impose rules, in connection with issuance of access to the Internet, that reflect widespread agreement on what constitutes wrongful action. And there is reason to think that the actions of users in selecting the on-line venues they visit and support will in general prevent such regulation from becoming either too oppressive or too lax. The on-line public will band together to electronically shun tyrants and detectable crooks. (We may need to worry more about due process, to protect unpopular minorities from mobs, than law enforcement.) Dens of thieves—and packets of data sent from known dens of thieves—can generally be avoided on line. If your concern is privacy, you can avoid Web sites that do not post verifiable tokens indicating that they observe rules that you deem satisfactory. If you do not want certain sites to link to your Web page, you can use software code to preclude such links. No matter what your policy goal, acting through the filtering power of sysops and users is much more likely to produce rapid and effective results than lobbying for the enactment of some rule by a new transnational legislative body.

To be sure, no decentralized, emergent lawmaking scheme of this kind could be 100 percent effective. But substantial consensus is, operationally and practically, quite important even when total compliance cannot be achieved (as, by the way, is always the case, even under centralized law enforcement regimes run by nondemocratic sovereigns). The reason is, again, that screening applicants for IDs and filtering out known sources of wrongful messages reduces the impact of wrongdoing even when these actions do not put the wrongdoer totally out of business. Trademark infringement tolerated on Web pages in a small corner of the Internet, and filtered out by most responsible sysops once they are aware of the problem, simply cannot cause very much confusion.

In contrast, efforts to use traditional top-down, centralized lawmaking to resolve the problems posed by the Domain Name System seem very likely to fail in more brittle ways. Take the question whether the establishment of alternative Top Level Domains should be allowed.[6] In the context of decentralized, emergent law, this question is decided in the marketplace by multiple independent decisions over whether to register with a new purported provider of a *.biz* domain or whether to point a local domain name server at another root lookup table. If, however, the United States were to attempt to exercise its powers to prohibit the establishment of alternative Top Level Domains, it would simply fail to attain jurisdiction over the actions of some host provider operating entirely outside the United States. Perhaps the United States could effectively prohibit all U.S. hosts from pointing their local domain name servers at that remote root table, but the First Amendment might constrain such restrictions, which in any event would look silly if they conflicted with practices in other countries and the desires of the U.S. market. If instead the United States sought to negotiate a new treaty governing the establishment of new Top Level Domains, it would likely still be defining the shape of the bargaining table while the issue was decided, de facto, by engineering decisions. If it sought to delegate decisions on Top Level Domain structure to a new international organization, it would face unanswerable questions about how to compel private actors to comply with that organization's decisions. And even if most countries agreed to defer to and enforce the decisions of such an organization, there would be a serious question of how to assure that its decisions reflected the needs and preferences of all participants in Internet-based commerce. The best indicator of those needs and preferences would be the independent actions taken by sysops and users to accept a new standard. Traditional lawmaking processes would become, in this context, a counterproductive extra loop that at most would delay or misdirect decisions otherwise likely to evolve rapidly from a decentralized process.

Similarly, contrast the likely outcome of traditional approaches to a problem involving potential conflicts between on-line behavior and the interests of those who may not even participate in Internet commerce: the use of domain names that overlap in some way with trademarks used on physical products. A U.S. statute outlawing the registration of a domain name by someone other than the holder of the corresponding copyright would face many problems. The registrant (and even the registry) might not be subject to U.S. jurisdiction, unless the United States is prepared to take the expansive view that anyone making use of pointers on computers in the United States can be governed by U.S. law (a position that would come back to bite the United States badly in its efforts to stave off regulation of U.S. businesses by foreign governments). Treaties on intellectual property rights might address this issue—but they would likely founder on the problem that multiple trademarks applicable to particular types of goods in particular geographic areas, and subject to differing local laws, might all seem equally entitled to preempt the others. As John Gilmore has said, you just cannot pour ten pounds of trademarks into a one-pound domain name sack. And some countries might well take the view that domain names should be treated somewhat differently from traditional marks. A new international organization might try to establish a uniform policy. But the unsatisfied trademark owners could still file suit in local courts, which might not defer to this new international organization. And in any event, dissatisfied domain name holders could support a competing registry. The apparent simplicity and uniformity of centralized, top-down solutions to the new issues posed by the Internet tend to vanish upon closer inspection.

The issuance of domain names is a good core problem in the context of which to consider Internet governance because this Internet "real estate" presents, by its very nature, the opportunity to resolve the governance problem more generally. Every domain name, and every subsidiary e-mail address, is issued by a registry or party that enters into a contract with the recipient. That contract, pursuant to which access to netizenship is granted, might contain various conditions that facilitate the growth of responsible self-governance by the Internet. The right balance between those conditions that ought to be imposed at the top level (on the domain name holder, by the registry) and those that ought to be imposed at lower levels (either on an ID holder, or as a condition for entry into a particular on-line space) will emerge as a result of a continuous negotiation between the various levels. We probably need competing domain name registries to allow this system to operate in a dynamic and responsive manner. While this contract-driven process will surely result in diversity, it (and the filtering and free movement provided by the Internet) will help to prevent conflicts and to limit the impact of any actions considered wrongful by particular constituencies.

Conclusion

Let's review the alternatives. Can territorial laws be applied to on-line activities that have no relevant or perhaps even determinable geographic location? We doubt it. Can international treaties set forth workable rules that provide good guidance for on-line commerce? Not in our lifetimes (now measured in accelerated Internet years). Should we allow the rules of the Internet to be encoded into software by a technical elite, with no mechanism of accountability to the on-line population? The question answers itself. Should we create a new international forum for Internet policymaking? Well, maybe not until we demonstrate that less formal mechanisms will not work. Has decentralized decision-making been demonstrated to produce unworkable chaos that threatens the vital interests of established governments? Not really. We have barely tried to conduct a collective conversation designed to allow responsible participants to set their own rules and to help all concerned—on line and off—seek to understand and respect others' vital interests. Yet that kind of conversation is precisely the kind of activity the Internet itself is designed—thanks to the engineers—to facilitate.

Of course, we know that this model can work in some contexts—it is called federalism, and we have witnessed its success in the U.S. constitutional system and elsewhere. Internet federalism looks very different from what we have become accustomed to, because here individual network systems, rather than territorially based sovereigns, are the essential governance units. The law of the Internet has emerged, and we believe can continue to emerge, from the voluntary adherence of large numbers of network administrators to basic rules of law (and dispute resolution systems to adjudicate the inevitable inter-network disputes), with individual users "voting with their electrons" to join the particular systems they find most congenial. Or perhaps we should think of this as the law of the *nets*, for one possible (or even likely) consequence of this evolutionary development is the emergence of multiple network confederations, each with its own "constitutional" principles—some permitting and some prohibiting, say, anonymous communications, some imposing strict rules regarding redistribution of information and others allowing freer movement—enforced by means of electronic fences prohibiting the movement of information across confederation boundaries.

This governance model does not, of course, solve all problems (any more than the existing system of international law perfectly administers and enforces rules in the real world), and these governance issues will not be sorted out overnight. Nor will they be resolved without a struggle; existing sovereigns are not about to blithely relinquish their lawmaking prerogatives and go quietly into that "Twilight of Sovereignty" that Walter Wriston presciently foresaw several years ago.[7] But the Internet itself is testament to the enormous power of this rule-making model that we ignore at our peril and to the likely detriment of all those seeking to take advantage of the remarkable potentials of the new medium.

Notes

1. An argument we make in more detail in our paper "Law and Borders: The Rise of Law in Cyberspace," 48 *Stan. L. Rev.* 1367 (1996), and available at <http://www.cli.org/X0025_LBFIN.html>.

2. Available at <http://ds.internic.net/rfc/rfc1591.txt>.

3. *ACLU v. Reno*, 929 FSupp 824 (ED PA 1996).

4. See the article by that name at <http://osf1.gmu.edu/~ihs/w91issues.html>.

5. See "Law and Borders."

6. See, in this regard, the Internet Drafts "New Registries and the Delegation of International Top Level Domains," available at <ftp://ds.internic.net/Internet-

drafts/draft-postel-iana-itld-admin-02.txt>, and "Creation of and Registration in the '.NUM' Top Level Domain," available at <ftp://ds.internic.net/Internet-drafts/draft-rfced-info-schultz-00.txt>.

7. See Walter B. Wriston, *The Twilight of Sovereignty: How the Information Revolution Is Transforming Our World* (New York, Scribner, 1992), which examines the challenges to sovereignty posed by the information revolution. On pp. 61–62 Wriston writes: "Technology has made us a 'global' community in the literal sense of the word. Whether we are ready or not, mankind now has a completely integrated international financial and information marketplace capable of moving money and ideas to any place on this planet in minutes. Capital will go where it is wanted and stay where it is well treated. It will flee from manipulation or onerous regulation of its value or use, and no government power can restrain it for long."

Factors Shaping Internet Self-Governance

A. M. Rutkowski

Introduction

The subject of governance is currently of great importance to the Internet because of a number of rapid transitions under way in the field. At this point, the Internet has reached a sufficient scale to constitute a very important public global infrastructure. Moreover, many significant new related services and capabilities are emerging, which constitutes an enormous market. It has become clear that the hidden governance role played by the U.S. government is no longer appropriate, and, as a result, different communities, including governmental bodies, are becoming involved in shaping new governance regimes. As in all rapid transitions, existing Internet institutions and regimes are adapting, and new ones are being created.

A kind of fable exists about Internet governance—namely that there is little or no governance, particularly under any kind of governmental aegis—and that this somehow has been the secret of the Internet's success. The reality is actually quite the opposite. Indeed, in terms of governance, the Internet shares many of the characteristics of all other kinds of communications networks past and present. The Internet requires a certain level of well-coordinated and uniformly applied technical standards, operational practices, user conduct, administration, and associated collective decision-making on a large scale. In fact, the level of coordination and cooperation in the Internet is far more extensive than in most other telecommunication networks because of the highly dynamic and interactive nature of network management information that constantly propagates through the network itself.

Strictly speaking, the Internet is just a collection of very flexible distributed networks that is optimized for computer communication "plumbing." Although we tend to talk about the Internet as if it were a single entity, it is important to recognize that it is merely a shorthand term that encompasses much more. It also includes intranets (also known as enterprise internets), extranets, on-line services, e-mail, the World Wide Web, and countless hundreds of other networks, applications, and services that are woven through the backbone networks constituting the Internet. Indeed, it is these ancillary components that produce the preponderance of revenue opportunities and innovations today, not the Internet.

The Internet's Complex History of Governance

Phase One: Total Governmental Governance

During the first half of the Internet's twenty-two year existence, it was both directly subject to the absolute governance and ownership of the U.S. Department of Defense (DOD), as well as indirectly through its contractors. Certain people and institutions employed by or funded and maintained by the government during this first phase had total control over the Internet, its operation, and use. No other communications medium has had this same genesis, and to a significant extent, certain attributes of the Internet's present governance stem from this heritage. The residual institutions include what are now called the Internet Assigned Numbers Authority (IANA) and the InterNIC.

Phase Two: Governmental and Academic Governance

During the next six years of the Internet's existence (approximately 1986–1992), governance derived from a combination of DOD and government research and education agency control and funding. This second phase of Internet governance resulted in a somewhat unusual hybrid of government-supported academic research institutions, practices, and values coexisting with first-phase institutions. This phase produced what are now called the Internet Architecture Board (IAB), the Internet Engineering and Research Task Forces (IETF and IRTF), the Internet Society, the Routing Arbiter, the Internet Engineering Planning Group, and the regional operators groups. Throughout this phase, governance was largely affected through U.S. government agencies and inter-agency activities. These institutions were very cleverly effected in a way that allowed governmental governance of all the key aspects of the Internet while at the same time encouraging open and highly active research and academic collaboration, innovation, and product and service development. The original masterminds of this two-pronged strategy—Bob Kahn and the "California Group"—referred to the process as "technology transfer," and the mechanisms as "collaboratories."

The intent of this elegant strategy was to provide a strategic industrial backplane in the form of the National Research and Educational Network (NREN), which had global reach and was managed quietly by what amounted to a distributed "civilian DARPA." (The notion of a "civilian DARPA" was advanced during the early 1980s as a means of advancing strategically important technologies for civilian applications. Although it never manifested itself as a definitive government agency, a variety of surrogate nonprofit organizations became vehicles for accepting and managing government monies to the same end.) It was a brilliant idea, but developments began to occur that its creators did not foresee or understand—commercial entrepreneurialism, PC-based applications, and public scaling. Early technology innovators are rarely, if ever, public-scale implementors. Thus began phase three of the Internet's history, a new phase of entirely entrepreneurial innovation and business models in virtual marketplaces.

Throughout the 1980s, a combination of Value-Added Network suppliers, major corporate users, and government regulatory agencies began designing and implementing policies and rules that allowed enterprise internets and the Internet to transcend their DOD and academic confines. In significant part, this government regulatory proactivity was a serendipitous result of the appointment of the original DARPA Internet leader, Steven J. Lukasik, as chief scientist of the Federal Communications Commission (FCC), where he helped craft the regulatory policies and strategies that were to eventually enable and nurture the Internet's emergence and growth in the public domain. These included the basic enhanced dichotomy device to exclude enhanced services from regulatory domains, the liberalization of network attachment rules, elimination of access charges, and simplification of underlying telecommunications transport capacity available at cost-oriented prices, and ideally flat-rate pricing. These activities developed not only in the United States, but were implemented internationally implemented over more than a decade through some of the most extensive and effective bilateral and multilateral regulatory forums and initiatives in U.S. history. They were rivaled in scope only by the actions taken in the 1920s to regulate radio, in the late 1940s with respect to multilateral telecommunications organizations, and in the 1960s for satellite communications. Most individuals involved in today's Internet activities have little cognizance or appreciation of the scope and magnitude of these regulatory strategies and activities.

Phase Three: Emergence of Industry Governance

In the late 1980s, some entrepreneurial individuals began to see a significant commercial Internet market emerging. PCs, Unix work stations, and Ethernet Local Area Networks, combined with increasingly frequent mergers and acquisitions, produced a demand for the kind of interoperability that the Internet provided. Increasing market competition produced a demand for "information and knowledge transfer" and collaboratories to maintain sustained competitive advantage. A robust and profitable enterprise internet (now called intranet) environment began to develop. New products with enhanced performance began to emerge, and prices were pushed down. Early provisioning service provider innovators like Performance Systems International and UUNET spun off from their research and academic networking origins to both meet and increase the demand for Internet and intranet services.

Then a number of critical developments began to unfold that made the Internet evolve beyond its status as a subliminal network for research and development. The activities that really made the Internet scale predominantly combined technical and commercial product developments that provided value and ease of use for large numbers of people and companies. These innovations include:

• the creation of the World Wide Web specification and the development of the Mosaic browser across all computer platforms, combining attractiveness, simplicity, and added value in hyperlinking;

• the availability of Transmission Control Protocol/Internet Protocol (TCP/IP) protocols for Windows operating systems—first from third-party vendors, then from Microsoft itself—combined with the agreement on Winsock specifications, allowing a flexible, open means of "gluing" any application to the Internet;

• the creation of SLIP and PPP protocols and services, enabling a widely distributed public user base to emerge, as well as an associated industry of Internet Service Providers;

• consistent publicity in the popular press that was fostered at high government levels with the assistance of an eager and interested press corps;

• seeding of the interest of an upcoming generation of users and innovators through access and use provided on a large scale in educational institutions; and

• the continued need among corporations and institutions of all kinds for the kind of simple internal and external connectivity, information sharing, and collaboration that the Internet, intranets, and associated applications provide.

As a result, governance of most of the Internet's significant facets was effectively transferred to companies operating in a robust marketplace, which invoked traditional government public governance and dispute resolution mechanisms. In these respects, the Internet is no different than any other activity in society. The only features that make it in any way unique are the complex and globally distributed nature of its infrastructure, and the dynamics of its evolution and development. However, even here, the Internet differs from existing communications systems only by a matter of degree.

In the future, it will primarily be major industry players, industry organizations, user response in the marketplace, and governmental agencies that determine the evolution and governance of the Internet. However, governance institutions, governmental controls, and processes from another Internet era may still be in place.

It is this complexity—past, present, and future—combined with the inherent characteristics of any major market and global infrastructure, that determines the nature and limits of Internet self-governance.

The Desire for Self-Governance

Every new technology that has been successful enough to become a public infrastructure and to generate a significant market has sought to maintain self-governance. Rarely do we create mature governance mechanisms out of whole cloth. Rather, these mechanisms begin to develop within a small community of users who devise their own cooperative governance approaches. Such evolutionary self-governance among those who are directly affected and knowledgeable is generally preferable to the extent that it is possible at any stage—particularly with complex technologies and markets. External mechanisms can provide public venues and neutrality; but they also introduce time delays, procedural complexities, potential manipulation, and decision-makers who face steep learning curves. However, at some point in the scaling of the players, infrastructure, and market, such external mechanisms become inevitable. Not all disputes can be handled among the parties themselves, and the external impact of the infrastructure becomes too significant.

Self-governance notions for the Internet present some ironic contrasts. The large-scale "public" networks were absolutely governed by the government agencies that built and developed them. Corporate enterprise internets required significant regulatory intervention for many years to ensure both their existence and viability. While they may have been internally self-governing, they certainly were not externally so. One of the first computer network criminal prosecutions involved harm to the Internet. The notion of Internet self-governance is in fact an illusion arising from the relative unfamiliarity of many people associated with the Internet, with either its history or the surrounding legal and regulatory constructs in which it exists.

Choice of governance mechanisms, however, is very important. Communications networks and computers in general, and the Internet in particular, are significant motivational devices. Those with the ability to use them are able to express their creations—whether ideas or products—and leverage that activity enormously. In addition, these capabilities allow for the creation of new virtual products and networks—even environments and communities—that have an instantaneous global reach. Those who can access and effectively use the Internet and its applications have advantages and incentives that go to the core of the individual and collective human psyche and what motivates people and ventures. Because governance is ultimately about shaping and managing collective human, machine, and institutional behavior in its most generic sense, it is important to both appreciate and promote entrepreneurial behavior, innovation, and other activities that are valuable in economic or societal terms.

How Wide is the Valley: Disparate Communities and Parties

One of the greatest challenges to Internet governance today is dealing with the disparate communities that now exist in the Internet arena, and finding institutional mechanisms that enjoin the Internet's largest and most important constituencies—Internet businesses and users.

Insularity

Computer and computer networking technologies have developed in a kind of golden nest over the past 30 years. In pursuit of numerous strategically important national objectives, special policies were crafted that not only insulated this entire sector from virtually every kind of public process or control, but also provided it with substantial public benefits, both directly through significant government funding, and indirectly by subjecting other related sectors like telecommunications to regulations designed to foster the development and growth of computer networking. However, this insulation has evolved into insularity, with precious little appreciation of this context, and a persistent belief by many in the immutability of these beneficial regimes. Indeed, it is easy to find people who believe that computer networks like the Internet exist in a world apart from all of the real world's social and legal norms, while at the same time receiving diverse and substantial forms of governmental largesse.

These policies and practices were predicated on several factors—some of which are beginning to change. One of the most significant is the "public" nature and scale of computer networking and use. In the past, the networks have been closed user groups.

Profoundly Different Skills, Values, Objectives, and Perspectives

Another persistent myth about the Internet is the notion that it is some kind of cohesive, collegial community with similar values, objectives, and skills that arbitrates its own affairs. In fact, there are dozens of different Internet communities today with very different objectives, values, skills, and perspectives that are frequently orthogonal at best, and antithetical at worst.

With the explosion of Internet applications and uses over the past several years, entirely new and isolated communities of institutions, people, and companies have come into existence. The most obvious is the World Wide Web, but others include, for example, electronic mail, file systems, as well as information discovery, multimedia, financial, and mobile agent sectors. Each typically possesses its own professional organizations, publications, conferences, channels of communication, and collaborative mechanisms. The isolation of these groups is significant.

Even within the same market arena—for example, Internet access service providers—there are major backbone providers, regional providers, local access providers, telecommunications providers, and more. The enormous variety of delivery options tends to assure that a multitude of competing providers will exist in most localities. A number of different organizations have been formed to represent the interests of these diverse constituencies. Similar divergences exist at different levels of the information food chain from low-level transport markets to high-level information discovery and integration services.

Other major divergences exist among the traditional educational, research and academic, government, and commercial sectors. Within each of these communities are still more divergent groups. For example, K-12 professional associations and educators have little in common with university-level groups; public policy government agencies and ministries look at things quite differently from defense ministries. In many instances, these subcommunities are competing for the same resources and funding. In general, they are likely to have different values, motivations, and perspectives on any significant issues relating to the Internet.

Government public policy communities in particular are likely to have very different perspectives as they look at the Internet in the context of high-level items like national security, economic and industrial development strategies, universal service concerns, anticompetitive practices, social and general public interest considerations. Somewhat unknown to most other Internet communities, government regulatory agencies have been involved in the Internet's development for more than 15 years, taking all the necessary steps to assure the emergence and development of the Internet as a public infrastructure. As long as the Internet operated on a small scale and was not generally available to the public, there was no reason for this nurturing regulatory role to change. However, this is no longer the case, and the role of government public policy and regulatory agencies is changing as well.

Perhaps the most extreme divergences in perspective are encountered among professional groups. For example, the very processes of observation, distillation of issues, analysis, and problem-solving in the engineering and legal communities effectively occupy different instances of the same reality. Engineers in general tend to focus narrowly on technologies and their development for their own sake, with little interest in or concern about surrounding applications, uses, and problems. Because they usually have direct control over the networks born of the most direct and intimate role in the development of the technology, engineers also tend to seek technical solutions for every problem. Lawyers and public officials, conversely, tend to focus on legal issues, disputes, due process, and political solutions—frequently with little understanding of the underlying technologies and the effects on or limitations of those technologies. Both communities and perspectives are important, and neither should dominate governance mechanisms.

The myth of a homogeneous Internet community arises from the Internet's origins. For nearly the first ten years of its existence, there was a single, cohesive, technical community through which the U.S. Department of Defense controlled every aspect of the Internet's funding and evolution. In this environment—a tightly knit community of distributed researchers—everyone helped each other, maintained their own ethic and processes for resolving disputes, complete with appeal to the ultimate authority, the DARPA program manager. These activities were very successful, and no other kind of governance was needed or appropriate. After the Internet was opened up to include a much larger open research and academic community in the mid-1980s as a result of industrial policy decisions to further strategically important research, a new, second-order community was grafted onto the original closed DARPA group, complete with its own institutions, governance mechanisms, and ethics. These included groups like the IAB, the IETF, and the Internet Society, EARN and RARE in Europe, and similar research and academic organizations worldwide.

Although much of this community still exists today, the past several years have brought profound change to the Internet environment. Large numbers of major users, Internet service, product providers, and developers of all kinds have emerged. Significant government programs have been aimed at Internet infrastructure. Yet few mechanisms have been instituted that are appropriate for these new entrants. Groups such as the Commercial Internet eXchange and Internet Law and Policy Forum are just emerging. As a result of these rapid shifts in affected parties and constituencies and a lack of effective or representative organizations, the existing governance mechanisms are in a state of considerable disarray.

The Internet Is Not Sovereign

In the real world, sovereign institutions with real plenary powers do exist, and they have the capability to enact and endorse strictures that exact sufficiently dire consequences so as to compel most nonsovereign institutions and individuals to conform to their dictates. Like it or not, neither the Internet nor anything associated with it is, or ever will be, sovereign. And only sovereigns have peer privileges.

Governance must rest with the will of sovereigns. Inherently global phenomena necessarily result in constant efforts to reconcile the different approaches taken by various sovereigns. These two factors intrinsically set limits on self-governance, and they apply regardless of whether we are dealing with the Internet, radio communication, air travel, or diseases, and have no doubt persisted since the dawn of human society and commerce.

Generally speaking, the more significant the infrastructure, services, and products, the more interested sovereigns become in their provisioning and use. Sovereigns also establish dispute resolution mechanisms, and intercede with other sovereigns. Numerous intergovernmental bodies have been involved for the past decade in matters of critical importance to the Internet. These include, especially, the Intellectual Telecommunication Union, the General Agreement on Tariffs and Trade, the Organization for Economic Cooperation and Development, and the European Union. Treaties and agreements have enabled the Internet to exist and to grow internationally. These provisions covered everything from multi-user international networks, unregulated enhanced services and networks, attachments to existing public telecommunications networks, cost-oriented tariffing, availability of leased lines, and spectrum allocations. Such developments could only occur through the activist intervention of sovereigns acting through intergovernmental bodies.

It is theoretically possible for sovereigns to significantly cede their sovereignty to some independent entity through the global commons concept that is applied to somewhat remote and relatively unoccupied territories like outer space, Antarctica, and the sea. However, it seems unlikely that a similar construct would attract many (if any) adherents in the Internet community given the immediate and potentially pervasive nature of computer communications networks. In any case, it would take many years to set such initiatives in motion—let alone to actually achieve any kind of meaningful result.

A somewhat innovative, but related alternative is being undertaken by the Clinton administration through its Framework for Global Electronic Commerce, which seeks commitments from sovereigns to temporarily forgo exercising their powers in selected matters like taxation. At the same time, this initiative is an example of why governments remain critical to Internet governance.

Conclusion

Internet governance exists in significant and diverse forms. However, it is presently quite unstable and ineffective in efficiently serving its present constituencies. For example, the huge, increasingly important Internet business sector has no effective way to manifest its collective needs and interests in any of the existing governance mechanisms. Fortunately, an open and highly robust market has reduced the need for institutional mechanisms.

We are now embarking on what can be characterized as the third generation Internet—a large-scale global public infrastructure and marketplace characterized by intense entrepreneurial activity and growth. However, the continued presence of residual first- and second-generation Internet governance mechanisms, coupled with increased government involvement in certain related public policy matters, poses a challenge that is just now being faced.

It is instructive to note that the kind of evolution that the Internet is undergoing is not unique. Many major technology platforms have undergone a similar evolution. What is different? It is the current rapid changes in every facet of the Internet, coupled with the large-scale public commercial character of nearly all those facets. Governance mechanisms need to reflect this reality.

Acknowledgment

This chapter was extracted from a more extensive unpublished analysis, "Limits of Internet Self-Governance," which was prepared to structure and articulate experiences, observations, and suggestions regarding a subject of growing interest and importance: Internet governance. It has been the author's fortune (and occasional bane) to have done a great many different things in a number of different institutions in the telecommunications and computer networking fields over the past 30 years as both an engineer and lawyer, including playing a number of different Internet-related leadership roles over the past ten years. The views and ideas expressed here flow from those diverse experiences.

Domain Names

Internet Domain Names: Whose Domain Is This?

Robert Shaw

Introduction

During the last year, debate has intensified in the press and on the Internet concerning the policy for allocation of "domain names," the Internet's on-line equivalent of telephone numbers. To entice the cybervisitor, everyone wants to have a short and easily remembered Internet address, preferably mnemonically related to an established company name, product, or service. In an increasingly commercialized Internet, the most coveted spot is the *.com* domain—the tag intended for commercial organizations. Domain names are used for everything from locating the World Wide Web site of a company (*www.ibm.com*) to the on-line marketing of Hollywood movies (*www.missionimpossible.com*), and it seems that everyone has suddenly woken up to the intellectual property value of a memorable Internet "brand name."

The principle for registration of domain names has been until now first come, first served. Therefore, it is not surprising that lots of names corresponding to well-known trademarks have been registered by nimble amateurs: sometimes with innocent intent—and sometimes in the hope of a quick payoff from a sleepy company which suddenly wants to go on-line. But the corporate world (especially in the litigious United States) is quickly waking up. Brandishing U.S. federal trademarks intended to protect anything from stuffed toys to Halloween costumes, corporate lawyers are aggressively appropriating domain names from their sometimes dazed owners.

In any case, trying to register directly under the narrow confines of *.com* will not work for much longer. With around 550,000 entries in *.com* as of September 1996, and registrations running at over 15,000 per week (see Figure 1), the possible permutations of easy-to-remember names is quickly running out. You don't have to be an Internet guru to see that the current system lacks sufficient meaningful name space for the eventual millions of registrants who will want their own mnemonic cybersite.

Even worse, what began as essentially a U.S. mess is turning into a global one. Unlike in the United States, domain name registrations in other countries are typically tagged with a country code. For example, France uses *.fr* and Japan uses *.jp*. But *.com* is a non-country-specific international Top Level Domain (iTLD) that can be used by anyone in the world. As of June 1996, non-U.S. entities accounted for about 75,000 of the existing iTLD registrations—and their relative percentage is rising.[1] What will happen when more non-U.S. companies want in and start waving their national trademarks too?

The rules for the Internet Domain Name System (DNS) are now overdue for reform. However, the related issues for a sensible evolution of DNS are very complex and there is far from unanimity on what to do next. The only consensus seems to be that something needs to be done—and fast. But what and how?

Perhaps even more important is the question of who? Because of the many policy issues relating to any modification of Internet name space, this problem particularly begs the question: Who should be setting Internet policy? After all, the Internet of today has little resemblance to the Internet of 1984 when the current DNS policy was defined. Who should set the new rules? Should it be the brilliant engineers who keep the Internet running? Should it be governments that have partially subsidized domain name registration services? Should it be the commercial sector, which depends increasingly on the Internet and is concerned about the relationship between trademarks and domain names? What about Internet Service Providers (ISPs) which also have a clear interest in a stable infrastructure? Shouldn't international multilateral organizations try to provide a forum for a neutral and international solution?

And what about the money involved? Internet domain names are a new form of intellectual property and insofar as they represent a

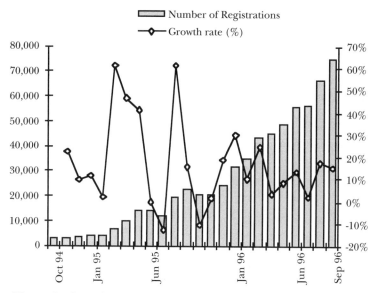

Figure 1 Growth of Internet Domain Name Registrations. Source: Monthly registrations from *Internet Monthly Reports* at <http://www.isi.edu/in-notes/imr> and *InterNIC News* at <http://rs.internic.net/nic-support/nicnews/>.

scarce resource, they are worth lots of money—in fact, very big money—both to those who hand them out and those who own them. Who, if anyone, should be profiting from the sale of international domain name resources?

This chapter discusses the background of the Internet Domain Name System and its problems, the organizations involved in "administering" the Internet (and their evolving relationships with each other), proposals for evolution of the DNS, as well as the question of who should be setting international Internet policy.

What Is the Internet Domain Name System?

The Internet Domain Name System basically provides a method to map a user-friendly name like *www.microsoft.com* to a numeric address like 198.105.232.6.

The suggestion of a hierarchical name space for the Internet was probably first publicly described in the Request for Comments (RFC)[2] document, "Internet Name Domains," which was written by

D.L. Mills of Comsat Laboratories in 1981.[3] In 1984, J. Postel and J. Reynolds, in RFC 920, "Domain Requirements,"[4] described a set of generic Top Level Domains (TLDs) that are still in use today:

.gov (government)

.edu (education)

.com (commercial)

.mil (military)

.org (organization)

Later, two more Top Level Domains were introduced:

.net (networking providers)

.int (international treaty)

(There is one more Top Level Domain; *.arpa*, which is solely used for Internet technical infrastructure needs.)

RFC 920 also defined Top Level Domains based on two-letter country codes from the International Standards Organization's (ISO) 3166 standard.[5] Examples include:

.af for Afghanistan

.ch for Switzerland

.fr for France

.us for the United States

.zw for Zimbabwe.

Delegation and management of ISO 3166-based TLDs have been typically assigned to national, or when not practical, regional[6] registries. These assignments have usually been made on a first come, first served basis. In some cases, the management of these TLDs has been delegated to individuals who have little or no association with the related countries.[7]

The usage of ISO-3166-based TLDs introduces a geographic and territorial (and therefore political) component to domain name space. However, since the Internet developed "bottom-up" from research and academic environments, governments have traditionally taken little interest in the national registries. This is slowly changing. In some cases, government authorities have begun to

give specific guidance to national name registries.[8] Other governments (often those with a restrictive political or highly regulated
communications environment) have insisted on total responsibility for TLD management. Recognizing the politics involved, it has
been one of those many unwritten Internet policies that if a
government requests TLD management for a country, it gets it.[9]

With the commercialization of the Internet, national TLD registries have been rapidly moving away from the previously informal
arrangements for domain name registrations. For example, both
the United Kingdom[10] and the Netherlands[11] have recently set up
new legally distinct entities to handle domain name registrations.
Naturally, the quickly developing relationship between domain
names and trademarks has also led registries to be more concerned
about potential legal liability. For example, the French Network
Information Center (NIC) advisory group on naming policy recently declared that "the majority of representatives judge that it is
necessary to apply legal criteria, exterior to the France NIC, for the
definition of the naming plan . . . in a manner to avoid direct
litigation."[12]

Another trend of the national registries is the widespread introduction of annual fees for domain name holders. For example,
Switzerland's registration authority, SWITCH, introduced an annual fee of approximately U.S. $80 after consultation with the Swiss
telecommunications regulatory authority.[13]

In Australia, France, Japan, the United Kingdom, and other
countries, the national TLD authorities have created subdomains
under the country code TLD to further classify and divide the name
space. Table 1 shows the subdomains that have been created in the
United Kingdom[14] and France.[15]

Although there is also a country code-based .*us* domain,[22] it is not
used very much and many do not even know it exists. Others
complain that there is a problem of access. The .*us* domain has an
elaborate subdomain naming scheme based on "political geography," but noticeable by their absence are functional equivalents of
the .*com, .net,* and .*org* subdomains that many other countries use.
In any case, the poorly developed use of the .*us* domain and what
Internet cognoscenti refer to as "domain name envy," ".*com* envy,"
or "international envy" have led just about everyone from individuals to megacorporations to register in the generic TLDs without the

Table 1 Subdomains in the United Kingdom and France

UK Domains	Intended Usage	FR Domains	Intended Usage
ac.uk	academic	*asso.fr*	associations
co.uk, *plc.uk*, *ltd.uk*	commercial	*barreau.fr*	regional barristers (barreaux régionaux)[16]
gov.uk	governmental	*cci.fr*	Chambers of Commerce and Industry (Chambres de Commerce et d'Industrie)[17]
mod.uk	Ministry of Defence	*cesi.fr*	Centers for Advanced Studies for Industry (Centres d'Etudes Supérieures de l'Industrie)[18]
net.uk	Internet networks	*dxxx.fr*	French numeric (xxx) geographical departments (départementaux)[19]
nhs.uk	National Health Service	*gouv.fr*	governmental[20]
org.uk	noncommercial organizations	*presse.fr*	press
sch.uk	schools	*tm.fr*	Trade Mark (Dépôt marque INPI)[21]

unesteemed addition of a national tag. Many perceive this is a great equalizer that reflects the spirit of the Internet. However, outside the United States, the lack of use of the *.us* country code tag is widely viewed as an abuse of the Domain Name System.

There is a widespread misperception that the generic TLDs *.com*, *.net*, and *.org* are U.S.-only domains. In fact, the rest of the world is learning that anyone can register in these domains and an increasing number of non-U.S. companies are doing so—from Swissair (*swissair.com*) to Ciba-Geigy (*ciba.com*).

It is not clear from RFC 920 that the initial intent of use for the "generic" non-country-specific TLDs was international (i.e., intended for non-U.S. registrants). When the DNS was deployed in the mid-1980s, the Internet was essentially a U.S. phenomenon and consisted of only about 50 networks. Arguing against an original international intent is that the .*edu*,[23] .*gov*,[24] and .*mil*[25] domains were eventually closed to all but U.S. registrants through allocation policies. The most recent Internet RFC document that describes Top Level Domain usage and administration is "Domain Name System Structure and Delegation" dating from 1994.[26]

The Internet Acronym Soup

Understanding the Internet acronym soup is a necessary rite of passage to understanding some of the players involved in the Domain Name System (or, for that matter, to be taken seriously among the Internet gliterati). Table 2 offers a basic primer on the key groups involved in "administration" of the Internet.

Domain Name Registrations

In a cooperative agreement[41] with the U.S. National Science Foundation, Network Solutions, Inc. (NSI), of Herndon, Virginia, has since 1993 administered the registration of the generic TLDs .*com*, .*net*, .*org*, .*gov*, and .*edu*. The .*mil* domain is managed by the U.S. Department of Defense (DOD).[42] The remaining .*int*, a specialized TLD intended for international treaty organizations will, pending final agreement, be administered by the International Telecommunication Union in Geneva, Switzerland.

As mentioned, the .*gov*, .*edu*, and .*mil* domains are restricted to U.S. applicants by allocation policy. Thus .*com*, .*net*, and .*org* can be considered as international TLDs.

The NSF and NSI have been struggling to deal with the astronomical growth and commercialization of the Internet. When NSI began registering domain names in the spring of 1993, approximately 400 domain names were registered per month. However, in September 1996 (see Figure 1), this number had risen to about 80,000 per month. Since the overwhelming percentage were in the .*com* category, the NSF found itself essentially subsidizing commercial registrations which did not fall under its mandate. Reacting to this, NSF amended its cooperative agreement with NSI, allowing NSI to institute an annual fee of U.S. $50 for domain name registrations from September 14, 1995.[43]

Table 2   The Internet Acronym Soup

Who?	What It Stands for and Where You Can Find out More	What You Really Need to Know about Them
IETF	Internet Engineering Task Force <http://www.ietf.org/>	These are the engineers who make Internet standards. You are considered a member of the IETF if you participate in its work or pay about US$240 to attend one of its meetings held three times a year.
IESG	Internet Engineering Steering Group <http://www.ietf.org/iesg.html>	The IESG handles the internal management of the IETF. Formed by area directors who handle working groups, an IETF chair, and an IETF executive director. The IETF secretariat is based at the Corporation for National Research Initiatives (CNRI),[27] which is principally funded by the U.S. government.
IAB	Internet Architecture Board <http://www.iab.org/iab/>	The IAB is a technical advisory group of the Internet Society (ISOC).[28]
ISOC	Internet Society <http://www.isoc.org/>	ISOC is a "non-profit, scientific, educational and charitable entity, incorporated in 1992 in the District of Columbia, separate from the Corporation for National Research Initiatives (CNRI), to which it formerly belonged."[29]
IANA	Internet Assigned Numbers Authority <http://www.isi.edu/iana/>	An "Internet Service" of the High-Performance Computing and Communications (HPCC) Division[30] of the Information Sciences Institute (ISI), part of the University of Southern California (USC) School of Engineering.[31]

FNC	Federal Networking Council <http://www.fnc.gov/>	FNC membership consists of one representative from each of 17 U.S. federal agencies (e.g., NASA, National Science Foundation, Dept. of Education, Dept. of Commerce—Telecommunications & Information Administration [NTIA]) whose programs utilize interconnected Internet networks.[32]
NSF	National Science Foundation <http://www.nsf.gov/>	The NSF provides support and grants for research in networking and communications including the NSFNET.[33] The relevant group is the Networking and Communications Research and Infrastructure (NCRI) Division[34] in the Directorate for Computer and Information Science and Engineering (CISE).[35]
InterNIC	InterNIC[36] <http://www.internic.net/>	A project comprised of two distinct services partially funded by the NSF: Directory and Databases Services[37] managed by AT&T and Registration Services[38] managed by NSI.[39]
NSI	Network Solutions, Inc. <http://www.netsol.com/>	The company that performs most generic domain name registrations in a cooperative agreement with NSF. NSI is a subsidiary of Science Applications International Corporation (SAIC).[40]

Internet Monikers and Money

Internet users initially reacted quite negatively to the introduction of the fee, but this has now died down somewhat. However, criticism continues to grow about the amount of money that NSI, a private corporation, is making in a monopoly situation "selling" what are essentially international name resources. During the 12-

month period from September 1995 through August 1996, the new annual fee generated on the order of U.S. $55 million in revenue (the fee for two years must be paid up front).[44] The average monthly growth rate of 15 percent over this period suggests, that by September 1997, the fee will potentially generate around U.S. $310 million in income. The actual overhead costs of performing a domain name registration are not clear. However, a significant revenue stream derives from the annual renewal fee, which involves little more than sending out a bill. Of the fees collected, NSI keeps 70 percent and 30 percent goes into an Internet "intellectual infrastructure" fund administered by the NSF.[45] At the end of 1996, this fund totaled close to U.S. $13 million.[46] Clearly, Internet domain name registries are a very big business.

Domain names in themselves are considered worthy intellectual property assets and are being brokered for increasing amounts of money. For example, when Microsoft wanted *slate.com* for its new Web-based interactive magazine of politics and culture, they supposedly purchased it for $10,000 (through a third party for obvious reasons). Undoubtedly greater amounts have been paid to obtain strategic domain names. Sometime the price is too high. An offer of U.S. $50,000 is reported to have been rejected for *television.com*.[47] Supposedly when AT&T wanted to launch their new Internet services, they attempted to purchase the domain name *worldnet.net* from a Paris-based Internet Service Provider. But even AT&T balked at the reported U.S. $500,000 asking price.

Domain Names and Trademarks

The relationship between trademarks and domain names has been described elsewhere. One of the best summaries is probably David Maher's "Trademarks on the Internet: Who's in Charge?"[48] Another useful survey is "What's In a Name?"[49] by students at the George Washington University Law School.

As mentioned above, domain names have until now been registered on the principle of first come, first served. Some domain names relating to famous trademarks like *7up.com* and *mcdonalds.com* were snagged early on by Internet aficionados and were handed over to their respective companies for token gifts or donations to charity.[50] However, the realization that big companies were often willing to pay thousands of dollars for a mnemonic cyberpresence has led to many cases of what has come to be known as domain name "hijacking." Many a company has discovered after requesting an appropriate domain name that it already belongs to somebody else. For instance, *coke.com* currently belongs to Rajeev Arora of California and *rolex.com* is registered to Janice Ard of Colorado. At least in the case of well-known trademarks (and the prospect of legal action), most amateur speculators can be bribed to amicably relinquish a valuable name.

Caught in the middle between domain name holders and trademark owners, NSI instituted a policy in July 1995,[51] with notable modifications in November 1995[52] and September 1996.[53] that gave trademark owners the possibility to reclaim a domain name if they could produce a corresponding federal (national) trademark.

But this policy has mollified neither trademark owners nor domain name holders. Many rightly point out that trademark law allows multiple entities to share the same name if they are not in competing businesses and/or in the same geographical area. For example, although there can be a McDonald's computer company and a McDonald's hamburger company, on the Internet, there can only be one *mcdonalds.com* (now owned by the latter). Trademark lawyers also discovered that a trademark from any country could possibly be used to defend the usage of a domain name. This led to trademark registrations by domain name holders in places like Tunisia, where in 48 hours a "federal" trademark can be produced. The NSI policy also does not deal with domain names that, although not identical to a trademark, constitute infringement, or U.S. common law trademarks not registered under the Lanham Act.[54]

The new NSI policy vis-à-vis trademarks has led to what some refer to as "reverse" domain name hijacking. For example, entertainment and toy companies obviously look at the Internet strategically as a vehicle for interactive entertainment. Naturally, these companies wish to leverage existing product lines, and an appropriate domain name is part of the package. For instance, Hasbro (*www.hasbro.com*) is using its trademark for the board games Perfection and Clue in an attempt to claim the domain names *perfection.com*[55] and *clue.com*.[56] Mattel is trying to claim *memory.com* because Memory is the name of one of its games. The current NSI policy makes it relatively easy for these companies to obtain the names they want.

One consequence of all this has been increasing litigation between trademark holders and domain name owners. And sometimes the registration authority, NSI, has also been dragged into the disputes. As of August 1996, NSI had been named party to ten related lawsuits.[57] Six domain name holders have brought suits against NSI, arguing that they should be allowed to keep their names. The remaining four were instituted by trademark owners, but none of these named NSI alone.

Criticism of NSI is surprisingly widespread in the Internet and trademark communities. There can be little doubt that much of the activity toward an evolution of DNS policy is a reaction to this. Among Internet users, the charge for name registrations has upped the ante considerably and led to different levels of service expectations. The trademark community (e.g., the International Trademark Association [INTA][58]) is not pleased that it cannot obtain facilitated access to the database of registered domain names to conduct trademark searches.[59]

Some have suggested using extensive geographical subdomain naming conventions as a solution to the trademark issue. But if we imagine an Internet that is someday as ubiquitous as the telephone, one only needs to take a look at a phone book to realize the scale of the problem. The necessary granularity to deal with all possible trademarks and homonyms in domain name space would lead to names that essentially resemble postal addresses, such as *www.mcdonald.apt23.54thstreet.nyc.ny.us*. And it is obvious that companies like IBM want to keep addresses like *www.ibm.com* (or even better have *www.ibm*) and have no interest in being designated as *www.ibm.armonk.ny.us*.

One of the basic problems that NSI faces is that it is handing out international domain names but existing trademark law is fundamentally national—there is no such thing as a widely recognized "international trademark." In the non-Internet world, there is an established tradition of dealing with trademarks on a national basis. The rules for dealing with trademark issues may be different in the United States, France, or Japan, but a procedure and clear jurisprudence for dispute resolution exist. These conditions are strongest at the national level with occasional provisions at the regional and international level.

The closest one can get to an international trademark is to file in the World Intellectual Property Organization's (WIPO)[60] International Register of Marks under the Madrid Agreement and Protocol.[61] About 47 countries are signatories, but conspicuous by their absence are the United States (over an objection to the European Union having an independent vote) and Japan. The WIPO database has about 310,000 marks registered and about 20,000 are added each year. However, filing in the WIPO register really only facilitates making multiple "national" filings through one procedure—it does not constitute an international trademark since any signatory to the WIPO agreement/protocol can reject filings at a national level—and of course, any resultant disputes are dealt with at the national level.

As of June 1996, the trademark conflicts concerning DNS were limited to U.S. registrants. What will be the result of a trademark conflict between two non-U.S. countries for control of a name in international Top Level Domain space? Which country's courts will have jurisprudence? Perhaps both will claim it? Conditions of access to international domain names could eventually require mandatory dispute arbitration through something like WIPO's Arbitration Center,[62] but on the basis of which laws would such a dispute be adjudicated? The mounting conflicts between trademarks and domain names with global significance will likely lead to increased pressure for a global trademark system.

Trademarks are only the first of many issues that will fundamentally pit territorially based legal systems against the Internet. Another eventual problem will be posed by each country's conventions to register or operate as a business. Domain names have already been fraudulently used to misrepresent associations. For example, until recently, *www.unhcr.org* took you to the Refugee Republic Corporation, incorporated in the state of Nevada, claiming to sell stock options in "refugees"—but having nothing to do with the United Nations High Commissioner for Refugees (UNHCR),[63] winner of the Nobel Peace Prize.[64] In e-mail to this author, the

Refugee Republic Corporation claims its intent was innocent, but this appears somewhat disingenuous when one examines its filed registration with NSI from the suspicious UNH Communications Institute. Equally damning is that the company has recently reappeared under *www.uno.org* (the United Nations is *www.un.org*) and its NSI registration claims that it is the United Nations Orchestra!

Climbing the Domain Name Space Authority Trail

What has made the Internet successful? There can be little doubt that part of the reason the Internet has been successful is that it is a cooperative effort over which nobody can assert control or jurisdiction. However, it is clear that a nominal amount of authority is required. How are blocks of Internet Protocol (IP) addresses allocated, and by what criteria? And more to the topic of this chapter, who has the authority to define the policy and administration of the root of the Top Level Domain name space? One of the most strange claims came from a U.S. government official who said that the U.S. Department of Defense (DOD), operating through the Federal Networking Council (FNC), "owns" the domain name space.[65]

Responsibility for the root of the domain name space is obviously an important international function. Responsibility for country code-based TLDs has been rightfully delegated to national registration authorities.[66] But who decides who in each country manages the potentially very profitable national domain name space? And who should define policy for evolution of the DNS?

This is clearly a delicate topic in the Internet technical community. According to the relevant Internet standards, "IANA is the overall authority for the IP Addresses, the Domain Names, and many other parameters, used in the Internet."[67] But who exactly is the Internet Assigned Numbers Authority (IANA)? Well, as all Internet insiders know, IANA is a small group of people, at the University of Southern California's Information Sciences Institute. Internet insiders also know that IANA policy is essentially defined by Jon Postel, one of the great Internet pioneers.[68]

There is little doubt that a sagacious IANA has played an important role in consolidating the stability of the Internet. But apart from historical precedence, where does IANA get its authority? According to the IANA Web site: "The IANA is chartered by the Internet Society (ISOC) and the Federal Network Council (FNC) to act as the clearinghouse to assign and coordinate the use of numerous Internet protocol parameters."[69] Now we have two bodies: the FNC (appearing again) and ISOC.[70] ISOC will be discussed later. Who really is the FNC and what is its charter? Besides the definition given in Table 1, the FNC says: "The purpose of the Federal Networking Council (FNC) is to provide a forum for networking collaborations among Federal agencies to meet their research, education, and operational mission goals."[71] Inquiries with the FNC indicate that there actually is no charter for IANA per se but there is a contract from the U.S. Defense Advanced Research Projects Agency (DARPA)[72] that is cost-shared by two FNC Executive agencies (NSF and NASA). In any case, the FNC also says:

The Federal Networking Council (FNC) is chartered by the National Science and Technology Council's Committee on Information and Communications (CIC) to act as a forum for networking collaborations among Federal agencies to meet their research, education, and operational mission goals and to bridge the gap between the advanced networking technologies being developed by research FNC agencies and the ultimate acquisition of mature versions of these technologies from the commercial sector.[73]

Now we have the National Science and Technology Council's (NSTC) Committee on Information and Communications (CIC). This appears to be essentially the end of the "authority trail" since the CIC is somewhat cryptically one of eight committees[74] of a U.S. "cabinet-level council [which] is the principal means for the President to coordinate science, space, and technology policies across the Federal government."[75] In fact, NSTC documents are located on the U.S. White House Web server.

The FNC's "Mission Statement" says: "The FNC supports the goals of the CIC, particularly those related to building the national information infrastructure (NII)."[76] On May 23, 1995, the FNC's Advisory Council (FNCAC)[77] made the following recommendation to the FNC on the "New Internet Paradigm":

The Internet is currently in a state of transition from a small set of federally subsidized networks to a large number of commercially run networks. The Federal Networking Council (FNC) is chartered to "oversee the operation and evolution of the Federal Internet Program in support of research and education". In this charter and in the recommendations that follow the term Internet is meant to refer to those unclassified networks that were initially sponsored by Federal agencies for the support of research and education computing, and which are either undergoing transition now or may be in the future.[78]

Specifically, the FNCAC recommended:

It is urgent that the FNC should study what Internet-wide committees and organizations are necessary for the successful operation of the Internet both during and after its transition to commercial providers. This study should be done in consultation with both domestic and international network service providers. Some of the necessary bodies may already exist and others may need to be chartered; in both cases it is important to ascertain who will charter and fund them, and to whom they will report. It is particularly important for the FNC to recommend the extent to which the government in its role as provider of research and educational networking should be involved with these entities. Some examples of relevant issues are . . . assignment of address space and domain names as currently done by IANA.[79]

Even more pertinent, on October 21, 1996, the FNC's Advisory Council made the following resolution on "Domain Name Service": "The FNCAC reiterates and underscores the urgency of transferring responsibility for supporting US commercial interests in iTLD administrations from the NSF to an appropriate entity."[80] This would seem to indicate that the responsibility for iTLD management still resides with the U.S. National Science Foundation.

The FNC mission statement mentioned its support for the U.S. National Information Infrastructure (NII) initiatives (consider this to be a sort of next-generation Internet). This brings in the U.S. Department of Commerce's National Telecommunications & Information Administration (NTIA), which has been designated to coordinate U.S. NII initiatives.[81] On the international level, the NTIA's Office of International Affairs (OIA) "advocates Executive Branch policy perspectives in bilateral and multilateral consultations with foreign governments, in international regulatory conferences, and in other forums dealing with *Global Information Infrastructure* issues."[82]

Finally, we return to ISOC's "charter" for IANA. Who is ISOC? As shown in Table 1, ISOC has defined itself as a "non-profit, scientific, educational and charitable entity, incorporated in 1992 in the District of Columbia, USA." For all intents and purposes, ISOC is a professional society analogous to organizations like the Institute of Electrical and Electronics Engineers (IEEE) or the Association for Computing Machinery (ACM). It is hard to fathom how such a society could claim to "charter" anyone with responsibility for international Internet name space. Since IANA existed before ISOC, such a charter (like the claimed FNC charter) appears to be somewhat dubious. The point being made here is not to question the important "trusteeship" role that IANA has played—only that any expansion of that role outside the traditional Internet technical community would be based on claims that could not bear much scrutiny.

Proposals for Evolution of Domain Name Space

Proposals for evolution of the DNS gained momentum with a series of workshops in 1995 and 1996. The first was "Internet Names, Numbers, and Beyond: Issues in the Coordination, Privatization and Internationalization of the Internet,"[83] which took place on November 20, 1995, in Washington, D.C. This workshop was sponsored by NSF's Networking and Communications Research and Infrastructure (NCRI) Division[84] and the Harvard Information Infrastructure Project (IIP).[85] A second workshop on "Internet Administrative Infrastructure"[86] sponsored by the Commercial Internet Exchange (CIX)[87] and ISOC was held in February 1996. A third related workshop on "Coordination and Administration of the Internet"[88] was held September 8–10, 1996, in Cambridge, Massachusetts, and was sponsored by the Harvard IIP, NSF's NCRI Division, CIX, ITU,[89] and ISOC.

Meanwhile, in November 1995, an Internet draft published by B. Carpenter et al., "Proposal for an ISOC Role in DNS Name Space Management" suggested that the "Internet Society take a formal role in the oversight and licensing of competitive registries for international Internet name space."[90] This was followed by another Internet draft in January 1996 by R. Bush et al., "Delegation of International Top Level Domains (iTLDs)."[91] More recently, Jon Postel, head of IANA, authored a proposal "New Registries and the Delegation of International Top Level Domains."[92] according to which up to 150 new international Top Level Domains (like .com, .net, .org) would be created and up to 50 new registries performing functions similar to NSI would be "awarded." In this scheme, ISOC would be the "international, legal and financial umbrella" of IANA.

There are both pros and cons to the creation of new international Top Level Domains (see Table 3). While the creation of additional international Top Level Domains may or may not be a good idea, the problems here seem to be process related. Who are the parties that should be consulted on the evolution of international Internet name space? Certainly many more than are currently involved. Many of the potentially concerned stakeholders have been listed by Tony Rutkowski, former executive director of ISOC, in "Parties of Interest in Internet Public Policy Matters."[96] It is also obvious that many governments want to have a say in issues related to a nascent GII. As Rutkowski has pointed out, even though any DNS policy decision would have an impact on international name space, no non-U.S. public policy officials have ever taken part in the public meetings held to date.

Has a fundamental shift in responsibility to a neutral solution for international name space been introduced by bringing ISOC into the process? Reading between the lines, it is hard to believe it. According to Postel's draft, these potentially multimillion dollar generating registries will be awarded by an "ad hoc working group" comprised of three people from IANA, two from the IETF and two from ISOC. These are, for the most part, engineers (albeit well-intentioned) who have no real legal or policy framework behind them. For ISOC (or any group) to claim responsibility for delegating international name space when there are such high stakes involved (e.g., financial) appears unsustainable. The Internet has become far too commercial and strategically important as a global communications tool to simply perpetuate the same informal arrangements that have kept it glued together until now.

It is not surprising that at the Montreal IETF/INET meeting in June 1996 the ISOC Board of Trustees voted,[97] *in principle*, to back

Table 3 International or National Top Level Domains?

Arguments for New International TLDs	Arguments for Country Code-Based TLDs
• Over 550,000 existing registrations in *.com*, *.net*, and *.org* would be impossible to "repatriate" to country code-based TLDs	• Respects national sovereignty in definition of National Information Infrastructure (NII)[93] policies
• Marketplace seems to have indicated a preference for domain names without country codes.	• Respects national naming conventions (e.g., *co.uk*, *plc.uk*, *ltd.uk*) and national language conventions (e.g., *.gov.uk*, *.gouv.fr*)
• Globalization of telecommunications services (e.g., international 800 toll-free telephone services)	• Provides a natural national registry-level basis to reject registrations with national trademark conflicts[94]
• Introduces competition among domain name registries (breaks NSI's monopoly)	• Provides a basis for dealing with domain names that are considered offensive[95]
• Facilitates alternative access to what has become a "scarce" resource (*.com*)	• International TLDs further complicate trademark issues—dispute resolution is a legal quagmire
	• New international TLDs would lead more users to acquire "rights" in international name space without a legal framework

the new proposal. Note that the last version of the proposal calls for ISOC to receive two percent of the annual income from the registries. It is very difficult to estimate how much revenue this will generate for ISOC. However, if 50 registries were awarded and they all eventually generated NSI's estimated U.S. $30 million annual turnover (which is not unreasonable considering Internet growth), the potential income for ISOC is on the order of U.S. $30 million a year. Because ISOC lacks any real legal framework for handling such an international resource, undoubtedly a good portion of any income would be necessary for liability insurance.

Conclusion

The Postel proposal is extremely controversial and it will be interesting to watch how it plays out. At least until now, the U.S. government, through NSF and Department of Defense contracts, has had a strong hand in guiding DNS policy. However, even with the ISOC umbrella, IANA's assertion that it can significantly evolve DNS policy and award multimillion-dollar contracts for registries will undoubtedly lead to some very serious legal and political challenges over their authority to do so. These challenges have already started: if you follow the related Internet mailing lists,[98] it is easy to glean that there are other groups that want to set up their own international Top Level Domains with absolutely no coordination with IANA or ISOC.[99] Technically it is possible they could succeed.

In a paper entitled "Law and Borders—The Rise of Law in Cyberspace," D. Johnson and D. Post, co-directors of the Cyberspace Law Institute[100] at the Georgetown University Law Center, make some thoughtful arguments on the problems of international domain names:

> The ultimate question who should set the rules for uses of names on the Net presents an apt microcosm for examining the relationship between the Net and territorial-based legal systems. There is nothing more fundamental, legally, than a name or identity—the right to legally recognized personhood is a predicate for the amassing of capital, including the reputational and financial capital, that arises from sustained interactions . . . Recall that the non-country-specific domain names like ".com," . . . lead to the establishment of on-line addresses on a global basis. And through such widespread use, the global domain names gained proprietary value. In this context, assertion by any local jurisdiction of the right to set the rules applicable to the "domain name space" is an illegitimate extra-territorial power grab.[101]

There seems to be a lack of consideration for the international implications of DNS policy evolution. It is hard to imagine that potentially concerned policy authorities from other nations are even aware of what is happening. As mentioned, the lack of use by Americans of the .us country code tag is widely regarded outside the United States as an anomaly of the Domain Name System. But the net effect of Postel's proposal will be to multiply this situation many times over. Therefore, it will not be surprising if many in the international Internet community react negatively to what they will perceive as an "illegitimate extra-territorial power grab."

A more formal legal and public policy framework is required for the Internet. Although somewhat orthogonal to the working methods of Internet "administration" bodies, it is fundamentally necessary. Without it, any DNS evolution is likely to be so controversial that it will probably lead to some form of government regulatory intervention to prevent Internet domain name space from fragmenting uncontrollably. As David Maher, former co-chair of INTA's subcommittee on Internet Trademark Issues, has written: "In order to maintain public confidence in any system of domain name registration, an adequate legal structure encompassing judicial review (whether by national or international judicial bodies) must be made available."[102] This would also appear to apply to the creation of any new Top Level Domains.

At the U.S. national level, one method to address Internet name space issues in a more formal legal setting would be to leverage the U.S. telecommunications policy framework—as has been suggested by the Commercial Internet Exchange.[103] Specifically, CIX has suggested that the Federal Communications Commission's (FCC)[104] Notice of Inquiry (NOI) process could be used to bring issues into a more public policy context. Other U.S. federal agencies could coordinate related input, including the Department of Commerce's NTIA (for NII/GII issues) and the U.S. Patent and Trademark Office.[105]

The next step would be to bring the issues into an international public policy context. U.S. Vice President Al Gore and the late Secretary of Commerce, Ron Brown, who also served as chairman of the U.S. Information Infrastructure Task Force,[106] released a paper, "GII: Agenda for Cooperation"[107] that described the U.S. government's vision for cooperation between nations in building the Global Information Infrastructure. In that paper, they wrote:

Multilateral organizations will play a vital role in this effort. In particular, the International Telecommunication Union (ITU), the Organization for Economic Cooperation and Development (OECD), the International Organization for Standardization (ISO), and the World Intellectual Property Organization (WIPO) are uniquely able to contribute practical solutions to problems affecting the development of the GII.[108]

One possible avenue to address international DNS policy issues would be for the FCC and NTIA to bring the discussions to the ITU which could provide a forum in which the views of other nations would be more fairly represented. WIPO, with valuable expertise in international trademarks, has also expressed interest in playing a role in an international solution. However, the challenge for these multilateral organizations is crafting an appropriate "light" regulatory framework that balances the dynamics of the Internet with the legitimate interests of other stakeholders.

The Internet is in a painful transition period and appears to be caught in a cross fire between the tremendous commercial, political, legal, and operational interests, on the one hand, and anarchistic Net individuals[109] who still want to "do their own thing," on the other. While "chaos" has recently been legally cited as one of the strengths of the Internet.[110] others seek a certain stability of infrastructure, international comity, respect for legal issues such as trademarks, and accountability that are standard in the "real world."

The Internet can no longer ignore the real world because it is rapidly becoming part of it. Therefore, the challenge is to find a path toward an international, balanced dialogue and legal framework while fostering the positive (and often chaotic) forces that have made the Internet the wonderful success story it is.

This chapter derives from a paper originally presented at the OECD/EC DGXIII/COMTEC Workshop on "Access and Pricing for Information Infrastructure Services: Communication Tariffication, Regulation and the Internet," Trinity College, Dublin, Ireland, June 20–21, 1996. The current on-line version can be found at <http://www.itu.int/intreg/dns.html>. The views expressed in this chapter are those of the author and do not necessarily reflect the views of the ITU or its membership.

Notes

1. See "Global Domain Names Grow Rapidly Worldwide" at <http://www.mids.org/prdomreg.html>.

2. "The 'Request for Comments' (RFC) document series is the official publication channel for Internet standards documents and other publications of the IESG (Internet Engineering Steering Group), IAB (Internet Architecture Board), and Internet community." See C. Huitema et al., *Not All RFCs are Standards*, RFC 1796 (April 1995), <ftp://ds.internic.net/rfc/rfc1796.txt>. Any RFC can be retrieved from the address <ftp://ds.internic.net/rfc/rfc**xxx**.txt> where xxx is the RFC number.

3. Mills, "Internet Name Domains," RFC 799 (September 1981), <ftp://ds.internic.net/rfc/rfc799.txt>.

4. Postel and J. Reynolds, "Domain Requirements," RFC 920 (October 1984), <ftp://ds.internic.net/rfc/rfc920.txt>.

5. ISO 3166, see <http://www.iso.ch/cate/d22748.html>. The standard defines two-character (alpha-2) and three-character (alpha-3) versions. The Internet Domain Name System uses the alpha-2 version.

6. Notably the Asian-Pacific Network Information Center (APNIC) at <http://www.apnic.net> and Réseaux IP Européens (RIPE) at <http://www.ripe.net>. Although somewhat out of date, a list of Top Level Domain delegation contacts can be found at <http://info.isoc.org:80/adopsec/domains.html>.

7. For example, the TLDs for the Republic of Zaïre (*.zr*), Republic of Rwanda (*.rw*), Republic of Burundi (*.bi*), and People's Republic of the Congo (*.cg*) are all delegated to an individual in Lausanne, Switzerland. See <http://www.ibpt.bi/> and note the high prices charged for name registrations.

8. See "5e REUNION DU COMITE DE CONCERTATION NIC FRANCE du 14/02/96" at <http://www.nic.fr/Presentation/CC/cc-960214.html>.

9. See notes from workshop on "Internet Names, Numbers, and Beyond: Issues in the Coordination, Privatization and Internationalization of the Internet" (November 20, 1995) available at <http://ksgwww.harvard.edu/iip/nsfmin1.html>.

10. See <http://www.nic.uk/press.html>.

11. See <http://www.domain-registry.nl/>.

12. See <http://www.nic.fr/Presentation/GT/gt-960320.html>.

13. See <http://www.nic.ch>.

14. See "Domain Names within the UK" at <http://www.nic.uk/new/domains.html>.

15. See "Pages Jaunes des Domaines de la Zone Française (FR)" at <http://www.nic.fr/Annuaire/index.html>.

16. See "2è REUNION DU GROUPE DE TRAVAIL SUR LE PLAN DE NOMMAGE DE .FR du 15/05/96" at <http://www.nic.fr/Presentation/GT/gt-960515.html>.

17. See "5e REUNION DU COMITE DE CONCERTATION NIC FRANCE du 14/02/96" at <http://www.nic.fr/Presentation/CC/cc-960214.html>.

18. Ibid.

19. Proposed; see "2è REUNION DU GROUPE DE TRAVAIL SUR LE PLAN DE NOMMAGE DE .FR du 15/05/96" at <http://www.nic.fr/Presentation/GT/gt-960515.html>.

20. See "Annuaire alphabétique de la zone française dédiée au gouvernement: gouv.fr" at <http://www.nic.fr/Annuaire/france/gouv/gouv.html>.

21. See <http://www.nic.fr/Presentation/GT/gt-960320.html> and "Pages Jaunes des Domaines de la Zone Francaise (FR)" at <http://www.nic.fr/Annuaire/index.html>. Note that for the moment France deals with homonyms in the *tm.fr* domain on the principle of first come, first served.

22. Cooper and J. Postel, "The US Domain," RFC 1480 (June 1993), <ftp://ds.internic.net/rfc/rfc1480.txt>.

23. Ibid.

24. FNC, "U.S. Government Internet Domain Names," RFC 1816 (August 1995), <ftp://ds.internic.net/rfc/rfc1816.txt>.

25. Engebretson and R. Plzak, "Registration in the MIL Domain," RFC 1956 (June 1996), <ftp://ds.internic.net/rfc/rfc1956.txt>.

26. Postel, "Domain Name System Structure and Delegation," RFC 1591 (March 1994), <ftp://ds.internic.net/rfc/rfc1591.txt>.

27. See <http://www.cnri.reston.va.us/>.

28. See <http://www.iab.org/iab/overview.html>.

29. Letter from the president of ISOC to the ITU secretary-general concerning ISOC participation in ITU activities, May 4, 1993.

30. See "High-Performance Computing and Communications Division (HPCC)" at <http://www.isi.edu/div7/>.

31. See "Information Sciences Institute" at <http://www.isi.edu/>.

32. See "FNC Members" at <http://www.fnc.gov/FNC_Members.html>.

33. See "NSFNET" at <http://www.cise.nsf.gov/ncri/nsfnet.htm>.

34. See "Networking and Communications Research and Infrastructure (NCRI) Division" at <http://www.cise.nsf.gov/ncri/index.html>.

35. See "Directorate for Computer and Information Science and Engineering" at <http://www.cise.nsf.gov/>.

36. Name adopted by awardees of NSF's tender for "Network Information Services Manager" for their unified services, see < http://www.rs.internic.net/nsf/review/appendix-D.html>.

37. See "InterNIC Directory and Database Services" at <http://ds.internic.net/>.

38. See "Welcome to the InterNIC" at <http://rs.internic.net/>.

39. See <http://www.netsol.com/>.

40. See <http://www.saic.com/>.

41. See "NSF Cooperative Agreement" at <http://rs.internic.net/nsf/agreement/>.

42. Engebretson and R. Plzak, "Registration in the MIL Domain," RFC 1956 (June 1996), <ftp://ds.internic.net/rfc/rfc1956.txt>.

43. See <http://www.isoc.org/adopsec/nsf-name-fees.html> and <http://rs.internic.net/announcements/index.html>.

44. See "NSF Cooperative Agreement No. NCR-9218742, Amendment 4" at <http://rs.internic.net/nsf/agreement/amendment4.html>.

45. Ibid.

46. See <http://rs.internic.net/announcements/iif-update.html>.

47. See <http://www.television.com>.

48. David W. Maher, "Trademarks on the Internet: Who's in Charge?" (1996), <http://www.aldea.com/cix/maher.html>.

49. Jonathan Agmon et al., "What's in a Name?" <http://www.law.georgetown.edu/lc/internic/domain1.html>.

50. James Romenesko, "University of Arizona Student Guards His Internet Domain Names," *Saint Paul Pioneer Press,* May 28, 1996. Also in *Telecom Digest* 16, No. 247 (back issues can be found at <ftp://mirror.lcs.mit.edu/telecom-archives/back.issues>).

51. See "NETWORK SOLUTIONS ANNOUNCES INTERNET DOMAIN NAME POLICY" at <http://www.saic.com/aboutsaic/news/july95/news07-28-95.html>.

52. See "NSI Domain Dispute Policy Statement," <ftp://rs.internic.net/policy/internic/internic-domain-4.txt>.

53. See "NSI Domain Dispute Policy Statement," <http://rs.internic.net/domain-info/internic-domain-6.html>.

54. David W. Maher, "Trademarks on the Internet: Who's in Charge?" (1996), <http://www.aldea.com/cix/maher.html>.

55. According to a post on the Internet mailing list *owner-domain-policy@internic.net* by Rick Wintersberger of Publishing Perfection (*rw@perfection.com*).

56. See "ROADRUNNER TO NETWORK SOLUTIONS: SHAME ON YOU" at <http://infolawalert.com/articles/960618.html>. Note that Hasbro could easily allocate itself third-level domain names such as *perfection.hasbro.com* or *clue.hasbro.com.*

57. See Carl Oppedahl, "Letter to the Editor of the San Francisco *Recorder*" at <http://www.patents.com/nsi/aug16.sht>. Also see <http://www.patents.com/nsi.sht> for considerable background and discussion of the NSI policies.

58. See <http://plaza.interport.net/inta/>.

59. See <http://infolawalert.com/corsearch/>.

60. See <http://www.wipo.int>.

61. See <http://www.wipo.int/eng/madrid/index.htm> and <http://www.law.gwu.edu/lc/internic/international/treat2.html>.

62. See <http://www.wipo.int/eng/general/arbit.htm>.

63. See <http://www.unhcr.ch>.

64. See *The Economist*, "The Internet—Names Writ in Water," June 8, 1996.

65. See "FNC Role in the DNS Issue" at <http://ksgwww.harvard.edu/iip/fnc.html>.

66. Although somewhat out of date, a list of Top Level Domain delegation contacts can be found at <http://info.isoc.org:80/adopsec/domains.html>.

67. Postel, "Domain Name System Structure and Delegation," RFC 1591 (March 1994), <ftp://ds.internic.net/rfc/rfc1591.txt>.

68. See <http://www.isi.edu/~postel/> for a list of Jon Postel's activities.

69. See "IANA Overview" (May 1996) at <http://www.isi.edu/iana/overview.html>. Also see "[Internet] Assigned Numbers Authority: known history" at <http://www.wia.org/pub/iana.html>.

70. It is unlikely that such a charter for IANA from ISOC really exists since it could not be produced.

71. See "Federal Networking Council Charter" at <http://www.fnc.gov/FNC_charter.html>.

72. See <http://www.darpa.mil/>.

73. See "Federal Networking Council" at <http://www.fnc.gov/>.

74. See "National Science and Technology Council Committees and Subcommittees" at <gopher://cyfer.esusda.gov:70/00/ace/nstc/nstc-comm/committee>.

75. See <http://www.whitehouse.gov/WH/EOP/OSTP/NSTC/html/NSTC_Home.html>.

76. See "Federal Networking Council Mission" at <http://www.fnc.gov/mission.html>.

77. See "FNC Advisory Committee" at <http://www.fnc.gov/FNCAC.html>.

78. See "Resolution—New Internet Paradigm" at <http://www.fnc.gov/FNCAC_Res.html#Paradigm>.

79. Ibid.

80. See "Resolution—Domain Name Service" at <http://www.fnc.gov/FNCAC_Res.html#DNS>.

81. See "National Telecommunications & Information Administration (NTIA)" at <http://www.ntia.doc.gov/>.

82. See "NTIA's Office of International Affairs" at <http://www.ntia.doc.gov:80/oiahome/oiahome.html>.

83. See <http://ksgwww.harvard.edu/iip/nsfforum.html>.

84. See "Networking and Communications Research and Infrastructure (NCRI) Division" at <http://www.cise.nsf.gov/ncri/index.html>.

85. See <http://www.ksg.harvard.edu/iip/>.

86. See "Internet Administrative Infrastructure—What Is It? Who Should Do It? How Should It Be Paid For?" at <http://www.aldea.com:80/cix/agenda.html>.

87. See <http://www.cix.org>.

88. See <http://ksgwww.harvard.edu/iip/internet.html>.

89. See <http://www.itu.int>.

90. Previously available (now expired) at <ftp://ds.internic.net/internet-drafts/draft-isoc-dns-role-00.txt>.

91. Bush, et al., "Delegation of International Top Level Domains (iTLDs)," Internet draft, <ftp://ietf.cnri.reston.va.us/internet-drafts/draft-ymbk-itld-admin-00.txt>.

92. Postel, "New Registries and the Delegation of International Top Level Domains," Internet draft (August 1996), <ftp://ds.internic.net/internet-drafts/draft-postel-iana-itld-admin-02.txt>.

93. Some would call the Internet a nascent Global Information Infrastructure comprised of National Information Infrastructure initiatives.

94. For example, if someone wants to register the domain name "migros" in Switzerland (*migros.ch*), the Swiss registration authority will know that Migros is the largest supermarket chain in Switzerland. Therefore, they should reject this application unless the applicant is Migros GB (Genossenschafts-Bund). However, if registrations are made at an international level (as NSI does with *.com*, *.net*, *.org*), it is very unlikely that the registry will have heard of Migros GB. (Migros wisely also registered *migros.com*.)

95. What set of moral values (and what language) would a registry use to reject "offensive" names? Clearly what is considered offensive in one country is not the same in another.

96. See <http://www.wia.org/pub/policy-orgs.html>.

97. See <gopher://gopher.isoc.org/00/isoc/bodies/trustees/documents/96-004.htm>.

98. To subscribe, send a message with "subscribe" in the message body to *newdom-request@ar.com*. Also see <http://www.iiia.org/> which hosted an earlier mailing list and has archives of the discussions. This list was shut down by the manager of the mailing list on July 30, 1996, due to its acrimonious nature and threats of legal action by participants.

99. See <http://www.alternic.net> and <http://www.mcs.net/nic/index.html> as examples of groups that want to set up "not officially sanctioned" international Top Level Domain services.

100. See <http://www.ll.georgetown.edu:80/lc/cli.html>.

101. Available from *First Monday: A Peer Reviewed Journal on the Internet* at <http://www.firstmonday.dk/>.

102. David W. Maher, "Trademarks on the Internet: Who's in Charge?" (1996), <http://www.aldea.com/cix/maher.html>.

103. See "White Paper: A Telecommunications Policy Framework for Internet Service Providers" at <http://www.cix.org/Reports/tcomm-wp.html>.

104. See <http://www.fcc.gov>.

105. See <http://www.uspto.gov>.

106. See <http://iitf.doc.gov/>.

107. See "GII: Agenda for Cooperation" at <http://www.ntia.doc.gov/oiahome/gii.html>.

108. Ibid.

109. See <http://www.alternic.net> and <http://www.mcs.net/nic/index.html> as examples of groups that want to set up "not officially sanctioned" international Top Level Domain services.

110. See "Federal Court Rules Communications Decency Act Unconstitutional" at <http://www.eff.org/pub/Alerts/960612_eff_cda_decision.statement>.

"Domain-ia": The Growing Tension between the Domain Name System and Trademark Law

Alexander Gigante

Introduction

The Domain Name System (DNS) adopted in the 1980s is having unanticipated repercussions as the Internet becomes more commercial. The alphanumeric names used as easy-to-remember alternatives to numeric Internet Protocols (IPs)—innocuous mnemonic tools when the Internet was primarily the province of governmental and educational institutions—face increasing conflict with assertions of trademark rights in such names, especially in the .com Top Level Domain. Unless changes in the DNS resolve this conflict soon, the entities responsible for administering the DNS will find themselves embroiled ever more frequently in trademark disputes to the detriment of their primary Internet functions.

Basic Trademark Concepts

What Is a Trademark?

A trademark is "any word, name, symbol or device . . . adopted and used by a manufacturer or merchant to identify his goods and distinguish them from those manufactured or sold by others."[1] A mark used in the sale or advertising of services is a service mark.[2] In our complex free-market economic system, in which consumers must make choices from among a variety of competing products and services, trademarks and service marks function to distinguish one competitor's goods or services from another, Identify those goods or services as having a single source, signify that the goods or services from that source are of a particular, known level of quality, and advertise the goods and services.[3] In addition, the trademark or service mark symbolizes the goodwill that the manufacturer, seller or service provider has acquired among consumers.[4]

Marks fall into four categories:[5] "arbitrary" or "fanciful,"[6] "suggestive,"[7] "descriptive"[8] and "generic."[9] Arbitrary, fanciful and suggestive marks are sometimes called "strong" marks, signifying that they presumptively have distinctive meaning in the marketplace. In contrast, a descriptive mark can be a valid trademark or service mark only if shown to have acquired "secondary meaning" identifying the mark with the provider of the goods or services. As a general proposition, a generic term can never be a valid mark: one competitor cannot preempt common words to the exclusion of others.

Registered and Common-Law Marks

The U.S Patent and Trademark Office (USPTO) registers trademarks and service marks pursuant to the federal Lanham Act. However, under the American trademark system, use of a mark in interstate commerce, not its registration, establishes ownership rights under federal law.[10] An unregistered mark established by use is sometimes called a common-law mark. Thus, the senior user of a mark—i.e., the first in time to use the mark—although not having registered the mark for itself, may obtain cancellation of a USPTO registration issued to a junior user.[11] A senior U.S. user also has priority over a junior U.S. registrant of a foreign mark, even though the mark was registered or used in the foreign jurisdiction before the senior user first used it in the United States.[12] In short, while federal registration confers many benefits, it does not by itself determine superior title in a mark.

Trademark Infringement

A valid mark is infringed by another's use of a similar name or symbol *likely* to cause confusion among or deceive consumers.

"Likely" means "probable." The party claiming infringement need not prove instances of actual confusion—a reasonable likelihood of confusion is sufficient to sustain an infringement claim.[13]

Although generic marks ordinarily cannot serve as valid marks, in cases involving "vanity" 800 telephone numbers, some courts have held that the number's mnemonic—though spelling a generic term—is a mark that can be infringed by a competitor's use of a similar 800 mnemonic.[14] One court even held that an 800 mnemonic infringed a competitor's service mark, although the competitor did not use the mark in a competing 800 number.[15]

Multiple Users of the Same Mark

Because the likelihood of consumer confusion is the benchmark of trademark infringement, noncompeting businesses generally may use—and acquire valid rights in—the same mark.[16] Thus, for example, the 1996 Manhattan telephone directory lists under the name "Acme": an awning company, belt manufacturer, cash register company, dry cleaner, exterminating service, nail salon, refinery, safe company and uniform supplier. Each operates in a separate, unrelated sector of the marketplace and it is not likely that a consumer would ever confuse one company for another. Thus, each of the Acmes may use the name freely within its limited sphere of business activity.

Dilution

One exception to the "Acme rule" just stated arises with the concept of dilution:

The dilution theory grants protection to strong, well-recognized marks even in the absence of a likelihood of confusion, if defendant's use is such as to diminish or dilute the strong identification value of the plaintiff's mark even while not confusing customers . . . . The underlying rationale of the dilution doctrine is that a gradual attenuation or whittling away of the value of a trademark, resulting from use by another, constitutes an invasion of the senior user's property right in its mark.[17]

Thus, a restaurant probably could not use the Tiffany name, or a shoe store Disney, even though such uses would be in fields unrelated to the businesses of the owners of those "strong" marks. Until recently, dilution was purely a matter of state law, as the federal Lanham Act made no provision for such a claim.[18] However, state dilution law cannot always afford complete relief, because state-court injunctions sometimes are unable to reach interstate activities.[19] In 1995, Congress closed this gap by amending the Lanham Act to provide the owner of a "famous" mark with remedies against diluting uses of the mark in interstate commerce.[20] With the new statute, a federal court can enjoin dilution occurring anywhere in the United States.

The Current Domain Name System

A Brief Description of the DNS and Domain Names

The Domain Name System is defined as

a set of distributed databases containing IP (Internet Protocol) addresses and their corresponding domain names. Each domain name is mapped to a particular numeric [IP] address. DNS, with servers located all over the Internet, performs the translation back and forth between names and numbers. This scheme enables users to invoke an easy-to-remember name . . . instead of a more mysterious string of numbers.[21]

A domain name is comprised of alphanumeric components, separated by periods ("dots"), that provide identifying information about the site. Reading from left to right, the first component identifies the host computer, the second component is the Second Level Domain and the last component is—in the United States—the Top Level Domain (TLD) that describes the purpose of the entity owning the Second Level Domain (e.g., .com for a commercial owner, .*gov* for a governmental agency, etc.). A domain name may include other components between the host name and the Second Level Domain called subdomains.[22]

The existing technical limitations of the DNS preclude two different registrants from using the same domain name, even though they have different underlying numeric IP addresses. Each "translatable" IP/domain-name pairing must be unique.[23]

Domain-Name Registration Disputes

Under a 1993 agreement with the National Science Foundation (NSF),[24] Network Solutions, Inc. (NSI) registers Second Level Domain names.[25] Within a short time after assuming that function, NSI faced the full brunt of the Internet's explosive growth, which today generates nearly 20,000 new registrations each month.[26]

Predictably, as an appreciation for the Internet's potential develops among business enterprises, real-world commercial disputes are beginning to intrude into cyberspace. Domain names are a particular source of contention because, as just explained, the DNS permits only one registrant per name in contrast with the real world, which can accommodate multiple users of a trademark based on the same name. These names often represent substantial real-world investment in goodwill, as well as an easily recognizable corporate identity among Net surfers, and trademark owners are thus sometimes understandably unwilling to lose a name without a fight.

NSI's Domain Name Dispute Policy

NSI has attempted to address the problem through adoption of a Domain Name Dispute Policy (NSI Policy) to deal with conflicting trademark-based claims to ownership of a domain name. The version in force until November 23, 1995,[27] generated many complaints from both trademark owners and domain-name registrants, and was replaced on September 9, 1996, by yet another incarnation (1996 Amendment).[28] The 1996 Amendment is the fourth change in the NSI Policy in little over a year, reflecting NSI's travails over domain-name disputes.[29] Despite NSI's continual reworking of the Policy, this latest revision perpetuates many of the flaws of earlier versions.[30]

For example, the 1996 Amendment still empowers NSI to suspend a challenged domain name on the complaint of a registered trademark owner, even though the domain-name holder might have its own trademark in the domain name, if the complainant shows that it registered its trademark before the domain-name holder activated its name or registered its mark in the name. These provisions ignore the basic trademark principles that, as shown above, allow many entities to validly use the same mark, and require more than a mere similarity of names to establish infringement.[31] The 1996 Amendment thus has not changed the fact that the NSI Policy is an invitation to mischief. By merely filing a complaint with NSI with proof of a registered trademark, a challenger can obtain what is in effect an NSI "injunction" disrupting the goodwill and recognition developed by the domain-name registrant.[32] In contrast, in court the challenger could obtain such relief only if it posted a bond, and only after persuading the court that it is likely to succeed on the merits of its claim *and* will suffer irreparable injury without issuance of an injunction.

The NSI Policy also continues to disregard the importance under American law of use of a mark *in the United States.* Thus, a domain-name holder failing to prove a use earlier in time than a foreign use or trademark registration faces suspension of the domain name,[33] even though trademark law would give priority to the domain-name holder if its use were senior in the United States.[34]

The NSI Policy harms trademark owners, too. An infringing domain-name registrant can avoid suspension if it shows a trademark registration for the domain name obtained anywhere in the world, as long as the registration is prior in time to the complainant's registration.[35] Whereas Bob Hope and Bing Crosby traveled the Road to Morocco, NSI sends trademark lawyers on the Road to Tunisia, a jurisdiction where a trademark applicant can obtain registration in a few days.[36] Yet, as shown above, under American trademark law, the senior U.S. user of a mark—albeit unregistered—could obtain cancellation of a foreign registration issued to a junior user. Thus, this aspect of the NSI Policy gives too much weight to registration.[37]

The NSI Policy also fails to address the concept of dilution, which is a separate issue from priority of use and likelihood of confusion.[38] However, with the new federal statute, large corporations holding "strong," "famous" marks can be expected to use dilution actions aggressively to police diluting uses of those marks on the Internet. For example, in February 1996, the federal court in Seattle issued an injunction in Hasbro's dilution action against the *candyland* domain name.[39] More recently, Avon Products brought a federal dilution suit against the *avon.com* domain name, and quickly obtained an injunction on the consent of the defendants.[40]

Finally, the NSI Policy is internally inconsistent. As shown above, even after the 1996 Amendment becomes effective, NSI will still be embroiled in trademark disputes despite its disclaimer that "Network Solutions does not act as arbiter of disputes between Registrants and third party complainants arising out of the registration or use of a domain name."[41]

The Need for Change in the DNS

The tortured history of the NSI Policy reflects the structural limitations in the current DNS. No matter how much NSI tries to stretch the DNS in response to rising claims of property rights in domain names, the current DNS requirement of domain-name uniqueness will always conflict with real-world trademark law, which tolerates multiple uses of commercial names.[42] Only changes in the DNS, in tandem with revisions in the law's treatment of domain names, can eliminate this inherent tension between cyberspace and the real world. The remainder of this chapter will demonstrate why the Internet governing bodies and the legal community should work together to address the issue, and suggest possible changes to accomplish this goal.

Changing the DNS to Accommodate Trademark Rights

A threshold question is whether the Internet governing bodies should concern themselves with trademark rights—or, for that matter, any legal issues—when establishing standards and protocols for domain names. Many participants at a November 1995 symposium sponsored by Harvard's Information Infrastructure Project evinced resistance—bordering on hostility—to addressing what some perceive as lawyer-created problems.[43] While this attitude may satisfy a Shakespearean lust for lawyer-bashing,[44] it will serve the Internet poorly in the long run. Despite the romantic notion of cyberspace held by some, the Internet is not a separate universe, but rather a subset of the real world governed by real-world laws and economics.[45] Practical, real-world considerations argue for greater sensitivity to the legal consequences of technical decisions.

Protecting the Trademark Value of Domain Names Is Consistent With the Spirit of the Internet

Whatever the original purpose of domain names, in today's commercialized cyberspace they fulfill many of the same functions that trademarks have in the real world.[46] As the cases involving 800 telephone numbers show, our flexible legal system quickly adapts existing concepts of intellectual property—including trademark—to new methods of doing business. Thus, the real world/cyberspace barrier has not been an insurmountable obstacle to application of basic trademark concepts to the Internet. Several courts have already recognized domain names as a species of trademark.[47] One of the earliest court decisions to address the issue declared that "[a] domain name mirroring a corporate name may be a valuable corporate asset, as it facilitates communication with a customer base."[48]

The U.S. Patent and Trademark Office will register a domain name (excluding its generic TLD) as a trademark.[49] Legal scholars accept domain names as trademarks: "Thus, domain names share many of the attributes of traditional trademarks. The value of trademarks in the traditional marketplace has carried over into the 'virtual marketplace,' as commerce has moved on-line."[50] The business world likewise views domain names as trademarks, as the growing number of disputes attests.[51]

In sum, whether viewed as classic trademarks or as a new species of intellectual property, domain names have acquired goodwill and commercial value analogous to trademarks.[52] The Internet "spirit" dictates that the Internet's rules and structures should accommodate—not resist—these evolving practices and usages of the Internet Community.[53] The Internet will be ill served if its governing bodies ignore—or worse, attempt to stifle—this important trend in the Internet's commercial development.

Protecting the Trademark Value of Domain Names Is in the Selfish Interests of the Governing Bodies

Avoiding conflict over this issue will also serve the selfish interests of the governing bodies. Today, a maze of boards, task forces, steering groups and the like "govern" interstate and international cybercommunication on the Internet.[54] This ad hoc system has functioned successfully in large part at the sufferance of the federal government and with the acquiescence of Internet users. However, if the perception develops that the governing bodies are treating valuable property rights cavalierly, the consensus could collapse.[55] For the reasons stated below, the existing Internet structure would be vulnerable to a legal challenge.

The National Science Foundation is the current source of authority for the existing system of Internet governance. In particular, the High-Performance Computing Act (HPCA)[56] authorizes the NSF—along with other federal agencies—to promote the development of network computing in cooperation with private network providers and the private computer and telecommunications industries. Significantly, the HPCA states that the computer network to be developed under NSF auspices shall "be designed and operated so as to ensure the continued application of laws that provide network and information resources security measures, including those that protect copyright *and other intellectual property rights.*"[57] Thus, the HPCA alone arguably requires operation of the Internet in a manner solicitous of real-world trademark law.

The NSF's basic charter,[58] as well as the HPCA, also provide the basis upon which the NSF has entered into the InterNic cooperative agreements,[59] which allow extensive NSF involvement in Internet governance,[60] including domain-name registrations.[61] Those questioning the federal government's proprietary claims to the Internet[62] need look no further than the statutory explanation of such cooperative agreements:

An executive agency shall use a cooperative agreement reflecting a relationship between the United States Government and a . . . recipient when (1) the principal purpose of the relationship is to transfer a thing of value to the . . . recipient to carry out a public purpose of support or stimulation authorized by a law of the United States . . .; and (2) substantial involvement is expected between the executive agency and the . . . recipient when carrying out the activity contemplated in the agreement.[63]

This interrelationship between the NSF and the private sector "to carry out a public purpose" may well mean that the governing bodies acting under NSF auspices are "state actors," i.e., private surrogates for the federal government.[64] If a court were to so hold on the complaint of a disgruntled trademark owner or domain-name holder, the governing bodies would thereafter have to conform their administration of the Internet to the U.S. Constitution.[65] Elements of the NSI Policy[66]—as well as proposed schemes to condition Internet access on the surrender of trademark rights[67]—probably would not pass muster under the Constitution's Due Process Clause.[68]

The gradual withdrawal of the NSF and other federal agencies from active administration of the Internet—as currently envisioned[69]—would probably eliminate the argument that the governing bodies are surrogates for the federal government. On the other hand, without the support of these governmental agencies, the governing bodies will lack any colorable legal basis for their activities. The result will be a structure vulnerable to a legal challenge that could undercut the entire Internet system of governance.

Thus, the selfish interests of the governing bodies dictate greater sensitivity to these trademark issues. The risk for not paying heed to the concerns of trademark owners could be the plague of lawyers that the Internet "organization" so earnestly wishes to avoid.

Some Short-Term and Long-Term Proposals for Harmonizing the DNS with Trademark Law

Proposals for the Internet Community

In the short run, NSI should remove itself from disputes arising under the current DNS.[70] No good reason exists for NSI to decide registration questions, make evaluations of competing claims, or preliminarily "enjoin" a challenged domain name.[71] Instead, NSI should follow the practice of the American Arbitration Association, which proceeds with an arbitration unless and until it receives a court directive to the contrary.[72] A legitimately aggrieved trademark owner does not need NSI's intervention, as the owner will be able to obtain in court injunctive relief prohibiting the infringing domain-name registrant from using the name.

If NSI is concerned about being caught in the middle of such disputes, it could institute a simple policy that should alleviate the problem. The U.S. Patent and Trademark Office publishes trademark applications for a period before issuing a registration to allow affected parties the opportunity to protest. NSI could likewise post domain-name applications on the Internet for a reasonable period, and at the same time afford the applicant the choice of either awaiting expiration of the publication period or using the name temporarily with the understanding that the name must be surrendered if challenged.

In the longer run, the DNS must be restructured to eliminate the grounds for domain-name disputes. Paul Vixie's proposal to issue meaningless "license plates" would do away with disputes by doing away with domain names.[73] His proposal is simple, albeit at the expense of removing a valuable tool for commercial sites and for consumers searching for those sites. Others have proposed adding depth to domain names with additional TLDs to permit multiple uses of a name with distinguishing geographical and business designations.[74] This proposal would work, but at the cost of creating a more cumbersome DNS. Most recently, the Internet Assigned Numbers Authority (IANA) has floated a proposal to flood the Internet with dozens of new TLDs,[75] despite indications that new TLDs will not alleviate the trademark issues raised by the DNS.[76]

In this author's view, the ideal solution—if technically feasible—would be to eliminate domain names, as suggested by Vixie, and instead embed depth in an Internet directory system.[77] As this system is envisioned, a user could access a directory screen with all the sites sharing a particular name (with the courts alone deciding any claims of infringement between directory registrants). The directory screen would provide the depth: either a Vixie "license plate" or the existing unique numeric IP for each site, the registrant's geographical location and business description, and other pertinent (and distinguishing) information. The many Acmes in the Manhattan phone book could then share the Internet in the same way.[78]

Proposals for the Legal Community

The legal community can assist in reducing conflicts between domain names and real-world trademark law. Some trademark owners feel compelled to challenge domain names because under trademark law, acquiescence in a competing use may weaken a mark's strength.[79] An amendment to the Lanham Act could eliminate this factor by providing that another's use of the mark as a domain name would not be admissible in court as evidence of acquiescence by the trademark owner.

NSI has involved itself in domain-name disputes out of the fear that it risks liability as a contributory trademark infringer if it does not exercise some policing over registrations of domain names.[80] This fear appears exaggerated, as a contributory infringer must act with knowledge to be liable in damages.[81] If anything, NSI would lower its risk if, as suggested above, it involved itself less in the domain-naming process. Nonetheless, the legal community can alleviate NSI's (and by extension, other registries') concern by pressing for legislation that will clarify the relative responsibilities of registries and domain-name registrants regarding trademark infringement.

International trademark law is more problematic. Generally, "a trademark is recognized as having a separate existence in each sovereign territory in which it is registered or legally recognized as a mark."[82] Thus, the legitimate owner of a mark in one country cannot use it in another country where the same mark belongs to a different owner. Yet the Internet transcends territoriality by projecting content into many legal jurisdictions worldwide.[83] Internet content lawful in its country of origin might violate the laws of other nations.[84] International trademark conflicts on the Internet therefore are a distinct possibility.[85]

Domain names registered in their countries of origin probably will not be a source of such conflicts because the country TLDs should be sufficient to avoid a likelihood of confusion. A protocol to the Paris Convention on trademarks nonetheless might be desirable to clarify this point.[86]

However, problems could arise from the current practice of allowing foreign entities to register domain names under the *.com* TLD.[87] Where the foreign registrant competes with the U.S. owner of the mark, the U.S. owner could have a claim for trademark infringement.[88] Changing existing *.com* registrations is probably not feasible.[89] Thus, the courts likely will have to resolve any trademark conflicts arising over existing *.com* registrations. However, future *.com* registrations could be coupled with country TLDs, which should eliminate this potential source of international trademark conflict in cyberspace.[90] Here, too, an amendment to the Paris Convention could be useful by providing that an infringement does not arise from identical domain-name registrations if differentiated by country TLDs.

Conclusion

Although the Internet is a new and evolving "space," real-world issues will intrude ever more frequently as it gains commercial importance. A failure to appreciate the real-world significance of these issues and address them constructively will generate legal disputes harmful to the Internet and its governing bodies. Cooperation between the governing bodies and the legal community is therefore essential to find solutions that can accommodate real-world commercial interests while preserving the Internet's specialness.

The current debate over domain-name conflicts should prove helpful in this regard. Domain-name disputes have provided the legal and Internet communities with the opportunity to observe how quickly this new "space" can spawn new concepts of property rights and commercial practices. Both communities should see in this experience the need to adapt to this rapid evolutionary process, rather than attempt to constrain it within traditional legal and technical concepts. Fortuitously, none of the techno-legal disputes over domain names has as yet set in motion an irreversible process that would preclude further experimentation and innovation. The way is still open for a cooperative solution of the domain-name problem. Such cooperation, in turn, would serve as an important precedent for resolving other—probably more difficult—issues that will arise in the future.

Notes

1. Section 45 of the Lanham Act, 15 U.S.C. §1127.

2. Ibid.

3. J. Thomas McCarthy, *McCarthy on Trademarks and Unfair Competition* §3.01[2] (Deerfield, Ill.: Clark Boardman Callaghan 1996).

4. Ibid.

5. Ibid., chap. 11, and 2 ibid., chap. 12.

6. "Arbitrary" and "fanciful" mean neither suggesting nor describing the good or service (e.g., Apple computers, Kodak films).

7. "Suggestive" means requiring some imagination to connect the mark with the good or service (e.g., Oracle software).

8. "Descriptive" means conveying a reasonably accurate picture of the good or service (e.g., Neva-Wet water repellant, Pocket Books paperback books).

9. "Generic" means the common name of the good or service.

10. McCarthy, note 3 *supra*, §16.01[1].

11. Ibid., §20.14[2]

12. Ibid., §§16.02[4], 16.07; 3 ibid., §20.04[3].

13. Ibid., chap. 23.

14. See, e.g., *Dial-A-Mattress Franchise Corp. v. Page*, 880 F.2d 675 (2d Cir. 1989); *Express Mortgage Brokers, Inc. v. Simpson Mortgage, Inc.*, 31 U.S.P.Q.2d 1371, 1994 WL 465842 (East. Dist. Mich. 1994).

15. *American Airlines, Inc. v. A 1-800-A-M-E-R-I-C-A-N Corp.*, 622 F.Supp. 673 (No. Dist. Ill. 1985).

16. McCarthy, note 3 *supra*, §§24.01–.12.

17. Ibid., §24.13[1][b], at p. 24-108.

18. Twenty-six states have dilution statutes, including New York and Massachusetts. Ibid., §24.14[2].

19. Cf. ibid., §24.23[3][b].

20. Section 43(c) of the Lanham Act, 15 U.S.C. §1125(c).

21. <http://rs.internic.net/help/domain/dns.html>.

22. Ibid.

23. Jon Postel, "New Registries and the Delegation of International Top Level Domains" (October 1996 IANA), available at <ftp://ftp.isi.edu/in-notes/iana/administration/new-registries>, para. A.1.1.

24. NSF Cooperative Agreement No. NCR-9218742, available at <http://rs.internic.net/nsf/agreement/>. The NSF is party to another cooperative agreement with ATT for fulfillment of Internet directory functions. NSI and ATT together form the entity known as InterNic. See <http://rs.internic.net/internic/index.html>.

25. In registering domain names, NSI operates within the parameters established by the Internet Assigned Numbers Authority (IANA), which is the central coordinator and clearinghouse for assigning parameter values for, among other things, Internet addresses and domain names. See <http://www.iana.org/iana>. See also RFC 1174, para. 1.2, available at <http://ds.internic.net/rfc/rfc1174.txt>.

26. See <http://rs.internic.net:80/announcements/press-release.html>; <http://rs.internic.net/nsf/fee-narrative.html>. See also Denise Caruso, "A Battle Over Internet Site Names Flares, With One Company at its Center," *New York Times*, July 1, 1996, p. D5.

27. The policy is available at <http://www.rs.internic.net:80/domain-infor/internic-domain-4.html>.

28. <ftp://rs.internic.net/policy/internic-domain-6.txt>.

29. See Carl Oppedahl, letter to *San Francisco Recorder*, available at <http://www.patents.com/nsi/aug16.sht>. See also Mr. Oppedahl's chapter in this book, "Analysis and Suggestions Regarding NSI Domain Name Trade Mark Dispute Policy," and Oppedahl & Larson's *NSI Flawed Domain Name Policy Information Page,* <http://www.patents.com/nsi.sht>.

30. Regarding problems with the earlier version of the NSI Policy, see, e.g., Carl Oppedahl, "Securing Your Domain Names Can Be Risky Business," *Network World*, May 27, 1996, p. 45, available at <http://www.patents.com/pubs/nw1.sht>; Carl Oppedahl, "NSI Domain Name Dispute Policy Puts Owners at Significant Risk," *New York Law Journal*, May 21, 1996, p. 5, available at <http://www.patents.com/ pubs/nylj6.sht>. See also Richard Zaitlen and David Victor, "The New Internet Domain Guidelines: Still Winner-Take-All," *Computer Lawyer* (May 1996), p. 12; Mark Voorhees, "Internet Name Policy Draws Suit it was Intended to Avoid," available at <http://www.infolawalert.com/stories/032996c.html>.

31. 1996 Amendment, para. 5, 6.

32. See Denise Caruso, "A Battle Over Internet Site Names Flares, With One Company at its Center," *New York Times*, July 1, 1996, p. D5.; Mikki Barry, "Is the InterNIC's Dispute Policy Unconstitutional?," available at <http://www.mids.org/legal/dispute.html>.

33. 1996 Amendment, para. 5, 6.

34. McCarthy, note 3 *supra*, §16.07. See also Mark Voorhees, "Internet Name Policy Draws Suit It Was Intended to Avoid," March 29, 1996, available at <http://www.infolawalert.com/stories/032996c.html>; David W. Maher, "Trademarks on the Internet: Who's in Charge?," available at <http://aldea.com/cix/maher.html>.

35. 1996 Amendment, para. 6(c). Paragraph 6(b) seems to say that *any* trademark registration held by the domain-name holder, irrespective of when registered, is sufficient to avoid suspension of the domain name. However, this reading of para. 6(b) would moot para. 6(c). NSI needs to clarify this point.

36. Oppedahl & Larson's *NSI Flawed Domain Name Policy Information Page,* <http://www.patents.com/nsi.sht>.

37. See Mark Voorhees, "Network Solutions to Rework Policy Governing Internet Domain Names," April 19, 1996, available at <http://infolawalert.com/stories/041996b.html>.

38. Cf. ibid.

39. *Hasbro, Inc. v. Internet Entertainment Group, Ltd.*, 1996 WL 84853 (West. Dist. Wash. 1996).

40. *Avon Products, Inc. v. Lew, et al.*, Injunction on Consent and Stipulation of Dismissal, 96 Civ. 1213 (SAS) (So. Dist. N.Y. June 17, 1996).

41. 1996 Amendment, Introduction.

42. Mark Voorhees, "Network Solutions to Rework Policy Governing Internet Domain Names," April 19, 1996, available at <http://infolawalert.com/stories/041996b.html>.

43. Mike Roberts, "The Future of Internet Infrastructures," available at <http://ksgwww.harvard.edu/iip/roberts.html>; remarks of Paul Mockapetris at the conference on Internet Names, Numbers and Beyond: Issues in the Coordination, Privatization, and Internationalization of the Internet (November 20, 1995), sponsored by NSF/DNCRI and the Information Infrastructure Project at Harvard University (November 1995 IIP Symposium), available at <http://ksgwww.harvard.eduiip/nsfmin1.html>.

44. "The first thing we do, let's kill all the lawyers." *Henry VI, Part 2*, Act IV, Scene 2.

45. "The Internet is no longer restricted to a small group of us who wrote some code. It's not ours anymore and we have to get over that." Remarks of Paul Mockapetris at November 1995 IIP Symposium.

46. See Paul Vixie, "External Issues in DNS Scalability," available at <http://ksgwww.harvard.edu /iip/vixie.html>; remarks of Vint Cerf at November 1995 IIP Symposium.

47. *Hasbro, Inc. v. Internet Entertainment Group, Ltd.*, 1996 WL 84853 (West. Dist. Wash. 1996); *The Comp Examiner Agency, Inc. v. Juris, Inc.*, No. 96-01213-WMB (Cent. Dist. Cal. April 26, 1996) (preliminary injunction enjoining plaintiff from using "juris" domain name on ground that it infringed defendant's registered "JURIS" trademark); *Sun Microsystems, Inc. v. Sunriver Corp.*, No. C-95 02340-CAL (No. Dist. Cal. September 28, 1995) (preliminary injunction enjoining defendant from using "SUNRIVER" mark as, among other things, a domain name on the ground that it infringed plaintiff's many "SUN-" trademarks).

48. *MTV Networks v. Curry*, 867 F.Supp. 202, 204 (So. Dist. N.Y. 1994).

49. See "Registration of Domain Names in the Trademark Office," available at <http://www.uspto.gov/web/uspto/info/domain.html>; 50 *Patent, Trademark & Copyright Journal* [BNA] 742 (October 26, 1995).

50. Richard Raysman and Peter Brown, "Domain Names: Protecting Trademarks on the Internet," *New York Law Journal*, June 11, 1996, p. 3, col. 1. See also, e.g., Dan L. Burk, "A First Look at the Emerging Law of Cybermarks," 1 *Richmond Journal of Law & Tech.* 1 (1995), available at <http://www.urich.edu/~jolt/vli1/burk.html>; Carl Oppedhahl, "Internet Domain Names That Infringe Trademarks," *New York Law Journal*, November 14, 1985 (revised February 2, 1996),

available at <http://www.patents.com/pubs/nylj1.sht>; Jonathan Agmon and Stacey Halpern, "The Relationship Between Domain Names and Trademarks," available at <http://www.ll.georgetown.edu/ lc/internic/introd1.html>.

51. David W. Maher, "Trademarks on the Internet: Who's in Charge?," available at <http://aldea.com/cix/maher.html>. See also *BellSouth Corp. v. Internet Classifieds of Ohio*, Civ. Action No. 1:96-CV-769-CC (No. Dist. Ga.), Complaint, available at <http://www.realpages.com/lawsuit/>; *Fry's Electronics, Inc. v. Octave Systems, Inc.*, No. C 95 2525 CAL (No. Dist. Cal.); *KnowledgeNet, Inc. v. Boone*, No. 94 C7 195 (No. Dist. Ill.), Amended Complaint, available at <ftp://internic.net/ netinfo/knowledgement.lawsuit>. For a comprehensive survey of domain-name disputes, see <http://www.ll.georgetown.edu/ lc/internic/recent/rec1.html>.

52. See authorities cited in notes 50 and 51.

53. See, e.g., David R. Johnson and David G. Post, "Law and Borders—The Rise of Law in Cyberspace," available at <http://www.cli.org/X0025_LBFIN.html>; Ann Wells Branscomb, "Anonymity, Autonomy and Accountability: Challenges to the First Amendment in Cyberspaces," 104 *Yale Law Journal* 1639, 1646–1647 (May 1995); Henry Perritt, "Dispute Resolution in Electronic Network Communities," 38 *Villanova Law Rev.* 349, 352–353 (1993).

54. See Robert Shaw, "Internet Domain Names: Whose Domain Is This?," available at <http://www.itu.ch/intreg/dns.html>.

55. David W. Maher, "Trademarks on the Internet: Who's in Charge?," available at <http://aldea.com/cix/maher.html>.

56. 15 U.S.C. §5501 *et seq.*

57. 15 U.S.C. §5512(c)(5) (emphasis added).

58. The NSF's basic charter directs it to foster the development of computer technologies. 42 U.S.C. §§1861(a)(4), 1861(b).

59. See NSF Cooperative Agreement No. NCR-9218742, Art. 1, NSF Cooperative Agreement No. NCR-9218742, available at <http://rs.internic.net/nsf/agreement/>.

60. Ibid., Arts. 6(b), 9, 10, 11, 14.

61. See *Roadrunner Computer Systems, Inc. v. Network Solutions, Inc.*, Civ. Dkt. No. 96-413-A (East. Dist. Va.), NSI Answer, para. 13, NSI Counterclaim, para. 4 (acknowledging that the NSF approves NSI policy regarding domain-name disputes), available at <http://www.patents.com/nsians.sht>.

62. Remarks of Vint Cerf and Mike St. Johns at November 1995 IIP Symposium.

63. 31 U.S.C. §6305.

64. See, e.g., *Lebron v. National Railroad Passenger Corp.*, 115 S.Ct. 961, 964 (1995); *Jackson v. Metropolitan Edison Co.*, 419 U.S. 345 (1974); *Burton v. Wilmington Parking Authority*, 365 U.S. 715 (1961); Mikki Barry, "Is the InterNIC's Dispute Policy Unconstitutional?," available at <http://www.mids.org/legal/dispute.html>.

65. Ibid.

66. For example, NSI's policy of suspending a domain name without a due-process hearing even after the domain-name registrant may have invested substantial time and money in and developed valuable goodwill with the name. Mikki Barry, "Is the InterNIC's Dispute Policy Unconstitutional?," available at <http://www.mids.org/ legal/dispute.html>.

67. Larry Landweber, Jon Postel and Nicholas R. Trio, "Domain Names and Network Numbers," available at <http://ksgwww.harvard.edu/iip/isoc.html>. See also David W. Maher, "Trademarks on the Internet: Who's in Charge?," available at <http://aldea.com/cix/maher.html>.

68. Mikki Barry, "Is the InterNIC's Dispute Policy Unconstitutional?," available at <http://www.mids.org/ legal/dispute.html>.

69. See the chapter written by Don Mitchell, Scott Bradner and Kimberly Claffy, "In Whose Domain: Name Service in Adolescence," also available at <http:// www.nlanr.net/Papers/Dnessence/>, indicating that the NSF and other governmental agencies will begin withdrawing support for Internet operations now that the Internet has matured. See also the Draft Minutes of the Federal Networking Council Advisory Committee, April 8 and 9, 1996, Part III(1), recommending that the NSF "begin the process of transitioning out of these [domain name/ addressing] responsibilities," available at <http://www.fnc.gov/ FNAC_4_96_minutes.html>.

70. As the DNS was originally conceived, the registering authority was not to involve itself in such matters. See RFC 1591, para. 4, available at <http:// ds.internic.net/rfc/rfc1591.txt>.

71. See <http://www.gpl.net/DomainNameUnderAttack/> for an example of how NSI's current activist role in dispute resolution is a no-win proposition.

72. In contrast with NSI, registries in other countries apparently do not involve themselves in domain-name disputes. Mikki Barry, "Is the InterNIC's Dispute Policy Unconstitutional?," available at <http://www.mids.org/legal/ dispute.html>.

73. Paul Vixie, "External Issues in DNS Scalability," available at <http://ksgwww.harvard.edu/iip/vixie.html>; David W. Maher, "Trademarks on the Internet: Who's in Charge?," available at <http://aldea.com/cix/ maher.html>.

74. Remarks of Vint Cerf and Mark Corbitt at November 1995 IIP Symposium; Jonathan Agmon, "The Problem and Criteria for a Solution," available at <http://www.ll.georgetown.edu/ lc/internic/prob1.html>.

75. Postel, note 23 *supra.*

76. See remarks of Vint Cert, Robert Frank and Robert Moskowitz at November 1995 IIP Symposium.

77. "The Internet badly needs a directory service." Paul Vixie, "External Issues in DNS Scalability," available at <http://ksgwww.harvard.edu/iip/vixie.html> See also remarks of Paul Vixie and Paul Mockapetris at November 1995 IIP Symposium.

78. Although domain names have served as convenient mnemonic devices, it may be time to acknowledge that their utility is outweighed by the growing legal confrontations over trademark rights. The average telephone user today is accustomed to dialing eleven numbers to access a long-distance number. Thus, Internet users should be able to use twelve-digit IPs without great difficulty. Moreover, as every major browser now allows the user to save Internet addresses, in reality most Internet users will be speed dialing to sites, further lessening the need for a mnemonic tool.

79. See 2 McCarthy, note 3 *supra*, §17.05. See also Postel, note 23 *supra*, para. A.1.4.1.

80. See Remarks of David Graves, NSI Business Manager, at ONE ISPcon conference, August 9, 1996, available at <http://domain-name.org/graves-ispcon.html>.

81. McCarthy, note 3 *supra*, §25.02[2]. An innocent (i.e., unknowing) contributor can still be subject to an injunction. Ibid. But the NSI Policy has hardly shielded NSI from injunction suits by disgruntled trademark owners and domain-name registrants.

82. McCarthy, note 3 *supra*, §29.01[1], at p. 29-92.

83. See Alexander Gigante, "Ice Patch on the Information Superhighway: Foreign Liability for Domestically Created Content," 14 *Cardozo Arts & Entertainment Law Journal* 523 (1996).

84. Ibid.

85. See *Playboy Enterprises, Inc. v. Chuckleberry Publishing, Inc.,* 939 F.Supp. 1032 (So. Dist. N.Y. 1996), holding that images available on an Italian magazine's Internet site violated a 15-year-old trademark injunction against distribution of the magazine in United States.

86. See Gigante, note 83 *supra*, regarding a proposed international convention for the Internet to address some legal issues raised by the Internet's extraterritoriality.

87. See Robert Shaw, "Internet Domain Names: Whose Domain Is This?," available at <http://www.itu.ch/intreg/dns.html>.

88. Cf. 4 McCarthy, note 3 *supra*, §29.11; *Playboy Enterprises, Inc. v. Chuckleberry Publishing, Inc.,* note 85 *supra*.

89. Postel, note 23 *supra*, para. A.1.4.2.

90. Cf. ibid.

Trademark Disputes in the Assignment of Domain Names

Carl Oppedahl

In Luna in 2075 phone numbers were punched in, not voice-coded, and numbers were Roman alphabet. Pay for it and have your firm name in ten letters good advertising. Pay smaller bonus and get a spell sound, easy to remember. Pay minimum and you got arbitrary string of letters.... I asked Mike for such a . . . number. "It's a shame we can't list you as 'Mike.'" "In service," he answered. "MIKESGRILL, Novy Leningrad. MIKEANDLIL, Luna City. MIKESSUITS, Tycho Under. MIKES" —Robert A. Heinlein, *The Moon is a Harsh Mistress*, 1966[1]

Heinlein not only wrote of something like the Internet's domain name system 20 years before its time, he also described what happens if the domain name you want is already taken. MIT registered its domain name in May 1985, and IBM registered its domain name in March 1986. But it was not until about 1993, when the World Wide Web brought the Internet to every computer screen, that domain names became a big deal. And only in 1995 did fights over domain names begin to hit the news.

This chapter discusses how certain types of trademark disputes on the Internet are handled now, and offers suggestions as to how they might be handled in the future. At present nearly all Internet domain names are administered by Network Solutions Inc. (NSI), which is the temporary administrator of domain names for the term of a five-year contract with the National Science Foundation that expires in 1998. Consequently, NSI's policies are very important and will be examined from several perspectives in this chapter, although the recommendations made here are of general applicability to other domain name registration authorities and to proposed new top-level domains.

This chapter assumes that the reader is knowledgeable about the Internet, the World Wide Web, and the system of domain names used on the Internet, and assumes further that the reader has some general familiarity with the law of trademarks.[2]

Domain Names Seem to Be Special

There are many ways in which someone on the Internet could trigger the ire of a holder of a trademark or some other form of intellectual property. A Web site could contain someone's registered trademark. A Web site could pluck an image (a trademark, or a Dilbert cartoon) from some other site and incorporate the image into its own Web page. A Web site could contain material protected by copyright without the permission of the copyright holder. A domain name could be similar to (but not identical to) some trademark. A third-level domain name (e.g., *exxon.oil.com*) could be identical to a famous domain name. Or a second-level domain name (e.g., *exxon.com*) could be identical to some trademark.

Each scenario has arisen many times in recent years, and in all cases but one, the intellectual property holder has had no choice but to resort to the courts if a simple request (or threat of litigation) did not yield the desired result. This hardly seems unfair, since intellectual property disputes in all other areas of human interaction (product packaging, product names, print media, television, radio), even if international in scope, are resolved in the courts.

The sole exception to this rule is the Internet second-level domain name. Historical accidents, recent trends in commerce, and clumsy policymaking by NSI have made the Internet second-level domain name the most hotly contested asset on the Internet, and have led to a dispute-handling regime that harms the Internet by injecting extraordinary uncertainty into the business plans of law-abiding members of the Internet community.

What is it that makes second-level domain names so different from everything else on the Internet? Why would a government contractor that otherwise keeps the lowest possible profile choose to inject itself into the public debate by enacting such a controversial policy regarding second-level domain names? Two factors provide at least part of the answer to these questions.

Getting a Particular Domain Name Is Often Viewed as Crucial

The Unum Corporation tried to obtain the domain name *unum.com*, learned that it had already been registered by someone else, and sued the holder to get it.[3] Explaining why they needed the domain name so urgently, Unum stated in court papers that:

> [I]nformation on companies and their products and services is usually located on the Internet by typing in a domain name containing the company's name or trademark followed by ".com" (e.g. "unum.com"). As such, a company's ability to use a domain name on the Internet consisting of its company name followed by ".com" is important to its ability to successfully market, promote and sell its products and services.[4]

It is important to appreciate that even if these views are not entirely justified (at the time Unum's papers were filed with the court it was easy, for example, to find all mentions of Unum on the Web through Alta Vista and other search engines), such views are nonetheless strongly held by many large companies.

Losing a Domain Name Can Mean Going out of Business

A domain name (note that for the balance of this chapter the term "domain name" will be used as shorthand for "second-level domain name") is important because its loss would at the very least cause disruption and monetary expense, and in many cases would put a company out of business. Roadrunner Computer Systems, Inc. (RCS), an Internet service provider in New Mexico, had some 700 customers who relied on *roadrunner.com* as part of their e-mail addresses.[5] After NSI wrote to RCS in December 1995 stating that its domain name would be deactivated[6] in 30 days, RCS sued NSI for a court order blocking the deactivation. The president of RCS stated under penalty of perjury that loss of the domain name "would be disastrous," and that one-fourth of the customers would be lost, in part because all of the customers would have had to change their e-mail addresses.[7]

The Triangle

Each trademark domain name dispute necessarily involves three parties—the domain name holder, the trademark holder, and the registration authority. Each party has interests differing greatly from those of the others.

The Domain Name Holder

For a domain name holder the predominant interest is predictability. The domain name holder does not want its domain name to be taken away precipitously any more than it wants to be evicted from its physical space or have its electricity cut off. In fact, for many Internet-related businesses, physical eviction or loss of electric power would be far more easily remedied than loss of the domain name. How can a domain name holder protect against loss of its domain name? Prior to NSI's July 1995 policy, a domain name holder could protect against loss of its domain name by the simple step of avoiding infringing anyone's trademarks. Starting in July 1995, however, that was no longer sufficient; one had to be prepared to sue NSI as well.

The Trademark Holder

For a trademark holder there are really two interest areas. The first arises if trademark infringement occurs, in which case the trademark holder would like to get the infringement stopped right away; a subsidiary concern is reducing the cost of halting the infringement. The second interest area arises solely as a consequence of the NSI policy, and involves the trademark holder that desires a particular domain name, and learns that the domain name has already been taken by someone else who is not infringing the trademark holder's trademark. (The law of trademark dilution is discussed below and presents special problems on the Internet.) A trademark holder in this situation will not get anywhere in court, but the NSI policy provides an alternative mechanism for denying the domain name holder the use of the domain name.

The Domain Name Registration Authority

The main interest of a domain name registration authority (of which there are several hundred around the world, one for each top-level domain) is getting its job done well. At present, about half a million domain names have been registered in the top-level domains administered by NSI; by comparison, all of the other domain name registration authorities of the world combined probably account for only a few tens of thousands of domain names. This makes NSI's interests of particularly great concern, and NSI has stated many times in recent months that it is not only interested in getting its job done well, but is also interested in trying to avoid being sued.[8]

Most of the domain name registration authorities of the world are volunteer organizations or are affiliated to some degree with universities and government agencies, and thus have few interests other than those of their users, the domain name holders. NSI, in contrast, is engaged in numerous lines of business in addition to the administration of Internet domain names including the installation and maintenance of computer networks. NSI's corporate parent, Science Applications International Corporation (SAIC), has revenues of U.S. $1.9 billion, has 20,000 employees and over 300 office locations around the world, and is a major contractor in information technology, systems integration, energy, environment, medical and health care systems, and transportation.[9] It may be more appropriate for domain name registration to be performed in an independent institution that is unlikely to have potential interests that may conflict with the interests of the Internet community.

In any event, the three parties to any dispute thus form a triangle, and it is important to consider the possible interests of all three parties when figuring out what to do about domain name trademark disputes.

History

The origins of the Internet lie in documents called Requests for Comment (RFCs), the very name of which communicated a consensus-based culture. RFC 1591, entitled *Domain Name System Structure and Delegation*, sets forth a simple role for the domain name registration authority:

In case of a dispute between domain name registrants as to the rights to a particular name, the registration authority shall have no role or responsibility other than to provide the contact information to both parties.

This remains, by definition, the default policy of any Internet domain name registration authority unless it establishes a different one. A compilation has been made of the domain name policies of the world's several hundred registration authorities,[10] and from the compilation it may be seen that most of the registration authorities follow RFC 1591 in whole or in part.

Of course it is possible to imagine a trademark holder suing a registration authority in connection with a domain name dispute, but in such cases the registration authority need not worry much about legal bills or financial liability. The reasons for this are simple. First, in most trademark cases (whether on the Internet or elsewhere) there is no award of money damages; instead, the only action taken by the court is to order someone to do something or to stop doing something. Second, if a trademark holder sues the registration authority, it is generally done merely for procedural reasons, to ensure that at the end of the case the registration authority will comply with whatever outcome is ordered by the court. Third, at least for the registration authorities that have a history of abiding by court orders and for living up to their own commitments and policies, there is little reason to think that a court would impose any financial liability on a registration authority. Fourth, there are no known cases of a domain name registration authority being sued (by a trademark holder) for damages as distinguished from being taken to court simply to be compelled to take particular action with the domain name.

It should be no surprise at all that neutral stakeholders such as telephone companies, stock exchanges, and domain name registration authorities have not been held financially liable in connection with squabbles over telephone numbers, ticker symbols, or domain names. Indeed, in one of the handful of cases touching on this issue, a U.S. District Court in 1994 reached the rather sensible conclusion that the New York Stock Exchange should not be liable for assigning a ticker symbol.[11] Citing the New York Stock Exchange case, a U.S. District Court recently ruled that NSI "is under no general duty to investigate whether a given [Internet domain name] registration is improper."[12]

By about 1994 there had been a few highly publicized cases in which individuals had registered domain names (e.g., *mtv.com*, *mcdonalds.com*) in ways that had angered trademark holders. Journalists quite cheerfully gave coverage to these mosquito-and-elephant stories in which large corporations that had been slow to appreciate the Internet found the domain names that they might have wanted already taken by others. The impression given was that the Internet was the site of a sort of Oklahoma landrush with enterprising individuals trying to stake out the likes of *coke.com*, *exxon.com*, and *kodak.com* in order to retire on the proceeds from the subsequent sale of the domain names to their namesakes.

The *com* domain name was administered by SRI until April 1993 when NSI took over that duty under a contract that will expire in 1998. In 1994, a company called Knowledgenet tried to obtain the domain name *knowledgenet.com* but found it was already taken. In December 1994, Knowledgenet sued several parties in Chicago federal court, including the domain name holder and NSI.[13] From court docket entries, it is apparent that NSI (represented by the Washington, DC law firm of Shaw, Pittman, Potts & Trowbridge) expended much lawyer time and money trying to get the case dismissed or transferred to Virginia. NSI did not succeed, and settlement talks dragged on until the summer of 1995. The last docket entries in the case, made in July and August of 1995, show that the court was waiting for NSI and the plaintiff to file settlement papers, yet give no indication that they were ever filed. Oddly, the court record shows the case as "terminated," yet nothing in the court record shows how the case ended, or if it ever did.

Meanwhile, in March of 1995 NSI was purchased by SAIC, based in San Diego. SAIC's outside counsel, the California law firm of Gray, Cary, Ware & Freidenrich, was given the task of drafting a domain name policy that would minimize the incentive for a trademark holder such as Knowledgenet to sue NSI. The result was the July 23, 1995, NSI domain name policy,[14] which created a decisionmaking process that existed separate from the regular court system, but was markedly beneficial toward trademark holders. A trademark holder that wanted NSI to deactivate someone's domain name had to do nothing more than write a letter to NSI stating that it held a registered trademark identical to the domain name, and NSI would deactivate the domain name after 30 days.[15] (NSI would send what is now referred to in the Internet community as a "30-day letter" to the domain name holder.) The intention was apparently to promise in advance to do almost anything a trademark holder would have asked for in court, thus making it unlikely that the trademark holder would bother to sue NSI. Moreover, the system also responded to the mosquito-and-elephant stories by enabling the elephants to get the domain names they had been slow to register. One of NSI's lawyers from Gray Cary has said "I represent [NSI] and assisted in drafting the domain name dispute resolution policy and this type of problem is the reason for the policy. It permits the holders of registered trademarks to have *special relief*"[16] (emphasis added). At the time that Gray Cary drafted the NSI policy, it was listed as the legal representative on more than 1,300 U.S. trademarks and trademark applications for various clients.

This policy proved to be quite popular with trademark holders (presumably because of the "special relief" designed into it by its authors), who immediately began writing such letters to NSI. NSI initiated some ten deactivation proceedings the following month (August 1995), and the number of deactivation proceedings increased to a peak of about 50 in March 1996. By May 1996 some 200 domain names had been deactivated at the request of various trademark holders. In addition, the new NSI policy resulted in many additional domain names changing hands privately since often a trademark holder merely had to threaten to use the NSI administrative procedure to coerce a domain name holder into giving up the domain name; the domain name holder knew that the nearly inevitable result would be the loss of the domain name anyway. In other words, the harmful effects of the policy went far beyond the several hundred domain names that were the direct subjects of NSI deactivation proceedings.

From the trademark holder's perspective, the NSI policy was a godsend. Instead of going to court with all the attendant drawbacks of doing so (the cost, the risk of a countersuit, and the risk of Rule 11 sanctions[17] or loss of the trademark if the court determined the case had been improperly brought), the trademark holder had merely to spend 32 cents on postage and NSI would (1) assume the risk of countersuit and (2) deactivate the domain name.

What the NSI policy ignored (and continues to ignore, despite two more policy revisions since the July 1995 policy) was that trademark holders were using its policy to win cases they could never have won in court. A trademark holder that had no bona fide case of trademark infringement against a domain name holder, but was merely covetous of a domain name, could quite easily get it taken away from the domain name holder simply by writing to NSI, or by threatening to do so.

Of course, each letter that NSI sent to a domain name holder stating that the domain name would be deactivated in 30 days at the request of a trademark holder represented a risk of litigation for NSI since it was possible a domain name holder would go to court to block NSI's threatened deactivation. But one can speculate that the drafter of the NSI policy considered who was more likely to sue (holders of well-known trademarks), and which side NSI had leverage over (domain name holders) in selecting a corner of the triangle to favor. And indeed this assessment proved sound: during the first eight months that the policy was in force, not one domain name holder fought back in court. The trademark holder always won, and NSI did not get sued.

Between March and October of 1996, however, seven different domain name holders (represented by seven different law firms) that received 30-day letters decided to fight back.[18] In each case, the domain name holder sued NSI and scheduled a hearing at which the judge would be asked to issue a court order blocking the deactivation. Significantly, in five of the seven cases, NSI contacted the domain name holder prior to the hearing date and agreed to scrap its policy so as to avoid being ordered to do so. In one of the cases,[19] NSI's counsel waited until the court hearing was in progress to relent and agree not to carry out its policy against the domain name holder. In the remaining case,[20] the judge signed an injunction ordering NSI not to deactivate the domain name and NSI is enjoined to this day from carrying out its policy.[21] It became clear that if a domain name holder that was not infringing anyone's trademarks received a 30-day letter from NSI, the most straightforward way of staving off loss of the domain name was to sue NSI. Indeed, for the domain name holder who sues NSI to keep from losing its domain name, the definition of "winning" is getting to keep the domain name, and on the basis of that definition, every domain name holder that has ever sued NSI has won.

NSI has said that it has placed about 350 domain names "on hold" under its policy. Seven of its decisions to place a domain name "on hold" have resulted in its being sued, and in each of those cases the domain name holder won, meaning that it has gotten to keep its domain name. This might suggest that NSI "gets the wrong answer" two percent of the time—that in two percent of the cases it reaches a different answer than a court would reach. In reality, however, the "getting the wrong answer" percentage is much higher, because there are many other domain name holders who have seen their domain names placed "on hold" but who do not have the financial resources to take on litigation with NSI or others. And as mentioned above, the harm flowing from NSI's policy extends far beyond the domain names that get put "on hold" due to its policy since many domain name holders have been coerced into giving up their domain names simply in response to a trademark holder's threat to use the policy.

Under NSI's second[22] and third[23] policies (in effect from July 1995 to September 1996), there was only one other means (besides suing NSI) by which a noninfringing domain name holder that had received a 30-day letter could keep from losing its domain name,[24] and that was to rush to a country in which a trademark registration could be obtained quickly. The reason was that, under the NSI policy, the recipient of a 30-day letter was invited to supply (prior to the expiration of the 30-day period) proof of that it was the holder of a trademark registration, in which case NSI would not deactivate the domain name. (The drafters of the NSI policy had presumably selected 30 days on the mistaken assumption that it was impossible to obtain a trademark registration in that short period of time.) Only one country—Tunisia—has been found that can provide a trademark registration (and the special "certified copy" of the registration which NSI demands) in such a short time, and several recipients of 30-day letters have used Tunisian trademarks to attempt to stave off loss of their domain names. NSI's fourth policy,[25] however, which went into effect on September 9, 1996, eliminates this option by stating that the domain name holder can use a trademark registration to halt the NSI proceeding only if the registration was obtained prior to the start of the NSI challenge proceeding. This leaves suing NSI as the only reliable remaining line of defense for a noninfringing domain name holder that does not already hold a trademark registration.[26]

Under NSI's fourth policy, the only safe harbor for a domain name holder (short of suing NSI upon receipt of a 30-day letter) is to do whatever is required to obtain a trademark registration identical to the text of the domain name. Obtaining a U.S. trademark takes a year or more, however. (Indeed, even a domain name holder that somehow learned of NSI's poorly publicized policy change in July 1995 and immediately commenced applying for a U.S. trademark would probably not have received it by now.) Thus the domain name holder that wishes to protect itself from NSI 30-day letters starting right now has no choice but to obtain a Tunisian trademark registration. Of course, most domain name holders will not do this—it seems silly to obtain a trademark in a country where one has no intention of doing business. Instead, it is fair to assume that many domain name holders will prepare and file trademark applications with the U.S. Patent & Trademark Office (USPTO) since most of the domain name holders in domains administered by NSI are in the United States. As there are presently about half a million domain names administered by NSI, this can reasonably be expected to result in tens of thousands of trademark applications filed with the USPTO that would otherwise never have been filed. This will result in a severe overload of the existing trademark examining corps within the USPTO. (The USPTO has indicated that it plans to conduct a public policymaking proceeding in the coming months to attempt to figure out what to do about this problem created by NSI.)

Fundamentally the problem with the present (fourth) NSI policy is that a domain name holder cannot protect itself from loss of its domain name merely by avoiding infringing anyone's trademarks.

(In all other areas of human endeavor, such as product packaging or naming, simply avoiding infringement does provide such protection; it is only in the specific area of NSI-administered domain names that this great risk presents itself.) The domain name holder is forced to obtain a trademark registration itself, a process that takes many months or years in most countries. A related problem is that, in the United States at least, trademark registrations are not available to all applicants as of right. To obtain the registration it is necessary to state under oath that one is actually using the trademark to indicate the origin of goods or services, and that this is taking place in interstate commerce. But there are probably a substantial number of domain name holders who do not in fact use their domain names to indicate the origin of goods or services, but merely use them in connection with a company name or line of business. And there are probably a substantial number of domain name holders who, even if they do use a domain name to indicate the origin of goods or services, do not do so in interstate commerce. All such domain name holders are stuck between the USPTO, which will not give them a trademark registration, and NSI, which maintains that nothing but a trademark registration provides defense against a 30-day letter.

It should be noted that while the NSI policy does give "special relief" to trademark holders, it does not do everything that a trademark holder could want. Most important, from the trademark holder's point of view, the NSI policy falls short because winning a domain name challenge proceeding does not mean the trademark holder gets to have the domain name. Instead, NSI places the domain name "on hold." To get the domain name taken off hold requires subsequent litigation, or paying the domain name holder enough money to induce it to give up the domain name. Let us see how this works out for trademark holders in the context of the various scenarios that prompt them to initiate challenges.

For the trademark holder that merely wants to bring a halt to some infringing activity, the NSI policy is fully satisfactory. By getting a domain name placed "on hold," the trademark holder achieves its goal of stopping the activity, and does so at nominal cost (less than a dollar), while leaving to NSI much of the risk of getting sued by the domain name holder.

But many trademark holders want more than simply a domain name placed "on hold"—they want the domain name itself. (As mentioned above, the reason can be either that the domain name holder's actions actually infringe the trademark holder's rights, or simply that the trademark holder is covetous of the domain name.) In this case, the trademark holder has no choice but to go to court, just as it would have if NSI had kept RFC 1591 as its policy. And the trademark holder might just as well sue not only the domain name holder but also NSI in order to make sure that NSI would comply with whatever court order might follow.[27] Indeed, this very situation has arisen at least four times since July 1995.[28]

Antidilution Laws and the Internet

Most trademarks are not unique. There is a Yale lock company and a Yale University, and neither one will ever be able to block the other from using the name "Yale." As a general rule, the holder of a trademark will only be able to block some other use of the mark if, in the opinion of the court, that other use gives rise to customer confusion. Because a court will not find customers of the lock company to be confused as to the origin of the university's services, and vice versa, trademark law will not allow either to block the other. A court may compare, for example, the goods and services offered by one company with the goods and services of the other, and if there is no overlap, the court may find that there is little likelihood of confusion.

A tiny fraction (probably less than one percent) of trademarks are indeed unique. Kodak, Xerox, and Exxon are all coined names used solely by their namesakes. Legislatures have responded to the requests of the Kodaks and the Xeroxes of the world by enacting so-called antidilution laws which permit the holder of a unique trademark to block someone's actions regardless of whether or not the actions give rise to confusion. The accused infringer in a dilution case will find it no defense that its goods or services have no overlap with those of the trademark holder; the only defense is to show that the trademark is not the kind of mark that is protectable by the antidilution law—e.g., that it is not unique. For the drafter of an antidilution law, the single most important task is to provide a cogent and workable criterion for determining whether a particular trademark deserves the special status of being "undilutable," namely, whether the court will enjoin accused infringers without the trademark holder's having to show that the actions cause marketplace confusion. Many U.S. states have antidilution laws, and the language of those laws often defines an undilutable mark as a coined mark (i.e., that it is not a word that was previously used) or as a unique mark (a mark that is used by only one company).

In January 1996, the U.S. Congress enacted a federal antidilution law.[29] In a move that virtually assured frequent collisions on the Internet for years to come, the law fails to provide any but the fuzziest language as to which trademarks deserve the special status of being federally undilutable. It merely states that such a trademark has to be "famous," and then provides a nonbinding list of eight factors which courts are free to apply or not as they see fit in their efforts to determine whether a trademark is "famous." Senator Patrick Leahy said this about the Act: "It is my hope that this antidilution statute can help stem the use of deceptive Internet addresses taken by those who are choosing marks that are associated with the products and reputations of others."[30] Thus it would not be surprising if every trademark holder were henceforth to claim that its mark is "famous" and thus argue that it need not show, in court, that an accused infringer was actually causing confusion. And that is exactly what has happened. Since the federal antidilution law was enacted, every single U.S. lawsuit by a trademark holder relating to a domain name has asserted the federal antidilution law. And each such lawsuit has been accompanied by a brief quoting the statement by Senator Leahy. Surely not all of the asserted trademarks are in fact "famous" (or unique, or coined), and yet the claim is uniformly made by the trademark holder for the simple reason that there is always some chance, however remote, that the court may find the mark "famous."

The U.S. Congress, by passing an antidilution law with such a vague definition of the term "famous," has fanned the flames of Internet domain name problems. As a practical matter this problem will only fade after some years as the U.S. courts interpret the term and eventually provide some sharper dividing line between the tiny handful of trademarks that deserve special antidilution treatment and the vast majority of other trademarks that do not. Until then one may predict with near certainty that every U.S. lawsuit asserting a trademark will invoke the federal antidilution law, which will exacerbate the problems with the present NSI policy. For example, under the present NSI policy, a trademark holder that wishes to have NSI deactivate a domain name must first write a letter to the domain name holder stating "unequivocally and with particularity that the registration and use of the Registrant's Domain Name violates the legal rights of the trademark holder."[31] Since the federal antidilution law is one of the "legal rights" that any trademark holder can assert (in the hopes that its trademark will be deemed famous), and since at present no one knows what constitutes "famous," then any trademark holder can quite easily make the assertion required by NSI based on the federal antidilution law, even if the domain name holder is not causing any confusion.

Proposed Solutions for the Domain Name Trademark Problem

It has often been stated, as if it sheds light on the matter, that the trademark system does not map onto the domain name system. There may be some truth to this, but if so the problem is neither new nor unique to domain names: there is likewise no workable mapping from trademarks to alphanumeric telephone numbers, to postal addresses, to radio and television station call letters, to names of pedigreed dogs or horses, or to stock exchange ticker symbols. (It often happens, for example, that a company making arrangements to be listed on a stock exchange finds that the ticker symbol it prefers has already been taken by some other company.)

One proposal for dealing with this problem is to establish new top-level domains corresponding to each of the several dozen international trademark classifications.[32] While the maker of York air conditioners and York Peppermint Patty candies cannot both have *york.com*, in this proposal one might have *york.mach* (for machinery, say) and the other might have *york.food*. Critics of this proposal have pointed out, correctly, that even within a single international trademark classification it is commonplace to find dozens of companies with the same name. They coexist (in the real world) because their lines of business do not in fact overlap even though they happen to be in the same trademark classification. Yet they would lead to collisions even if this proposal were implemented. Critics of this proposal also point out, correctly, that trademark holders tend to want to protect not only their present line of business but also all possible future lines of business. Thus, if the trademark-classification domain names were announced, the Disney company (for example) would presumably instantly sign up for *disney.food* and *disney.mach* simply to protect possible future brand name extensions.

It has also been stated that from its beginnings the domain name system was never intended to be a directory system. This statement is slightly disingenuous, however, since no one has ever expected, for example, that *mit.edu* would map to anything other than MIT, or that *harvard.edu* would map to anything but Harvard University. Likewise it is fair to say that once the *com* domain was defined, nobody would have expected *xerox.com* to map to anything but the Xerox Corporation. Indeed, since the introduction of the domain name system there was a not-very-clearly-articulated hope that domain names would be easily guessed, just as Unix commands are (*mv* means "move," *cp* means "copy," etc.). And until Web search engines became common in about the summer of 1995, there were only four ways to find out somebody's domain name (and, for example, their e-mail address): (1) wander from site to site in Gopherspace hoping to find the answer; (2) use Whois to search for the organization name; (3) guess that the domain name might be the organization name or some variant of it; or (4) call the individual or organization on the telephone and ask.

These four ways of finding a domain name (and/or e-mail address) led to a perception by large corporations that the only acceptable domain name is the corporation name followed by *com*. (Recall the statement by the Unum Corporation to this effect, quoted above.)

Many people have remarked upon the great speed with which the World Wide Web transformed the ways people use the Internet, and probably very few of us imagined, even as recently as five years ago, that a hypertextual environment with free access to a meaningful fraction of the sum of human knowledge would become a fixed part of society in 1996. But even after the force of the Web became clear a couple of years ago, few would have predicted the almost instantaneous development of search engines (e.g., Lycos, Infoseek, Alta Vista) that would offer extraordinary searching power and convenience *for free* to everyone.

The fact is that in 1996 one can find the domain name for any large corporation quite easily even if it happens not to be the corporate name followed by *com*. It is a trivial matter to plug in the company name with any search engine and very quickly to find the company's Web site. One may then make a bookmark in one's Web browser, and thus never need to type in the domain name even once.

It is likely that new metalevels (in addition to the search engine capabilities) will be developed and imposed between the user and the domain name system, making it less and less important for a company to have its exact name as its domain name. Such developments will probably be as difficult to foresee as the search engines were.

Still other commentators have suggested that the way to lessen or eliminate domain name trademark disputes is to add new top-level domains (TLDs) that would compete with com and would be administered by registration authorities other than NSI. Frequently mentioned proposals for new TLDs include *alt*, *biz*, and *corp*. It has been suggested that the availability of such TLDs would relieve pressure on *com* by providing other places where companies could obtain domain names identical to their company names. But there are several reasons to predict that adding such new TLDs will not alleviate this problem.

First, if you have spent years developing a business that relies upon some particular com domain name, it is no comfort whatsoever to be told that if you want to, you can register with some other TLD. To do so would undermine all the accumulated goodwill and render useless the Web browser bookmarks that have assured a future for the business.

Second, there are already over 100 top-level domains (including, for example, over 100 two-letter domains corresponding to countries). Many hundreds of domain name challenges (and many lawsuits) have been brought by trademark holders who could have registered in any of those hundred-odd domain names, but wanted a *com* domain. Nothing else was good enough for them. There is little reason to think that adding more top-level domains will change this perception that *com* is the place to be.

Third, it is not true that the present domain name trademark problems stem from pressure on the *com* domain; it is simply wrong to say that *com* is full or that the present addressing space is not big enough to accommodate all who wish to have distinct domain names. Any proposed additions or changes to TLDs to the right of the "dot" that supposedly would cure some problem, could just as well be added or changed to the left of the "dot." Suppose that United Air Lines wants a domain name, but that *united.com* is taken already. While some proponents of additional TLDs would assert that the best (or only) way to accommodate the airline would be to create a new TLD *air* (to permit the airline to have a domain name *united.air*), the reality is that the tinkering could take place to the left of the dot, yielding perhaps *united-air.com* or *unitedair.com* or *unitedairlines.com*. The address space in *com* will never run out.

This is not to say that it would be a waste of time to set up new TLDs. It would probably be quite desirable to have a number of new, nongeographic TLDs, distinguished not so much by the connotations of the letters making up the domain, but rather by differing policies or levels of service of the registration authorities. One registration authority might distinguish itself by price, charging little in the way of annual fees. Another might distinguish itself by promising not to deactivate a domain name unless ordered to do so by a court. Yet another might promise to have efficient and accurate billing and invoicing.

Perhaps with the passage of years the perception that it is crucially important to have an easily guessed com domain will fade. This may happen because of a more widespread appreciation of search engines, or by shifting fashions in top-level domains, or because of some future metalevel change (e.g., a shift away from character-based input to speech recognition) in the way people interact with the Web and the Internet. But for the near future there are half a million stakeholders, present-day domain name holders who need predictability and stability to be able to justify further investment of money and sweat and human creativity into their Internet-related businesses. The present regime, in which a domain name can be taken away on only 30 days' notice from someone who is not doing anything wrong, has to change. That is one reason why meaningful debate on developing good domain name trademark policies needs to take place. NSI, the holder of a position of public trust regarding nearly all of the domain names on the Internet, cannot be permitted to continue to develop its policies with no meaningful stakeholder involvement.

A second reason why such debate is important is that it can help the hundreds of present domain name registration authorities as they continue to fulfill their duties, and as they consider whether to make any changes to their policies. A third reason is that such debate can help the founders of newly created top-level domains as they draft their policies.

Designing a Good Domain Name Trademark Policy

This chapter now turns to the question of how to design a better domain name trademark policy. It is fashionable nowadays to say that the pace of technological change is so great that the legal system cannot keep up. This view is offered in support of any number of propositions, such as that it should not be copyright infringement to copy what is found on the Internet, that the patent system should not be applied to the works of computer programmers, and that we should simply declare that the world of domain names has no connection to the world of trademarks.[33] Leaving those debates aside, this chapter reflects the author's view that whether we like it or not, the legal system is in fact the mechanism through which disputes in modern society are decided if and when other approaches (asking nicely, negotiation, mediation, NSI challenge proceedings, etc.) do not work. Thus we have little choice but to consider how a particular dispute (or class of disputes) would be decided in a court of law, as we consider how to design a policy. When a policy yields outcomes that differ from what a court would do, the policymaker is certain to be sued. When the policy yields the same outcome, the policymaker is much less likely to be sued.

This simple observation helps to show how wisely RFC 1591 was drafted. Under RFC 1591, a registration authority does not take action, and thus it does not contradict what a court would do. Implicit in RFC 1591 is that the registration authority will obey the order of the court. This means that by definition the registration authority does exactly what a court would do (because it does what the court tells it to do). Under RFC 1591, there is little reason to sue a registration authority (other than for the mere procedural purpose of making sure that it is a party to the case and thus can be relied upon to obey the court order).[34]

In every case to date in which a trademark holder sued a registration authority, the trademark holder did not merely sue the registration authority but also sued the domain name holder. However, it would not be unrealistic to suppose that a trademark holder might sue the registration authority alone, perhaps seeking a court order directing that the domain name be given to the trademark holder. In such a case, how would the registration authority deal with the lawsuit? How could it bring the lawsuit to an end? Where would the money come from to deal with months or years of active litigation? The answer, it turns out, can be found in a corner of the legal system that most lawyers hear about for part of one day in their first year of law school, and promptly forget: the doctrine of interpleader.[35]

The law of interpleader had its origins in banking law. If two parties (would-be heirs of a deceased account holder, for example) both wanted the contents of a bank account, one party might sue the bank to try to get the money. Under the doctrine of interpleader, the bank does not have to expend any money or lawyer time defending the lawsuit. The bank instead simply makes a formal tender of the asset to the court (the asset itself normally does not physically change hands) and advises the court that it will dispose of the asset in accordance with the court's orders. The other party (the one that did not sue the bank) is served with papers inviting it to participate in the interpleader action. The parties present their cases, the court decides who gets the money, and that is the end of the matter.

For the bank, the interpleader procedure cuts its legal costs to a minimum. Upon being sued, the bank presses a button on its word processor and prints out the interpleader papers. From that point onward the bank's lawyers have no duty other than to watch the incoming mail for a court order informing the bank that the case is over and that the money should be paid out in some particular way.

Interpleader works just as well when one of the parties sues not only the bank but also the other party. In that case, too, the bank merely interpleads the asset and waits for the dust to settle and for the court order to arrive.

A domain name registration authority could do the same. If sued, it could simply tender the asset (the domain name) to the court, stating that it will comply with the final order of the court. In this way it could minimize legal expense. A domain name registration authority that behaved in this way consistently for a period of months and years would eventually find that trademark holders would not bother to name it as a defendant since they would trust it to obey the court order anyway.

It is intriguing (but futile) to wonder what would have happened if NSI had responded to the Knowledgenet lawsuit by means of interpleader rather than with the costly jurisdiction and venue battle. NSI's legal fees would presumably have been far smaller, and perhaps it would not have felt the need to enact what was apparently a hastily contrived policy in response to those fees. NSI has not, to this day, used interpleader properly.

Which Court?

The preceding discussion ignores the fact that the Internet has no boundaries, and that the three corners of the triangle of dispute may be in three different countries. It refers to "the court" as if there were only one. But it is necessary to consider what could happen if several countries were involved. Suppose the registration authority is in country A, the domain name holder is in country B, and the trademark holder is in country C.

From the trademark holder's point of view it would, of course, be desirable if the lawsuit were filed in country C, but there are at least two reasons why C is likely to be unsuitable as a forum: it might not have jurisdiction over the domain name holder, and its court's orders might not be enforceable outside of C's territory. Alternatively, the trademark holder could sue the domain name holder in country B, seeking an order directing the domain name holder to transfer the domain name. After all, this is what the trademark holder would have to do in the case of most other types of disputes. Finally, the trademark holder could simply sue the registration authority in country A, and wait for the registration authority to interplead the domain name and serve its interpleader papers upon the domain name holder. The proposed domain name policy would not harm the trademark holder because its only effect would be to add to the number of places where the trademark holder could file its lawsuit (two countries in total), in comparison with the list of places where the trademark holder could sue if the dispute were in some other area (e.g., a fight over a third-level domain name), namely the country where the domain name holder is located.

From the domain name holder's point of view, the proposed policy might seem unfair. After all, the domain name holder would receive interpleader papers inviting it to defend itself in some other country (the country where the registration authority is located). The expense and disruption of traveling to that country to defend itself could be great. This would not be much of a problem in the simple case in which a top-level domain was newly created and the registration authority disclosed the policy from the outset. In such a case the domain name holder would presumably have taken the policy into account when choosing the top-level domain in which to register. If the domain name holder did not like the notion of having to travel to country A to defend itself, or did not trust the courts of country A to decide cases fairly, then the domain name holder would presumably have chosen a different TLD in the first place.

The more complicated case would be one in which a registration authority announced for the first time that it planned to use interpleader, and the domain name holder had not previously been told this. It might be suggested that this would be unfair. One must take into account, however, that if a domain name holder selects a registration authority located in a foreign country, it cannot claim to be surprised if it finds itself having to deal with the courts of that country. Moreover, the law of interpleader is old, and in particular is older than the Internet. No one can claim to be surprised if some well-established legal procedure is followed in a case in which it is applicable.

NSI's recent implementation of its third policy uses a backward variant of interpleader. In each of two recent cases,[36] NSI wrote to a domain name holder stating that its domain name would be deactivate in 30 days, and the domain name holder responded by suing NSI and requesting a court order to prevent the domain name from being deactivated. NSI's response in each case was to file a separate lawsuit initiating an interpleader action against both the domain name holder and the trademark holder. In a case in which the domain name holder was not infringing any trademarks, this would be doubly unfair, since it would force the domain name holder to incur the expense of defending itself in not one but two actions. (In one of the cases the domain name holder is having to defend itself not only in two actions but in two different courts in two different cities.) NSI's use of this backward form of interpleader has failed, however. In the *clue.com* case, the federal court dismissed NSI's interpleader action, likening NSI to "a wrongdoer with respect to the subject matter of the suit," saying that NSI is not "free from blame in causing the controversy," and concluding that NSI was improperly seeking "to escape adjudication of its contractual duties, and possible liability, in the state court action [that had been initially filed by the domain name holder]."[37]

Third-Level Domains Should Be Emphasized

From the beginnings of the domain name system, it was contemplated and desired that third-, fourth-, and higher-level domain names would be commonly used. For example, the Kennedy School of Government at Harvard University uses a third-level domain (*ksgwww.harvard.edu*) rather than a second-level domain (e.g. *www.ksg.edu*) for its Web site. This is a very good thing for the Internet for several reasons. First, it saves some work for the root-level servers because they need only answer lookup requests for *harvard* and not for *ksg*. Instead, servers operated by Harvard answer lookup requests for *ksgwww*. This spreading out of the domain name server workload was intended by the designers of the Internet. Second, it saves work for the administrator of the *edu* domain, because the creation and deletion of third-level domains such as *ksgwww* can be done locally by the administrator of the *harvard.edu* domain. Finally (and most important for Internet policymakers), the use of third- and higher-level domains expands the domain name address space and reduces pressure on the root-level domains.

Some of the most highly visible domain name disputes have involved companies that already have one or more Internet domain names (for example, the company name followed by *com*) but also want to possess domain names based on the names of products made by the company.[38] Hasbro, a maker of children's games, has had the domain name *hasbro.com* since 1994. Hasbro's products include a game called Clue. If Hasbro wanted to set up a Web site for its game Clue, the most Internet-friendly way to do this would be to program its *hasbro.com* domain name servers to create *clue.hasbro.com.*

Instead, Hasbro went to NSI and attempted to register *clue.com*, only to find that a company called Clue Computing in Colorado had beaten it to it. Further investigation apparently yielded no evidence that Clue Computing was infringing any trademark of Hasbro (because Clue Computing and Hasbro were in very different lines of business). If Clue Computing had been infringing, then Hasbro could have used an ordinary lawsuit to attempt to obtain the domain name. Given that an ordinary lawsuit was apparently out of the question, then were it not for NSI's policy, Hasbro would have had no choice but to accept that someone else held *clue.com* and that perhaps *clue.hasbro.com* was the way to set up a domain name for the board game. Stated in different terms, if Hasbro had simply filed a lawsuit to attempt to obtain *clue.com*, Hasbro would have had the case dismissed and might have faced sanctions. There are hundreds of businesses called "Clue" and none of them has legal grounds for taking *clue.com* from another.

NSI's policy, however, provided another avenue for attempting to obtain the domain name. Hasbro simply wrote to NSI stating that it held a trademark registration for "Clue," and NSI sent a 30-day letter to Clue Computing. Clue Computing now faces not only the expense of the lawsuit it brought against NSI to block the deactivation of the domain name, but also the expense of the additional suit that NSI filed against it and against Hasbro. These are expenses that Clue Computing would never have faced if NSI had retained RFC 1591 as its policy.

In its early days of domain name administration, NSI urged domain name holders to try to get by with only one or two domain names each. Now that NSI is collecting annual fees it has stopped making such recommendations. The Internet community and policymakers should find ways to exert pressure or at least moral suasion on those who try to amass second-level domains when their needs could better be served by a single second-level domain and a number of third-level domains. Domain name registration authorities should encourage their customers to consider the use of a third-level domain rather than a second-level domain when possible. Lawyers advising domain name holders and trademark holders should try to help their clients understand the purpose of third-level domains.

This chapter refers repeatedly to conflicts over second-level domains, and recommends among other things that members of the Internet community that already have a second-level domain be urged and/or shamed into using third-level domains (e.g., *clue.hasbro.com*). The terminology is driven by the historical accident that nearly all of the highly publicized conflicts have been in the *com* domain and have involved second-level domains such as *clue.com*. But in many countries, the two-letter top-level domain (e.g., *au* for Australia) is subdivided into content-related second-level domains such as *edu.au* for educational institutions in Australia, *com.au* for commercial entities in Australia, etc. The recommendations of this chapter apply *mutatis mutandis*. For example, if there are conflicts in Australia, they are likely to be over third-level domains (e.g., *clue.com.au*), in which case what should be encouraged is the use of fourth-level domains (e.g., *clue.hasbro.com.au*).

Policies Should Be Diligently Communicated to the Stakeholders

Diligently communicating any and all policy changes to the stakeholders should be a standard practice of the registration authority. While this might seem onerous at first blush, the fact is that the registration authority can use e-mail for this purpose at little or no cost. The registration authority already has contact information for each domain name holder including e-mail addresses. Failure to communicate policy changes leads to profoundly unfair results. For example, the NSI policy enables the trademark holder to surprise the domain name holder. The trademark holder will have been able to take as much time as desired to prepare for the eventualities of a domain name challenge. In contrast, of the many recipients of NSI 30-day letters with whom the author has spoken, almost without exception the domain name holders reported that they only found out about the NSI domain name policy when NSI sent the 30-day letter (which has a copy of the policy attached). Many recipients of 30-day letters are domain name holders that registered their domain names long before July 1995 and thus could not have known about the policy at the time they registered. Had NSI done a trivially simple broadcast e-mailing to all of its domain name holder customers in July 1995, some of them would have filed trademark applications at that time with the USPTO, and might now have trademark registrations and thus be able to defend themselves against 30-day letters.

Policies Should Not Be Changed Retroactively

One of the most controversial aspects of NSI's policy is that it makes a drastic change in the rules and purports to apply the change to domain names that were registered long ago. A domain name holder who registered a com domain in, say, 1994 did so at a time when the only way a domain name could be taken away was by court action, and a court would only take away a domain name if the domain name holder had done something wrong. The domain name holder presumably chose to invest time and money in its business with that in mind. Then came the July 1995 policy, and suddenly a domain name could be deactivated even if the domain name holder was not doing anything wrong.

If a registration authority chooses to change a policy retroactively, extreme care should be taken in the design of the policy to avoid causing harm to those who registered domain names earlier in good faith and are not infringing any trademarks.

The Registration Authority Should Deliberate Openly

Courts conduct their proceedings on an open record for two important reasons. First, it promotes settlement, since parties to a dispute can predict how their case would come out and thus can settle on those terms, thereby saving the social cost of going to court. Second, it permits members of the public to reassure themselves that the court's decisions are fair.

For the same reasons, the registration authority should keep an open record. This permits domain name holders and trademark holders to see that disputes have been decided fairly. It likewise permits domain name holders and trademark holders to reach their own resolutions without having to involve the registration authority or the court, because they can simply predict for themselves what the likely outcome would be, and settle on those terms. Keeping an open record is particularly important if the registration authority has interests that are not fully disclosed and may conflict with the interests of its domain name holders. Indeed, any proposed new registration authority should be strongly encouraged to reveal its other interests.

NSI conducts its decisionmaking (regarding the disposition of individual requests from trademark holders to deactivate domain names) in secret, and its past and present policies contain vague areas (e.g., what counts as "identical" between a trademark and a domain name, and how strongly worded a trademark holder's letter must be to trigger an NSI domain name deactivation proceeding). This leaves the public with no way of knowing whether NSI is fair in its decision-making, and leaves disputants unlikely to be able to settle their differences because each may have a different guess as to how NSI would decide the dispute.

Ideally a registration authority would leave it to the courts to decide disputes about the domain names that it administers, which would leave very little for the registration authority to disclose on its open record, since it would make few, if any, decisions.

Immunities Are Not Needed

It has been suggested from time to time that domain name registration authorities should be granted a legislative immunity from suit for domain name registration authorities. They are special, so the argument goes, because they hold a position of trust with respect to this extraordinarily important part of our modern society, the Internet. This chapter argues otherwise, and for several reasons.

First, there are many ways a domain name registration authority might be sued other than by some trademark holder having a gripe about the actions of a domain name holder (or that merely covets a domain name). A domain name registration authority might be sued by a visitor who slips and falls in the reception area, or by a creditor who claims a bill has gone unpaid. Such lawsuits are a simple fact of doing business with the public. There is no compelling reason why any particular category of lawsuit should be specially blocked by some legislative immunity.

Second, giving a domain name registration authority immunity from suit essentially grants a blank check to the registration authority to engage in arbitrary and capricious conduct without fear of having to answer for its actions. Domain name holders who have viewed NSI's past conduct with alarm are aghast at the prospect of having the court system taken away from them as a way of protecting themselves from NSI.

Third, as described above, the specter of liability arising out of the conduct of a domain name holder, cited by NSI as a justification for its controversial policy, is greatly exaggerated. No domain name registration authority has ever been held liable for the conduct of a domain name holder, nor has any trademark holder ever sued a domain name registration authority for an award of money damages from the registration authority. Trademark suits in analogous situations (for example, suing a publisher for a trademark infringement by an advertiser) have uniformly sought no more relief from the publisher than an injunction against future conduct, not an award of money damages. Indeed awards of money damages in trademark cases are quite rare; in most trademark cases, if any remedy is awarded at all it is merely an injunctive remedy. As discussed above, courts have held that neither the New York Stock Exchange nor NSI itself has a general duty to investigate the possibility of trademark infringement.

Fourth, to the limited extent that a domain name registration authority has any legitimate concern about getting sued by a trademark holder, the registration authority can put a cap on its legal expenses by simply tendering the domain name to the court in an interpleader action. What follows is a period of little or no legal expense for the registration authority.

Conclusion

This chapter suggests that domain name registration authorities should simply adopt a first come, first served policy for registration of domain names. Alternatively the registration authority could impose a simple, objective, first-level screen by asking that the applicant show organizational papers (e.g., articles of incorporation, doing-business-as statement, birth certificate) indicating a putative right to use the proposed domain name, thereafter granting the registration on a first come, first served basis. The policy should further provide that if someone sues the registration authority over a domain name (and if the suit is brought in a competent court in the jurisdiction in which the registration authority is physically located), then the registration authority will simply agree to obey the court's order. Interpleader should be invoked to bring before the court the parties to the dispute. The registration authority should not presume to grant preliminary relief, deciding by itself when to deactivate a domain name; such grants of preliminary relief should come only from competent courts. To the extent that the registration authority does make any substantive decisions about the granting or cutting off of domain names (and this chapter suggests that the registration authority should avoid doing so), the decisions should be duly memorialized on an open record. Policy changes should not, generally speaking, be retroactive in application unless there is no other way to proceed, and then only if due provision is made for the rights and interests of stakeholders. Policy changes should be communicated most diligently to affected domain name holders, by direct e-mail for example.

Notes

1. I thank Bruce Albrecht <bruce@zuhause.mn.org> and Dale Worley <worley@ariadne.com> for pointing out this historic reference.

2. A number of excellent papers set forth basic trademark principles and their connection with the Internet. See, for example, Jonathan Agmon, et al. "What's in a Name?" <http://www.law.georgetown.edu/lc/internic/domain1.html>; and Robert Shaw, "Internet Domain Names: Whose Domain Is This?" <http://www.itu.ch/intreg/dns.html>.

3. *Unum Corp. v. Sanfilippo et al.*, N.D. Cal. 96-civ-1369. The author was counsel for the domain nameholder in that litigation, now concluded on confidential terms.

4. Motion for Preliminary Injunction, *Unum Corp. v. Sanfilippo et al.*, N.D. Cal. 96-civ-1369, <http://www.patents.com/fogbelt/mpi.sht>.

5. The author was counsel for RCS in that litigation, now concluded. RCS got to keep its domain name.

6. The threatened deactivation was pursuant to NSI's trademark domain name policy, discussed at length below. NSI's terminology is that the domain name is "placed on hold" pending the outcome of litigation. The terminology is disingenuous, however, because (1) at the time NSI places a domain name "on hold" there is, by definition, no litigation pending, and (2) in the vast majority of instances in which NSI places a domain name "on hold", no litigation ever follows. Of the 350 or so cases in which NSI has placed domain names "on hold", only about a dozen have seen litigation. The remainder (about 97% of the domain names) remain on hold forever, waiting for the outcome of a litigation that never comes. The author's firm has counseled several dozen domain name holders whose domain names have been placed on hold, who cannot afford to litigate, and who will presumably never again have the use of their domain names.

7. Declaration of Jane Hill, *Roadrunner Computer v. NSI*, E.D. Va. 96-civ-413A, <http://www.patents.com/nsidecl.sht>.

8. As will be discussed below, NSI's policy has failed at this task.

9. <http://www.saic.com/aboutsaic/facts.html>. SAIC has announced that it will purchase Bellcore, the organization that allocates area codes and telephone exchange prefixes in North America. It is interesting to note the parallel with its acquisition in 1995 of NSI, which allocates Internet domain names.

10. Geoffrey Gussis, "Global Top-Level Domain Dispute Resolution Policies" <http://www.digidem.com/legal/domain.html>.

11. *MDT Corp. v. New York Stock Exchange, Inc.*, 858 F.Supp. 1028 (C.D.Cal. 1994).

12. *Panavision Int'l L.P. v. Toeppen*, ___ F.Supp. ____ (96 civ. 3284, C.D. Cal., December 2, 1996). Indeed it is difficult to see how the Court could have ruled otherwise, since any other ruling would have placed upon NSI the burden of searching all the trademark records of every country of the world, each time a new domain name registration application was received. There are some 180 countries with trademark systems, and the majority of them do not provide the information online, so that manual searches would be required. This, together with the sheer volume of applications processed by NSI (several thousand per day) makes it pragmatically impossible to review every application for possible infringement.

13. *Knowledgenet, Inc. v. Boone et al.*, N.D. Ill, 94-civ-7195; docket record at <http://www.patents.com/knowledg/knowledg.sht>; complaint at <ftp://internic.net/netinfo/knowledgenet.lawsuit>.

14. NSI Domain Dispute Resolution Policy Statement, July 23, 1995, <ftp: //rs.internic.net/policy/internic/internic-domain-1.txt>.

15. The policy provided (and its successors, the third and fourth policies provide) the (largely illusory) impression that the deactivation of the domain name at the end of the 30 days is not automatic. The policy stated that the domain name holder could avert loss of the domain name by producing a trademark registration before the 30 days had expired. What the policy ignores is that before bringing an NSI 30-day challenge, the trademark holder will have done a search and will have found no indication of the domain name holder holding a trademark registration. Thus the loss of the domain name at the end of the 30 days is indeed generally a *fait accompli*. Stated differently, if a trademark holder that covets a domain name finds, in a search, that the domain name holder does have a trademark registration, then there is no reason to bother to bring the challenge since the trademark holder will not win. History has borne out the *fait accompli* nature of 30-day challenges—there is no publicly known case in which a domain name holder who received an NSI 30-day letter managed to keep from losing the domain name by proffering a trademark registration.

16. Mark Radcliffe, partner in Gray Cary Ware & Friedenrich, posting to Net-Lawyers discussion group, December 17, 1995.

17. Rule 11 of the Federal Rules of Civil Procedure provides sanctions under certain circumstances if a lawsuit is brought, or some other court paper filed, without reasonable inquiry having been made as to the basis for the lawsuit or paper.

18. The cases are *Roadrunner v. NSI*, E.D. Va. 96-civ-413-A; *DCI v. NSI*, M.D. Tenn. 96-civ-429; *Giacalone v. NSI*, N.D. Cal. 96-civ-20434; *Clue v. NSI*, District Court, Boulder County, Colorado 96-civ-694-5; *DISC v. NSI*, D. Colo. 96-civ-1551; *Regis v. NSI*, N.D. Cal. 96-civ-20551; and *Juno Online v. NSI*, E.D. Va.96-1505-A. As noted above, the author was counsel in the Roadrunner case. Much information about these seven cases is available at <http://www.patents.com/nsi.sht>.

19. *juno.com*. Astonishingly, if it had not been for the domain name holder bringing suit, NSI's stubborn adherence to its policy would have resulted in the cutting off of over half a million e-mail addresses, namely the e-mail addresses of all of the customers of *juno.com*.

20. *clue.com*.

21. *Clue Computing v. NSI*, District Court, Boulder County, Colorado, Case No. 96 CV 694, Division 5, <http://www.clue.com/legal/index.html>.

22. <ftp://rs.internic.net/policy/internic/internic-domain-1.txt>.

23. <ftp://rs.internic.net/policy/internic/internic-domain-4.txt>.

24. There is one other fact pattern which can be imagined, namely the case in which a domain name holder that happens to already have a trademark registration finds itself the recipient of a 30-day letter. As mentioned earlier, in real life this would not happen, because the would-be challenger would do a trademark search first to see if the domain name holder had a trademark

registration, and would not bother to initiate the challenge if a trademark registration held by the domain name holder were found in the search.

25. <ftp://rs.internic.net/policy/internic/internic-domain-6.txt>.

26. Otherwise one must be concerned as to whether the registration authority will comply with orders of the court.

27. It might be thought that the trademark holder could dispense with naming NSI as a party because NSI's present policy says it will obey court orders. But NSI could change its policy in this regard at any time; recall that NSI is now on its fourth policy in 13 months and has repeatedly said that it is entitled to change its policy at will on a mere 30 days' notice. It is a very trusting litigator indeed who would choose *not* to name NSI as a party when suing a domain name holder, given NSI's unpredictable behavior.

28. The cases are *Porsche Cars North America, et al. v. Chen, et al.*, E.D. Va. 96-civ-1006 (*porsche.com*); *American Commercial, et al. v. Sports & Leisure, et al.*, C.D. Cal. 96-civ-713 (*mikasa.com*); *Panavision International. v. Toeppen, et al.*, C.D. Cal. 96-civ-3284 (*panavision.com*); and *Prestone Prods v. Maynerd Collision, et al.*, E.D. Va. 96-civ-234 (*prestone.com*). Much information about these six cases is available at <http://www.patents.com/nsi.sht>.

29. Federal Trademark Dilution Act of 1995, 15 USC § 1125(c).

30. Congressional Record, December 29, 1995, S19312.

31. <ftp://rs.internic.net/policy/internic/internic-domain-6.txt>, para. 5(b).

32. David Collier-Brown, "On Experimental Top Level Domains," <http://java.science.yorku.ca/~davecb/tld/experiment.html>.

33. See, for example, Mike Doughney, posting to domain-policy@internic.net, message ID <199612130312.WAA10610@sadie.digex.net>, December 12, 1996.

34. NSI has justified its domain name trademark policy on the grounds that it is supposedly stuck between the widely divergent demands of trademark holders on the one side, and domain name owners on the other side. NSI says that its policy is an attempt to balance these allegedly polarized views, and that NSI should thus be forgiven for adopting a policy which neither camp finds acceptable. It is therefore extraordinarily significant that the Internet Subcommittee of the International Trademark Association (INTA) has released a policy recommendation for domain name trademark disputes that turns out to be in substantial agreement with the policy recommendations of parties that are supposedly at the opposite end of the spectrum (e.g., the recommendations of this chapter). Proposed Domain Name Registry Policy, <http://plaza.interport.net/inta/intaprop.htm>. The policy recommendations of the Internet Ad Hoc Committee are likewise in substantial agreement with those of the INTA subcommittee and with those of this Chapter. Draft Specifications for Administration and Management of gTLDs, <http://www.iahc.org/draft-iahc-gTLDspec-00.html>.

35. In the United States there are two sources of federal interpleader—so-called "Federal Rules" interpleader (Rule 22 of the Federal Rules of Civil Procedure)

and statutory interpleader (28 USC § 2361). In addition, most U.S. states have interpleader laws, and many other countries have similar laws.

36. *clue.com* and *disc.com.*

37. *Network Solutions, Inc., v. Clue Computing, Inc., and Hasbro, Inc.,* 1996 U.S. Dist. LEXIS 18013 (96-D-1530, October 29, 1996).

38. Another example of the pursuit of second-level domains when third-level domains use Internet resources more efficiently is a well-known automobile maker that is trying to take away from others the second-level domain names corresponding to its car models.

Network Solutions and Domain Name Disputes: A Reply to Carl Oppedahl

Philip L. Sbarbaro

Picture yourself in a wide, fast-running cold water creek between two mountainsides, one populated by the Hatfields and the other by the McCoys. As you stand knee-deep in that freezing current, which seems to be rising rapidly, look up to one side at the McCoys, rifles loaded, cocked, and aimed. Directly across the creek stand the Hatfields, equally prepared. Some of those rifles, more than you can count, are aimed directly at you. Call yourself "the registry."

Network Solutions, Inc., the worldwide registry for the .com Top Level Domain on the Internet, finds itself caught between nearly 12 million trademark owners on one side and 900,000 domain name holders[1] (increasing at a rate of approximately 80,000 holders per month) on the other side.

The Trademark Owners' Position

According to the trademark owners, "the real McCoys," who have spent many generations and many millions, if not billions, of dollars, lire, kroner, pounds, marks, etc., instilling their good names with meaning and identification, there is no new issue presented by the phenomenon known as the Internet. It is simply just one more medium, just one more marketplace, where all normal legal constraints and precedents apply. There is nothing "special" about a domain name. Take someone's trademark as a domain name at your peril; ignorance is no excuse. Correctly or incorrectly, trademark owners assume that a domain name is synonymous with a trademark. Once that assumption is made, causes of action against domain name holders are limited only by the creativity of the trademark owners' marksmen. Infringement, dilution, unfair competition, and that perpetual favorite, "interference with prospective economic advantage," in all of the various federal and state varieties, tend to be most popular and effective.

On occasion, trademark owners sue domain name holders who also have nearly identical trademarks.[2] The causes of action tend to be the same as described above, with the addition of claims for breach of contract. In some cases, the two trademark owners have met before and have some sort of bilateral agreement which predates the Internet conflict, and it is this agreement that is alleged to have been breached.

The Domain Name Holders' Position

According to the domain name holders, who are very intelligent, aggressive, vocal, and, perhaps most important, Internet-literate, first come, first served has always been the rule on the Internet. Someone has applied for and obtained a domain name, has been using it unaccosted and without interruption for months or years, either in business or simply as a communications device, is confronted and affronted by some "wealthy trademark owner" who, only now, sees the benefit of a new technology which will forever change the way the world communicates.

When attacked or even threatened by a trademark owner, domain name holders respond in kind by suing for declaratory judgment, alleging, inter alia, an actual and justiciable controversy, "senior rights" and prior use on the Internet, no violation of law concerning infringement or dilution, and the right to continued use.

It has been estimated that as many as 50 trademark owner-domain name holder cases are now before the courts. Like any other lawsuits, some move quickly, while some move more slowly and become quite expensive. Eventually, they all end and the losers are told by the court, through an injunctive decree, what to do. These cases do not involve the registry; the registry is not named as a party. When Network Solutions receives a file-stamped copy of the injunction, it dutifully assists either the loser or the prevailing party in complying with the court's order.

Eventually, precedent will be set that a trademark either is or is not the same as a domain name; that use of another's trademark as a domain name on the Internet either is or is not trademark infringement and/or dilution; that a domain name holder either can or cannot register a domain name for the purpose of selling it;[3] that a domain name either is or is not bound by technical classifications or geographic boundaries; and will determine all of the other various intellectual property rights and jurisdictional issues. At the moment, however, few legal precedents exist for these issues. There is nothing but the sound of gunfire across the creek.

The Internet Registry

Faced with overwhelming odds from both sides, Network Solutions, or any registry for that matter, stands squarely in the middle of that creek. Without legal precedent, and without immunity from suit for alleged intellectual property right violations, Network Solutions must fend for itself.

On the one side, as of January 16, 1997, 11 trademark holders (out of approximately 12 million) have included Network Solutions, as registrar, in their suits against domain name holders. Causes of action, even more imaginative than the allegations against the domain name holders themselves, include contributory infringement or dilution, unfair competition, breach of contract based upon a theory of third-party beneficiary, and negligent interference with prospective business relations.[4] Some have sought damages, compensatory and punitive; some have sought injunctive relief. None have succeeded.

On the other side, as of the same day, seven (out of approximately 900,000) domain name holders have sued Network Solutions when faced with the possibility that the use of their domain name would be suspended, pending resolution of their dispute with an owner of a federally registered trademark. These domain name holders have believed it necessary or appropriate to sue the registry along with the trademark owner, or sometimes to sue the registry alone. Causes of action have included breach of contract based upon third-party beneficiary, detrimental reliance, and interference with contractual relations. Some have sought damages, compensatory and punitive; some have sought injunctive relief. Only one has been partially successful.[5]

Network Solutions assigns second-level domain names, in the Top Level Domain .com, on a first come, first served basis. This process is totally automated with an electronic application form which simply calls for the requested domain name and, if it is available, permits its assignment in a matter of hours, sometimes minutes. No human intervention is involved. No trademark analysis is performed. In contrast to the pendency of an application for a trademark (16.7 months, according to U.S. Patent and Trademark Office statistics),[6] a domain name is assigned within anywhere from five minutes to three or four days. Network Solutions' process is not unlike that of the New York Stock Exchange (NYSE), in its assignment of trading symbols. The Federal District Court in Los Angeles held that the NYSE registration process does not constitute "contributory infringement" of anyone's trademark.[7] The court additionally held that the NYSE had no duty to police the mark for a trademark owner. "The owner of a trade name must do its own police work."[8]

On December 2, 1996, the Federal Court in Los Angeles[9] held that Network Solutions "is under no general duty to investigate" whether a given domain name registration is improper, citing the *MDT Corp. v. New York Stock Exchange, Inc.* decision.

All told, 18 suits out of 900,000 registrations (or two-thousandths of one percent) have included the registry as a defendant. Eight of the 18 suits have been dismissed (46 days on average) and one has been stayed. Some commentators would say that the system seems to be working; others would say that the chaos is clear. It depends upon one's frame of reference. It should be apparent from these actual statistics, however, that only the fringe element or the uninformed believe it in their interest to sue the Internet registry. Such a tactic makes an adversary of the registry, which is simply a stakeholder in the dispute, with no financial or other interest in the assignment of the particular domain name in dispute; increases litigation costs; and generally deflects attention from the true controversy between the two claimants. However, until precedent exists to dissuade such plaintiffs, or registries receive immunity from suits for contributory infringement or dilution for performing their registration function, there will be advocates who will continue to chase this ambulance.

The Dispute Policy

Without precedent or immunity to protect the registry from attack by potentially 12 million trademark owners, and to give domain name holders a certain amount of time to determine their own future, among other reasons, Network Solutions implemented a Dispute Policy with the oversight and concurrence of the National Science Foundation. The Dispute Policy does not resolve any dispute; it was not intended to resolve disputes. It was and is intended to benefit Network Solutions and to present a domain name holder with five possible responses to an attack by an owner of a federally registered trademark. Only in certain circumstances will the registry use its limited discretion to place the domain name on "hold."[10] As of this writing, approximately 580 domain names out of 900,000 (or six-thousandths of one percent) have been placed on hold pending resolution, either way, of the dispute. When placed on hold, the domain name registrant is *not* changed and the domain name is *not* "deleted," as has been suggested by some authors. The domain name is simply placed in suspension so that neither claimant can use it. This is the provision to which domain name holders have objected. Some domain name holders believe that it is the registry's duty to permit the domain name to continue unobstructed and to thus incur liability as a contributory infringer or diluter. The registry, on its own behalf and that of the National Science Foundation, the Internet Assigned Numbers Authority, the Internet Activities Board, the Internet Society, and all of their directors, officers, employees, and agents, has declined to incur such potential liability.

Section 7 of the Dispute Policy makes three points abundantly clear: (1) that the registry, although not named in a particular case, will immediately abide by any court order which is issued in the case; (2) that the registry will deposit the domain name, through notarized declaration, with the registry of the court which will then have complete dominion and control over it; and (3) that, regardless of which party first sues the other claimant, *before* the registry places the name on hold, the registry will maintain the status quo and not touch the domain name.

Conclusion

Someday there may be no need for a domain name Dispute Policy. Sufficient legal precedent or legislative immunity will have been set in place to eliminate the necessity. At present, however, nothing other than the Dispute Policy protects the Internet registry and its governing organizations from the power, as yet unused, of the trademark owners of the world.

Pike County, Kentucky, is quiet these days. Perhaps the Hatfields and the McCoys grew tired of the feud after 25 years, or are so intermarried that you can no longer tell one from the other. Time has a way of resolving things. Participants in the present feud can choose to attack each other and the registry. They can choose to communicate and to govern themselves. They should choose wisely, before the governments of the world choose for them.

This chapter is a general response to the factual and legal positions presented in the chapter in this volume by Carl Oppedahl. Mr. Oppedahl was opposing counsel against Network Solutions in *Roadrunner Computer Systems, Inc. v. Network Solutions, Inc.*, Civil Action No. 96-413-A (U.S.D.C. E.D. Va.), filed on March 26, 1996, and dismissed by the Federal Court on June 21, 1996, on a motion for summary judgment brought by Network Solutions.

Notes

1. A domain name is assigned to an applicant who then becomes a "registrant." "Holder" rather than "owner" more clearly describes the relationship between a registrant and the assigned domain name. Telephone numbers are also assigned to holders rather than owned.

2. *American Commercial Inc. d/b/a Mikasa and Mikasa Licensing, Inc. v. Sports and Leisure International d/b/a Mikasa Sports*, Civil Action No. 96-713LHM (U.S.D.C. C.D. Cal.); *Mattel, Inc. et al v. Hasbro, Inc. et al.*, Civil Action No. 96-7635, (U.S.D.C. C.D. Cal.).

3. A November 1, 1996, scholarly opinion by the federal court in Los Angeles in

Panavision International, L.P. v. Dennis Toeppen, et al., Civil Action No. 96-3284 DDP (U.S.D.C. C.D. Cal.) may end "piracy" of famous trademarks.

4. A December 2, 1996, opinion by the federal court in Los Angeles in *Panavision International, L.P. v. Dennis Toeppen, et al.*, Civil Action No. 96-3284 DDP (U.S.D.C. C.D. Cal.) granted Network Solutions' motion against the trademark holder's sole cause of action against Network Solutions for "negligent interference with prospective economic advantage."

5. One preliminary injunction was issued in state court proceedings in Boulder, Colorado, without presentation of documentary evidence or any witnesses. The court then immediately stayed the proceedings pending the result of parallel interpleader proceedings in federal court.

6. According to the 1995 Annual Report of the U.S. Commissioner of Patents and Trademarks, 75,375 United States trademark registrations were issued in fiscal year 1995 (averaging 6,281 registrations per month), and the pendency of a trademark application for the same period was 16.7 months from filing to registration.

7. *MDT Corp. v. New York Stock Exchange, Inc.*, 858 F. Supp. 1028 (C.D. Cal. 1994).

8. *Id.* at 1034.

9. *Panavision International, L.P. v. Dennis Toeppen, et al.*, Civil Action No. 96-3284 DDP (U.S.D.C. C.D. Cal.).

10. The British registry has substantially more discretion. Under the rules for Nominet UK, dated July 25, 1996, the British registry can "withdraw or suspend delegation of a name" under five broadly defined situations:

• if the name is administered in a way likely to endanger operation of the DNS

• if the basis on which the name was registered has changed (e.g. the organisation making the application no longer exists). This does not include a change in UKNIC rules for names subsequent to the name being delegated, but does include the case where the automaton failed to correctly apply the existing rules

• if it is drawn to Nominet UK's attention that the name is being used in a manner likely to cause confusion to internet users

• where Nominet UK has been informed that legal action has been commenced regarding use of the name

• where Nominet UK is of the opinion that one of the above events is likely to occur.

Registering the Domain Name System: An Exercise in Global Decision-Making

William A. Foster

Internet domain names have become valuable properties. During the past two years, conflict has grown over the rights to these names and over who has the rights to create them. There is the potential that these conflicts could destabilize the domain name system itself. Efforts to bring the domain name system into alignment with trademark law are complicated by the fact that trademark law is generally national while domain names are inherently global.

One approach to these challenging issues would be to register the domain name system with the appropriate organs of the United Nations. This would build legitimacy for the Internet's naming and registration conventions under the trademark laws of each country and would give the world's governments an "appropriate" role in decision-making regarding the Internet infrastructure. Organizations with a vital stake in the Internet should invest the time and energy to insure that the world's governments acknowledge the domain name system.

The domain name system includes not only the actual Internet domain names, but the administrative and technical infrastructure that makes them possible. The domain name registries impose order on the name application process by preventing duplicate name assignments and by fitting them into a distributed hierarchy. These registries also provide a server from which remote programs may inquire and retrieve authoritative pointers to the domain name servers which contain details about a domain. The Domain Name Service (DNS) is the server program that provides this function and allows the servers to coordinate with each other and with the root servers to provide a comprehensive view of the entire Internet. Though this chapter is primarily concerned with the administrative aspects of the domain name system, it is important to keep both the administrative and technical infrastructure in mind when referring to the domain name system.

National Trademarks—Global Domains

The Internet domain name system was set up to create a more "human-friendly" means of accessing Internet hosts than just using a long string of numbers. It also has created a plenitude of marks that are being treated as trademarks or service marks in various countries. There has been a growing number of court cases in the United States over the rights of the holder of a trademark to a domain name that has been registered to someone else. Agmon, Halpern, and Pauker at their Web site "What's in a Name?" provide an excellent overview of recent disputes over the rights to various domain names.[1] Many of these disputes have involved Network Solutions, Inc. (NSI), which is responsible for registering domains under the *.com* Top Level Domain (TLD). NSI has gone through four iterations of a domain dispute policy and has enraged many in the Internet community in the process. At the same time, the U.S. Patent and Trademark Office is developing its rules on registering domain names as trademarks.[2] But, as David Maher of the International Trademark Association points out, the real dilemma is that trademarks are governed by national rules but domain names can—by virtue of the Internet—immediately appear in almost every other country.[3] There is nothing to prevent a second country from judging that a domain name violates the rights of a trademark holder. This has already occurred in Germany, where an American company was sued for using a domain name on the World Wide Web that was registered in the United States but infringed on a trademark claimed by a German company.

Though domain names appear globally, there are no global trademarks. Currently, trademarks need to be registered in each and every country where they are used. The only way to register a mark globally is to register it in every country. The World Intellectual Property Organization (WIPO) does have a process for facilitating multiple registrations, but only for states that have signed the

Madrid Agreement Concerning the International Registration of Marks. The Madrid agreement is limited to 46 states and does not include the United States or Japan.[4] Signatory countries have the right to reject a filing under the Madrid agreement and disputes are settled at the national level.

Though there are no global trademarks, the Internet community does have international Top Level Domains (iTLDs). For the most part, these iTLDs, such as *.com* and *.net*, are currently controlled by the Internic, the registry run by NSI. The rest of the registries are either country or region specific and issue TLDs that are based on International Standards Organization (ISO) 3166 two-letter country codes (i.e., *.fr* for France). Organizations that register a domain name with a national registry will have the country code appended to the right of their second-level domain. However, for historical reasons, the *.us* TLD is rarely used and most U.S. businesses and organizations register under the *.com* or *.org* iTLDs. Businesses outside the United States have been allowed to register under the *.com* TLD regardless of where their host is situated. Thus *.com* is considered an international TLD. The *.com* iTLD has developed a snob appeal that has attracted many non-U.S. companies to register under it, but non-U.S.-based companies have also registered out of fear that someone else might register a domain in the *.com* TLD and dilute the value of their trademark within their own country.

With the incredible explosion of interest in the Internet on the part of the business community, many businesses are finding that when they try to register a second-level domain that the name that they would prefer, a name based on their own trademark, is already taken. U.S. law allows many companies to use the same word in their trademarks (e.g., Acme toys, Acme books, Acme cookies). But because of the way the Internet is currently configured, there can only one *Acme.com*.

There has been considerable discussion in the Internet community on how to restructure the domain name system to meet the needs of the commercial business community and the realities of trademark law. The Kennedy School of Government along with the National Science Foundation hosted a symposium on November 29, 1995, at which leaders from different sectors of the Internet community exchanged ideas on a number of proposals.

One proposal from the Internet Assigned Number Authority (IANA) and the Internet Society (ISOC) called for the creation of new iTLD registries that would compete against each other and would provide businesses with multiple opportunities to use the same second-layer domain (e.g., *Acme.com, Acme.bus, Acme.ind*). These registries would be chartered by IANA and ISOC.

Tony Rutkowski, former director of the Internet Society, presented a paper noting that the TLD debate touches on a range of international and domestic legal issues. Any TLD solution, he argued, needs to recognize the legal ramifications and include the major stakeholders in the decision-making process. Rutkowski has developed a list of the "parties of interest" in Internet public policy matters which includes both international business associations and international governmental bodies such as the International Telecommunications Union (ITU), the World Trade Organization (WTO), the World Intellectual Property Organization, and the United Nations Educational, Scientific, and Cultural Organization (UNESCO).[5] He sees the need for a new body to oversee the administrative functions of the Internet that would incorporate the key stakeholders and effectively tap their expertise.

While many have debated the question, Eugene Kashpureff has set up a registry called Alternic to issue TLDs for a fee. The TLDs that Alternic registers are not in the Internet root servers, so most users cannot access hosts that have them as TLDs. However, Alternic does offer an alternate root server for those who will point to it which will give users access to the Alternic-registered TLDs along with the IANA-approved TLDs. At the Internet Engineering Task Force (IETF) meeting in Montreal in June 1996, Kashpureff questioned the right of IANA to stifle competition and even threatened to go to court to gain access to the root servers.

Internet Decision-Making?

We reject Kings, Presidents, and Voting:
We believe in rough consensus and working code.
—David Clark, IETF (1992)

Robert Shaw's "Internet Domain Names: Whose Domain Is This?" gives an excellent overview of the organizations that are involved with Top Level Domains.[6] David Maher in "Trademarks on the Internet: Who's in Charge?" reviews the key proposals for overhauling the system.[7] However, neither Shaw nor Maher fully resolves the questions their titles pose.

Internet Assigned Number Authority

The Internet Assigned Number Authority has historically played the key role in coordinating the domain name system. The IANA states on its home page that it is "chartered by the Internet Society (ISOC) and the Federal Networking Council (FNC)[8] to act as a clearinghouse to assign and coordinate the use of numerous Internet protocols."[9] IANA is not legally incorporated. It is run by John Postel of the Information Sciences Institute (ISI) at the University of Southern California (USC). According to Postel, he is the voice for a "low level of effort" task that is staffed by himself, Joyce Reynolds, Nehel Bhau, and Bill Manning.[10] ISI receives its funding from the U.S. Department of Defense's Advanced Research Projects Agency (ARPA). Though it is not clear how much the U.S. government is involved in, there is some speculation that, in the event that it is ever sued in court, IANA might claim that it is a U.S. government activity to remove the case from the court's jurisdiction.

IANA's authority does not stem from its relationship with the U.S. government but from its historical relationship with the Internet Engineering Task Force and its steering group (the IESG). The Internet protocols that are defined by the IETF contain numerous parameters (Internet addresses, domain names, Management Information Base [MIB] identifiers, etc.) that must be uniquely assigned. John Postel has a long history of making technically sound decisions that have worked for the IETF, Internet Service Providers (ISPs), and users of the Internet. It is this history that has given IANA its authority.

Postel and IANA have not demonstrated parallel skills when forced into the public policy arena. Much to his dismay, Postel has watched as the domain name system has become wrapped up with trademark law. Postel's August 1996 "Memo on New Registries and the Delegation of International Top Level Domains" recognizes "trademarks are a complicated problem in their own right."[11] He hopes that there are aspects of his plan that "may ease the problems involved with the interaction of trademarks and domain names by giving more access to domain names for holders of the same trademark in different business areas."

It is very disconcerting that Postel never acknowledges in his memo the reality that, though domain names are used globally, trademark law is national. In his side remarks on "Trademarks and Domain Names," he states that we will have to wait until a "high-level court" makes a decision as to whether domain names are trademarks. In fact, courts all over the world are going to have to make this determination along with their governments and international organizations.

To his credit, Postel requires in section 6.1.1 that new iTLDs must not be trademarks. It is the responsibility of the new registries to research their proposed iTLDs to insure that they have not been trademarked. He states that new iTLDs may be required to not be on the international list of national trademarks maintained by WIPO. In the memo, he is unclear as to whether WIPO's trademark list is readily available and does not seem to be cognizant of the limitations of this list, such as the fact that it does not include trademarks of the United States, Japan, and other nonsignatories.

The Postel memo calls for IANA, ISOC, and the IETF to create a joint committee to oversee the selection of new iTLDs and registries. The contracts used to create new registries will include a "statement indemnifying the IANA and the ISOC for any infringement of trademark which may be created in this process." Processes for arbitrating conflicts are mentioned along with an appeals process that escalates from IANA, to IETF, and finally to ISOC. It seems that IANA and IETF have no intention, however, of becoming involved in trademark disputes though they do allocate legal funds in case they are dragged in to such disputes.

Internet Society and Internet Engineering Task Force

The Internet Society board of trustees voted during its June 1996 meeting to support the Postel TLD proposal. ISOC's mission is to further the Internet, which it tries to do by providing a legal and financial umbrella for the Internet Engineering Task Force, the Internet Engineering Steering Group (IESG), the Internet Architecture Board (IAB), and IANA. In his memo, Postel acknowledges that ISOC provides IANA with an international legal and financial umbrella. Given the importance of the domain name system to the Internet community and to the businesses that are investing in it, the ability of the umbrella to withstand potential conflicts over the legitimacy of the domain name system must be examined. ISOC's strength comes from its dues-paying members, but also—and more important—from the success and vibrancy of the IETF which it serves. The IETF sets standards for the Internet but has shied away, for good reason, from trying to govern the operational infrastructure of the Internet or to work directly with government to address public policy concerns surrounding the Internet.

ISP Organizations

Internet Service Providers that operate much of the infrastructure have created trade associations such as the Commercial Internet Exchange (CIX)[12] to organize and influence the public policy debate on such key issues as ISP liability for indecent content and copyright violations. Over the past two years, CIX has repeatedly demonstrated an ability to track issues, articulate issues to policymakers, and influence the course of legislation. Though CIX focused primarily on U.S. issues during 1995, in 1996 it began to actively work with a wide range of global and regional bodies that impact ISPs such as the ITU, WIPO, the European Commission, the OECD, and others. CIX has also been active in the debate over the domain name system and jointly hosted with ISOC the well-attended February 1996 conference on the "Internet Administrative Infrastructure—What Is It? Who Should Do It? How Should It Be Paid For?"

In addition to CIX there are a number of national and regional associations of Internet Service Providers. Some of these associations have developed to meet national and regional infrastructure needs for exchange points and registries, but some have also been active in the public policy concerns of their members.

There is also a wide assortment of associations that have sprung up to represent various interest groups and around specific technologies. The nature of the Internet dramatically lowers the costs of putting together an organization, especially at a national or global level. The ability of these Internet organizations to build consensus and make decisions varies widely, as does their ability to work constructively with other organizations and government. There is certainly no hierarchy into which all these groups fall, nor is there one organization that represents the interests and the expertise of all stakeholders in the Internet. This is not to say that the Internet community cannot focus on common goals such as the creation of an environment where the global domain name system can coexist with various national trademark laws. In working toward this goal there are many potential allies among business associations and businesses themselves which are concerned about the stability of the Internet and their own domain names.

United Nations?

The United Nations and its specialized bodies have a critical role to play in registering the Internet domain name system. Registering the domain name system would help to establish its legitimacy as a global system, even in the absence of global trademark law. Most countries have decided to participate or at least to allow their citizens to participate in the Internet. Though many nations are wrestling with how to set up barriers to illicit content, few have developed policies to deal with foreign domain names that might infringe on local trademarks.

In "Law and Borders," Johnson and Post argue that cyberspace needs and can create new laws and legal institutions of its own.[13] However, they neglect to discuss how to persuade national governments to accept limitations on their own jurisdiction. The Internet community ought to actively engage representatives of the world's governments in dialogue over the domain name system with the goal of registering the system. The goal should not be to make the domain name system a government-mandated convention for all electronic communication or even for the Internet itself. Rather, stakeholders in the Internet should work with those responsible for maintaining trademark law to insure that the domain name system can coexist with the various national trademark laws.

Part of the dialogue that needs to occur is over how to protect the rights of both domain name holders and trademark holders in this global environment. Postel's new memo seems to suggest that the venue for protecting a trademark is the country in which the iTLD registry is located even if the trademark infringement occurs in another country. Hopefully, IANA will not charter any registries that are not dutifully registered in a particular country or in countries which do not respect the rights of foreign trademark holders. Unfortunately, there is little evidence to suggest that IANA significantly engaged world governments in a discussion as to whether this would be an acceptable solution.

International Telecommunication Union

Such dialogue needs to occur and it would occur much more effectively if the Internet community focused on the goal of United Nations registration. There are a number of UN bodies that ought to be engaged. The International Telecommunication Union (ITU) and particularly its Telecommunications Standardization Sector (the ITU-T) have as their mission the coordination and facilitation of telecommunications between countries. The ITU-T has been active in setting many telecommunications standards, including the Open System Interconnection (OSI) standards such as X.400 and X.500 that attempt to provide some of the same services as the Internet domain name system. There are some in the IETF who are contemptuous of the ITU-T and its standards processes. There are major differences in how the two organizations set standards. The ITU-T votes on standards, while the IETF relies on rough consensus. The IETF requires at least two separate implementations before a draft can become a standard, whereas the ITU-T can draft a standard without an implementation. The IETF is open to all based on their ability to participate, while the ITU-T is controlled by representatives from the government ministries that control telecommunications with input from large telecommunications carriers and manufacturers.

Despite the differences in organizational cultures, at this point in time the Internet community needs to learn how to work through the ITU to build support for the Internet in general and the domain name system in particular. By attempting to register the domain name system with the appropriate UN bodies, the Internet community would introduce a feedback loop that would be very educational for IANA, ISOC, the IETF, and other members of the Internet community. The experience might even result in IANA growing into, or being supplemented by, the kind of body that Tony Rutkowski envisions in which the key stakeholders in the Internet make the decisions regarding its administration.[14]

If the ITU-T registered the key Requests for Comments (RFCs) associated with the domain name system and how it is administered, the world's governments would take a step toward acknowledging the system's legitimacy. The ITU cannot force any country to do something it does not want to do. However, through its decision-making processes the ITU can create powerful forces for consensus.

The process of registering with the ITU could also be very helpful to the Internet community. Though there are certain Request for Comments such as RFC 1591 that describe domain name system structure and delegation, Postel's memo and the Internet draft that preceded it have not gone through the IETF's RFC processes. IANA needs to update RFC 1591 if it is in fact going to proceed with creating new iTLD registries. The Internet community needs a current set of RFCs dealing with the domain name system for which it can build international support.

Parts of the Internet community are wary of giving the ITU a role in the Internet administrative infrastructure. There are people who fiercely guard the IETF's decision-making processes. In addition, given the potential for competition between ISPs and telephone companies, ISPs may be concerned about the amount of power that national telephone monopolies have in the ITU. Instead of seeing the ITU as a threat, the IETF and the ISPs should recognize the value of utilizing the ITU to build relationships with the world's governments. The ITU can serve as an excellent resource for gathering information and driving debate. The ITU should not define Internet protocols or administrative procedures;

rather it should be challenged to explicate what it would take for a global system, in particular the Internet, to coexist with the world's governments.

The ITU now accepts International Standards Organization standards through a cooperative agreement. It is possible that such an agreement could be arranged with ISOC and the IETF. ISOC and the ITU have become members of each other's organizations. Nevertheless, the mistrust in parts of the Internet community of the ITU in particular and government in general may limit ISOC's ability to build this relationship.

World Intellectual Property Organization

The Internet community should also consider working through other United Nations organizations, such as the World Intellectual Property Organization. WIPO's objective is to promote the protection of intellectual property throughout the world through cooperation among states and, where appropriate, in collaboration with other international organizations. Though there might be a question as to whether IANA is an international organization, there is a potential role for WIPO in harmonizing the domain name system with trademark law.

The WIPO Convention does give the WIPO director general the power to be involved in, subject to the General Assembly's consent, agreements to promote the protection of intellectual property.

Agmon, Halpern, and Pauker suggest that a potential solution to the trademark/domain crisis would be for WIPO to facilitate an international domain name treaty.[15] There is a concern that treaties often take five or more years to write and ratify and no one has any idea where the Internet and its naming conventions will be five years from now. Working through WIPO to register the domain name system is a more realistic short-term goal. WIPO could be very helpful in developing a set of procedures for registries that would minimize the chance that their TLDs or the domains created under them would be contested. WIPO could also be very helpful in setting in place adjudication mechanisms for businesses that countries would not contest and that would minimize litigation. The business community would like the assurance that if a company registers a domain name in a registry in one country, it will not be sued for having that domain name appear in another country. Finally and most important, working through WIPO could help to diffuse tensions that might threaten the stability of the domain name system itself.

The Internet community ought to explore with WIPO ways of protecting the rights of domain name and trademark holders in iTLDs on a multilateral basis. For many of the same reasons mentioned with respect to the ITU, it would be a worthwhile exercise to register the domain name system with this different UN specialized agency that has expertise and authority that are relevant to the trademark/domain name dilemma. It is not a matter of choosing WIPO over the ITU or vice versa; they have different expertise and represent different interests (trademark offices vs. telecommunications ministries). It is recommended that the Internet community both engage in a dialogue with and work for registration in both bodies.

The International Ad Hoc Committee

At the September 1996 Harvard Conference on "Coordination and Administration of the Internet," Don Heath, president of ISOC, presented John Postel's proposal for creating new registries and iTLDs.[16] Heath made a major change to Postel's proposal by suggesting that one representative each from the ITU, WIPO, and the International Trademark Association (INTA) should join the International Ad Hoc Committee (IAHC) that would set the rules and select the new registries and iTLDs. Under Postel's proposal the Internet Society, IANA, and the IETF would each choose two members of the committee. Heath's revision includes these six committee members and adds three more from the international organizations.

By including the ITU, WIPO, and INTA on the committee, Don Heath has internationalized the iTLD decision-making process. It is not totally clear whether each of these institutions will agree to serve on the IAHC. More important, just because a representative of the institution is on the IAHC, it is does not mean that the institution and the member-states it serves necessarily accept the decisions of the IAHC. Building an international consensus might involve not only working with a representative of the ITU and a representative of WIPO, but might also require working through the institutions themselves. The Internet Society under Don Heath's leadership is proposing to take an important first step.

Conclusion

A general "Law of Cyberspace Treaty" or a more specific convention dealing with domain names may eventually come into reality. However, currently the technology and the business are outstripping the ability of stakeholders to organize and make sound decisions. The Internet community should focus on having the world's governments formally recognize the domain name system. Governments and businesses need to be convinced that domain name disputes can be arbitrated or adjudicated even if a domain name is owned by a business in another country and used in a third country. Given the stakes involved, a business or government might out of frustration choose to attack or destabilize the domain name system or the organizations that support it.

The Internet community should work at the national and international level to build consensus behind the domain name system and to minimize the possibility of actions that destabilize the system and the businesses that depend on it.

Notes

1. Jonathan Agmon, Stacey Halpern, and David Pauker, "What's In A Name?" <http://www.law.georgetown.edu/lc/internic/recent/>.

2. Jessie Marshall, "Domain Names and Trademarks: At the Intersection," <http://www.isoc.org/isoc/whatis/conferences/inet/96/proceedings/f4/fr_3.htm>.

3. David Maher, "Trademarks on the Internet: Who's in Charge?" <http://www.aldea.com/cix/maher.html>.

4. *WIPO General Information*, Geneva: 1996.

5. "Parties of Interest in Internet Public Policy Matters," <http://www.wia.org/pub/policy-orgs.html>.

6. Robert Shaw, "Internet Domain Names: Whose Domain Is This?" <http://www.itu.ch/intreg/dns.html>.

7. David Maher, "Trademarks On The Internet: Who's In Charge?" <http//www.aldea.com/cix/maher.html>.

8. FNC membership consists of representatives from 17 U.S. federal agencies whose programs utilize interconnected Internet networks.

9. IANA, <http://www.isi.edu/iana/overview.html>.

10. John Postel, e-mail re "issues on the table" posted in newdom@iiiia.org on July 16, 1996.

11. "New Registries and the Delegation of International Top Level Domains," <ftp://ftp.isi.edu/in-notes/iana/administration/new-registries>.

12. See CIX, <http://www.cix.org>.

13. David Johnson and David Post, "Law and Borders—The Rise of Law in Cyberspace," *First Monday*, <http://www.firstmonday.dk/issues/issue1/law/top.html#bdtb>.

14. Tony Rutkowski, "By-laws of the Internic Committee," <http://www.agent.org/pub/cnic-charter.html>.

15. Agmon, Halpern, and Pauker, "What's in a Name?" <http://www.law.georgetown.edu/lc/internic/domain1.html>.

16. Don M. Heath, "Adding New Registries and International Top Level Domain Names," <http://www.isoc.org/whatsnew/itlds.html>.

Addressing and the Future of Communications Competition: Lessons from Telephony and the Internet

Ashley Andeen and John Leslie King

Introduction

There are many ways one might distinguish broadcast communications from interactive communications: purpose, content, technological requirements, and so on. However, at both the practical and conceptual levels, the critical distinction is the fact that interactive communications require addresses whereas broadcast does not.[1] In the analysis that follows we consider the evolution of communications services addressing in the North American Numbering Plan (NANP) for the telephone system of World Zone 1, and the Domain Name System (DNS) developed for the Internet. Addressing is the boundary zone between the technical features of communications networks, on one hand, and the socio-institutional behaviors that arise from new technological opportunities in those networks, on the other. In time, these socio-institutional behaviors become embedded, creating powerful path dependencies that shape future technological developments within the given technological "regime."[2] The world of communications services provision is undergoing radical change in both the technical and socio-institutional dimensions. Addressing issues reflect many of the fundamental tensions that will face communications services providers, regulators, investors, and users in the next decade.

There is no better measure of the penetration of interactive communication media into everyday life than the number of addresses a person "owns." For many centuries, most people had only a residential locator, if that, to serve as an address. In many countries this locator was no more precise than the name of the building in which the person lived. Going the "last mile" of communications meant finding someone within the immediate environment who could locate the individual in real time, or at least pass along a message. The advent of uniform street addressing, which was not common until the 19th century, was an elaboration on the same theme. By the middle of the 20th century a person might have two addresses: a street address and a telephone number. A person in business or the professions might have in addition an office street address and telephone number. Within the past few years, three more addresses have been added to the list: a second telephone number dedicated to receiving facsimile transmissions, an Internet address used mainly for electronic mail, and a World Wide Web address referring to the location of one's Web site. "With this proliferation of addresses, one wonders what Horrocks and Scarr meant in 1993 when they predicted that, in the near future: An end-user will have a single identification. This identification will be independent of the location of the user and the services used by the user. Thus it will not need to change but it may cease if the user ceases to exist. Thus ultimately there will be provision for only a single end-user identification on business cards."[3]

Aside from the questions of whether anyone wants a single address, and if so, why, there are several compelling problems with achievement of this vision. We can start with the fact that the term "address" has two meanings, and they are easily confused.[4] As the quote above suggests, one meaning of the term is "identification," or a direct pointer to one's identity (in which case one's proper name is an address, though we do not usually think of it as such). But by implication, another means of identification is a reference to one's "location" in physical space (a street address) or in a communications network (a telephone number). An individual is thus Joe Jones, who lives at this address, who has this telephone number and this fax number, who uses this email address, and whose Web site can be accessed by the following Universal Resource Location (URL) string. Most people have little trouble understanding how this all works conceptually, but this conceptual simplicity belies the technical and managerial challenges involved in communications addressing.

Addressing is so routine and commonplace that its fundamental importance in all interactive communications is overlooked. Well-organized and properly functioning addressing schemes are necessary for communications, as we know it, to function. A careful look at the current state of communications services addressing reveals that it is not the mundane task that it may appear to be. On top of complex technical issues there are contentious social and political issues. Addresses are not merely technical collections of numeric or alphanumeric characters; they now have economic and social value as any real estate agent will confirm. Why does a huge population of people in many countries know the zip code for Beverly Hills? Because that zip code constitutes one of several "names" for Beverly Hills, particularly one embedded in a syndicated television program broadcast in dozens of countries. The prestige or disgrace associated with an address often can substantially add to or subtract from the economic value of a real property.

Similarly, other addresses have become identifiers in ways that extend their worth far beyond the value of their functionality in the addressing scheme they occupy. Many toll-free 800 telephone numbers are now more than addresses within a routing scheme.[5] American Express has invested millions of dollars in advertising and promoting "1-800-THE-CARD" as one of the company's "names" by which it can be "called," and it is only one of thousands of vanity numbers in the 800 number system. Any seven digits might replace "THE-CARD" (843-2273) or any other vanity number with equal functionality, but those digits would not identify American Express or another company in the same way. The subculture of 800 number assignment is rife with examples of individuals who have secured special sequences of seven-digit numbers, hoping that a company desiring a particular number will be forced to buy the right to use it from them.

This phenomenon has hit the Internet. Enterprising individuals registered names like *ronald@mcdonalds.com* and *coke.com* before the Internet had developed sufficiently to attract much corporate attention, much to the dismay of McDonalds and Coca-Cola. The food processor Kraft recently registered over 150 Internet domain names, most of them the names of Kraft products. Procter & Gamble registered not only many of their product names, but went on to claim as reserved addresses names of body parts and health ailments, including *diarrhea* and *badbreath*. It is not yet clear what Kraft and Procter & Gamble intend to do with these names, but it is noteworthy that they are willing to pay an annual per-name fee to maintain the rights to the names. Addresses are identifiers, even if they were not designed to be identifiers. The significance of addressing in communications becomes obvious when the original technical requirements of addressing clash with subsequent identification issues.

Addressing has often proven to be more complicated than the designers of the addressing schemes intended or suspected. Downstream behaviors involving identity with particular addresses cannot be foreseen. The development of new technologies for communications, and the new demands for communications services, confound the underlying logic of addressing designs made during earlier eras. The phenomenal success of 800 numbers for everything from advertising and customer support to toll-free means for college kids to call home created a run on the assignment of the finite supply of 800 numbers, necessitating, first, rationing of the remaining toll-free numbers, and finally the introduction of a new access code—888—to provide a new pool of numbers. Similarly, as the fax machine and cellular telephony became popular the number pools within area codes began to dry up, necessitating area code splits and overlays. The growth in the number of area codes exhausted the old area code structure, in which the middle digit was either a 1 or a 0, and a new system allowing any digit 0–9 for the middle number was introduced (with considerable difficulty) to provide additional area codes. While Internet addresses are somewhat less constrained because they use alpha as well as numeric characters and have longer field lengths, there are other problems with the Internet addressing scheme that portend real trouble as the phenomenal growth of the Internet proceeds.

The Challenge of Communications Addressing

As suggested earlier, the term "address" can be used in a variety of ways. In addition to the lexical confusion, there is further confusion when comparing the use of the term in the telephone and

Internet worlds. The key distinction to bear in mind is between "logical" and "physical" addressing. Logical addressing is essentially an address-as-name; it is what we call a given location, and it seldom specifies much information about where the location is. The physical address is a specification of a location within some context that permits delivery to the address.

A regular telephone number, often called a POTS (plain old telephone service) number, is very precisely defined by Bellcore, the administrator of the North American Numbering Plan, as "that portion of the dialed digits that conforms to CCITT Recommendation E.164 and can be transmitted across 'national', i.e., numbering plan boundaries (WZ1)."[6] Depending upon where a call originates and terminates within World Zone 1, this number is either the ten-digit NANP number or the country code followed by the national number. Addressing, by contrast, "is the total string of digits/characters dialed by the calling party and required by the public switched network to translate, transport, terminate, and bill the call."[7] Numbering is subsumed by each particular addressing scheme. Dialing some local calls using only seven digits instead of the full ten-digit number succeeds because the local switching system recognizes what is intended by the dialed number (e.g., a local call within the NPA, or number plan area) and completes the call accordingly.[8]

For most telephone users, it is sufficient for near neighbors to use only seven-digit telephone numbers, even though that is not the complete number. In fact, what people in the United States and other countries of World Zone 1 have long considered a complete (i.e., ten-digit) telephone address is no longer complete under the NANP description above. The introduction of competitive long-distance services in the United States required establishment of a means for users to specify for each toll call which preferred provider they wished to use. This was accomplished by providing an initial strings of digits at the beginning of dialing to notify the system regarding appropriate routing and billing for the call (e.g., 10288, or "10ATT" for AT&T service). Similarly, user blocking or release of caller identification requires insertion of a code prior to the called number. For users with calling cards, a full address for a call requires the initial provider identification code, the called number, and the number of the calling card plus a user personal identifier.[9] A telephone address can now be much longer than ten digits when it includes all information necessary to translate, transport, terminate, and bill the call.

A similar story can be told about addressing in the Internet world. Strictly speaking, an Internet address is a number 32 bits in length, divided into groups through the insertion of periods and other codes. Early Internet designers believed that most people have difficulty remembering long numeric strings, so they permitted the substitution of alphanumeric codes corresponding to actual addresses. These alphanumeric codes were logical addresses invoked in an effort to connect to a specific person or location via a physical address. Both the logical and the physical address are specific and unique codes, recognizable by the infrastructure that makes the connection. The actual connection is accomplished through invocation of a "routing" protocol that builds or chooses a pathway through the network from the unique physical address of the sender to the unique physical address of the receiver. This allows establishment of a communication path that links two atomic, unique physical addresses within the network. In the circuit-switched telephone network, the physical path has to be built and then torn down following the completion of the communication. In the packet-switched Internet world, the path is instantaneous and disappears as the packets pass by the nodes in the network. The logical address is not necessary for the operation of the physical system, and it is usually possible to bypass the logical addressing scheme altogether to complete the connection. It is never possible to bypass the physical address. Ultimately, all communications operation depends on the successful functioning of the physical addressing scheme. But, as we shall see, the logical addressing scheme can be exceedingly important as well to the practical functioning of communications services.

In the discussion that follows, most of our references are to the evolution of addressing for telephony and the Internet within the United States particularly, and within North America more broadly. These schemes also are historically relevant for other countries, but we do not specifically concern ourselves with other countries. We begin with a historical account of the evolution of addressing schemes, which illustrates the complex interplay of technical and socio-institutional issues that led to the addressing schemes seen today in both telephony and the Internet. Through this analysis we highlight the successes, failures, path dependencies, and commonalties of the two addressing schemes. We conclude with the suggestion that addressing issues provide a uniquely valuable opportunity to see simultaneously both the technical and socio-institutional aspects of the complex changes now under way in the communications sector.

Telephony Addressing in World Zone 1

One cannot understand the evolution of telephony addressing, or the complexities it now poses for telephony deregulation, without a review of the idiosyncratic industrial organization of the U.S. telephone industry over the past century. As this discussion will show, the telephone company and telephone addressing evolved in a monopolistic, paternal, "top-down" manner that achieved the goal of ubiquitous service provision.[10] Ubiquitous service provision required a uniform addressing scheme; the construction of that addressing scheme put in place impediments to subsequent schemes for deregulation and competition because it vested in the incumbent service provider a special relationship with the industry standard that competitors would have to work to overcome.

Alexander Graham Bell was awarded a patent for the invention of the telephone in 1876, and shortly thereafter joined the three men who had financially backed his research in the creation of the Bell Telephone Company. Early on, these men made an important decision to control "both the service and the consumers' equipment," thus shaping the formation not only of their company but also of the entire telephone industry.[11] The Bell Telephone Company grew as local franchises popped up everywhere. Although Western Union, already in the telegraph industry, initially threatened to compete against Bell in the telephone industry, an agreement in 1879 between the two companies established that Bell alone would continue telephone service while Western Union alone would pursue telegraph service. By the early 1880s, the Bell Telephone Company was on its way to creating a near-monopoly on the U.S. telephone business. The company invested heavily in technical innovation, obtaining numerous patents that presented a barrier to competitive entry. Although thousands of small telephone ventures sprang up when some of Bell's key patents expired, Bell's strategies of technical innovation, horizontal growth, and vertical integration enabled it to remain dominant in the industry.

In 1899, the assets of the Bell Telephone Company were transferred to one of its own subsidiaries, the American Telephone and Telegraph Corporation (AT&T), which was providing long-distance service. The resulting complex, which we refer to henceforth as the AT&T Bell System, had four primary components: Western Electric Company, Bell Telephone Laboratories, Long Lines, and local Bell Operating Companies (BOCs). Western Electric, responsible for manufacturing and supplying all equipment to the Bell System, had begun as its own company and had ironically been Western Union's ally in the early struggle against Bell. It was the largest component of the Bell System, and by vertically integrating it into the system, Bell hindered smaller competitors from purchasing telephone equipment. The second component, Bell Telephone Laboratories (or Bell Labs), formed the central research and development arm of the company. Technical innovations that emerged from Bell Labs were sent to Western Electric where the new technology was manufactured. The third component of the system was Long Lines, the long distance service operator. The final component was a group of 24 local Bell Operating Companies responsible for local telephone service.

By the early 1900s, the AT&T Bell System controlled everything from the research and innovation phase to the provision of end-user telephone service. Institutional control over the company was provided for by a hodgepodge of governmental regulations at the federal and state levels. Because of its technical skill and financial power, the AT&T Bell System generally was subject to relatively weak institutional regulation. The company could point with pride to its established technical success, its important and growing role in national security, and the obvious economic and social benefits of getting the whole country onto the same reliable network. Potential competitors and zealous regulators occasionally challenged the company's supremacy, but for nearly a century Bell triumphed over these attacks, justifying its position with one or more of these three arguments. It is useful to examine each of these arguments in greater detail, for taken together they illustrate much about the complex technical and socio-institutional interactions relevant to addressing.

The AT&T Bell System was able to argue convincingly that it was technically as good as, if not better than, any other telephone company in the world, whether government or privately owned, in a competitive or monopoly market. Revenues from the monopoly operation went into pathbreaking research and development that had rapid and material effects on the quality of telephone services. A monopoly could afford to make such "public goods" investments. Breaking up the monopoly would require a greater company focus on profits and competition, and technical excellence would suffer. America seemed to have the best telephone service in the world, and in fact, much of the world was buying expertise from the company. Why ruin a good thing? As the company matured, its record of technical achievements grew, thereby strengthening this argument.

One powerful argument used by the AT&T Bell System to avoid competitive breakup was its importance to national defense. The company had more than rhetoric behind its position on this matter. At the start of World War I, Bell supplied all communications for the Navy Department, and after the war, Bell equipment and employees were shipped to France, where they established a complete American telephone network. The requirement for a reliable and secure telephone service was so strong that, in 1918, the U.S. government took over the operation of the telephone industry in the United States—a common practice in other countries where telephony had been subsumed by governmental postal departments. This action produced a major outcry, and in fact, government ownership proved to be a disaster. AT&T resumed ownership within a year.[12] A key result of this fiasco was the institutionalization of the view that a private, regulated telephone company operating with minimal government interference would best serve the public interest. Congress declared that telephony was a natural monopoly, and that telephone competition was an endless annoyance.[13] Thus, World War I had demonstrated not only that AT&T's network was critical to national security, but that the network functioned best as a private regulated monopoly.

For years the AT&T Bell System maintained a powerful position, shielded by the institutional regulators themselves. The Federal Communications Commission (FCC) was responsible for overseeing the monopoly; it had to approve all tariffs and new communications services. But due to a lack of time and manpower it was unable to stay abreast of the developments at Bell Labs and therefore exerted little control over the innovations. Similarly, state regulatory commissions relied on information obtained from the industry rather than through their own investigations. "Regulation had become a comfortable environment for the telephone companies."[14] As one senior staffer in the FCC expressed in interviews with us, "The setup at the FCC was simple: AT&T ran the phone system and the commissioners went to lunch with the broadcasters."[15]

Powerfully reinforcing the AT&T Bell System's monopoly argument was the fact that, as more people joined the network, its utility rose for everyone. Such positive network externalities argued strongly for extending the system toward ubiquitous service. This concept was embodied in the 1934 Federal Communications Act under a provision for "universal service," and is embedded in the regulatory reforms passed in the 1996 Telecommunications Act.[16] In principle, a competitive industry might enhance universal service by competing for customers, but the AT&T Bell System responded with two counterarguments. First, the company argued that its monopoly status enabled it to cross-subsidize the growth of residential services with revenues from more lucrative business services, thus extending residential services more rapidly than a competitive market would.[17] Competition would require lower prices in urban areas and higher prices in rural areas, a notion that not only stood in the way of universal service, but was contrary to the well-established model of the U.S. Post Office, which charged a single price to mail a first-class letter anywhere in the country. Second, the company argued the danger of what became known as "network harms," in which low-quality "foreign attachments" to the network could cause failure of the entire system. This too was a successful defense, but it began to come apart in 1949 when the

Department of Justice sued AT&T, seeking the divestiture of Western Electric on grounds that the company "had a 'captive monopoly' in the phone equipment business."[18] In a 1956 consent decree, AT&T was able to preserve its Western Electric subsidiary, and therefore its near monopoly on telephone equipment development, only by sacrificing all activity in the computer industry. This replay of the deal with Western Union to stay out of telegraphy worked for a while, but eventually gave way before stronger arguments in favor of equipment competition and, more important, the increasing interrelationship of computing and communications that made the separation of the two an unworkable fiction.

In the late 1950s and early 1960s, the attitude of AT&T Bell System customers began to change. The comfortable image of "Ma Bell" as a provider of needed services had taken on a nasty parental aspect, with rising complaints of poor service and indifference toward customers. Calls for deregulation and competition arose as customers grew unhappy with requirements that they lease their telephone equipment from AT&T as opposed to being able to buy their own equipment from other manufacturers and tie into the network. Bootleg telephone equipment became available to consumers and grew in popularity. The FCC finally turned against the AT&T Bell System on the crucial "network harms" argument in the 1968 Carterfone decision, in which AT&T's protest over the use of a device manufactured by Carter Electronics Corporation of Dallas, Texas, to interconnect private two-way radios with the telephone system via a base station was overturned. The Commission ruled that such equipment could be connected to Bell lines as long as the company was allowed to install protective equipment between the line and the alien device.[19] As independent companies connected their equipment to the AT&T network and the disasters that had been predicted did not occur, AT&T lost credibility. The decision marked the end of the comfortable environment provided by regulators; the regulators saw equipment competition as ultimately beneficial to the consumer, and the other defenses of the monopoly were threatened.[20]

Only one year later, in 1969, the FCC approved MCI's application to provide "private lines." Through a series of savvy legal and political maneuvers, MCI eventually won the right to compete in the long-distance market. During the next two decades, the AT&T

Bell System lost two major anti-trust lawsuits—one to MCI and the other to the federal government. In 1984, AT&T, already divested of Western Electric, was forced to divest itself of its regional operating companies. The 22 local operating companies were consolidated into seven geographic Regional Bell Operating Companies (RBOCs) that, together with a large number of smaller Local Exchange Carriers (LECs), continued to maintain monopolies on their respective local telephone services.[21] Meanwhile, AT&T continued the business of Long Lines although it no longer had a monopoly on long-distance services. Bell Labs became AT&T Bell Laboratories, which continued to be owned by AT&T and focused on the new company's products and services, while much of the telephone communications-related research went into a newly created company, Bell Communications Research (Bellcore), jointly owned by the RBOCs.[22]

Competition, firmly present in the long-distance market since the 1980s, is beginning to move into the local service market. A principal objective in creating the climate for competition is to "level the playing field." This quaint sporting metaphor sounds ideal when the playing field is a bit of bumpy prairie that can be swept clean with a few passes of a road grader. It takes on an altogether different meaning when the playing field looks like the Sierra Nevada, a granite batholith rising from the desert. Leveling the playing field in the telephony market means reducing the advantages of incumbents, the players who have long dominated the market and who have learned to like the bumps and valleys. The challenge of doing so can be illustrated by the evolution of telephony addressing into the North American Numbering Plan, and the implications of that evolution for competitive toll-free number services. This story has major lessons for local numbering in the face of competition in the local loop that is now materializing as a result of the 1996 telecommunications legislation and the FCC's pro-competition rule-makings.

The Legacy of the North American Numbering Plan

In the early days, telephone numbering and addressing were not necessary. A call was placed by ringing the local operator and requesting a line to the called party. The operator could manually make a local connection on her switchboard; a remote connection required calling the called party's local operator, who then put the call through. Operators served a number of roles, but in the 1920s a combination of labor shortages, union demands, and inflation prompted the AT&T Bell System to begin automating its major exchanges. Dial telephones and mechanized switching equipment were installed that enabled the user to directly dial local calls, although it was still necessary to go through an operator for calls outside the local area. By the 1940s the AT&T Bell System began to implement dial switching for toll calls outside the local area, with the goal of permitting the subscriber to either go through an operator to complete toll calls or to dial toll calls directly. AT&T's Bell Laboratories took on the job of developing the direct distance dialing (DDD) system to accomplish this, and in 1945 a writer for Bell Labs eloquently promised, "Plans are now under way to insure that the expansion of toll dialing will be guided by principles in harmony with the ultimate incorporation of all networks into an integrated network of nation-wide scope."[23]

In fact, it was not that simple. Direct distance dialing required the forging of a single numbering system from the bewildering array of existing local numbering systems. Central office names had to be converted to dialable digits, and letters of the alphabet were placed on the dial. An office was reached by dialing the digits that corresponded to the first letters of the office name. Unfortunately, with letters assigned to only eight digits on the dial (0 was reserved to reach the operator and 1 was disqualified because the pulse switching system meant that a fumble of the switchhook could produce a false pulse and result in a wrong number), there was to be overlap. For example, the names ADams and BEacon would both correspond to the digits 2-3-2. In large cities like New York, the number of useful office names producing nonconflicting codes was inadequate, so numerals instead of letters were assigned to the third position. Adams might be ADams 2 (2-3-2) and Beacon, BEacon 3 (2-3-3), allowing subscribers to dial the three-digit office code followed by the four-digit code of the terminal they wished to reach.[24]

This scheme worked at the local level, but seven digits did not provide a sufficient supply of telephone numbers for the entire country. The AT&T Bell System's coverage area, meaning the United States and Canada, was therefore divided geographically into 83 numbering plan areas (NPAs) to be addressed using newly created three-digit NPA codes. The North American Numbering Plan began to take shape. Shortly thereafter subscribers were allowed to dial long-distance calls directly. Englewood, New Jersey, initiated direct distance dialing on November 10, 1951. Customers and operators were introduced to a ten-digit NANP format represented symbolically as N0/1X-NNX-XXXX (N = digits 2–9; X = digits 0–9; 0/1 = digits 0 or 1). "Dial 0" remained a familiar backup for nondialable calls, but the ten-digit DDD format, while shortened to seven digits for use within the home NPA, became the dominant addressing scheme.[25]

In addition to changes in the technical infrastructure, implementation of the NANP required the establishment of a NANP Administrator (NANPA), and the training of millions of users to do the work that operators had formerly done for them. The establishment of the NANPA was relatively easy: Bell Labs took on that function. The training was more of a challenge, and the fact that it was accomplished is testimony to the vision and capability of the AT&T Bell System. However, it is necessary to remember that the transition occurred over decades, from the 1940s through the 1970s. The standardization of the plan at the national level also meant that, once people learned it, they could use it from anywhere to call anywhere within World Zone 1. Finally, the backup option to connect to the operator was always available.

Bell's unique position and technocratic vision enabled the company to create and successfully implement the NANP throughout much of North America. The NANP has evolved since 1951, but today's format (NXX-NXX-XXXX) remains strikingly similar to the original format. The concept also had reach beyond its original borders. The United States and Canada were the original NANP participants, but physical proximity to and trade relations with the United States and Canada, combined with their recognition of the ingenuity of the plan, led a number of Caribbean nations to request inclusion as a geographic area in the numbering scheme. As a result, the area actually served by the NANP now includes 19 countries, though not the other major country of North America,

Mexico.[26] The NANP community was a strong institutional force by the 1970s, when the International Consultative Committee on Telegraph and Telephone (CCITT) set out to establish guidelines that would enable International DDD (IDDD). In order to assign regional and country codes as number prefixes, the CCITT divided the globe into nine world zones (using digits 1 through 9), within which countries would be assigned unique one- or two-digit country codes to follow the world zone number. The only exception was the already consolidated NANP area, which was simply allocated the code 1, and thus became World Zone 1.

The creation and implementation of the NANP were made possible in part by the enormous power of the Bell System, which possessed the means to do the job. The AT&T Bell System was not forced to create the NANP for competitive reasons. Rather, from all appearances, it did so because the NANP scheme was technically sensible, efficient (it allowed replacement of human operators with automation), and it improved universal service. These were technocratic goals that might have been hindered by competition, at least at that time when the concepts for the scheme were still being worked out. The introduction of competition into the NANP scheme caused by regulatory reforms since the mid-1980s has brought unforeseen addressing problems, especially the problem of "number portability" that is considered to be a key to successful competition in local telephone services as directed by the 1996 telecommunications regulatory reform legislation.[27]

The problem of number portability did not originate with the effort to introduce competition in the local loop. It arose following the "modified final judgment" (MFJ) in 1984 that brought competition to long-distance services.[28] By the late 1960s, the AT&T Bell System had three basic components of technical infrastructure in place. The first was DDD, enabled by the NANP scheme, that made it possible for users to be their own operators. Second was the automated Trunk Inventory Record Keeping System (TIRKS), which allowed assignment of calls to trunks, thus enabling automated long-distance service. Third was a set of highly sophisticated billing systems developed by the BOCs that allowed precise charges to be imposed on toll calls. Together, this infrastructure enabled the establishment of Wide-Area Telephone Service (WATS); a scheme that allowed a customer to buy flat-fee toll service for long-distance calling from one number to many. The infrastructure later allowed the creation of a "reverse WATS" service, in which toll-free calling was possible from many numbers to one. Unlike WATS, which simply altered the billing scheme using the existing numbering structure, a reverse-WATS system had to create a single number to be dialed from many remote locations so that the local billing systems would know how to bill the call. The result was the creation of the first nongeographic area code, designated 800, to which the standard seven-digit number could be attached.[29] The 800 service was a major success, growing rapidly as the advantages in marketing and other applications became clear. It became obvious that the pool of approximately eight million 800 numbers would be exhausted far earlier than anyone had anticipated. But that was a secondary concern compared to the problem that arose following the MFJ.

The 800 service was unusual. By definition, it was toll-free long-distance service, and thus subject to deregulation and competition under the MFJ. As AT&T left local service behind and became a competitor in long-distance service, it held a complete monopoly on all interLATA[30] 800 service, and it owned the addresses the customers used. This created an odd situation. For decades telephone numbers had essentially belonged not to the customer, but to the service providers as implemented through the NANP and Central Office code administration. Now a competitor in the newly competitive 800 service market, AT&T, owned the interLATA 800 telephone numbers. A federal court order required the NANPA to issue NXX codes to AT&T's competitors for 800 services, but this was only part of the problem. Under the old scheme, AT&T still owned the telephone numbers. Customers who would switch their 800 service from AT&T to a competitor would have to relinquish their number and receive a new number from their new service provider. Companies with long-established 800 numbers such as "1-800-THE-CARD" would have to remain with AT&T or give up their established 800-number identity in the marketplace. This was rightly seen as a disadvantage for AT&T's competitors.

The solution to this problem was service provider portability: placing the 800 number under control of the 800 service subscriber rather than the service provider. Unfortunately, there was no easy way to make the telephone numbers portable within the existing switching technology. Addressing had grown up entirely under the institutional regime of the AT&T Bell System in which provider portability was never an option. Technically, the switching system could not support the automatic information-sharing that portability would require if calls were to be completed accurately and quickly. Central offices would not be able to tell what POTS number to give to an outgoing 800-number call because the owners of 800 numbers could switch 800 service providers at any moment. That problem was overcome when the FCC mandated the full deployment of a switching technology that would enable information sharing. There were several technical competitors for this duty, but the FCC was aware of the advantages of one such system developed by AT&T Bell Labs—Signaling System 7 (SS7). The commission issued a mandate requiring deployment of the necessary switching technology, and wrote its requirements in a way that ensured the deployment of SS7.

SS7 brought about "the ability to use a database lookup to route 800-number calls to more than one physical location" and the ability to "allow customers to mix and match carriers at will. SS7 [allows] users to shift traffic at will, at any time, to any provider."[31] A schematic of how SS7 operates in the so-called Intelligent Network (IN) configuration is shown in Figure 1.[32] SS7 is built upon the interplay of service switching points (SSPs), signaling transfer points (STPs), service control points (SCPs), and service management systems (SMSes). The SCP provides local access as well as an Integrated Services Digital Network (ISDN) interface for the STP. The STP provides packet switching of message-based signaling protocols for use by an SCP. The SCP, in turn, provides access to the SMS, which provides a human interface to the database of numbers as well as updating services.

The implementation of SS7 provided a system of Inter-eXchange Carrier (IXC) operated SCPs that received inquiries for routing information on outgoing 800 calls from Local Exchange Carrier central offices and sent back correct routing instructions. The SCPs were updated about every 15 minutes by the Service Management System-800 (SMS-800) mainframe computer, which managed the

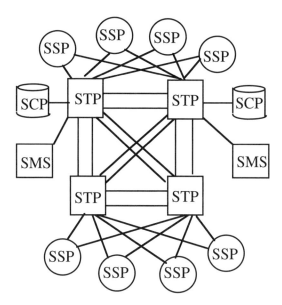

Figure 1   The Signaling System 7 Scheme.

master routing tables. Technically speaking, centralized addressing was thus maintained, but distributed operation was enabled.
SS7 enabled the SMS-800 solution for 800-number portability, but
it opened the door to competition in the local loop and to
communications competition more broadly because it provided, at
least in principle, a technical means for making addresses the
effective property of the subscriber within that LATA, while maintaining the accuracy of routing information.

SMS-800 technology by itself did not solve the problem altogether, however. The SMS-800 mainframe was merely the repository of the centralized addressing information. Also needed was a
centralized coordinator to assign numbers, match customers with
their chosen service providers, and update the SMS-800 mainframe. Since none of the 800 service providers wanted their
competitors to be able to see into their customer profiles and
records, it was decided that an independent, third-party administrator, the Number Administration Service Center (NASC), be
created to manage the boundary between the 800 service customer
base and the 800 service providers. The NASC works with NANPA

to assign 800 numbers to 800 service subscribers. It maintains the vital tables on the SMS-800 mainframe.[33] The NASC, by regulation, cannot hold a common carrier license and thus cannot be a competitor for service provision. In order to enable the NASC contractor to undertake the business without undue exposure, the NASC function was informally extended by the FCC to include the liability indemnification granted to common carriers under the 1934 Communications Act. This was the first time such indemnification was granted, and the action opened the door for so-called third-party service provision in an industry that traditionally was handled entirely by common carriers. The implementation of this solution is illustrated in Figure 2. Full portability of 800 numbers took over seven years to achieve.[34]

The solution to the 800-number problem indicates the importance of maintaining a centralized coordinating apparatus for addressing to enable competition. It also illustrates the complexity of the institutional changes arising from competition in a previously uncompetitive realm. Following the MFJ, the FCC made Bellcore the NANPA "subject to the plenary jurisdiction and oversight of the appropriate regulatory agencies within the 19 countries served by the NANP."[35] When the NASC was created, the NASC operations were performed by a contractor under contract to Bellcore. Bellcore was owned jointly by the RBOCs, which were themselves formerly part of AT&T, and thus by tradition aligned with a major competitor in the 800 service industry. By the mid-1990s, the RBOCs themselves were lining up to be major competitors in both long-distance and local loop competition under the new regulatory regime. The fact that Bellcore controlled the NANP and governed the contract for the NASC created conflict of interest concerns. Neither Bellcore, the IXCs, the RBOCs, the competitors to the RBOCs, the FCC, or the federal courts were happy with this situation, and many efforts were made to find a solution, but the situation persisted much longer than those involved desired simply because finding workable alternatives was so difficult.

To ensure fair competition, the NANPA and the NASC must be impartial. Assuming that a technically capable neutral party is prepared to take over these tasks, who has the authority to assign the tasks to them? Remember that the NANP grew up at a time

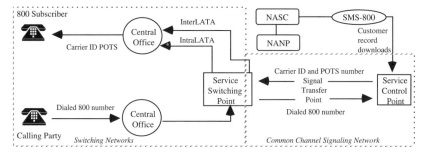

Figure 2 The SMS-800 Scheme.

when a privately owned, powerful, multinational service monopoly literally owned and ran the telephone infrastructure for the vast majority of people living in the 19 countries of World Zone 1. AT&T was, in a very real sense, transnational; it could do the work normally reserved for multilateral treaty organizations operating at the diplomatic level. Since the dominance of the AT&T Bell System has declined, no institutional entity has emerged capable of claiming jurisdiction or oversight over the NANP. As a technical matter, NANP oversight has always been split among numerous regulatory agencies in the NANP countries. As the NANPA noted in 1993, "The regulatory agencies within [the countries governed by the NANP] have joint NANP oversight of general policy, planning, procedural issues and individual NANP oversight of specific numbering issues uniquely impacting their respective territory."[36] But practically, the AT&T Bell System was able to act in lieu of those regulatory agencies. Bellcore, a weak residual of the once monolithic AT&T Bell System, continued to function as the NANPA simply by inheritance. Similarly, the NASC was established before the RBOCs had regulatory authority to enter into long-distance service, so there was no clear conflict with the RBOC-owned Bellcore providing oversight over the NASC, which provided long-distance-related 800 system services. With the 1996 reforms, the RBOCs were granted the right to offer long-distance service, and Bellcore's oversight of the NASC became problematic. Yet Bellcore retained oversight of the NASC.

The selection of the next NANPA is central to the issue of local number portability. This agency will receive from customers directions about the provision of telephone service, and in turn, instruct the computerized systems that run switching, routing, and billing what to do with the customers' calls. This bears similarities to the number portability solution of the 800 system, but the sheer magnitude of numbers in local service raises questions about whether the technical solution provided for the 800-number system will work in the local loop. If it does, the extensive software developed by AT&T to support the SMS-800 system will have to be provided for the local loop, further raising questions about AT&T's role as both a competitor and a crucial infrastructure provider to its competitors. If the SMS-800 strategy does not work, another technical solution must be found. Despite the rhetoric surrounding competition in the local loop, local number portability remains the key enabling factor and it has not been solved satisfactorily.[37]

The 1996 reform legislation, in Section 251(e), specified the FCC's plenary jurisdiction over all numbering matters in the United States. In late 1996, the FCC ordered the creation of the North American Numbering Council (NANC), comprising 20 individuals from the telephone industry, to set policy for and issue the contract for NANPA. The FCC ordered the NANC to appoint the NANPA within 180 days of its first official meeting. It further ordered that, beginning in the fourth quarter of 1997, the NANC must take over responsibility for the Number Portability Administration Center (NPAC) model for local number portability that was prototyped in Illinois. Many industry principals believe that the NPAC should operate a standardized SMS-like operation for permanent number portability administration throughout NANP. However, others argued that the rapid movement of the states to implement local competition in the various RBOC regions has already demonstrated that centralized schemes could give way to local and regional schemes for handling number portability. The states have already set up limited-liability corporations to serve as NPACs, under the direction of industry officials who will oversee the NPAC contracts. This, in effect, is creating a set of mini-NANCs that might or might not merge smoothly under the control of the overall NANC. Although the stage is set for the long-awaited transfer of NANP oversight from the legacy of the AT&T Bell System to a new governance structure, it is by no means clear what that new governance structure will be.

In all, the story of telephone addressing in World Zone 1 illustrates the subtle and complex interplay of technical and socio-institutional forces alluded to earlier. Addressing is never simply a technical issue. Addresses carry identity information that sometimes goes far beyond the simple networking requirements, as complex as they might be. That identity information has important social and economic implications, and these have become increasingly important within the telephone sector since the advent of 800 service. The issues have become much more critical given the move to deregulate service in the local loop. Moreover, as we can now see with the effort to move the NANPA out of its traditional home in the AT&T Bell System (and descendants) and place it in the control of the NANC, addressing is raising complicated problems of structure, governance, accountability, and control. The following section discussing the Internet world illustrates some of these governance problems, and further elaborates the underlying technical and socio-institutional complexities of communications addressing.

The Evolution of Internet Addressing

The history of the Internet is significantly shorter than that of the telephone industry, spanning only a few decades. Yet even in this brief period of time important precedents have been established, and a legacy of prior decisions shapes the path dependencies of the Internet into the future.[38] The origin of the Internet lies in the fact that computers are capable of processing data quickly and storing large amounts of data for ready retrieval. When attached to one another, groups of computers can accomplish more than a single computer. The first major computer network systems were the Semi-Automated Ground Environment (SAGE) air defense system in the early 1960s and the SABRE airline reservation system in the late 1960s.[39] Both systems, like all subsequent wide-area computer networks, were built by linking computers to components of the telephony infrastructure. Database-driven transaction processing systems such as airline reservation systems and automatic teller machine networks usually must support simultaneous database retrieval operations from multiple users. According to Irwin Lebow,

Since the applications varied and the computers themselves were not all of the same type, this meant that the communications network had to be general enough to allow for the idiosyncrasies of a variety of computers and tasks. The desire to provide computer network support useful to a wide array of individuals for a variety of purposes stimulated the creation of the precursor of the Internet, the ARPANET, named after its research sponsor, the Department of Defense Advanced Research Projects Agency (ARPA).[40]

The ARPANET was not a substitute for the existing, reliable telephone system. It was supplementary. As Lebow notes, the telephone system was ideal for instantaneous, real-time voice communications between individuals. The path between these individuals had to be constructed rapidly, maintained for the duration of the conversation, and then torn down, which was accomplished through circuit switching. Communications between computers were typically for exchange of data and text strings, and often took place asynchronously from their human users. Hold times were often not extensive—only whatever was required to move the data. It made sense to multiplex as many data streams onto a single carrier as possible. This was accomplished by packet switching, which divided data into discrete chunks called packets which were then routed to their destination on an individual basis. Circuits were held only during the time that a single packet was sent. A full-fledged and working ARPANET was in place by 1972, connecting universities, government laboratories, and commercial organizations involved in ARPA projects. The ARPANET was originally envisioned as a testbed for a robust communications system that could survive war damage, and also as a device to link scientists doing work on Defense Department projects so they could share computer resources. Before long, however, it became clear that the ARPANET was being used primarily for interpersonal communication, and by the mid-1970s administration of the network was turned over to the Defense Communications Agency.[41]

The ARPANET exhibited astonishing growth in use. Starting with a few hundred connected computers in the 1970s, by the 1980s it interconnected several thousand computers. It demonstrated the potential of networking so convincingly that it ignited a computer networking frenzy. Other computer networks sprang up to interconnect subscribers who were not allowed to participate in the ARPANET. Similar to the linking of regional networks in the development of the national telephone system, these various computer networks were eventually connected to one another via gateways to extend communication potential. But the similarity ended there. Because of the AT&T Bell System, local telephone networks were all based on the same technology and protocols. The emerging computer networks were heterogeneous, using many different machines, operating systems, networking protocols, and so forth. It was nearly impossible for the emerging networks to communicate effectively. It was not feasible to force the computer networks to conform to a uniform structure, so commonality and standardization were achieved at the level of the links between the computers. The strategy was to develop a Transmission Control Protocol (TCP) that would standardize exchange of data, and an Internet Protocol (IP) that would allow different systems to recognize one another in the network. The resulting TCP/IP protocol allowed each network to maintain its own computer architecture while sending and receiving messages conforming to TCP/IP. TCP/IP did not permit creation of a single network, but rather a network of networks, the ARPA-Internet. Unlike the evolution of the telephone system in the United States, the ARPA-Internet vision was born from the "anarchy of independently owned and managed networks."[42]

Due to its federally supported origins, the Internet initially served only the military, government, research, and university communities; commercial uses were prohibited. As the network grew, the military component, largely for security reasons, split off into MILNET, for military use, and ARPANET, for ARPA researchers. Subscribership to these networks was still limited, and many research and university communities remained excluded. In 1988, the National Science Foundation (NSF) created the NSFNET to include these researchers. NSFNET grew so rapidly that in 1990 the ARPANET structure was subsumed into NSFNET and disappeared, while the NSFNET became the primary carrier of what was becoming known generally as "the Internet." Commercial uses were eventually admitted to the Internet, and use of the network began to grow even more rapidly. The large growth of commercial subscribers persuaded the NSF to abandon its sponsorship in favor of emerging Internet Service Providers (ISPs), both for profit and nonprofit.

The differences in the evolution of the telephony and Internet systems are striking. The telephone system evolved with a clear concept of universality from the start; the Internet stumbled into it. The telephone system was created by a strong monopoly with a professed goal of providing telephone service to the nation; the Internet was designed to serve an idiosyncratic and elite community—university-based researchers working on military contracts. Telephone equipment was relatively simple and cheap to manufacture, which fit with the goal of universal service—a telephone in every home was a realistic goal. In the late 1960s, when the ARPANET started, computer equipment was so expensive that it could only be bought by organizations that could justify the expenditure in light of organizational operations and goals; no one imagined that people would someday have computers in their offices, homes, schools, churches, and so on. Had the ARPANET builders foreseen the personal computer revolution, they might have given more thought to universality; but it is easy to understand why they did not.[43] Despite these clear differences in the history of the telephone and Internet, we find that addressing issues are remarkably common across them.

Compared to the development of the telephone addressing system, the development of the Internet addressing scheme was a haphazard affair. Bell Labs rationalized the manually operated local exchanges by ensuring that standard hardware was installed and standard switching protocols were instituted. The ARPANET builders began with an installed base of heterogeneous hardware and an almost complete lack of interconnection protocols. The design of the networking solution would inevitably be the result of compromise. ARPA essentially controlled the development of the Internet addressing scheme, as the AT&T Bell System controlled the telephone addressing scheme, but for different reasons. ARPA was the first major financial supporter of computer networking research, and thus controlled the distribution of funds to developers. It had no mandate to provide networking service, but it did have the means to influence researchers to develop networking capability across a heterogeneous population of computer systems and users. When ARPA wanted a scheme implemented, it simply chose a particular research group, provided the funding to develop the scheme, and then facilitated its diffusion. Generally speaking, technically effective solutions were considered "good" by the development community, and the ARPA-supported schemes were widely adopted.[44]

The Internet addressing scheme is based on logical-to-physical address translation. Logical addresses consist of alphanumeric characters, and physical addresses are 32-bit numbers. Just as the terms "number" and "address" carry very specific meanings in terms of telephone addressing, the terms "name" and "address" have distinct meanings in Internet addressing. The name refers to the logical Internet address, while the address is the physical translation. All ARPANET users were on the same network with the same protocols. Logical addresses of the form *user@host* were assigned in a flat structure. But as internetworking began through the gateways, addressing grew complicated. To send a message from one network to another, the sender had to specify the routing information in the address "by hiding some sort of 'other-system' addressing information in the local-part of the mail address and using a mail-relay host in the host-part of the mailbox."[45] For example, if Jones on the ARPANET wanted to send a message to Smith on BITNET through the original ARPANET/BITNET gateway at the University of Wisconsin, he might have had to send the message to the address *smith%itivax.bitnet@wiscvm.wisc.edu,* which basically mailed a coded address (with % substituting for @) to the gateway, which stripped out the coded address, corrected it, and sent it on. The sender had to know something about the topology of the destination network and specify that information in the address. As the size and complexity of the internetwork grew, this form of addressing was increasingly difficult to maintain. Discussions in the early 1980s led to the implementation of a new naming scheme.

The solution, which emerged in 1983, was to switch to a hierarchical naming structure of the form *local-name@domain.domain. ... .domain,* referred to as the Domain Name System.[46] From highest to lowest levels, the domains are increasingly specific. The highest level was the Top Level Domain (TLD)—one of seven generic TLDs (e.g., .edu, .com., org, .gov) or a two-letter country code. A hierarchy of names could be created under each TLD. The generic structure of most TLDs was expected to be flat, with many organizations registered directly under the TLD, with further structure left up to the individual organizations under the TLD.[47] To make this work, the centrally maintained database containing the logical-to-physical address mappings referred to as the InterNIC was created, and copies of the database or parts thereof were then distributed. Originally, the InterNIC structure maintained the table of all name-to-address translations, which was then copied by hosts throughout the network, in much the same manner as the updating scheme involving SMS-800. As the database grew it was partitioned, and portions were given to other servers to maintain in a distributed fashion. While sensible from a processing standpoint, this confused the reconciliation process because name-to-address translations had to be handled dynamically by an elaborate set of name servers and "resolvers" dedicated to locating the right name server.

There are many details that must be managed to achieve successful DNS operation, but the primary scheme can be described as shown in Figure 3.[48]

Four kinds of software are used to manage the DNS: user programs, interface routines, resolvers, and name servers. User programs (File Transfer Protocol, electronic mail, TELNET, etc.) make a subroutine call to an interface routine that ties the local system to the Internet. The interface routine then makes a subroutine call to a resolver, which is a computer on the network that will either have the required routing information stored in its cache (usually because earlier requests have shown that specific routing information is needed by local systems), or will make a UPD or TCP query to a name server. The name server might interact with other name servers to get the required information. When the name server has the required information, it sends a UDP or TCP response to the resolver, which sends a subroutine return to the interface routine, which issues a subroutine return to the user program.

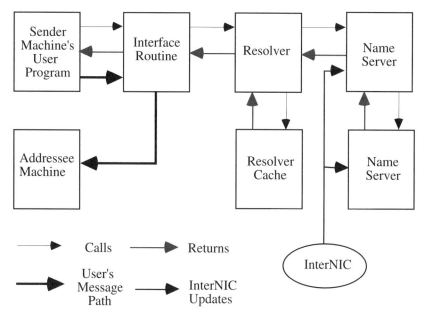

Figure 3 DNS Scheme.

As with the telephone system, however, the Internet's success has made mockery of the carefully developed addressing scheme created when the network was comparatively small. The huge growth in use of the Internet, especially since World Wide Web has come into widespread use, has resulted in a drastic increase in demand for addresses. The problem of restricted combinatoric possibilities for physical addresses found in the telephone system proved to be a problem, and resulted in the expansion of the 32-bit address to a 128-bit address. However, the Internet always allowed long string lengths which could be used for logical Internet addresses and Web addresses, so there were many possibilities for naming. Nevertheless, other problems abound. One is the congestion in the TLDs, where exponential growth in some domains (especially .com) has made assignment and management difficult, and more seriously has raised problems about the governance structure required to make the reforms. It is useful to contrast the evolution of the naming problems of the Internet with the numbering problems of the telephone system. In a sense, the nearly monolithic telephone numbering system is now being deconstructed, with authority being devolved to the NANC and the states, while the previously loosely coupled governance of the Internet is searching for a solution to the need for some top-level authority while not damaging the traditional decentralized character of the Internet community.

When the ARPANET's governance structure was guiding the newly evolving Internet DNS scheme, authority for addressing was consolidated within the relatively coherent Interent development community that King, Grinter and Pickering have called "Netville."[49] Decisions were made mainly as a result of consensus-building through technical deliberation in a body called the Internet Engineering Task Force (IETF), which still exerts considerable influence on the evolution of the Internet, although as an open meeting, it has grown to almost unwieldy proportions. When the National Science Foundation inherited primary responsibility for the Internet in the United States it issued a request for proposals for the establishment of a network information services manager.[50] The result of this contracting effort was the creation in 1993 of the InterNIC, a collaborative venture involving Network Solutions, Incorporated (NSI), AT&T, and General Atomics.[51] Almost immediately, complaints were raised regarding the authority of the InterNIC to make critical decisions about name assignment, and alternatives such as the ALTERNIC emerged to challenge the conventional naming authority by using "experimental" TLDs to assign new domains.[52]

At a more official level, various agencies and associations involved in the Internet began to create special authorities to guide the evolution of key aspects of the Internet. For example, the Internet Society (ISOC) and the Federal Network Council (FNC) created the Internet Assigned Numbers Authority (IANA) to work with the IETF. In turn, the ISOC, the IANA, the Internet Architecture Board (IAB), the FNC, the International Telecommunication Union (ITU), the International Trademark Association (INTA), and the World Intellectual Property Association (WIPO) have joined together in the Internet International Ad Hoc Committee (IAHC), working to "satisfy the requirement for enhancements to the Internet's global Domain Name System (DNS)."[53] As the membership of the IAHC suggests, much of the concern about naming arises from trademark and intellectual property issues, and the problems in adjudicating disputes arising from such concerns. As yet, there is no agreement among the Internet community regarding which organizations should have authority to govern naming issues, and there is evident dissension within the community over whether there should be any ultimate authority.[54] Whatever new organizations and authorities are created, the real test will come when an attempt has been made (as suggested by the IAHC and others) to subordinate the current incumbents in the DNS scheme. In particular, it remains to be seen how the traditional TLDs (*.com*, *.edu*, etc.) will be subsumed under a new, higher-level TLD structure, and whether organizations holding trademarks will be persuaded to accept a "trademark" domain designation (.tm) to secure their trademark rights in lieu of forbidding use of their trademarked names by other addressees.[55]

On the physical addressing side, things have become equally complicated. Physical Internet addresses are 32-bit numbers, written as four groups of eight bits each, ranging from 0.0.0.0 to 255.255.255.255. Addresses were initially broken into three classes: Class A, ranging from 0.0.0.0 to 127.0.0.0; Class B, ranging from 128.0.0.0 to 191.255.0.0; and Class C, including 192.0.0.0 through 223.255.255.0. Class A represented 50 percent of the total IP host addresses, but there were only 126 Class A addresses, and their allocation had to be restricted. There were only 16,383 Class B addresses, constituting 25 percent of the total IP addresses, and these were allocated only when specific criteria had been met. Class C addresses made up a mere 12 percent of the total, but because they were relatively unrestricted, they were regularly allocated and in danger of being rapidly exhausted. It is not surprising that this happened; as Bradner puts it,

Address assignments were made assuming that the Internet world consisted of numerous small organizations containing fewer than 250 computers each (Class C networks), a smaller number of larger organizations with up to 64,000 computers each (Class B networks), and a few very large companies with up to 15 million computer each (Class A networks). Using this inefficient address assignment method, the Internet was running out of the most popular type of address assignment, Class B networks.[56]

In response, the Internet Engineering Task Force (IETF) introduced a scheme called Classless Inter-Domain Routing (CIDR) that would essentially permit the aggregation of smaller network addresses, so that organizations could have more that 250 computers but the routing tables would still contain one entry for a given organization. CIDR eliminated the need for allocations in the Class A, B, and C framework, permitting assignments of blocks in virtually any power-of-two size, and it enabled aggregation of continuous smaller blocks into one larger block for the purpose of creating routing hierarchies in which groups of lower-level net numbers are routed as a unit in upper levels of routing hierarchy.[57] This required considerable efforts to update the routing tables, but it successfully prolonged the useful life of the current addressing scheme.

As with name assignment, governance regarding numbering for the Internet has become controversial. Key concerns are how to deal with the explosion in demand for IP numbers, and strategies for handling that growth. NSI recently proposed the creation of the American Registry for Internet Numbers (ARIN) to manage IP address space for the territories NSI administers.[58] In the NIS plan, has ARIN would be a nonprofit corporation derived from the InterNIC IP group, to be initially supported by NSI and governed by trustees selected by NSI with advice from an advisory council. The key to the scheme is the establishment of membership fees for those organizations that join the registry, and registration fees for the allocation of address space to registry members. Not surprisingly, this proposal has met with considerable controversy. In addition to the difficulties always faced when imposing significant fees where none were previously required, ARIN would charge only for new allocations, thus providing an enormous benefit to incumbent address holders.

Lessons for Communications Competition

The preceding review of addressing in the telephone and Internet worlds reveals four fundamental requirements of all communications addressing:

- Atomic addresses—i.e., each address must refer to a single point of termination that may be either a physical station or a particular recipient. If there are both logical and physical addresses, each must be atomic, and the mapping between them must be unique.

- A single point of control to handle address allocation and disputes, even if the volume of addresses grows so large that instruction is delegated to regional agents.

- A properly operating and reliable infrastructure to perform routing, especially if there is both logical and physical addressing.

- Users who know how to use the addressing scheme efficiently, including workarounds and fallbacks to addressing failures.

As the previous sections suggest, there are remarkable similarities between the schemes used to handle addressing in the telephone and Internet worlds. In fact, it is striking when one looks at the diagrams of the SMS-800 scheme and the DNS scheme to realize that these highly different networks, which evolved from very different origins and for different purposes, exhibit such remarkable similarity. It is particularly interesting to note that, as far as our research has been able to discover, there was no direct connection between the social worlds of work that designed the two schemes. They appear to have evolved quite independently, without even documentary connections to join them.[59] Both the telephone and Internet addressing schemes use logical and physical addresses, and most of the complexities of the technical and socio-institutional interface from these two worlds show up in three areas: logical addresses, physical addresses, and translation and resolution. We will discuss each of these.

Logical Addresses

For many years the logical addresses of the telephone system were very close to the physical addresses. The only masking was provided by the fact that the Central Office switching system allowed a caller to dial the local seven-digit number (i.e., without the area code) to make a local call. In effect, the Central Office translated the local number into the full address by recognizing that the incoming sequence of digits could not be a long-distance call and thus, by default had to be a local call. The Central Office then matched the three-digit prefix to the list of all local prefixes, and sent the call to the appropriate central office. A step toward more separated logical addresses was the introduction of special three-digit codes that could be dialed by themselves for directory assistance (411), telephone repair service (611), and emergency service (911). But these codes were relatively simple because they merely pointed to other local telephone numbers. The introduction of 800 service changed telephone addressing fundamentally by creating the first nongeographic area code, and introducing the concept of the Service Access Code (SAC).

Three lessons arise from the 800-number experience. First, the popularity of 800-numbers has been so overwhelming that a second SAC with the same functionality (888) has been introduced to cope with the addressing requirements. While this might seem merely an extension of the practice of splitting area codes to provide for more local numbers, the issue is more complicated. Because the SAC is nongeographic, its coverage is the entire network, and to the user it is uniform in function (i.e., dialing 800 has the same effect everywhere in World Zone 1). As new SAC services such as 900 (pay per call) and 500 (universal personal communication) grow, it is likely that two fundamentally different logical addressing schemes will emerge: one tied only to geographic areas irrespective of service, and another tied only to service characteristics irrespective of geographic area. Many individuals and organizations will have more than one of each. All must be reconciled, because in the end, calls must reach discrete destinations regardless of where they originate. But because of the similarity in appearance between the logical and the physical addresses, there is great opportunity for confusion among users as to just what a given telephone number represents. This will not matter if the technical infrastructure is sufficiently robust to "black box" the relationship between logical and physical addresses, which the telephone system did very successfully for many years. However, changes in the telephone industry have weakened the powerful centripetal force of the AT&T Bell System, which was critical to maintaining the robustness of the black box, and it is not clear how this strategy will fare in the future. The Internet world, in contrast, seems to be having serious difficulty implementing its addressing structure, and controversy over naming and addressing is running at a fever pitch.[60]

A second lesson from the 800 experience is that logical addresses take on the property of proper names, and thus must be seen as much more than mere functional addresses. The deregulation of long-distance service required, for the first time, transferring the property rights inherent in the logical telephone address from the service provider to the customer—i.e., the introduction of number portability. Although the matter is not yet settled legally, there is no reason to believe that logical telephone addresses might not be bought and sold like trademarks and brand names. There is nothing particularly disturbing about this in principle—we know how to deal with such transactions. But trademarks and brand names outside of telephony do not play a functional role in the operation of huge, technically complex communications networks.

This brings us to the third lesson of the 800-number experience. As the evolution of the SMS-800 system shows, a workable regime to link both the technical and the socio-institutional components of logical addressing requires considerable technical and institutional reform. The SMS-800 reforms worked well in the comparatively small and circumscribed 800 service world. It is not clear whether or how such a strategy would work in the much larger and more complex world of local telephony. Given that competition in the local loop absolutely depends on local number portability, a solution must be found if deregulation in the local loop is to succeed. Beyond that, there is serious discussion underway about extending the SMS model directly to the N00 domains of nongeographic SACs (500, 600, 700, 900), and turning over the authority over SACs to the NANC.

Logical addressing on the Internet has always been clearly separated from physical addressing. The DNS concept of domain names using alphanumeric strings of varying lengths almost completely masks the underlying 32-bit numeric IP addresses. The DNS scheme has two clear advantages over telephone addressing. One is that logical and physical addresses are distinct by design, and thus cannot be confused with one another. Another is that domain names may be arbitrarily long, providing a huge potential supply of logical addresses. Given the confusion and address exhaustion faced by the telephone system, why not introduce something like the DNS scheme for telephony? Here, again, the path dependencies of telephony become evident: the change to alphanumeric addresses would require that all telephone users be provided with new telephone instruments incorporating keyboards or similar interfaces. Another alternative would be to simply allow telephone numbers to vary in length up to very large strings, but current switching technologies—even the advanced digital switches—were designed on the assumption of fixed address lengths. An "overlay" translator could be used to interpret what the new logical address means, but this would almost certainly introduce significant post-dial delay in routing and call completion. This is not a major issue in the Internet, but it is a serious problem in telephony.

In fact, any limit on length, no matter how long, reduces the number of available addresses to a finite set. How do we determine how big the limit will be? The current telephony scheme provided for what its developers thought was a set of addresses that far exceeded the most optimistic predictions of demand, yet we have repeatedly exhausted that supply largely due to the advent of unforeseen technologies. The simple fact is, we must make decisions now based on available information and our best guesses. Those kinds of decisions often prove to be suboptimal given what evolves later, but the infrastructure and institutional arrangements put in place as a result of those decisions carry on and shape the path of future evolution in profound ways.

One of the most fascinating examples of this problem is the difficulty faced in finding a new administrator for the NANP. The NANP, like the DNS and the InterNIC in ARPANET's administrative legacy, grew up under the protection of a powerful, rich, technically proficient, paternalistic institution that simply decided for its constituents how things would be handled. The AT&T Bell System and ARPA were institutions with sufficient status to prevail in a decision regime of "status wins." Both institutions have disappeared, and there are no institutions of sufficient stature to take their places. Despite the ordering of the NANC, it is not clear how successful the NANC will be in designing and implementing of the NANP to "impartially consider and meet the combined interests of the public user community and the entire communications sector within WZ1" so that no "segment of [the] industry should be advantaged or disadvantaged by the design or administration of the NANP."[61] The reality will be more difficult to achieve. There is no ideal solution, making the "truth wins" alternative to "status wins" unattainable. And it is not clear that the third decision principle— "majority wins"—is desirable given the complexities of the problem and the fact that the decision would have to be made by "voters" representing governments, the private sector, consumers, and other interests from 19 countries.

A sense of how difficult the issues can become is found in the Internet version of the problem presaged by vanity numbers in the 800 system. As in the telephone system, Internet addresses were originally assigned on a first come, first served basis. The DNS administrators sought to remove themselves from responsibility, claiming that in disputes between name registrants over the rights to a particular name, the "registration authority shall have no role or responsibility other than to provide the contact information to both parties," and further, that the "registration of a domain name does not have any Trademark status."[62] In fact, however, a number of lawsuits have been filed by plaintiffs holding trademarked names claiming that certain Internet addresses have infringed on those trademarks, and there has been an ongoing dispute in the Internet community over the practice of some local domain administrators who have revoked names for some users when business interests have presented documentation that they own the same or similar name as a trademark.[63]

Whatever institutional and technical resolutions to logical addressing problems might be forthcoming, there are still important problems of social learning entailed by any proposed changes. Given that addresses confer identity, it is not surprising that individuals are almost as reluctant to part with their addresses as they are to part with their names. For example, in the telephone industry it has taken up to five years to split an area code: equipment vendors have to develop equipment modifications and network operators have to implement the network and support system modifications, but most important, users must adjust to the changes that are to be made.[64] This adjustment is sometimes not easy for political reasons. For example, some years ago when New York

Telephone proposed splitting Staten Island off from New York City's 212 area code, a protest was led by the borough president who, in response to an explanation about the limited set of numbers possible under the 212 code, stated that a company as technically sophisticated as the New York Telephone Company should be able to get more than 10,000 numbers from four digits. The time required to migrate to a new master addressing scheme, say one with 15 digits, is difficult to estimate, but there is no doubt that such a change would take years, and the best guess is that it will not occur until it is absolutely necessary.[65] A much smaller challenge that still had complex effects arose from the change to area codes with any digits 0–9 in the center, which opened up hundreds of millions of new telephone numbers for use.[66] This required the retrofitting of software and sometimes hardware on hundreds of thousands of pieces of customer premise equipment, such as PBXs, that were built on the assumption of NNX. It is not clear how future changes in addressing in the telephone system will be made given the huge costs that might be imposed on distributed providers and customers to implement such a change. Under the single authority of the AT&T Bell System, and even the reduced authority of the Bellcore-run NANPA, such changes could be made even if they took a while to implement. Now it is not clear how they will be made at all. Put simply, who will have the authority to force them through if there is strong opposition from within the industry or among consumer groups?

It has been a long, slow march from the manual operation of the original telephone system to the present state. It is difficult to estimate how long it would take to migrate to a completely new Internet naming convention. The evolution of the current conventions has been highly incremental, and the number of Internet users even under the most optimistic scenarios is far below the number of telephone users, so fewer people would have to change. Nevertheless, there is every reason to believe the change would be difficult and time-consuming because of the entrenchment around the existing system in embedded infrastructure, social learning, and the establishment of property rights to certain specific addresses. Nevertheless, the rather ad hoc process by which Internet addressing evolved and the already rickety conditions under which it is being implemented suggest that continued rapid growth in Internet use will reveal problems so severe that a new logical addressing scheme will be necessary. More important, as the next section shows, the physical addressing that underlies the logical addressing of the Internet is already showing signs of strain, and this alone might compel changes in the logical addressing scheme.

Physical Addresses

The foundation of any addressing scheme lies in functional physical addressing. Both the telephone's ten-digit addresses and the Internet's original 32-bit addresses constitute finite pools of possibilities. The Internet world went to a 128-bit scheme, which greatly increased the available number pool, but this pool is also finite. When it is necessary to expand such pools, the questions arise regarding what is an appropriate replacement scheme and who decides which scheme to choose. One commonality of both existing conventions is that physical addresses are allocated with strong attention to geography. This is obvious in the telephone system, but even in the Internet world geography plays an important but not intended role through the allocation of addresses to organizations that are, in fact, geographically located in one or more locations and that provide opportunities to optimize by geographical clustering.[67] This is not surprising: geography is the oldest foundation for addressing, as shown in street addressing and telephone addressing. Geographic addressing is somewhat new to the Internet—it is now being introduced as a result of the desire to delegate allocation authority, in much the same way that the NANP delegated authority to the NPAs.[68] A new, strictly geographical IP addressing scheme might resolve some issues, but there are still problems of deciding on a reasonable string length and reaching industry consensus. Although consensus was finally reached on string length and many of the feature enhancements that will go into the next-generation IP Version 6 (IPv6), persistent problems remain regarding implementation plans and a scheme for efficient address allocation.[69]

Physical address changes are inhibited mainly by existing infrastructure, but they are also tied to the logical addressing structure, and are thus subject to problems with that structure. As logical addressing grows, the underlying physical addresses can be increasingly hidden from the end-user, making knowledge of them unnecessary. The largest obstacles to physical address changes are the time, cost, coordination, and user education efforts required to replace or upgrade the infrastructure on which physical addressing operates. Yet the need for such upgrades, and by implication a grounds for tolerating disruptions from the upgrades, will largely be hidden from end-users. It is easy to think of the Internet as similar to the telephone system, which is still governed by a legacy of protocols from the days of the AT&T Bell System monopoly. In fact, the Internet has never been more than a melange of infrastructures owned by many different entities, and the telephone infrastructure is becoming more like the Internet all the time. The simple fact that there are many possible routing paths ignites conflict about whose paths are to be used for what purposes, under what conditions, and according to what terms for payment, security, and so on. These issues are already contentious on the Internet, and are likely to become more so as the volume of traffic and cost of handling it increase. In the telephone system, increased confusion is the likely short-term result of an ever more competitive and deregulated industry.

An interesting legacy of both the AT&T Bell System and Internet cultures is the quaint assumption that competing parties in the network want to cooperate with one another. This assumption is based on two factors. First, there is the goal of universal service, which requires a significant amount of cooperation to achieve coordination and interoperability. As long as everyone wants universal service, this cooperation is ensured at least to some degree. The other is the long experience of individuals from the AT&T Bell System and Internet worlds of living in comfortable, paternalistic institutional environments from which they have recently been ejected. In the new, competitive worlds of telephony and the Internet, addressing decisions are likely to be dramatically affected by property rights. For example, although the Internet is often thought of in terms of a single, open network, it is actually a conglomeration of thousands of private networks. The altruistic vision of universal service would suggest that the structure of all networks should be available to all network administrators, to ensure smooth operation across the whole network of networks. In fact, the structure of proprietary networks is proprietary information, and even now it is virtually impossible to create a "map" of Internet topology of the sort one can easily find for the telephone system because one cannot get the information to do so.[70] The success of the Internet's infrastructure depends solely on each network's compliance with the common protocol, but there is no way to enforce such compliance or even to determine whether the networks are in compliance except indirectly by monitoring traffic going into or coming out of them. Another interesting example is found in the growing popularity of cellular telephony, which requires widespread deployment of cellular stations. Each station is a critical infrastructural component in the physical addressing scheme, and one must have sufficient, well-located stations to achieve both radio coverage and channel capacity. However, locating these stations is difficult given that some people do not want a cellular station on or near their property.

Address Translation

Any addressing regime that depends on logical and physical addresses requires a translation capability to link the logical to the physical addresses. The telephone system has evolved a relatively efficient translation scheme in which large numbers of executed logical addresses are identical to their physical addresses (e.g., a full ten-digit call with the required "1" prefix is a full physical address), and vanity numbers (e.g., 1-800-FLOWERS) are translated by the user into a string of digits using the telephone keypad, which contains the alphanumeric assignments on the faces of the keys. Control over the master addressing scheme has been maintained centrally, but because the deployed infrastructure of physical addresses and the social conventions for use of logical addresses were so rigid and predictable, actual final address allocation was left to the NPA level. The appearance of the SACs and number portability drastically changes this situation, however, by separating the logical and physical addresses. The result is a centralization-decentralization conflict. On one hand, the integrity of the master addressing scheme, which is essential to overall operations, requires centralized control. On the other hand, the proprietary ownership of the infrastructure by multiple, competing parties suggests considerable diversity that might conflict with the centralized authority.

The Internet, by contrast, has been quite decentralized in operation for a long time. The conversion to a distributed database was essential because there was no organizational structure within the ARPANET world (in contrast to the world of AT&T Bell System) to provide centralized control. However, decentralized operation created problems due to local mistakes in local domain configuration that led to error propagation.[71] Distribution of the database presumes the cooperation of local administrators and diligence in carrying out tasks, but problems occur through inadvertent slips, blatant carelessness, and other mishaps. It is virtually impossible for the network-wide coordinators to supervise the work of the many domain administrators, and as a result, the Internet addressing function is far less reliable than that of the telephone system. Another interesting problem with the decentralization of the DNS operation is linked to the black boxing of the system. It is easy within the current system for a user to trigger an excessive number of queries in order to get one response without even knowing a problem is being created. This creates a huge amount of excess traffic on the Internet. It is estimated that the DNS consumes about 20 times more bandwidth than it should due to deficient resolver and name server implementations on every kind of computer, from all over the world.[72] With a small number of users such excess traffic could go unnoticed, but the rapid growth of the Internet makes it likely that excess traffic will be generated more often and will become increasingly annoying as congestion rises.

Conclusion

The Internet and telephone addressing schemes evolved independent of one another, yet they share many features and problems. We believe that a close study of the issues related to communications addressing provides a powerful perspective for developing an understanding of fundamental operational challenges in both telephone and Internet services. This is desirable because, to all

appearances, the two worlds are increasingly being drawn together. The Internet already runs upon elements of the telephony
infrastructure, from dial-up lines that link PCs to ISPs, to the trunks
of the IXCs that carry backhaul traffic. Equally important, the
service provision worlds that serve both telephony and the Internet
are on a collision course as the barriers separating LECs, IXCs,
cable television providers, ISPs, and so forth come down. The
whole purpose of deregulation is to allow everyone to play in every
market, and it seems highly likely that a large number of conflicts
and disputes will arise. The disputes within the telephone industry
over interpretation of the 1996 Telecommunications Act and the
FCC's implementation of it illustrate these problems. The FCC
sparked the ire of the state telephone regulatory establishment by
attempting to set fee ranges for incumbent LECs which must
provide access to competitive LECs, raising many questions about
where jurisdiction over such matters should reside.[73] The implementation of the universal service provision clauses of the act are
also controversial because it is not clear what should be included in
the basic service package.[74] We have already seen the incumbent
LECs complaining that the telephone service structure is unfairly
subsidizing ISPs, and others have argued that use of the Internet
over the telephone infrastructure is interfering with telephone
service.[75] It is not absurd to argue that the Internet is a part of the
telephone system, at least with respect to the fundamental transmission features of the network.

More intriguing is the argument that telephony and the Internet
will merge because the Internet will swallow telephony. Already
there is the prospect of "Internet telephony," in which the use of
special hardware and software on an Internet-linked computer
allows a user to open duplex voice channels to similarly equipped
Internet users at other locations. The spread of this technology has
already caused some financial analysts to declare that telephone
companies are financially threatened by this development.[76] It is
also interesting to note that the IAHC's proposal for a new TLD
scheme suggests adoption of the ITU World Zone telephone
numbering scheme, thus moving the addressing of the Internet
toward geographic addressing along the telephone model.[77] Thus,
one could argue that in the technical, administrative, and gover-

nance dimensions the Internet will absorb and subordinate the telephone world. As intriguing as this speculation might be, it is highly improbable that the Internet could subsume, much less handle, anything near the scale of the existing telephony infrastructure, particularly since that infrastructure carries most of the Internet's traffic. Nevertheless, this development suggests why the continuing blending of telephone and Internet form and functionality calls for more penetrating assessment of the challenges of communications under competition. A focus on addressing provides a special window into the technical and socio-institutional problems at the heart of this transition.

It is noteworthy that the long separation between the addressing communities in the telephone and Internet worlds might be ending. As noted earlier, the IAHC has proposed adoption of the ITU World Zone scheme for the basis of a new set of Internet TLDs. The NANC has taken under consideration the prospect of the creation of a new generic TLD called .num, which would allow assignments to Internet users of Internet addresses based on their in-service, assigned telephone number.[78] Such a scheme would require at least a set of mechanisms whereby Internet numbering authorities could verify in-service telephone numbers, but it raises questions about the fundamental link between telephone and Internet addressing. Perhaps most interesting, in late 1996 SAIC, a major defense contracting firm, announced plans to purchase Bellcore. As noted earlier, Bellcore served as NANPA and remains the residual repository of much of the intellectual and technical knowledge behind the NANP and its administration.[79] The proposed merger prompted concern because SAIC owns Network Solutions, Inc., which runs the registration functions of InterNIC, the central authority for Internet address assignment. Both Bellcore and NSI had been accused by critics of having too much power in the allocation of critical addresses in communications services. Suddenly, it appeared, one company might own both Bellcore and NSI, and thus have control over addressing in both worlds. In some ways, such a merger would make technocratic sense: the telephone and Internet worlds are being pulled together, and perhaps a uniform governance and administrative structure for addressing in both worlds would be helpful. However, placing such power in the hands of a single entity is disturbing to those who believe in greater decentralization and competition in all aspects of the communications world. Whatever the outcome, the peculiar combination of attraction and anxiety at the very prospect of such an occurrence illustrates the ways in which addressing is critically tied to the future of communications competition.

Ultimately, the fundamental technical driver of addressing is that Top Level Domains of any addressing scheme must be under the authority of a single, superordinate power if the network is to be globally effective. There is no way to avoid this. The problem facing the architects of the new, competitive, global information infrastructure is how to create this single, superordinate power in a manner that holds the respect and compliance of all the subordinate participants in the networks under its control. As Baer notes, the global information infrastructure concept faces a basic dilemma in reconciling transnational forces and national regulatory regimes.[80] At present, the global telephone addressing system remains under fairly effective control of a hierarchy rising up through the layers of formerly monopolistic service providers to regional authority structures, such as the NANPA in World Zone 1, and ultimately to the authority of the ITU. However, as we have noted, the long-term character of this hierarchy is open to speculation. In the case of the Internet, the center that gave birth to the DNS and guided its use for a decade is clearly weakening in the face of the radical changes in Internet use and control brought about by the growth in the network's popularity and, in particular, by the rise of commercial users as dominant forces. There are many areas of uncertainty regarding the future of communications competition, but few are so fundamental in origin or far-reaching in implication as the rudimentary issue of addressing.

Acknowledgments

The authors wish to thank David Niklaus for his essential assistance in the area of telephone addressing, and Paul Mockapetris for his assistance in the area of Internet addressing. We thank the many others we interviewed in the course of this research who choose to remain nameless. The authors are responsible for all errors and omissions.

Notes

1. The term "communications" can be used in many ways. We use it in this chapter to refer to interactive communications that take place over electronic channels. We include the telephone system as used in support of real-time voice communications (dyadic and conference calls), the telephone system as used in asynchronous voice communication through voice mail and answering machines, the complex of technologies used to provide digital data communications linking computer systems together, and the computer technologies linked together in networks that enable so-called computer-mediated communication in the form of computer conferencing, computer video conferencing, file transfers, electronic mail, World Wide Web services, and so on. Although related, we do not explicitly include video conferencing.

2. General background for these assertions can be found in P.A. David, *Technical Choice, Innovation and Economic Growth* (Cambridge: Cambridge University Press, 1975), and in P.A. David, "Clio and the Economics of QWERTY," *American Economic Review* 75, No. 2 (1985): 332–337. For a broader discussion of the relationship between technical change and institutional order, see John Leslie King, Vijay Gurbaxani, Kenneth L. Kraemer, F. Warren McFarlan, C.S. Yap, and K.S. Raman, "Institutional Factors in Information Technology Innovation," *Information Systems Research* 5, No. 2 (July 1994): 139–169.

3. Horrocks and R.W.A. Scarr, *Future Trends in Telecommunications* (New York: John Wiley & Sons, 1993): 394.

4. The word "address" comes from the conjunction of the Latin *ad* to the Middle French *dresser*, itself derived originally from the Latin *disagere*, meaning to lead straight. The transitive verb "to address" therefore derives from something close to "the act of leading straight." An archaic use of the word "address" means to direct, to aim, to send, to make ready. In time, the term evolved an elaborated set of meanings along these lines (to get ready, to put on clothes, to speak to a group, to give instruction), as well as into a noun involving the process or object implied by such actions (the name of an article of clothing, the text of the speech given, the destination to which someone is directed to go, the location at which someone or something can be found). See *Webster's Third International Dictionary of the American Language.*

5. The toll-free 800 number scheme has been augmented by the addition of the 888 service access code. In the rest of this chapter we refer to both the 800 and the 888 toll-free access structure as simply the 800 system.

6. *North American Numbering Plan Administrator's Proposal on the Future of Numbering in World Zone 1,* Second Edition (Morristown, NJ: Bellcore, 1993).

7. Ibid.

8. There was a long period of time when local calls could be completed by dialing only a four-digit number because the Central Office (CO) used a single prefix, and an incoming four-digit number not preceded by a 1 would by default be

destined for a called party served by the CO. Similarly, it was customary in many calling areas to dial a 1 prior to the seven-digit "local" number to indicate that the call was a toll call not covered under the fixed-price service area. It has been proposed that all WZ1 users move to routine use of the full ten-digit number.

9. As an example, a 36-digit string must be dialed to call the authors' voice mail boxes from the Netherlands using the AT&T service USA-Direct.

10. We use the term "ubiquitous service" to refer to what is often implemented under the more specific and institutionally complicated term "universal service."

11. Claude S. Fischer, *America Calling: A Social History of the Telephone to 1940* (Berkeley, CA: University of California Press, 1992): 37.

12. John Brooks, *Telephone: The First Hundred Years* (New York: Harper & Row, 1976): 150–159.

13. Fischer, *America Calling*: 51.

14. Ibid.

15. Interview at the FCC headquarters, Washington, DC; name withheld on request.

16. The 1996 telecommunications reforms require that the FCC and the state regulators overhaul universal service provisions. At present a portion of Inter-eXchange Carrier (IXC) access charges plus special fees collected by Local Exchange Carriers (LECs) go into the Universal Service Fund, which is used to subsidize high-cost service areas to ensure that prices for service in those areas are within about 20 percent of average for other service areas. There is agreement that "universal service" means tone dialing and 911 service, but there is great controversy over whether it means Internet access. The actual costs of providing local service are difficult to ascertain because the LECs guard the data in anticipation of local loop competition and the competitive advantages of cost-based pricing information in a competitive market.

17. Fischer, *America Calling*: 51.

18. Steve Coll, *The Deal of the Century: The Breakup of AT&T* (New York: Athenaeum, 1986): 58.

19. Brooks, *Telephone*: 299.

20. Coll, *The Deal of the Century*: 104.

21. As of 1996 there were about 14,000 LECs and 400 IXCs in the United States.

22. Considerable information regarding the NANP can be found on the Bellcore WWW site <www.bellcore.com>.

23. Shipley, "Nation-Wide Dialing," *Bell Laboratories Record* (October 1945): 368. We are told in personal correspondence with Henry Fagin that a principal force behind this strategy was Chester I. Bernard, an AT&T executive who also is well known for his writings in the management field. Fagin reports that Bernard recognized that the long-term future of the telephone system required turning the customer into the operator.

24. Ibid.: 369.

25. *North American Numbering Plan Administrator's Proposal on the Future of Numbering in World Zone 1*: 5.

26. Ibid.

27. See Appendix IV: "Ensuring the portability of telephone numbers poses a challenge," in General Accounting Office, *Information Superhighway: An Overview of Technology Challenges* (Washington, DC: General Accounting Office report GAO/AIMD-95-23, January 1995).

28. There are actually three kinds of number portability issues. One is service provider portability, in which the customer keeps the number in order to move freely from one provider to another in a competitive market. Another is service portability, in which a customer uses one number (or address, more broadly) across several different kinds of communications services (e.g., land line, cellular, Internet). The third is location portability, which frees the customer from geographic addressing and allows regional or global "roaming" using the same number. We concentrate in this section and most of the rest of this chapter on service provider portability, but the other issues are equally important to the larger story.

29. The 800 prefix thus became the first nongeographic Service Access Code (SAC).

30. A LATA is a Local Access and Transport Area, a geographic service area defined in the MFJ that restricted LEC operations to within, but not between, LATAs. Long-distance service within a LATA was provided by the LEC, while service between LATAs was provided by an IXC.

31. Dave Powell, "Signaling System 7: The Brains Behind ISDN," *Networking Management* 10, No. 4 (March 1992): 36–40.

32. From Russell Travis, *Signaling System #7* (New York: McGraw-Hill, 1995): 21.

33. The NASC also provides technical and user support to 800 service subscribers, and provides training in the use of the system for those subscribers who do not conduct their own training.

34. General Accounting Office, Appendix IV: "Ensuring the portability of telephone numbers poses a challenge."

35. *North American Numbering Plan Administrator's Proposal on the Future of Numbering in World Zone 1* (January 4, 1993): 6. Note that under the 1996 Telecommunications Act the FCC was given plenary jurisdiction over numbering only in the United States, but as a practical matter, the other countries of World Zone 1 have gone along with the FCC's decisions after discussion of any problems that have arisen.

36. Ibid.

37. In addition to the governance problems, the basic challenges in implementing local number portability are significant. Rubin notes that the estimates for the costs of nationwide number portability in the United States range between

U.S. $2 billion and 16 billion, and the technical, managerial, and social learning difficulties are considerable. Paul Rubin, "Take a Number . . . Any Number," *tele.com* (an electronic publication of McGraw-Hill) (1996) <www.tele.com>. There is some experience with number portability in various countries, including the United Kingdom, Australia, and Hong Kong, in addition to the United States; the experiences to date suggest major challenges in the establishment of charging schemes to distribute the costs for number portability. See Cutler and Company, "Foreign Country Experience of Number Portability" (Melbourne, Australia: Cutler and Company, 1996).

38. A complete history of the Internet is not workable or necessary here. The institutional history of the Internet enterprise can be found in J.L. King, R. Grinter, and J. Pickering, "The Rise and Fall of Netville: The Saga of a Cyberspace Construction Boomtown in the Great Divide," in S. Kiesler, ed., *The Culture of the Internet* (New York: Erlbaum, 1997); a detailed analysis of the origins of the Internet is found in J. Abbate, "From ARPANET to Internet: A History of ARPA-Sponsored Computer Networks, 1966–1988," unpublished doctoral dissertation, University of Pennsylvania, 1994; an interesting colloquial account is V. Cerf, "How The Internet Came To Be" (interviewed by Bernard Aboba), *Internaut Magazine* (1993). A good general source for watching the evolving controversy over numbering is the Alliance for Telecommunications Industry Solutions (ATIS), which maintains an Industry Numbering Committee as one of its active groups <www.atis.org>.

39. Moreau, *The Computer Comes of Age: The People, the Hardware, and the Software* (Cambridge, Mass.: MIT Press, 1984).

40. Irwin Lebow, *Information Highways and Byways: From the Telegraph to the 21st Century* (New York: IEEE Press, 1995): 177.

41. Ibid.: 181–182.

42. Ibid.: 190.

43. Ibid.: 191.

44. King, Grinter, and Pickering, "The Rise And Fall of Netville."

45. Jon Postel, "Domain Name System Implementation Schedule," Request for Comment (RFC) 897, Information Sciences Institute (ISI), February 1984.

46. Mockapetris, "Domain Names—Concepts and Facilities," RFC 882, November 1983. See updates RFC 1034 and RFC 1035.

47. Jon Postel, "Domain Name System Structure and Delegation," RFC 1591, ISI, March 1994.

48. This figure and description are based on P. Mockapetris, "Varian: The Domain Naming System (DNS) and Internet Naming Directory Services" (1996): 25–27.

49. King, Grinter, and Pickering, "The Rise and Fall of Netville."

50. Solicitation for Network Information Services Manager, NSF92-94 (Washington, D.C.: National Science Foundation, March 1992).

51. See <rs.internic.net>.

52. See <www.alternic.net>.

53. See <www.iahc.org>.

54. *Evolving Internet Infrastructure,* (The Cook Report): 157–188.

55. See International Ad Hoc Committee, "Draft Specifications for Administration and Management of gTLDs" (Washington, D.C.: IAHC, December 19, 1996), <www.iahc.org>.

56. Scott O. Bradner and Allison Mankin, eds., *IPng: Internet Protocol Next Generation* (Reading, Mass.: Addison-Wesley, 1996): 4.

57. This description comes via personal correspondence with Paul Mockapetris.

58. See <rs.internic.net>.

59. The authors will be grateful for any insight that can be provided on influences of the telephone addressing world on the Internet addressing world, or vice versa.

60. See, for example, Ed Foster, "Prehistoric Systems Crossed with Centralized Control Create InterNIC Chaos," *Infoworld,* January 13, 1997: 58.

61. *North American Numbering Plan Administrator's Proposal on the Future of Numbering in World Zone 1,* Second Edition, January 4, 1993.

62. Jon Postel, "Domain Name System Structure and Delegation," RFC 1591, ISI, March 1994.

63. These reports have been circulating mainly in various Internet news groups and distribution lists.

64. *NANP Expansion Report,* Draft 4, June 1, 1995.

65. *North American Numbering Plan Administrator's Proposal on the Future of Numbering in World Zone 1,* Second Edition, January 4, 1993.

66. This switch removed the requirement that the middle digit of area codes be restricted to 0 or 1, permitting any digit to be used.

67. Internet addressing has not been done according to geography, as telephone addressing has, but it has been suggested that a solution to some Internet addressing problems would be to move toward a geographic scheme.

68. Gerich, "Guidelines for Management of IP Address Space," RFC 1466, Network Working Group, May 1993.

69. A significant contribution toward deciding on the new string length was something called the "H ratio," proposed by Christian Huitema, which describes the limited efficiency of address allocation procedures. H = log(number of addresses)/number of bits. In perfect address allocation one bit would number two hosts, while ten bits would number 1024 hosts. The value of H was determined by finding saturation points in address allocation in other networks and working backward. The H ratio varies between 0.22 and 0.26. The French telephone system moved from eight to nine digits when the number of tele-

phone numbers reached 10^7, which produced an H ratio of 0.26. The U.S. telephone system added area codes when subscriptions reached 10^8, and produced an H ratio of 0.24. SITA, the international network supporting airline information systems, expanded its seven-character address with 64,000 addressed points and reached an H ratio of 0.14, but SITA represents an extreme case because it uses fixed-length tokens in its hierarchy. DECnet, with 16-bit addresses, stopped growing at 15,000 nodes, for an H ratio of 0.26.

70. We received this information via an Internet posting written by Steve G. Steinberg, an editor at *Wired Magazine* (steve@wired.com).

71. Romao, "Tools for DNS Debugging," RFC 1713, FCCN, November 1994.

72. Ibid.

73. The access fee question reflects the complexities involved in developing a new governance structure for a world in transition from one regime to another. The crux of the issue is the problem of finding out exactly what local telephone service provision costs and then apportioning those costs fairly among the various service providers through pricing schemes. As an example of just one issue in the controversy, some argue that the fees assessed the new competitors for access to the existing network should be based on the costs of whole installed base rather than on just the incremental costs of adding new competitors to that installed base.

74. The question of whether Internet service should be included in the basic package is one major issue raised by those who are concerned that access to the Internet will soon become essential to full citizen participation in the economy and society. Brian Kahin, "The U.S. National Information Infrastructure Initiative: The Market, the Web, and the Virtual Project," in Brian Kahin and Ernest Wilson, ed., *National Information Infrastructure Initiatives: Vision and Policy Design* (Cambridge, Mass.: MIT Press, 1997): 179.

75. Bell Atlantic has conducted a major study that, it claims, demonstrates conclusively that ISPs benefit at Bell Atlantic's expense under the current tariff structure. The report is available at <http://www.ba.com>.

76. The London stock brokerage firm Durlacher has made such a claim. See *Financial Times,* January 15, 1996: 6.

77. International Ad Hoc Committee, "Draft Specifications for Administration and Management of gTLDs" (Washington D.C.: IAHC, December 19, 1996).

78. Schultz, "Creation of and Registration in the "NUM" Top Level Domain" (Network Working Group, August 1996).

79. See <www.bellcore.com> and <www.saic.com>, which as of January 1997, carried detailed information regarding the proposed merger.

80. Walter Baer, "Will the Global Information Infrastructure Need Transnational (or Any) Governance?" In Brian Kahin and Ernest Wilson, eds., *National Information Infrastructure Initiatives: Vision and Policy Design* (Cambridge, Mass.: MIT Press, 1997): 532–552.

In Whose Domain?: Name Service in Adolescence

Don Mitchell, Scott Bradner, and K Claffy

"When you read RFC 1, you walked away from it with a sense of, 'Oh, this is a club that I can play in too . . . . It has rules, but it welcomes other members as long as the members are aware of those rules.'"
—Brian Reid[1]

The Problem

The Internet grew from a small research experiment to the huge global enterprise it is today in a relatively closed and protected environment whose cultural ethics were based on cooperation and collegiality, and where bureaucracy was minimal. Such an environment allowed its participants to handle many things informally with strategies like placing important responsibilities in trusted hands, like those of Jon Postel who almost singlehandedly serves as the Internet Assigned Numbers Authority (IANA). The pro bono provision of the root domain servers is another example. It is no accident that the only record of operational "rules" for the Internet are called Requests for Comments (RFCs), which were originally intended for communal discussion among interested parties until they reached "rough consensus and running code."[2] However, its incredible growth has rendered the Internet important enough to the (commercial) world that we can no longer rely on this protected environment to shelter its existence and preserve its cultural ethic. If the Internet community wants to preserve the culture and customs upon which it has thrived, we must find ways to institutionalize them, both legally and operationally. Only by doing so can we enable our collaborative and collegial culture to survive in an environment that is ever more adversarial and competitive.

Further, if the Internet community wants to preserve the present culture and mechanisms, what we will call its underlying intellectual infrastructure, these mechanisms must become economically self-sufficient. The National Science Foundation (NSF) decision to require Network Solutions, Inc. (NSI), to impose fees for registration of second level domain names within the international Top Level Domains (iTLDs) was an emergency "patch" on a financial crisis in domain name registration services. It was decidedly not an articulation of long-term policy or approval of the status quo. Nonetheless, many in the community seem completely unable to separate this action from the larger issue of how to move the Internet to an operational mode of self-sufficiency. Tactical responses have taken precedence over a strategy for arriving at rough community consensus concerning which segments of the intellectual infrastructure to preserve and which funding mechanisms should be used to secure their future.

Historically, U.S. federal government support of the intellectual infrastructure effectively separated operational from governance or policy activities in the Internet community mindset. For instance, much of the community has now accepted the need to pay for Internet connectivity, but fails to understand that the U.S. government also supported development of the protocols and policies that frame the provision of that connectivity, and that their continued evolution will be necessary to facilitate sustained scalability. Thus, as the U.S. government withdraws support from the provision of visible operational services (e.g., NSFNET or domain name registration services), there is little appreciation of the fact that they still finance a majority of the invisible (to the end-user) infrastructure underlying Internet services.

The Challenge

Under the auspices of a cooperative agreement with the U.S. National Science Foundation, since March 1993 Network Solutions, Incorporated (NSI), has managed the registration of Internet Top Level Domains and second level domain names within a few special existing top level domains (e.g., .*com*, .*net*, .*org*). This agreement has fostered the continued rapid expansion of the Internet, but this growth has not come without a cost. Indeed, the explosion in registration requests inevitably stressed the existing institutions and procedures, which were neither self-sustaining nor officially (legally) recognized either nationally or internationally. In September 1995, in response to nearly two orders of magnitude of growth in demand over a 30-month period, NSI, at the NSF's request, began charging a registration fee of $50 per domain per year. An emergency measure to solve an immediate critical funding problem, this action made no attempt to establish longer-term policies for supporting Internet registration. Indeed, the NSF has no official position on specific issues beyond the actions it has already taken. Its intention is to follow the recommendations of the September 1994 IEEE workshop on .com domain name registration[3] and the November 1994 InterNIC performance review panel[4] that NSF extricate itself from Internet registration activity.

The NSF and other U.S. federal agencies also provide support for other core Internet functions (e.g., IANA and the Internet Engineering Task Force [IETF] Secretariat). The Internet has grown beyond any possibility of supporting its operational components as either an experiment or a service unique to the U.S. government and academic research and education communities. Furthermore, although there is recognition of and appreciation for the prominent role of the U.S. government in Internet evolution thus far, a more international scope has clearly emerged, and government funding for such critical activities as the IANA and IETF is becoming inappropriate. The U.S. government has already begun to withdraw support for such activities; it is clear that only some form of governance balanced among and representing the interests of governments, providers, vendors, operators, users, and academia will be viable in the long term.

Just as the NSF had to withdraw from providing production-level backbone services, for the good of the taxpayer as well as the long-term vitality of the industry, the NSF and other U.S. federal agencies must now gradually withdraw support for Internet registration and other core administrative functions. To relinquish support for this intellectual infrastructure carefully, with minimal disruption to the community, the NSF critically depends on the

Internet community to develop mechanisms for full recovery of direct and indirect costs associated with the administrative functions of the Internet. If the community can reach consensus in the next few months on a long-term strategy to cultivate the continued growth and health of the Internet, it will forestall the possibility that communities outside the traditional Internet may feel compelled to impose their solutions on what they perceive as its problems.

Registration Services and the Intellectual Infrastructure

Much of the current discussion of the intellectual infrastructure of the Internet is distorted by a focus on the least challenging aspects of its ad hoc governance structure. The apparently sudden privatization of the domain name registration services currently provided by the InterNIC has caught many by surprise, and served as a catalyst for those dissatisfied with any number of administrative aspects of the Internet.

Commentators range from anarchists who do not believe in any form of central organization or support of the Internet to those who see the requirement for unique domain names as a potential revenue source, either for civic purposes such as expanding community access, or for private profit.

In reality, the registration of domain names is only peripheral to major unresolved issues. Fixating on the domain name registration will only exacerbate finding solutions to more fundamental difficulties. Indeed, the whole issue of the Domain Name System (DNS) will greatly depreciate with an inevitable movement toward universal directory services. But other issues—vital support functions required to continue development and operation of the Internet— will remain. In addition, the community has not yet addressed the question of who should set rules, coordinate processes, and arbitrate resolutions in this most international of systems. No one has even formulated a process for determining what functions are fundamental to Internet operations.

The community's volatile reaction to the imposition of DNS registration fees by the InterNIC has distorted the discourse. The most modest proposals to have users of the Internet help pay for some of the intellectual infrastructure have encountered charges of unconstitutional imposition of taxes. The shortsightedness of those who rely on a functioning Internet to ascertain how to keep the Internet working and growing in the future is astonishing if not depressing, particularly since questions surrounding definition and support of the Internet intellectual infrastructure are still in very early, exploratory stages. The success of the haphazard growth of the Internet has been nothing short of stunning, but a careful examination of the structures, relationships, and responsibilities of the evolving Internet, of which the DNS is only a single component, is long overdue.

These strong reactions to the InterNIC's action also neglect the international scope of the Internet, now of fundamental importance to political and economic health in a growing part of the world. Discussions of changes in Internet structure or processes must occur in an international context, and with the understanding and acceptance of existing regulatory authorities. Otherwise those authorities will see the actions as a threat to the stability of an increasingly critical infrastructure in their countries, and will take active measures to secure that stability.

Registration Services

The single critical ingredient to participating in the Internet is obtaining an Internet Protocol (IP) address, which is essentially a number used to identify and route to a given destination.

In the interests of routing table efficiency, most Internet users obtain their IP addresses from their Internet Service Providers (ISPs), which in turn obtain their IP addresses from either their upstream ISPs or a central registry. Limitations imposed by current technology on the total number of IP addresses available and the supportable size of routing tables render centralized registration the most reasonable approach to managing this limited resource. Although users do not currently have to pay the IANA or the InterNIC directly for IP address registration, the function must be supported; indeed, part of the NSI fees for registering domain names in the iTLDs currently help defray the costs of registration of IP addresses, as well as autonomous system numbers, which we will not cover here.

Less critical to Internet participation but in a far brighter spotlight is the issue of domain name registration. We do not discuss the history of the domain name system[5] or domain name specifications[6]; we refer interested parties to the relevant documents. In simplest terms, the Domain Name System establishes an association of a domain name (ASCII character string) with an IP address of a particular machine. Domain names provide a convenient addressing mechanism for people and machines to identify resources without having to remember long strings of numbers. Registration of the mapping between domain name and IP address confers no ownership or legal rights to the name beyond establishing this relationship for Internet addressing purposes.

Conceptually, the Domain Name System is hierarchical, with one of the top levels of the hierarchy depicted in the last suffix of a fully qualified domain name, and each suffix toward the left representing a level lower in the hierarchy. Note that, outside of the United States, Internet registrations typically use the two-letter country codes defined by the International Standards Organization (ISO) as the set of top level domains, allowing for a geographically based naming hierarchy at the root level. Within the Unites States, however, largely as a historical anachronism related to the fact that the United States housed the first segments of the Internet, the use of three-letter (nongeographically based) iTLDs predominates.

In addition to IP address and autonomous system registration, other administrative services also rely on a portion of the $50 annual fee for domain name registration in the iTLDs to defray their costs, in particular the administration of the .us domain and the cost of some of the root domain servers. Additionally, 30 percent of collected fees go into an interest-bearing account designated for support of portions of the intellectual infrastructure that U.S. federal agencies have historically supported.

Because the imposition of domain name registration fees represented a visible change from the previous government-supported model, tremendous discussion is now taking place over how to "fix the domain name problem." No clear consensus has yet emerged and we do not intend here to add to the current cacophony. Presently on the table are approaches that recommend:

• rapidly creating more iTLDs (which we believe will likely cause a flood of litigation and lead inevitably to restrictive regulation by national regulatory authorities);

- phasing out the use of the existing iTLDs and placing the domains currently registered under the existing iTLDs under the two-letter country code TLDs;

- placing the two-letter country code TLDs under the iTLDs; and

- adding new TLDs to denote appropriate areas or fields for purposes of intellectual property or trademark/service mark considerations.

Although we admit finding only the second of the above solutions amenable to an international context with existing regulatory authorities, we emphasize that we do not intend in this chapter to make any specific recommendation for resolution of the domain name problem. The most important point we want to leave with the reader is a caution that solutions to this immediate "problem" that exacerbate the larger issues will not be helpful to the Internet community.

In the Long Run: Domain Name System versus a Directory System

Domain names serve two distinct purposes. As mentioned above, they are used as a "handle" for users to specify a particular computer. A domain name server supports database queries to map these handles to the corresponding IP address and insert that address into the packets that comprise the data stream sent to that computer. The second use is one that was not originally envisioned: domain names have fallen into the role of a rudimentary directory system. Rather than looking up the name of a specific computer in a directory, the way one uses a phone book, users tend to assume that the domain name itself is strongly related to a company name or service offering. The problem with this assumption is that company and service names are far from unique, even in a local context and far less so on the global Internet. Many companies can conceivably have the same name. In other environments one differentiates among these companies by the geographic locality or field in which they do business, e.g., an Olympic Pizza shop in Cambridge, Massachusetts, is not likely to be confused with a similarly named establishment in Seattle, Washington, or Athens, Greece, nor is the coexistence of Apple Records and Apple Computer a problem. But the Internet is not bounded by geography or line of business. A domain name of *olympic-pizza.com* does not tell the user where the shop is (or its delivery area), nor does *apple.com* inform the user the associated company's line of business. The advent of the Hyper Text Transport Protocol (HTTP) protocol has acutely exacerbated the situation since it uses the DNS to find Internet sites on the World Wide Web, resulting suddenly in an immense perceived value of mnemonic domain names, and leading to a number of bitter disputes over specific desirable domain names.

We believe that the reliance on the DNS for a directory service only indicates our desperate need for a real directory service; it does not prove that the DNS should be that service. We also believe that facilitating the use of the DNS as a directory service is the wrong goal and that the Internet needs a universal directory system to continue to move forward.

Several factors complicate the development of such a directory service. First, an Internet directory service must support both interactive and noninteractive modes, to support browsing as well as batch processing (e.g., sending to an email list). Business cards, for example, would do best with resolvable addresses that are relatively easy to remember; a digit string is less than ideal. A second inhibiting factor to Internet directory service deployment is the fact that a several-year-old effort in this very task has created some community distaste for the idea. Although based on detailed investigation of requirements for an international, network-based, universal directory system, the ISO X.500 directory system, relying on Distinguished Names (as best exemplified in X.400 email addresses), has received widespread criticism for being overly complex and resulting in addresses much too long to be usable by the general Internet user population. Nonetheless, the underlying tenet of this system seems inescapable: it is not realistic to rely on names themselves to provide sufficient information to differentiate multiple entities with the same name. One must add some way of incorporating categorization information along with the entity name. The categories might include geographical, type of enterprise, or type of service information, but in any case entity names by themselves are not sufficient.

We believe a reexamination of the requirements for a universal directory system is in order, specifically with an eye toward ease of use by those from a wide range of technical backgrounds. Until we have such a directory system for this exploding infrastructure, we will continue to overload functionality onto the DNS with increasingly frustrating results.

Possible Models for Infrastructure Support

We strongly believe that the Internet community must identify the portions of the intellectual infrastructure it deems critical to preserve, and then pursue agreement on the appropriate models for sustaining these functions. We identify three alternative approaches to achieving a self-sustaining model for the IANA and other parts of the intellectual infrastructure of the Internet as the U.S. government withdraws its support:

• *Laissez-faire.* Each individual registration activity would pay for itself. Achieve by having multiple registries for addresses, ASNs, domain names, routing information—all of which would charge for service. These registries, to which would accrue de facto authority, could somehow coordinate their activities to avoid contention or possible duplication. This approach would avoid the question of how to support infrastructure costs not directly related to individual registration services, but would still allow for robust commercial registration activity.

• *Patronage.* Interested parties would volunteer support to portions of the intellectual infrastructure germane to their interests. Under such a model, registries might support a registration guild or the current IANA as a self-governing body; ISPs and router/switch manufacturers might be willing to support a routing/switching guild to facilitate uniform routing and switching policies; and equipment or other companies with an interest in the adoption of particular standards might support groups in those areas (e.g., the ATM Forum). The disadvantage of this model is that it could allow powerful interests with large installed bases of a particular technology to skew standards development to slow the introduction of new technologies and allow them to amortize installed equipment over the longest possible period. However, it would avoid direct charges to those not directly interested in a particular standard.

• *Democratic/taxation.* Those most likely to have an interest in the decision-making and governance processes would be charged. Commercial or other entities with an active Internet presence would pay a tax on some registration or another fee. This would allow those dependent on the Internet for financial or intellectual well-being to be visible participants in directly supporting the policy groups that influence future operational conditions. However, it would incur visible and possibly contentious costs to large numbers of individuals and organizations that have a stake but no interest in the decisions of policy-making groups.

It is also possible, of course, to use some combination of the above or to apply different models to different portions of the infrastructure.

The Internet community prides itself on its anarchic nature. Withdrawal of U.S. government support and authority for its intellectual infrastructure will render inadequate the boundaries that have isolated and protected that anarchy. The community must create new authorities and/or coalesce around globally credible institutions of governance, and determine and establish mechanisms most likely to insure the long-term viability of these institutions. And all of this must occur quickly. We fear, and thus caution the community, that there is much truth to the old adage that those who are unable to govern themselves will be governed by others.

We see a critical need to institutionalize the IANA function as quickly as possible, both to relieve the enormous pressures on Jon Postel and to insure continuity. We stress that there is absolutely no implication that anyone other than Jon should lead the effort. Rather, the concerns are that he and the IANA staff should have more help, and that a small secretariat should exist to formalize and document the decisions he makes so that they can be used as legal precedents in the future when this becomes necessary.

The Internet community should at the same time be identifying other portions of the infrastructure critical to Internet governance and policy, and also be working to build a strong consensus on an optimal model for insuring their sustainability.

Organizational Issues

It is difficult to identify any existing organization as ideal to assume responsibility for the tasks outlined here. Numerous discussions have revealed a reasonably strong consensus among knowledgeable participants that such an organization is needed, but this agreement breaks down at the level of particulars. Some believe that no existing organization is up to the task, others disagree. Unfortunately the latter typically nominate an established organization in which their own capacity is other than that of a disinterested observer.

The Internet is a new phenomenon, not amenable to regulatory processes developed over the years to guide traditional communications infrastructure. Much underlying Internet technology derives from the open and deliberative working group process of the Internet Engineering Task Force, where standards are not developed by majority vote, but rather by persuasion and consensus building. Those with expertise, the necessary background, and solid arguments are likely to convince their working group on the best technical solution to a given problem (especially if the common interest is simply in developing a solution that works). This process has largely facilitated the selection of the best technology for many aspects of Internet operations, but it proves less effective when discussing policy instead of technology since it permits anyone, even someone without an understanding of the relevant issues, to voice an opinion and even dominate a discussion.

It is necessary that any group attempting to address the underlying issues of governance and sustainability of the Internet should be globally credible and include representation from major stakeholders, including vendors, network operators, technology developers, governments, academia, content providers, and traditional regulatory authorities, all on an international scale. The group must hold Internet stability and growth as primary goals, avoid doing harm to the larger community in the interests of solving parochial problems, and, whenever possible, adopt solutions that adhere to the existing standards and generally accepted practices of the international communities involved.

Conclusion

For the reader who wishes to leave this chapter with a clear understanding of its major conclusions, they may be stated bluntly.

1. The future of the Domain Name System is essentially irrelevant to strategic issues of Internet governance and sustainability.

2. The DNS is almost equally irrelevant to the tactical issue of resource location on the Internet.

3. Domain names, including iTLDs, are simply a flawed handle for grappling with either of these larger issues.

Although there is obviously some benefit to a reasonably architectured naming system, even the best solution will prove insufficiently scalable to handle the Internet's projected growth if it continues at anything approaching the current rates. It is not just the indefinite scaling of the DNS as a resource location tool that is technically unworkable. It is also that the legal conflicts inherent between this informal and local system now adopted for global use and the hierarchy of established national and international laws are severe. We should accept the DNS for what it is: an artifact designed to serve a colloquial system that was in no way scalable, and insufficiently compatible with trademark and other intellectual property law (anywhere) to permit its perpetuation in the current evolving environment. We view attempts to force it to shoulder this functionality as misguided.

In the longer run, only a well-designed and implemented directory system will be effective for locating people and resources on a vastly expanded Internet. As such we find it unsettling that the DNS issue is receiving disproportionate attention since it is the wrong tool to solve the lack-of-directory-service problem. Further, it is at best unhelpful, and most likely destructive, to delineate the DNS as a central focus in discussions of the future of Internet governance and sustainability, to which we believe it is largely irrelevant.

As with other facets of technology in society, solving the social issues is frequently harder than solving the technical issues. The Internet is a stunning example; even entire fields of law and public policy may ultimately prove inapplicable to a cybersphere. As we see an inevitable trend to a point where most human exchange will be virtual rather than physical, there is sure to be a wide variety of systemic stresses, and we may have no choice but to simply unlearn some notions that have tied infrastructure together in the past. It is wiser to work from the assumption that a larger social context will, and should, frame Internet governance, which will in turn be eventually incorporated back into the Internet architecture. DNS is hardly a sufficient lever to effect global societal change, and obsession with this issue will create more problems than it solves.

The opinions expressed in this chapter are those of the authors themselves and do not reflect any opinions held by their respective organizations.

Notes

1. Brian Reid quoted by Katie Hafner in *Where Wizards Stay Up Late* (New York: Simon & Schuster, 1996): 144.

2. Coined by Dave Clark of MIT.

3. <gopher://ds0.internic.net/11/nsf/cise/>.

4. <http://www.rs.internic.net/nsf/review/review-toc.html>.

5. Mockapetris, Paul. 1987. Domain Names—Concepts and Facilities, RFC 1034.

6. Mockapetris, Paul. 1987. Domain Names—Implementation and Specification, RFC 1035.

Network Numbers

Financial Incentives for Route Aggregation and Efficient Address Utilization in the Internet

Yakov Rekhter, Paul Resnick, and Steven M. Bellovin

Introduction

Growth of the Internet is limited both by the availability of Internet Protocol (IP) addresses and by the capacity of routers. Several interventions can relax these limitations. New routing protocols can expand the pool of available addresses. New technology can improve the capacity of routers. Organizations can give up unused addresses and they can renumber their computers (assign them new addresses) in a way that reduces the burden on routers. None of these interventions, however, is cost-free.

Internet growth results from the actions of many independent decision-makers whose perceptions of individual costs may not reflect the global impact of their actions. The most effective way to induce socially responsible behavior is to introduce financial incentives that make global effects visible to individual decision-makers. Where a trade-off must be made between conflicting goals, financial incentives will permit local decisions that take into account local differences, thus leading to better choices than could be made by any centralized administrative body. This chapter presents a framework for property rights and contracts so that prices for addresses and route advertisements can arise through natural market forces, without the need for a global authority or tax collector.

Growth While Minimizing Resource Utilization

When a new host computer joins the Internet, it needs full connectivity and an unambiguous address. That is, from every existing host there must be at least one path by which packets can travel to the new host. At each step along each of those paths, a router examines the host's address and forwards packets to the correct next hop.

There are two limits, then, on growth. First, there must be an unambiguous address available for each new host. In particular, the IP address used by the new host should never be simultaneously used by any other host. There is a limited number of addresses, determined by the length of an address. The current IP address length is 32 bits, implying that 2^{32} (approximately four billion) addresses are available. Second, each router must maintain a table that indicates the correct next hop for each destination address, and routers have a limited amount of the fast, expensive memory needed to store entries in the forwarding table.

New protocols and technology can expand these limits. For example, dynamic address allocation and Network Address Translators[1] permit reuse of addresses in some circumstances and Internet Protocol version 6 (IPv6)[2] has longer, and thus more, addresses. At least in principle, routers with more memory could keep track of extra routes. Protocol changes and additional technology, however, are costly and not always available when needed. The technology growth curve may also be unable to keep up with the growth of the Internet. Sometimes it will be either cost-effective or just necessary to make more efficient use of existing resources instead.

Hierarchical route aggregation[3] is one way to make more efficient use of existing resources. In particular, if all packets destined for addresses with the same prefix get forwarded to the same next hop, a router can maintain just one entry in its router table for that prefix, rather than a separate entry for each individual address. This method can be applied recursively to create larger and larger address blocks that share shorter and shorter prefixes.

Hierarchical route aggregation is widely used on the Internet today and was the main motivation behind Classless Inter-Domain Routing (CIDR).[4] Hierarchical aggregation only works, however, if traffic destined to all the addresses covered by a particular address prefix should be routed to the same next hop. Thus, the assign-

Original
Allocation

Final Allocation

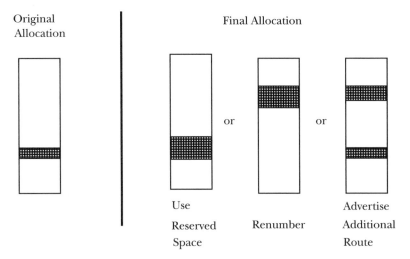

or

or

Use

Reserved   Renumber
Space

Advertise

Additional
Route

Figure 1   Three Ways to Accommodate Growth. Each vertical block represents the entire address space; the small rectangles represent address space used by a particular organization. The first two methods allow advertisement of an aggregate route because the addresses used are contiguous.

ment of addresses to hosts must follow the connection topology of the network in order for hierarchical aggregation to be successful.

Even when address assignments match connection topology sufficiently at one point in time, it is hard to keep them aligned. Difficulties arise both from networks that grow and shrink, and from changes in network topology that occur when customers switch providers or peering arrangements change.

Consider first a growth scenario. An organization initially has some hosts to connect, but at a later time may need to connect an as yet unknown number of additional hosts. There are three ways to handle this, as shown in Figure 1 and described below.

The first method assigns the block of addresses but, in anticipation of future needs, reserves spare addresses with the same prefix. When the reserved addresses are eventually used, they all can be routed as a single aggregate. For example, the current practice of RIPE NCC, the European address registry, is to allocate a 19-bit address prefix to a new Internet Service Provider (ISP), but to reserve the companion 19-bit address prefix so that it can also be given to that ISP in the future, thus creating a single 18-bit address prefix that can all be routed to the same destination. However, this may waste addresses if the ISP never needs the reserved addresses, or it may not completely solve the problem if, alternatively, the ISP eventually needs more addresses than those that have been reserved.

In the second approach, when additional addresses are needed, the existing hosts are renumbered into a larger block that accommodates both the existing and additional hosts. The cost of renumbering the existing hosts, however, may be quite high. In many organizations, this requires manual entry of a new address in each host, and administrators may no longer remember how to enter addresses for hosts such as printers that have been running successfully for years. Horror stories abound of networks shut down for hours or even days during a changeover.

In the third method, when additional addresses are needed, they are allocated separately and an extra route is advertised. This is a common practice, but it imposes a cost on the organizations that must carry the additional route.

The best choice among the three growth options will depend on time-varying and local circumstances. If addresses are plentiful, the inefficient address space utilization of the first method may be acceptable. If renumbering costs are low, the second may be appropriate. If routers are not overloaded, the last method may be fine.

Consider also how to accommodate changes in network topology. In particular, suppose that an organization switches Internet providers. If the organization keeps the same addresses (such addresses are called "portable"), then the new provider will have to announce a separate route for those addresses, as shown in Figure 2. However, switching to addresses that the new provider can easily aggregate requires renumbering existing hosts. Again, the best choice will involve trade-offs between the costs of handling an additional route throughout the Internet and the costs of renumbering.

Distributed Decision-Making

To complicate things further, the Internet consists of many independent participants (e.g., providers, subscribers). The self-inter-

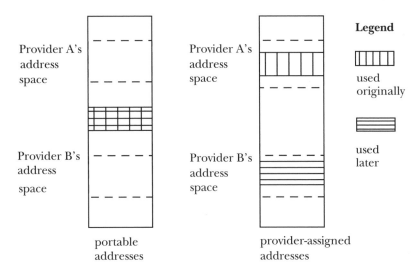

Provider A's address space

Provider A's address space

Provider B's address space

Provider B's address space

portable addresses

provider-assigned addresses

Legend

used originally

used later

Figure 2 Portable Addresses Avoid Renumbering but Complicate Routing.

est of these participants may not always align with the interests of the Internet as a whole. In the growth scenario, the costs of reserving address space accrue to others who are not able to use those addresses, and the costs of additional routes are borne by routers throughout the network. The costs of renumbering, however, are borne locally. This creates an incentive for a decision-maker, acting in its own local self-interest, either to reserve lots of addresses or to advertise additional routes, rather than renumber. Similarly, portable addresses impose a cost on the rest of the Internet, but are attractive to a subscriber because they reduce the local cost of renumbering.

The "spirit of cooperation" is often invoked when self-interest does not align with the larger interest. It calls on everyone to cooperate with each other and do whatever is necessary "for the good of the Internet." This appeal to altruism has been remarkably effective so far: that the Internet is still operational is largely due to the spirit of cooperation.

It would be unwise, however, to rely solely on this spirit, especially as the Internet grows larger and anonymous commercial ties replace the personal ties that bound network operators together in the old days. In a competitive environment, moreover, organizations that place the common interest ahead of their own self-interest will be at a disadvantage.

Sometimes rules, or policies, can align individual behavior with the common good despite a misalignment of interests. While reliance on policies solves some of the problems associated with the spirit of cooperation, it introduces its own set of problems.

To begin with, it is becoming more difficult to agree on policies as the Internet grows. There is no clear chain of authority for dictating policies. Consensus-based processes move slowly and may result in weak policies that are not effective.

Second, policies are difficult to enforce. Even where there are well-recognized authorities, as with the address registries today, they may not have sufficient resources to investigate whether individual entities are following the rules. For example, it is difficult for a registry to verify whether addresses are used for the purposes stated by the organization that requested them. Authorities may also lack coercive powers to punish rule violations even when they are detected.

A final problem with policies is that it is difficult to make them reflect the heterogeneity of the Internet. A policy about advertising aggregate routes that is appropriate for organizations with low renumbering costs may not be appropriate for those with higher costs. Similarly, a blanket policy determining the number of addresses to allocate to a new provider does not take into account the likely growth of the provider, while an allocation policy that takes into account business plans requires sophisticated, and sometimes subjective, decision-making rules.

Alternatively, financial incentives can align individual self-interest with the global interest. In the scenarios described above, an organization would reserve addresses or advertise additional routes only when its own benefits outweighed the global costs. As an added feature, the money collected could compensate those entities that actually bear the costs.

Decisions based on financial incentives will naturally take into account local and time-varying factors. If there are charges both for addresses and for advertisement of routes, organizations will trade off these costs against their own costs of renumbering. Since the cost of renumbering will vary among organizations, different organizations will make different trade-offs. If the charges for route advertisements and addresses change over time, reflecting changes in scarcity, this may cause organizations to make different trade-offs.

Charging for Route Advertisements

The primary goal of introducing charging for route advertisement is to limit the number of routes within the Internet routing system while still maintaining full IP connectivity. To put it differently, the goal is to propagate each route to as few domains as possible while maintaining connectivity among as many domains as possible.

In order to understand the framework for charging, it is helpful to understand how routing information is disseminated on the Internet. In particular, it is helpful to distinguish between the distribution of routing information that is necessary to provide connectivity, and routing information that results in improved connectivity (i.e., better paths). Figure 3 illustrates both types of route distribution.

Route "push" occurs when one provider knows a path to some destination and offers to neighboring providers to forward transit traffic to that destination. Each of the neighbors can carry on the process by pushing the route to its neighbors. This is the natural way to expand the region of hosts with connectivity to a destination. In the context of hierarchical routing, a route has to be pushed only until it is aggregated with other routes whose destination addresses share a common prefix. In the worst case the route may never be aggregated and will have to be pushed to every provider in the default-free zone of the Internet.[5]

Route "pull" occurs when a provider chooses to use a better route to a destination than the route that was pushed to it, in effect asking other providers along the new route to provide transit service. Thus, route pull is not necessary to provide connectivity. A pull route might reflect private peer-to-peer connections between two ISPs, or even between two end-users. If one provider pulls a route from the other, it can use that private connection for such traffic instead of sending it via the possibly slower route that the data would otherwise take. The decision on when to pull a route is

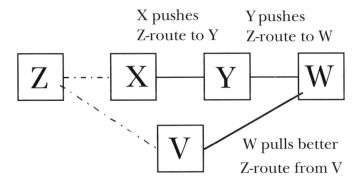

Figure 3 Dissemination of Routes. X has a path to Z and pushes it to its neighbor Y, which pushes it on to W. But W may also choose to pull a better route to Z from V.

influenced by the trade-offs between path optimality and the possibly increased volume of routing information if the pull involves disaggregating a large block of addresses that has been pushed as a single route.

Use of Bilateral Agreements

Both route push and pull cause resources to be consumed at providers all along a route: at every hop, a router needs to record the route advertisement in the forwarding table, and to forward packets. Yet it is only the endpoints of the route that benefit from the connectivity. Moreover, choices that the endpoints make, such as using addresses that permit route aggregation, or requesting the pull of optimal paths, influence the amount of resources consumed at the transit points. One possibility would be to devise charges whereby the endpoints directly compensate all the transit providers. Such a scheme, however, would not scale well, as it could involve settlements between every pair of providers on the Internet, even those which do not exchange packets directly.

Instead, route dissemination (and hence financial charges) can be realized as a composition of bilateral agreements between directly connected organizations. Such agreements can be made between providers and subscribers or between peers. As described below, composition (including subcontracting) of bilateral agreements enables extension of the scope of "push" or "pull" beyond those who are directly connected. Each organization, however, need only negotiate and settle charges with those organizations directly connected to it. This follows the principle of "edge pricing."[6]

The Push Contract. Suppose X has a route to Z, as shown in Figure 3. For X to push the route to another provider Y (directly connected to X), X and Y would sign a "contract" of the form, "I, Y, promise that the following providers: _____, will be able to reach destination Z by sending traffic to me (Y), which I will forward to X." Typically, Y will fulfill its promise by subcontracting with its neighbors to further push the route.

The Pull Contract. Suppose V has a route to Z. For a provider W (directly connected to V) to pull a route from V, W and V would sign a "contract" of the form, "I, V, promise to forward traffic from W to Z via the following sequence of providers: _____." This would require a bilateral agreement between V and the first organization in the sequence, which would then subcontract with the next organization in the sequence, etc.

When an organization Y contracts to accept traffic from another organization X (through either a push or pull contract), the routing information controls the destinations X can reach through Y. This would impact the amount of traffic Y would receive from X. For example, X could push to Y just one route stating that it accepts traffic for all destinations (a default route), but that could result in X carrying a lot of transit traffic.

Both the sign and magnitude of payments accompanying a contract are open to negotiation. Since a contract would involve X adding an entry to its router forwarding table and Y agreeing to carry transit traffic, the settlement payment could flow in either direction, depending on which party most wants the agreement. One typical scenario would involve a subscriber paying a provider to push its route to the entire Internet. The provider would then disburse some of that money to its neighbors when it subcontracted with them to push the route. The recursive subcontracting provides a mechanism to disburse the subscriber's payment among all the providers who kept track of the subscriber's route and carried transit traffic to the subscriber.

Interaction with Hierarchical Routing

Any time routes to two or more sets of destinations are aggregated, a neighboring provider that accepts a push of the aggregated route will need to keep only one entry in its forwarding table. If memory in the forwarding table is scarce, as it is today in many Internet routers, the charge for pushing an aggregate route will be smaller than the combined charges for pushing the separate components. This will create a natural incentive for aggregating routes.

Interaction with Address Portability

Recall the scenario of a subscriber switching providers and considering whether to renumber to addresses in the new provider's pool or whether to keep the old addresses. Renumbering to the new provider's pool would permit the new provider to push the subscriber's route as part of an aggregate. Keeping the old addresses would force the provider to push a separate route. If router table space is scarce, the provider would have to pay extra for pushing a separate route, and would presumably pass this cost on to the subscriber in some form. One likely outcome is that subscribers who accept provider-based addressing will pay less than they do today, while those who use portable addresses and advertise additional routes will pay more than they do today. The optimal choice still will depend on local factors (such as the cost of renumbering for that subscriber), but the subscriber will take into account the costs imposed on the rest of the Internet.

Charging for Addresses

While charging for route advertisement may motivate address assignment that is suitable for aggregation, it does little or nothing to produce efficient address space utilization. Separate charges for addresses would motivate organizations not to reserve too many addresses for future growth and to transfer addresses that were no longer needed.

Transferable Address Ownership Policy

Currently there are two address allocation policies for the Internet, portable and nonportable ("address ownership" and "address lending" in the terms of RFC 2008.)[7] Portable addresses are acquired directly from Internet Registries, including InterNIC, RIPE NCC (for Europe), and APNIC (for the Asia Pacific region). When an organization acquires portable addresses, it can keep the addresses when switching providers, as illustrated in Figure 2. They are not, however, transferable to another organization. The only officially sanctioned transfer is to return an address to the registry that initially allocated it.

A second policy, address lending, covers nonportable addresses. Under this policy, Internet Service Providers lend addresses to their subscribers, but the transfers are temporary and are coupled with connectivity between the provider and its subscribers. That is, the provider lends addresses to a subscriber as part of a contract to provide routing to the rest of the Internet.

Neither of these policies is ideal for introducing charges for addresses. The registries could impose a tax on portable addresses,[8] but there would be no market forces operating to discover the appropriate level of charges. Charges are a natural part of the service contract when a provider lends addresses to a subscriber, but then when a subscriber changes its provider, it has no way to trade off the costs of renumbering against additional routing costs that come with address portability.

A third policy, "transferable ownership," is needed, which would combine the best features of both policies. It would add transferability to the portable address policy: an organization could give away, barter, or sell addresses that it owned. It would add portability and indefinite duration to the lending of nonportable addresses: a subscriber could keep its addresses when switching providers.

If addresses were scarce, it is likely that money would change hands in compensation for address transfers, but no central authority need decree a price. The monetary value of addresses would create a natural incentive for minimizing their use. An organization that could, at some inconvenience, get by with fewer addresses, might choose to sell some, depending on the level of inconvenience and the going price. An organization that wanted to reserve addresses for planned future growth would be able to do so, but only if it were willing to pay for the addresses, thus compensating the organization that gave them up.

If, however, addresses were not scarce, perhaps because of a transition to IPv6, the market price might drop nearly to zero. In that case, there would be no incentive for conservation, but without scarcity there would also be no reason for conservation.

Scope of Ownership

Transferable address ownership is defined with respect to a particular set of organizations (what we call a "club") that honors the ownership right. Ownership of an address implies exclusive use of that number as a destination address for routing within the club. Ownership does not imply that data packets bearing that address will be routed to a host owned by the address owner, merely that data will not be routed anywhere else. In essence, the property right results in unique address assignment within the club.

An operational definition of the address property right can be expressed in terms of a database consisting of ownership deeds for blocks of IP addresses. The club is defined as the set of organizations that agree to respect the database entries, refusing to route data (within the club) destined for a particular address except as authorized to do so by the owner of the address.

The most interesting club, of course, is the "public Internet," operationally defined as those organizations that respect the current NIC databases of address registrations. There appears to be great value in having a single Internet club, so that networks everywhere can be interconnected. Private intranets, however, would be free to form their own clubs and reuse the same IP numbers used in the public Internet. Clubs could even be interconnected using Application Layer Gateways or Network Address Translators (NATs).[9]

Note that this description of the property right immediately makes clear that no entity can exert control of the IPv4 address space without the cooperation of the ISPs that form the club. If, for example, the U.S. government claimed that it owned the IPv4 address space[10] and tried to raise revenue by auctioning it off, ISPs could simply agree en masse to form a new club with its own address allocation mechanisms.

Address Ownership without Connectivity

A transferable address ownership policy would decouple address ownership rights from actual connectivity. Owning a (transferable) address without having global routability might have what economists call "option value." That is, there would be value in having the option of global routing some time in the future. For example, this would permit an organization to change its style of firewall, making formerly hidden hosts visible to the Internet, without incurring the cost of renumbering.

Interactions with Hierarchical Routing

The market price of address blocks is likely to be influenced by route charges. In particular, a large block of addresses that can be aggregated into a single prefix is likely to sell for more than an equivalent number of addresses that do not share a common prefix because it will be cheaper to contract for routing of the large block than the collection of smaller blocks. In fact, the mere prospect of future route charges or the prospect of some providers refusing to route to small address blocks may be sufficient to create an immediate price premium for larger address blocks.

Address Ownership Registry

If addresses are to be owned by individual parties, it is necessary to have some way to ascertain who owns—and has the right to have routed—each address. At present, registries already maintain databases of allocations; transferability merely requires a method of updating the database when an allocation is transferred. The registry database could list a cryptographic public key with each address block; all change requests would be signed by the corresponding private key, thus ensuring that the current owner authorized the transfer. Transaction types would include rekeying, to allow for ownership changes; additionally, address blocks could be subdivided, in which case a new public key would be specified for each new block. If desired, change requests could even be accompanied by anonymous digital cash payments, to reimburse the registry for its administrative overhead.

Dangers of Hoarding

One danger in any market is the accumulation of power by one or a few players who corner the supply of a scarce resource and artificially inflate its price. While theoretically possible, this is unlikely to happen in the market for IPv4 addresses. There is a natural ceiling on the price that anyone can charge, which is determined by the cost of alternative technologies. In particular, higher prices for addresses would spur the use of NAT boxes and IPv6.

Conclusion

The current routing and addressing situation on the Internet is inadequate to support continuous growth. Space in router tables and unallocated IPv4 addresses are scarce enough to have prompted conservation measures already, but these measures are unlikely to be sufficient because the problem is a tragedy of the commons: individuals benefit from consuming these resources without directly bearing the costs. Transferable property rights to addresses and bilateral routing contracts can make the costs of common resource depletion visible to individual decision-makers. The appropriate level of charges will emerge naturally in the marketplace, based on demand and the degree of resource scarcity. Pricing will not suddenly make free resources costly; it will merely expose the hidden costs, so as to encourage conservation.

Acknowledgment

We would like to thank Noel Chiappa, David Conrad, John Curran, Mike O'Dell, Sean Doran, Peter Ford, Geoff Huston, Tony Li, Peter Lothberg, Bill Manning, Daniel Karrenberg, Andrew Partan, and

Hal Varian for useful discussions and critiques of the ideas presented in this chapter.

Notes

1. P. Francis and K. Egevang, The IP Network Address Translator (NAT), Request for Comments 1631 (1994).

2. S. Deering and R. Hinden, Internet Protocol, Version 6 (Ipv6), Request for Comments 1883 (1996).

3. L. Kleinrock and K. Farouk, "Hierarchical Routing for Large Networks," *Computer Networks* 1 (1977).

4. Y. Rekhter and T. Li, An Architecture for IP Address Allocation with CIDR, Request for Comments 1518 (1993); V. Fuller, T. Li, J. Yu, and K. Varadhan, Classless Inter-Domain Routing (CIDR): An Address Assignment and Aggregation Strategy, Request for Comments 1519 (1993).

5. The default-free zone of the Internet is the maximal set of interconnected routers that do not advertise default routes to or accept default routes from each other. Advertising a default route expresses a willingness to carry transit traffic to any destination on the Internet. For example, a provider typically advertises a default route to its subscribers. Thus, the subscribers would not be part of the default-free zone, though the provider might be.

6. S. Shenker, D. Clark, D. Estrin, and S. Herzog, "Pricing in Computer Networks: Reshaping the Research Agenda," *Telecommunications Policy* 20(3) (1996).

7. Y. Rekhter, and T. Li, Implications of Various Address Allocation Policies for Internet Routing, Request for Comments 2008 (1996).

8. G. Huston, Management of Internet Address Space, Request for Comments 1744 (1994).

9. Francis and Egevang, RFC 1631.

10. Because of the U.S. military origins of the ARPANET, the U.S. government does lay claim to the address space, though it rarely attempts to exert control. (See, for example, <http://ksgwww.harvard.edu/iip/fnc.html>).

Address Administration in IPv6

Eric Hoffman and K Claffy

"Humans have not inhabited Cyberspace long enough or in sufficient diversity to have developed a Social Contract which conforms to the strange new conditions of that world. Laws developed prior to consensus usually serve the already established few who can get them passed and not society as a whole."
—John Perry Barlow

Introduction

As the Internet begins to enter the popular scope, portending large-scale changes in how society will operate, important questions of fairness and responsibility have emerged regarding several aspects of the base Internet architecture.

These questions are many, and all have cumbersome legal, financial, and cultural ramifications. We focus here on only one: the addressing model. Addresses are the technical cornerstone of the Internet's ability to move data from sender to any connected receiver. The shape of the address space ultimately determines the effective scalability and constrains the financial model of the network. We contrast two models of address assignment, provider- and geography-based, expanding on Tsuchiya's analysis,[1] and explore their ramifications.

One difficulty in discussing address space is that although its effective use is essential for the technical feasibility of Internet operation, the ownership of address space and the responsibility for justifying its use remain ill-defined. There are several revealing analogies in other spheres, e.g., spectrum assignment and international telephony. Like spectrum bands, Internet Protocol (IP) address space is a finite and contended resource that requires careful assignment and management. We note also that it has been, and continues to be, particularly challenging for regulatory bodies to create and enforce equitable and consistent policies for spectrum allocation.

Internet addressing policy must be constructed out of a careful balance among:

- service requirements of end-users;
- base technology of the network;
- cost-effectiveness of service provision;
- ability of providers to regain infrastructure costs; and
- use of the Internet as a technology as fundamental to society as a the phone system.

Although the Internet Engineering Task Force (IETF) has entertained discussion of addressing policy that has included all of the above issues, the Internet has reached a stage of maturity and breadth of scope that require wider debate of these issues.

Addressing and Routing

Routing in the Internet requires network elements to proactively exchange information concerning reachability to sites on the Internet. Each of these sites is described by an *address*, much as a phone number or street address describes a location in its respective network. Information about how to reach any destination in a given part of the network is referred to as a *route*. These routes are summarized into a table, which the switching element in the center of the network, the *router*, uses to decide which output interface to use for each arriving packet.

The two most performance-critical tasks for the Internet router are processing routing updates and consulting this forwarding table on a per-packet basis.

The costs of memory to store both the routing and forwarding tables, and the processing power needed to update and consult them, place economic constraints on table size. These processing costs are becoming dominant as the backbone routing table size grows and other components such as high-speed line interfaces become cheaper. One other important design factor is that as interfaces become higher speed, routing systems have increasingly less time to make a forwarding decision for each packet.

Rather than maintaining information about each attached host in the forwarding tables of backbone routers, routers can summarize, or *aggregate*, reachability information. *Aggregation allows the Internet to scale.* The basic form of aggregation, collecting groups of hosts into subnets, collapses routing information for the hosts within the subnet into a single route describing reachability to the entire subnet. This base level of aggregation has become insufficient for reducing the size of routing tables in the backbone, and the operational Internet is now trying to aggregate further, by collapse routing entries into larger blocks of contiguous addresses with the same reachability.

Aggregation minimizes the amount of information exchanged among routing elements in the Internet, which is generally considered helpful to promote scalability. However, this loss of information can hinder systems that use such distinctions to implement routing policy. *Routing policy* generally refers to the ability to steer traffic based on external constraints, such as those reflecting specific mission-oriented networks or transit contracts.

Provider-Based Addressing

In the early 1990s, an extrapolation of exponential address allocation trends thus far predicted two catastrophes: a depletion of usable address space around the year 2000, and an explosion in the size of routing tables beyond what current technology would be able to accommodate.

The grim nature of the prediction sparked the development of a next-generation IP protocol (IPng) with a larger address space. But because it was clear that the situation would become unmanageable before IPng deployment, the IETF also undertook a short-term measure: closer examination of address allocation policy and usage. IETF working groups, including the Address Lifetime Expectancy (ALE) group, proposed Classless Inter-Domain Routing (CIDR)[2] as a more sensible address allocation scheme that would mitigate the growth in backbone routing table size.

Although the CIDR proposal originally only made allocation more flexible by eliminating rules about which sized address blocks could be allocated, it soon became synonymous with a form of aggregation called *provider-based.*

Provider-based addressing curtails routing table growth through address aggregation: coalescing multiple routes from different organizations that are connected to the Internet through the same provider into a single route table entry. In order to accomplish this, control over parts of the address space is given to providers, who in turn allow customers with connectivity through them to use contiguous regions of addresses based on need.

Development of the next generation Internet Protocol version 6 (IPv6) has occurred in parallel to these efforts to slow the Internet protocol version 4 (IPv4) routing growth. IPv6 simplifies and rationalizes the forwarding semantics of earlier versions (IPv4), but the primary motivation for its development was its larger addresses. With enough space to address some 10^{38} interfaces, proper address space management would allow the space to last humanity quite a long time.

However, the ability to address so many nodes is not the same as the ability to route to them, and it seemed natural to start allocating the IPv6 address space in a manner consistent with the best existing practices.

Provider-based addressing for IPv6[3] uses prefixes of variable size, just as in IPv4, to give providers blocks of an appropriate size given their usage patterns (see Figure 1). Since service providers depend on their ability to number customers, this decision concerning who qualifies for blocks and what sizes they should be granted is one of the most difficult issues involved with provider-based addressing today.

Assuming users of the network nestled properly under the large aggregation blocks of their providers, hierarchical aggregation would insure that the routing system at the top level was as terse as possible. Proper address management under this scheme would insure that the curve relating total number of attached hosts to

FP	Registry	Provider	Site	Intra-site
bytes: 1	Variable Length			

Figure 1 Provider-Based Addressing Hierarchy.

backbone routing table size would be as flat as possible. This growth would hopefully remain within the ability of routers with increasingly better technology to manage routing tables of that size.

Renumbering

Renumbering is a term used to describe the changing of addresses of the hosts in a network. Sites sometimes renumber in order to reorganize internal network topology, but it is most often the case that renumbering results from changing providers or requesting a larger address block from the current provider. Because changing the network address of nodes involves reconfiguring nodes, services, and routing systems, sites generally prefer to avoid paying the administrative cost of renumbering. Since provider-based addressing assigns addresses out of larger provider blocks, sites have a strong disincentive to change providers. This situation can substantially hinder free competition, not only by making it less likely that a customer will continually seek better valued service, but also by making providers that can offer relatively stable larger address blocks much more attractive to customers.

IPv6 efforts have focused considerable attention on making renumbering as automatic as possible.[4] However, renumbering equipment in the current Internet still imposes a significant burden on even small organizations. Furthermore, many Internet applications still use host addresses as unique identifying keys; such applications range from transient sessions such as Transmission Control Protocol (TCP) connections, to globally cached information such as Domain Name System (DNS) mappings, to near permanent relationships such as tunnel endpoints and Network News Transport Protocol (NNTP) and (AFS) configurations.

Although such applications could use DNS records in place of IP addresses for these functions, software designers have preferred to avoid reliance on the DNS since transient DNS failures are quite common. Currently DNS itself requires manual configuration of server address information in the forward direction, and an external registry to handle changes in the reverse direction.

Efforts to alleviate the renumbering burden have primarily focused on mechanisms to facilitate the assignment of arbitrary addresses to end systems, but another alternative, Network Address Translators (NATs), has also received attention. IPv6 itself has rules for dealing with multiple sets of addresses associated with an interface, primarily for phasing out old sets of addresses in deference to new prefixes. While these mechanisms can somewhat automate a transition, it is clear that without serious changes to hosts and application semantics, renumbering will never be fully transparent. Ultimately, the degree of transparency will determine the perceived customer cost of changing providers; if renumbering is sufficiently disruptive, provider-based addressing will seriously damage the purity of competition in the Internet service market.

Individual customer renumbering is not the worst case. Singly homed resellers of Internet service, i.e., those fully dependent on a parent provider for transit service, bear a compounded risk. Current provider-based schemes, including Request for Comments (RFC) 1887,[5] allow service providers their own address blocks, but this policy will be unsustainable as the number of leaf providers grows enough to inhibit routing scalability. Continued growth will inevitably involve *recursive aggregation*, resulting in singly homed smaller providers using address space allocated from the blocks of their parent providers. If such a smaller provider needed to change transit providers for business or legal reasons, it would have to impose renumbering on every one of its customers.

Settlements for Route Propagation

In order to insure that the networks they serve will be universally reachable from the Internet, providers must arrange with one another for propagation of their routes through the system. Carrying transit routes incurs a load on provider infrastructure, and there is as yet no direct financial incentive to control the number of routes one announces. Unabated growth in routable entities with no feedback mechanism to control their proliferation has threatened the ability of current backbone routers to maintain the necessary routing tables. In order to limit routing table size and promote aggregation, at least one provider has already resorted to imposing a lower limit on the size of route blocks that it will announce.

Rekhter, Resnick, and Bellovin, in their chapter, propose creating a market around route advertisements, so that closed loop economic feedback can balance between the global costs of route maintenance and the selfish desire to consume large amounts of address space rather than renumber. In the limit, this scheme requires that settlements to carry individual routes occur on a contractual basis.

Internet reachability to prefixes increasingly involves contractual and legal relationships that stretch far beyond the customer and immediate provider. Although providers need some mechanism to recover transit costs, whether usage-based or flat-rate, it is far less clear that their reachability should be subject to second-order business dynamics over which customers have no control.

Furthermore, although the economic ramifications of Internet access outside the major industrialized states is still slight, it is naive to assume they will remain so as more and more countries and businesses rely more fully on electronic information exchange. Although any provider-based addressing scheme will probably involve allocating blocks to countries for local administration, control over route propagation will likely still fall under the control of a set of multinational contractual relationships. Considerable debate over this concern in the context of the current IPv4 provider-based addressing policy has already occurred.[6]

Multihoming

Multihomed sites attach to more than one provider, as shown in Figure 5. Sites multihome to enhance network reachability or to connect to task-specific (e.g., research) networks.

Multihoming has traditionally complicated provider-based aggregation, since by definition multihomed sites do not fit neatly underneath a single aggregate prefix of a parent provider. To multihome in the current Internet, a site must get its own Autonomous System Number (ASN) in order to advertise its own reachability directly into a default-free, or core, routing table.

The extent to which this is a problem depends on how many sites require this level of multiprovider connectivity. Multihoming is not supported well by the provider-based model since it requires that customers peer directly with providers, something which providers are only willing to support for sites with enough experience and responsibility to manage wide area routing. It is not an option available to everyone.

The Metro Addressing Scheme

One alternative approach to provider-based addressing uses network address prefixes that correspond to major metropolitan areas.[7] These area prefixes are allocated underneath country prefixes to facilitate aggregation at country boundaries when possible. Sites on the Internet are assigned addresses out of the metropolitan region to which they belong, and all such sites are aggregated outside of that region for purposes of routing abstraction.

Because routers outside a metropolitan region by definition cannot distinguish among reachability to individual sites within a metro, the metro addressing scheme structures Internet backbone service around Metropolitan Exchange Points (MIXes). These exchange points resemble the Network Access Points (NAPs) of today's Internet but serve also as aggregation points for each of the defined metropolitan regions. The size of these metros is a trade-off between the number of required MIXes and the number of destinations that need routing support within the metro.

The essential design goals of the metro addressing scheme are: (1) achieving the ability to easily change providers without renumbering; and (2) creating terse backbone routing tables. The first goal requires essentially flat addressing within a MIX, with no structure to exploit for aggregation. The proposed metro address scheme allocates three bytes within the IPv6 address field to represent this flat space. Providers permanently attached to the MIX receive a *site identifier*, more dynamic, address-on-demand customers can receive identifiers from the site through which they connect. Each site within the metro area will receive a site identifier

FP	Country	Metro	Site	Intra-site
bytes: 1	2		3	10

Figure 2 Proposed Metro Address Format.

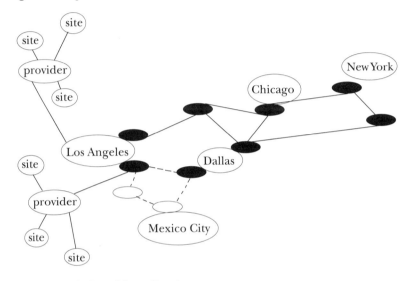

Figure 3 Wide Area Metro Routing.

out of a pool of sites within its MIX. Each site will have 80 bits, or 10^7 addresses with which to number hosts and implement internal hierarchies.

The underlying assumption of the metro addressing scheme is that indefinite recursive aggregation is not necessary; rather, only a high level of aggregation in backbone routers, based on short geographic prefixes, is needed. Since the number of countries is small, and hierarchical aggregation can optionally occur across country boundaries, backbone (core) router forwarding tables will be much smaller than current ones, while serving a subscriber base several orders of magnitude larger.

This scheme bears a strong resemblance to the *stratum* addressing that Rekhter has outlined.[8] In both schemes addresses cluster around interchange points and allow arbitrary movement within the exchange point. The major difference between the approaches is that the stratum approach does not impose any geographic context on the interexchange address space, instead choosing to number around interchange points convenient to providers. This allows less constrained interactions between the members of the stratum with a corresponding loss of permanence in the addresses assigned. Stratum addressing thus has the aggregation and multihoming properties of metro addressing, but retains renumbering problems associated with the provider-based model.

Intra-MIX Routing

Metro addressing drastically simplifies the backbone routing problem, but requires careful engineering to solve the *intra-Metro* routing problem. Provider independence requires that any site identifier be reachable through any provider from the MIX. This routing space is completely flat and corresponds in size to the total number of sites active within the region. As this number grows, the traditional dynamic routing system for dealing with frequent changes in a small number of network prefixes will no longer be appropriate for exchanging reachability information among sites. The size of this table also creates a special role for MIX routers, requiring them to maintain large routing table capacity and the ability to handle a large volume of routing information.

Deering proposes a relatively static MIX-wide broadcast protocol that would result in the exchange of customer identifiers on a daily basis.[9] These routes would allow traffic between sites with different providers and traffic entering the metro from the wide area to travel to the correct destination provider for the destination customer site.

An alternative solution would involve an on-demand mechanism: if a packet arrived at a provider's MIX router and there was no destination provider, the router would send a message to a special broadcast group, and the provider serving that customer would respond with its router's address. Other routers would cache this information for some interval to avoid subsequent remote lookup delays for each packet they transit for that customer.

A third possible solution would include a centralized server as part of the base MIX service. Providers would register customers with the server and could obtain partial or complete dumps of

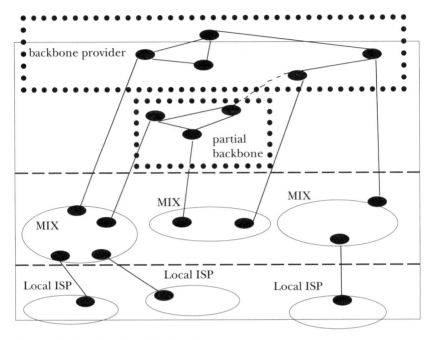

Figure 4 Metro Routing Relationships.

intra-MIX routing information. Although servers that maintain such mappings are single points of failure and often architecturally unnecessary, a single synchronization point for this information would enforce a consistent customer policy across the MIX.

Any of these solutions would be adequate for the simplified routing problem of distributing the information about which provider router to use to reach a customer. All of these techniques are similar to those used in another well-understood networking problem domain, that of address resolution.

Multihoming under Metro Addressing

Metro routing has as a beneficial side effect its simple support for multihoming within a metro region. Since aggregation occurs above the interchange point, multihoming within a metro area will not affect the routing table size outside the MIX.

Multihoming under metro routing has good high-level aggregation properties, but it does require implementation changes. As the normal MIX routing system leverages off the fact that customer-provider bindings do not change more often than once a day, there is no way to support instantaneous failover within the basic intra-MIX routing model. However, application of a redirection technique is appropriate if one only needs to redirect a small number of sites at one time.

Redirection can take the form of explicit messages, sent by the MIX exit router toward the entry point into the MIX, which create a transient routing entry to direct future traffic to the backup router.

Redirection is not the only solution to providing failure robustness. Encapsulation could be used to create a temporary virtual link between the primary and failover router. This has the advantage of relying completely on the local information of the primary provider, but can result in undue traffic consumption as each packet has to enter and exit the primary provider on the path to the backup route.

Provider Constraints

Many providers are convinced that metro addresses and the implied two-layer MIX routing are topologically constraining and thus impose undue expense to supply the same service. This concern stems from the perception that metro routing forces a fixed style of interconnection and routing without adequate means of expressing policy.

We submit that there is no architectural constraint preventing backbone providers from peering directly with each other using appropriate settlements for transit to metros that they do not serve directly. These peer relationships would be very similar to existing direct peerings, and could occur directly off the MIX or in some other context. Routing exchange across providers at such points traditionally benefits from provider-based aggregation, but the metro addressing model treats provider-based routes as exceptions rather than the rule, and supporting nondefault inbound metro connectivity implies exchanging them as full customer routes. Since involved providers typically have some kind of agreement between them, they should be able to arrange for mutual recovery of costs.

While the profit model for a provider that serves end-users is straightforward, it is less clear which business model will best serve providers acting solely in a backbone transport capacity. For current large-scale backbone providers, subscriber fees from leaf customers cover much of the cost of maintaining the long-haul resource. This cost is justified to end-users by the end-to-end service they receive from transitting dedicated resources.

However, there is no reason why a backbone provider should not also serve as an intra-metro provider, in which case it could bypass the MIX for inter-metro traffic to customers within the metro region. Although not strictly required, such a provider would likely use metro aggregation within its own routing system to prevent the insertion of nonscalable customer routes into its global routing system.

Direct second-tier clients of a backbone provider can also arrange transit along dedicated links bypassing the MIX, as shown in Figure 5. If a second-tier client is a provider, it would need to form an intra-MIX routing adjacency with the backbone provider and advertise its customers in the providers intra-MIX routing tables. These routes would allow traffic in both directions to use the dedicated link, but would not prevent the backbone provider from aggregating the entire metro across the wide area, or force traffic from other sites within the MIX to traverse the backbone.

Singly connected smaller providers can still use regional backbones by arranging to get their customers' routes carried to and advertised at the MIX by their parent provider. These small providers gain added leverage from the metro addressing scheme, since they have the ability to move their customers directly to another parent without disruptive renumbering.

Providers that must carry each other's customer routes when implementing direct peering relationships might see this as an inherent scalability problem with metro routing. However, in this case the metro scheme maintains a valuable property: scalability of policy. Although the providers involved must do extra work to peer directly, they do not impose any added complication in the routing system on entities outside the arrangement. Also, it is likely that if the provider spans multiple metro regions, providers can use metro aggregation using their own routing system to increase internal routing efficiency.

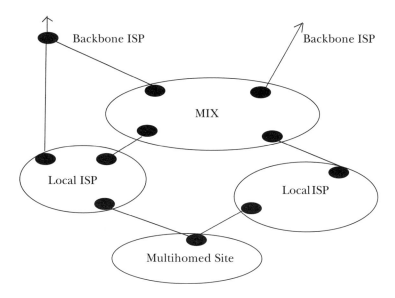

Figure 5 Routing Relationships within a MIX.

Establishment of Exchange Points

Metropolitan Exchange Points play a central role in the proposed metro architecture, and their establishment and maintenance merit careful consideration. The nonmonopolistic nature of the exchange point is essential. Any second-tier provider capable of meeting some generally accepted criteria must be able to connect to the MIX. Without this constraint the MIX itself would breed monopolistic behavior and encourage providers to violate the geographic locality of the address space. Possible models for insuring this property include mediation by a loose cooperative or government body.

Physically, the MIX resembles either a centralized switched backbone or a physically dispersed shared media, analogous to NAPs or Metropolitan Area Ethernets (MAEs) today. Also similar to the NAP model, the MIX serves a dual role, as a concentration point for traffic in the metropolitan area as well as a central point for the exchange of routing information. As noted above, it is not necessary that all traffic across the metro region cross this wire, but it will be the rule, especially for inbound traffic, rather than the exception.

In the San Francisco area there are currently several exchange points, including MAE-West, the Pacific Bell NAP, PCH, and FIX-west. Each of these has arisen out of the differing needs and business models of the providers that serve that region.

Metro routing does not preclude the creation of multiple exchanges in a Metropolitan area; accommodating all the service providers in a dense region might require more than one exchange point. Unless every regional provider attaches to each of these exchanges, they will all need links among them. These links carry traffic entering the metro region at one MIX, but destined to providers at some other MIX in the metro, as well as traffic between the exchange points within a geographic region.

These interexchange links are already difficult to manage in today's Internet, given that they are essentially public resources with no reasonable mechanism for cost recovery from traffic across large exchange points. However, metro-based routing imposes one additional burden: the maintenance of a coherent, fully qualified intra-MIX routing table consistent among all of the exchanges.

Proxied metros would relax the constraint of having backbone connections at each defined MIX, thus providing a crucial mechanism for any initial metro-based deployment. Assigned metro regions without an exchange would select a nearby exchange as a parent. Although they would number out of their assigned metro, each provider in the proxied metro would procure its own link to the nearby exchange. As soon as there were enough providers in an area to justify an independent exchange point and attract a backbone provider, the network could incrementally rearchitect itself around the new MIX without any address reassignments.

Addressing Authority

Responsible use of allocated space in the provider-based model creates an interesting issue for resellers of Internet service who negotiate address space for their leaf customers. Although less critical in IPv6, scalability of provider-based addressing requires active management by addressing authorities and providers to insure conservative use of space. An organization capable of demonstrating that it serves a large number of end-users and other providers can receive large blocks, with future allocations based on growth of the top-level provider as well as effective use of previous allocations.

In contrast, the site identifiers used by the metro addressing scheme are neither scarce nor structured; assignments are not highly dynamic and are subject to much less policy consideration than in a provider-based scheme. Since the topmost bits are assigned to countries, it is perfectly natural to delegate the addressing authority for each country to a national government or cooperative institution. Within each country, metropolitan regions themselves can use local registries or number out of the national registry. This natural match of the allocation problem to the region gives local governments and business cooperatives tools with which to shape the local networking landscape without having to contend with policy decisions elsewhere. Regardless of the scheme used locally for address assignment, it seems reasonable to permit providers to assign site IDs to new customers that need them as they purchase service, as long as these IDs are still fully transportable.

At the top level, some global organization should manage the country portion of the address space. Appropriate initial allocation should allow this address space to remain static over time scales that leave it amenable to management by a global treaty organization.

The Charging Problem

As the Internet continues its transition to a fully commercial framework, viable underlying business models remain unclear. Yet one cannot really design a routing framework without analyzing its effect on the ability of providers to charge for service.

Most differentiation among current backbones derives from their ability to effectively transit for large leaf customers and directly attached, singly homed providers. Since attachment points are a potential source of revenue, there is little economic incentive to provision a backbone to provide transit for default traffic.

Although some networks offer usage-based billing at rough granularities, and other proposals for usage-based pricing are emerging, the most common charging mechanism uses base connectivity fees with implicit corresponding transit policy. Internet Service Providers (ISPs) typically operate in two directions, carrying packets from an attached customer to the backbone, and providing routes at major exchange points to their customers. ISPs use explicit route filtering as well as route announcements to provide symmetric control over which routes to accept.

Since metro-based addresses contain no provider information, and site IDs are flat and fully aggregated at the exchange boundary, advertising routes for directly attached customers is no longer possible. A provider could inject nonaggregated site routes to retain this policy flexibility, but it certainly would not scale to a large number of such routes. Service within the metro model is thus necessarily constrained to providing settlements based on the sender, not the receiver. Ultimately, this unidirectional service model may turn out to be insufficient to express whatever charging policy may evolve. While it does offer providers the ability to instrument attachment and usage-based policy for transmitters, it deliberately restricts the ability to filter based on receiver in the wide area.

An additional challenge to charging in the metro model comes from the need to provision outbound service from second-tier providers transiting the MIX. Since backbone providers currently only receive revenue from the destinations to which they explicitly route, they are unlikely to be willing to continue carrying traffic toward noncustomers without some mechanism for revenue recovery. Unless each second-tier provider is willing to negotiate separate interconnect agreements for outgoing traffic with each provider, the group of attached second-tier providers will have to collectively subsidize default outbound connectivity. Enforcement in the first case, and in the second case if there are second-tier providers that will not contribute to the subsidy fund, would require using layer-two information to verify conformance to the agreement.

Conclusions

The IPv6 address space will host the Internet for some time to come. Careful consideration should precede initial numbering to insure that routing in the IPv6 will scale in usage as well as routing table size. Most discussions of addressing models to date have focused on the problem of allocation to support maximal aggregation. While aggregation is absolutely essential to maintaining a scalable infrastructure, it is not the only aspect of the wide area Internet that address assignment directly impacts.

Renumbering and route distribution policy are tools that can help improve the efficiency of the global routing system, but they also place the burden of implementation on the end-user, and could actually encourage a complete or partial monopoly over some segment of the market. Provider-based addressing optimizes routing assuming a relatively static, hierarchical routing system that is uniconnected at the edges. Metro-based addressing offers an interesting alternative, although it presents a simplified costing model and requires further investigation into the details of intra-MIX routing.

We concede that excessive interference by regulatory agencies can be harmful to technological development, but in this case the ramifications are too broad to be debated on technical merit alone. The deployment of an addressing model, whether provider-based, metro, or some other alternative, will largely determine the Internet's ultimate utility to society.

Notes

1. Paul Tscuchiya, "Comparison of Geographical and Provider-rooted Addressing", INET '93 (1993).

2. Yakov Rekhter and T. Li, "An Architecture for IP Address Allocation with CIDR," RFC1618, 9/24/1993.

3. Yakov Rekhter and T. Li, "An Architecture for IPv6 Unicast Address Allocation," RFC1887, 1/04/1996.

4. S. Thomson and T. Narten, "IPv6 Stateless Address Autoconfiguration," RFC1971, 8/16/1996.

5. Rekhter and Li, "An Architecture for IPv6 Unicast Address Allocation."

6. K. Hubbard, M. Kosters, D. Conrad, D. Karrenberg, and J. Postel, "Internet Registry Ip Allocation Guidelines" (work in progress).

7. S. Deering and R. Hinden, "IPv6 Metro Addressing" (work in progress).

8. Yakov Rekhter, "Stratum-Based Aggregation of Routing Information," INET '95.

9. Deering and Hinden, "IPv6 Metro Addressing."

Interconnections and Settlements

Scalable Internet Interconnection Agreements and Integrated Services

Joseph Bailey and Lee McKnight

Introduction

The growth of the Internet can be measured by the number of users and hosts, the amount and types of traffic, and the size of the Internet industry. Growth has not been a result of one provider dominating the industry. In fact, the Internet industry is very fragmented and some expect it to become even more fragmented, although others see evidence of a trend towards consolidation.[1] Save for a few centralized functions such as allocation of Internet Protocol (IP) addresses, Domain Name Service (DNS), and distribution of routing tables, the Internet has consistently followed the ARPANET's philosophy of decentralized administration.[2] Plans for further decentralization of Internet functions are being discussed.[3] Decentralization allows for heterogeneity of users and applications ranging from electronic mail to World Wide Web browsing. Decentralization has also led to heterogeneous network designs and interconnection agreements.

The point of interconnection is an illuminating focus for Internet analyses. Interconnecting networks must cooperate to exchange information to help the Internet function. Interconnection points must also relay the bits and bytes of an e-mail message or a Web session across different networks. Assessment by Internet Service Providers (ISPs) of a range of technology, policy, management, and economic factors determine how and where interconnections occur.

This chapter examines interconnection agreements and explores how to extend present agreement models[4] to include new technological developments such as integrated services.[5] Integrated services represent an important development because they may make possible new applications, such as real-time video, voice, and data conferencing. Integrated services also fundamentally change the economics of Internet interconnection agreements.

This chapter presents four models of interconnection agreements for Internet Service Providers and then describes the different pricing policies that can be adopted at interconnection points. It also details the emergence of integrated services. Finally, the chapter uses incomplete contracts theory to provide an integrated analysis of these elements. By integrating the technology of the Internet (interconnection models and integrated services) and the economics of interconnection agreements (pricing policies and incomplete contract theory), we are able to determine which interconnection models will be sustainable by an integrated services pricing policy. This analysis suggests that usage-sensitive pricing policies, which have been very rare in the Internet community to date, will become more pervasive as integrated services expand. Along with this development, new accounting and billing methods must be implemented. We conclude that only by adopting new pricing policies can the Internet become scalable to new services, new applications, and new users.

Interconnection Agreement Models

Interconnection of networks that exchange Internet Protocol (IP) traffic is the glue that holds together the Internet as a "network of networks." However, interconnection occurs between numerous types of networks at many different locations. Many different companies and user groups can be affected by the terms of interconnection agreements. Although sending an e-mail message or a Web transmission between two computers can span numerous networks (and therefore will take advantage of the existence of many interconnection agreements), the details of the interconnection agreement do not have to be known by those who use it. Rather, it is up to the connecting parties to decide how they wish to interconnect with other networks.

In this chapter, we describe four basic models of Internet Service Provider interconnection agreements: peer-to-peer bilateral, hierarchical bilateral, third-party administrator, and cooperative. Each of these models exists in the Internet. It is very likely that all four types of interconnection agreements will exist in the future. An interesting feature of the models and of the Internet is that different models for interconnection can coexist and interoperate without one model dominating. This permits networks and firms with different technologies and customers to select the model for an interconnection agreement that suits them best. The four interconnection models are described in detail below.

Peer-to-Peer Bilateral

The peer-to-peer bilateral interconnection model consists of two Internet networks owned by different firms of approximately the same size, experience, technology, and customer base that interconnect via a two-party contract governing their agreement. An example of this model is the interconnection of two Internet Service Providers that both have a national reach and are of similar size. Even though these providers are competing in the same market for the same customers, they must provide interconnection between their networks so that their customers will realize the benefits of positive network externalities.[6]

The network externalities are symmetric in the peer-to-peer bilateral agreement since both networks have approximately the same customer base. Although the users are the ones who actually derive the benefit from the network externality, the value of a network (and therefore the price that can be set for being connected to the network) is proportional to the network externalities that it has. Consider an ISP that is deciding whether to enter a peer-to-peer bilateral agreement with either a company of equal size or with one that is half its size. If the ISP connects to the one of equal size, it will double the number of users to which it can directly connect through this interconnection point. If the ISP connects to the one half its size, then it is only increasing the number of possible direct connections by 50 percent. Both connections may connect the ISP with the Internet "cloud,"[7] but connection with the network that is half its size will make more of the connections *indirect*. Direct connections are more desirable than indirect connections since traffic must traverse fewer links and must pass through fewer intermediaries. Therefore, having indirect connections would make the indirect traffic susceptible to the reliability of the intermediary network. However, it may still make sense for the ISP to connect to the smaller network in a hierarchical bilateral agreement, which we discuss below.

The elements that make two firms peers as opposed to placing them into more of a customer-provider relationship are important: size, experience, technology, and customer base. The customer base and its implications are apparent in the discussion of network externalities above. The size of a network is very important since one network may have a national reach whereas another may have only a regional reach. All else being equal, an interconnection agreement with a network which has a larger reach is better than one with a small reach since larger networks can help transport packets a farther distance and reduce the number of networks a packet must traverse (i.e., it decreases the "indirectness" of connections to other Internet locations).[8] Experience is very important because the parties entering the interconnection agreement must be able to trust each other to transport the data that is exchanged between them. If the interconnecting parties have asymmetric experience, the party with greater experience (or knowledge) may act as a mentor or teacher to the less experienced party. A similar argument can be made for technology. If there is a large difference in the level of technological development, the capacity of the network with more developed technology to benefit from the interconnection is less.[9] This effect is magnified by the introduction of new services such as integrated services.

Hierarchical Bilateral

Similar to the peer-to-peer bilateral agreement, the hierarchical bilateral agreement is governed by a two-party contract, but it interconnects firms of a discernible difference in size, experience, technology, and customer base. We distinguish this bilateral agreement from the peer-to-peer case since the economics and technology of the interconnection are very different. Both differences usually lead to a customer-provider relationship rather than a peer-to-peer relationship. An example of this interconnection model is an Internet Access Provider or a corporate network connecting to an ISP.

The technology leader, usually the firm with the larger network, benefits less from the interconnection agreement than the technology follower. The leader may also have more experience or network links with greater capacity. The network externality benefits are greater for customers of the smaller network provider. The experience of the technology leader can be of great benefit to the firm with the smaller network, but the experience and knowledge benefits do not flow in the opposite direction. For these reasons, we find that the firm with a smaller network takes on the role of the customer and pays a larger amount of the costs of interconnection.

The hierarchical bilateral model of interconnection is the most pervasive in today's Internet. Customers connect to Internet Access Providers. Internet Access Providers and corporate networks connect to Internet Service Providers. All of these interconnection agreements follow the hierarchical model since they aggregate users and interconnect them with networks which have superior technology and larger network externalities.

Third-Party Administrator

The third-party administrator model is followed when an interconnection point consists of more than two networks exchanging packets and the administration of the interconnection is operated by a firm that does not operate a network. Examples of this include the Commercial Internet eXchange (CIX), the Network Access Points (NAPs) established by the National Science Foundation, and MAE-E (pronounced "may east"). The roles of the third party are to route traffic between the interconnected networks and to serve as a trusted party to facilitate communication and promote nondiscrimination. Because of these roles, a third-party administrator often acts as a common carrier, offering consistent prices to all customers and not refusing interconnection by any party. The objective of the third-party administrator is to cover the operating expenses of the interconnecting points and profit from the endeavor.

The network externalities for the third-party administrator are characterized by positive feedback. If the number of people connecting to the third-party administrator's interconnection point is zero, the first network to connect receives zero benefit. As the number of networks that connect to the interconnection point increases, the network externalities also increase. It is difficult, therefore, for a third-party administrator to establish an interconnection point, but once it attains a critical mass of firms, it can provide a very real benefit to new networks. A wise strategy for such third-party administrators would be to secure a critical mass before establishing an interconnection point.

The third-party administrator must establish trust, which results partially from a technological edge. Because the third-party administrator does not compete with the networks it interconnects, it does not benefit from information it obtains about its customers (the interconnecting networks). Furthermore, the third-party administrator is likely to keep this information about its customer confidential because it benefits from keeping this information private—this is the administrator's competitive advantage. Sharing information in confidence establishes the administrator's trustworthiness. The administrator's ability to impart some kind of experience or knowledge to their customers also builds trust. A third-party administrator that knows less than its customers is unlikely to provide adequate service.

Cooperative Agreement

Similar to the third-party agreement, the cooperative agreement has more than two parties sharing an interconnection point; however, with a cooperative agreement, the operation of the interconnection point is run by a committee of the interconnecting firms. This interconnection model was the sole example of interconnection when the Internet comprised government-supported networks. The Federal Internet eXchanges (FIXen) were created to interconnect government agency networks that had a shared purpose and incentive to promote research and education.

While it is unclear that this model works in the commercial sector, it is worth mentioning since the FIXen still exist and remain successful. Unlike the third-party administrator, the cooperative agreement is run by committee and does not need to make a profit—only cost-sharing is necessary.

The cooperative agreement is more desirable than many bilateral agreements because there are fewer coordination costs and greater economies of scale. This is especially true because there is an incentive alignment between the parties involved that makes them willing to cooperate and have very incomplete contracts (discussed further below), and use their trust in each other to facilitate coordination. Also, multiple bilateral agreements are not only more expensive to coordinate, but may cost more in terms of hardware and leased lines than a single interconnection point of n networks. This gives the cooperative agreement an economies-of-scale benefit that is the same as the benefit realized by the third-party administrator.

Since information is not a competitive advantage for the cooperative firms, experience and information are shared among all parties involved. Instead of information being absorbed by the administrator, all parties can benefit from committee participation and shared learning.

Pricing Policies

Pricing for Internet service is one of the most critical issues to emerge from the commercialization of the Internet following the NSFNET. Two of the first articles to suggest pricing based upon actual usage initiated a debate over the cost recovery and business of providing Internet service.[10] Economists and technologists continue to debate, and disagree, on how and whether to implement new pricing policies.[11] There are still more research and potential business opportunities to explore to further our understanding of pricing and Internet economics.

In this section we describe three pricing policies: flat-rate, capacity-based, and usage-sensitive pricing.[12] These pricing policies coexist today and our analysis that follows indicates that they will continue to coexist in the future Internet infrastructure.

Flat-Rate Pricing

The pricing model that most people think prevails on the Internet today is flat-rate pricing. With flat-rate pricing, a user does not pay for each transmission of data but only has to pay for the initial cost of the connection. The flat rate is set independent of the speed or configuration of the connection.[13] Because configuration and speed of connection are very important in a heterogeneous Internet, we find that flat-rate pricing is not as common as pricing based on capacity.

One of the benefits of flat-rate pricing is that it is easy to set prices and bill for services. No accounting is necessary to track usage. Also, no price discrimination has to be determined for pricing based on the speed of connection. Flat-rate pricing is easy to administer and easy for customers to understand. Furthermore, it encourages usage since users do not have to pay any additional fee to upgrade the speed (bandwidth) of their connection or reduce their usage because of billing.

Capacity-Based Pricing

Capacity-based pricing relates pricing to usage by setting a price based on the bandwidth or speed of the connection. This policy is based on the *expected* use of a circuit because no accounting is done on the link, and this is accomplished by charging for the configuration (i.e., bandwidth) of the connection but not the actual bits sent and/or received. Capacity-based pricing differentiates classes of users (price discrimination), so network providers can charge more where there is more benefit.

Capacity-based pricing is the currently prevailing pricing policy for the Internet. While it requires a more complicated billing policy than does flat-rate pricing, it helps the network provider increase its revenue. As users or other networks connect with bigger (i.e., greater bandwidth) connections, they are charged more because they can increase congestion on the shared portion of the network. The larger revenues from higher-capacity links help cover the costs of infrastructure improvements.

The one weak point of capacity-based pricing is that it does not track the customer's actual usage. Therefore, the customer may be inflicting a higher congestion cost on the network when he or she sends and/or receives traffic during the middle of the day instead of using the network during the off-peak evening hours. Capacity-based pricing does not change the behavior of the customer by encouraging use of the network at night. Furthermore, not all customers that have the same capacity connection use the network in the same way. Some users prefer the low latency that a larger capacity link offers, but do not use it often (many periods of zero traffic on the link). Other users fill their capacity and have less sporadic use. Both types of customer would pay the same price in a capacity-based pricing model. It would take a usage-sensitive pricing model to differentiate these users.

Usage-Sensitive Pricing

Unlike capacity-based pricing, usage-sensitive pricing policies charge for *actual* rather than expected usage. This distinction is important because usage-sensitive pricing requires accounting as well as billing, whereas capacity-based pricing only requires billing for cost recovery.

How the accounting is implemented for usage-sensitive pricing will determine pricing, and thus the incentives for users and network providers as well. For example, if accounting is done at the connection level (i.e., TCP layer), then billing for network traffic will also be done at that level.[14] Accounting for packets at the IP layer will lead to billing for packets, not bits. This accounting and billing will then be reported back to the users who may in turn change their behavior to save money.

Usage-sensitive pricing gives the network provider more flexibility when designing its price discrimination model. Pricing by time of day or priority of traffic will help the network provider reduce congestion on its network by shaping the behavior of users. This is, in essence, a form of load management. The difficulty with this kind of pricing policy is that users are not used to a variable price for their Internet service (note that capacity-based pricing would have the same cost per billing cycle regardless of use). It is difficult to get people to accept usage-sensitive pricing when capacity-based pricing is easier (and requires less accounting overhead from the network provider).

However, usage-sensitive pricing is possible and does exist. For example, in New Zealand an expensive link to the United States is supported by charging users based upon their actual use of the network.[15] Users pay for the bits they send and receive. It is a nonlinear pricing scheme with discounts for high-volume users which reflect the fact that there is an overhead for billing users that does not change with their actual use (the cost is just averaged over more volume). For best effort service, we believe the New Zealand case is a unique example of a successful usage-sensitive pricing policy. In places where there is competition based on pricing policies, it is less clear that usage-sensitive pricing will be acceptable to users. However, it may be the only way to implement integrated services.

Integrated Services

As described in the chapter in this volume by Gillett and Kapor, one of the greatest benefits of the Internet is its ability to incorporate new protocols and technologies—it is very dynamic. Recently more attention has focused on the ability of the Internet to provide integrated services.[16] Because not all applications have the same bandwidth requirements, the integrated services model allows for different applications to call on different protocols to deliver different qualities of service. The current quality of service, best effort, is seen as the most basic integrated service, while guaranteed service (suitable for a lossless, constant bit rate transmission) is the most demanding. Today the Internet only delivers reliably very-low-quality video or voice in real time, but a future Internet may be able to offer a guaranteed quality of service that is consistent with the public switched telephone network. The capacity of integrated services to offer better quality seems likely with development of the new Internet Protocol version 6 (IPv6).

This chapter concentrates on the reservation process for providing integrated services, such as guaranteed service. A reservation is the set-up procedure for allocating bandwidth from the source to destination. It conveys a priori information about the data stream to tell the network to set aside capacity. Every interconnection point through which the traffic passes must have the reservation supported in order to provide true guaranteed quality of service. At the time of writing, the protocols for reservations such as RTP and RSVP are currently being developed and tested.

The reservations affect the interconnection analysis because not all traffic is handled equally. The ability of these protocols to reserve bandwidth on networks other than their own is necessary to ensure consistent quality, but may be detrimental to the business models of Internet Service Providers. For example, consider a hierarchical bilateral agreement in which the larger network reserves bandwidth on the smaller network. It is possible for the larger network to reserve *all* of the bandwidth on the smaller network for integrated services.

Analysis

By determining which pricing policies are consistent with different interconnection agreements in adopting integrated services, we will now integrate the models for interconnection agreements, pricing policies, and the introduction of integrated services. Our methodology will be analysis through incomplete contract theory.[17]

Incomplete contracts are a result of a firm's bounded rationality. It is impossible for people or firms to know everything that will happen in the future—they are bounded by their rational thinking. However, they are aware of this when they enter into a contract, thus, by definition, the contract will not take into consideration all future events. The contract cannot be complete because events exogenous to the contract are unknown and firms participating in the contract may act beyond the limits of the contract. Analysis stemming from incomplete contract theory looks at the exogenous changes affecting the contract and determines where a firm can act opportunistically.

Analysis through incomplete contract theory is a useful methodology because the Internet and, consequently, the interconnections between networks are very dynamic. The development of new applications like the World Wide Web change the use and behavior of the network but have little effect on the actual protocols that affect interconnection. The introduction of integrated services, however, has a large impact on interconnection because it makes it possible to impose a large opportunity cost on an interconnected party by reserving bandwidth on its network. Furthermore, network providers can find new ways to act opportunistically in an interconnection agreement since they often compete with the firm with which they are interconnecting.

Table 1 summarizes the analysis already presented in this chapter and presents the findings of the analysis below. The first row of Table 1 lists examples of the different interconnection models. The second row indicates the nature of the network externality benefits for each model (this analysis is also described earlier in this chapter). The third row indicates which pricing policies are possible for best effort service for the various interconnection models.[18] Furthermore, the accounting overhead associated with usage-sensitive pricing is too great for a cooperative agreement since the incentive for all interconnected parties is very much in alignment. Therefore, the flat-rate, third-party administrator and the usage-sensitive cooperative model are not sustainable, scalable interconnection agreements, as the third row of Table 1 shows.

We now turn our attention to the last four rows of Table 1 (reservation pricing policies, costs, agreement, and accounting), which summarize the analysis in this chapter.

As the fourth row of Table 1 indicates, it may not be possible for flat-rate or capacity-based pricing schemes to be consistent with any of the four interconnection models when integrated services are introduced. The ability of any one user to reserve bandwidth on any other network means imposing a very high congestion cost (in some cases, taking away the entire capacity of the network) without incurring any cost (under a flat-rate or capacity-based pricing scheme). In fact, as the table indicates, perhaps only a usage-sensitive pricing scheme may prevent a tragedy of the commons.[19] This is especially true in cases where the interconnecting parties are competing, but it may also be true in cooperative agreements. While the National Science Foundation and NASA might agree on a cooperative interconnection, they may have two users who do not get along (rarely does the U.S. government agree on anything!). One user could establish a reservation without incurring a cost and take away the bandwidth from the other user.

Another issue that arises is the capacity of usage-sensitive pricing to be based on the current congestion level of a network. While this is only one method for setting a price, it has been suggested

Table 1 Comparison of Interconnection Models

	Peer-to-Peer Bilateral	Hierarchical Bilateral	Third-Party Administrator	Cooperative Agreement
Examples	ISP-ISP	IAP-ISP	MAE-E	FIX
Network Externalities	mutually beneficial	asymmetric— more beneficial to the smaller firm	positive feedback	positive feedback
Best Effort Pricing Policies	capacity-based, usage-sensitive, and flat-rate	capacity-based, usage-sensitive, and flat-rate	usage-sensitive, capacity-based	capacity-based, flat-rate
Reservation Pricing Policies	usage-sensitive	usage-sensitive	usage-sensitive	usage-sensitive
Costs	equal split	smaller firm pays more	all firms pay total cost plus profit	all firms pay total cost
Agreement	contract	contract	common carrier	committee
Accounting	possible	possible	probable	not likely

before.[20] It offers incentives to create artificial congestion on a network so that the network can raise its price and increase its revenues. This is less likely in the cooperative case, but it may be likely in all the other cases since the artificial congestion is promoted by a party that stands to make more money. The third-party administrator may be less likely to create artificial congestion since it does not own a network, but it is also trusted more than peers trust each other (since they are competing in the same markets).

The table's last three rows (costs, agreement, and accounting) detail differences between the parties in the interconnection agreement. Although most of this analysis is included earlier in this chapter, we wish to highlight the last row—accounting. Accounting is the most probable outcome in the third-party administrator case for best effort service, since third-party administrators are the most ready to adapt to usage-sensitive pricing. Therefore this model will incur the lowest costs in a transition to reservation policies.

Conclusion

Internet interconnection agreements are as heterogeneous as the users of and the traffic on the networks connected by the Internet. No single model of interconnection dominates on the Internet. However, changes in interconnection agreements and pricing policies are evident as new services such as integrated services are introduced. The interaction of technology and economics which shapes the evolution of the Internet has never been as apparent as it will be when users can establish reservations and potentially tremendously increase the congestion costs of other users. A usage-sensitive pricing policy that is introduced simultaneously with integrated services has a good chance of being successful. A usage-sensitive pricing policy provides a new Internet platform for integrated services that is scalable for new applications.

Acknowledgments

The authors thank David Clark and Scott Marcus for their contributions. This work has been supported in part by NASA (fellowship no. NGT-51407), the National Science Foundation (grant no. NCR-9307548), and the Internet Telephony Interoperability Consortium. The views expressed as well as any errors of fact or omission are those of the authors, and not their sponsoring institutions.

Notes

1. J. Maloff, *1994–1995 Internet Access Providers Marketplace Analysis*, The Maloff Company, 1995.

2. D. Clark, "The Design Philosophy of the DARPA Internet Protocols," *Computer Communication Review* 18, No. 4 (1988): 106–114.

3. See, for example, "Draft Specifications for Administration and Management of gTLDs," International Ad Hoc Committee, December 19, 1996, available at <http://www.iahc.org/draft-iahc-gTLDspec-00.html>; and Y. Rekhter, P. Resnick et al., "Pricing for Internet Addresses and Route Assignments," paper presented at Telecommunications Policy Research Conference, Solomons, Maryland, October 6, 1996.

4. J. P. Bailey, "The Economics of Internet Interconnection Agreements," in L. W. McKnight and J. P. Bailey, ed., *Internet Economics* (Cambridge, Mass.: MIT Press, 1997).

5. S. Shenker, "Service Models and Pricing Policies for Integrated Services Internet," unpublished paper, Xerox PARC, 1993.

6. A network externality is a benefit to incumbent users of a network as an additional customer joins the network. For example, a telephone system involving only one person has zero overall benefit since this one individual cannot call anyone else. If a second person joins the network, the first user will benefit since he or she now has someone to call. The network externality is positive when the benefit is positive, and negative as the additional user becomes a cost. For more information see J. Farrell and G. Saloner, "Competition, Compatibility and Standards: The Economics of Horses, Penguins and Lemmings," in H. L. Gabel, ed., *Product Standardization and Competitive Strategy* (New York: North -Holland, 1987), and M. L. Katz and C. Shapiro, "Network Externalities, Competition, and Compatibility," *American Economics Review* 75, no. 3(1985): 424–440.

7. The Internet "cloud" is the network of networks that comprises the Internet. It is drawn as a cloud as opposed to a specific diagram since no one actually knows what is inside the cloud! Because the interconnection points and technology within the cloud are very dynamic and have distributed control, it is impossible for anyone to know what is inside. Traffic is injected at one point of the cloud and it exits from a different point of the cloud depending on the technology, interconnection points, and congestion at the time of transmission.

8. There may be a benefit to having a smaller network of people to decrease the "noise" from the many users on a large network—or information overload, as it is sometimes called. However, we are focusing our discussion on the Internet where users connect to every other user on the network, thus making them susceptible to this noise anyway.

9. An example of this is the interconnection of two countries with the United States. Even though these countries may be adjacent and have similar technology, they both will benefit greatly by connecting to a network with greater technology (such as networks in the United States) than they do with each other. The effect this has is that countries that are very close route traffic through the United States and experience longer delay paths and cause more congestion in the U.S. portion of the Internet. For example, Australia and New Zealand had to traverse the U.S. backbone in the early 1990s to exchange traffic.

10. R. Bohn, H.-W. Braun, et al., "Mitigating the Coming Internet Crunch: Multiple Service Levels via Precedence," Applied Network Research technical report, 1994; and J. K. MacKie-Mason and H. R. Varian, "Pricing the Internet," in B. Kahin and J. Keller, eds., *Public Access to the Internet* (Cambridge, Mass.: MIT Press, 1995): 269–314.

11. L. W. McKnight and J. P. Bailey, eds., *Internet Economics* (Cambridge, Mass.: MIT Press, 1997).

12. Our use of the terms *flat-rate, capacity-based,* and *usage-sensitive* here differs somewhat from our usage in McKnight and Bailey, eds., *Internet Economics.* We continue to struggle to identify the most salient characteristics of Internet service pricing and hope that the definitions offered here add some clarity to a still-muddy issue.

13. See Anania and Solomon, "Flat—the Minimalist Price," in McKnight and Bailey, eds., *Internet Economics,* for an analysis of the benefits of flat-rate pricing for data networks such as the Internet.

14. R. J. Edell, N. McKeown, et al., "Billing Users and Pricing for TCP," unpublished paper, University of California at Berkeley, 1994.

15. N. Brownlee, "New Zealand's Experiences with Network Traffic Charging," in McKnight and Bailey, eds., *Internet Economics.*

16. Shenker, "Service Models and Pricing Policies for Integrated Services Internet."

17. R. H. Coase, "The Nature of the Firm," *Economica* 4: 386–405; and O. Williamson, *Markets and Hierarchies: Analysis and Antitrust Implications* (New York: Free Press, 1975).

18. This analysis is discussed in detail in Bailey, "The Economics of Internet Interconnection Agreements." In summary, he finds that there is an incentive for customers to aggregate their traffic before reaching an interconnection point when a flat-rate pricing policy is used. Bailey also describes the ability of policing to eliminate aggregation of traffic or resale of the interconnection service but that, he argues, is very costly and reduces the trust between the interconnecting firms. Therefore, this chapter does not explore the ability to police for the enforcement of contracts. Furthermore, it should be added that the CIX tried to use a policing policy to prevent aggregation and resale with little success.

19. The "tragedy of the commons" occurs when a public good, which can be shared among many people, is overused since each individual benefits more from more use of the public good. Eventually, the overuse of the good (or commons) leads to its eventual destruction. See G. Hardin, "The Tragedy of the Commons," *Science* 162(13): 1243–1248.

20. MacKie-Mason and Varian, "Pricing the Internet."

Internet Exchanges: Policy-Driven Evolution

Bilal Chinoy and Timothy J. Salo

Introduction and Motivation

Internet Exchanges (IXes) are systems within the Internet[1] that enable networks to meet and exchange data and control information. In order to carry out these functions, Internet Exchanges must do much more than merely forward packets. They must provide a robust environment in which differences between the attached client networks, such as in technologies used by different networks or in administrative and operational policies and procedures, do not become barriers to interconnection. Moreover, they must have policies that do not hinder competition between classes of attached networks (such as the often conflicting business interests of large, nationwide networks versus smaller, regional networks).

Internet Exchanges exist in many different forms, often because of differences in the available technology or because they were created with different objectives. Some of the characteristics that can be useful in classifying different types of Internet Exchanges are explored below. For example, some exchanges are collocated in a single room, while others are physically distributed. Access to some exchanges is relatively free, while other exchanges are open only to certain networks. Likewise, the focus of some exchanges is interconnecting regional networks, while other exchanges provide interconnections for nationwide networks.

Major policy decisions have also had a strong effect on the structure of many Internet Exchanges. Conversely, some exchanges

enabled certain policies, or made other policies difficult to implement or enforce. Two policies that have had a tremendous effect on
the configuration of today's Internet are commercialization, the
use of the Internet for commercial as well as research and educational purposes, and privatization, the implementation and operation of the Internet networks by the private sector rather than by
government agencies. The interaction between the policies of
commercialization and privatization and the evolution of Internet
Exchanges is examined here in detail.

The Internet has been growing at an explosive rate for several
years, with no end to its growth in sight. This rapid expansion has
placed considerable stress on the Internet infrastructure. Many of
these strains are visible at the Internet Exchanges. For example,
some Internet Exchanges are experiencing sustained aggregate
traffic loads of 200–400 megabits per second. At some point,
existing products and technologies will be inadequate. Several of
the significant issues facing Internet Exchanges are summarized in
this chapter.

Historically, the U.S. federal government has played a significant
role in funding the development of much of the key technology
used in the Internet, funding the early deployment of some of the
networks which comprise the Internet, particularly the NSFNET[2]
backbone and regional networks, and coordinating much of the
operations of the Internet, again largely through the NSFNET
program. With the privatization of the Internet, exemplified by the
decommissioning of the NSFNET backbone network in April 1995
and the dramatic rise in commercial Network Service Providers
(NSPs), the role of the U.S. federal government has considerably
diminished. But these changes beg the question of what the role of
the federal government ought to be in today's Internet. We do not
claim to know the answer to this extremely complex question, but
we do believe that there are a few specific aspects of Internet
Exchanges that could effectively leverage federal funding.

It should be noted that most of the examples cited in this chapter
are from the experiences of the U.S. portion of the Internet and the
NSFNET in particular. Nonetheless, we believe that most of the
lessons learned in this part of the Internet are applicable to a wide
variety of environments.

A final note on terminology: we use the term "Network Service Provider" to denote an organization that provides Internet connectivity services. "Network" generally refers to an NSP's network. We occasionally use the term "national NSP" when referring to those NSPs which provide service nationwide and operate their own nationwide network, and "regional NSP" to identify NSPs which provide Internet services only in a limited geographical region and depend upon a national NSP for interregional transport.

The Purpose Of Internet Exchanges

Internet Exchanges have been created to allow independently administered networks to connect with each other and exchange data and routing information in a controlled manner. Figure 1 represents a typical Internet Exchange. The interconnect allows the attached networks to exchange data and routing information. Note that the IX exists apart from the networks that connect to it, and in many cases, it is administered independently of the attached networks. Similarly, the NSP networks are not connected directly to each other. Rather, each NSP is connected to the interconnect, which in turn enables the networks to communicate. This structure provides a useful isolation between, for example, NSPs that use different technology internally or compete with each other, or have other reasons to prefer not to be directly attached.

NSPs establish bilateral connectivity by exchanging routing information using a routing protocol, a process termed "route peering." NSPs may choose to advertise reachable destinations to peer NSPs or decide to filter announcements (i.e., not announce destinations even thought they are reachable via the NSP) based on some technical or policy criterion. Similarly, an NSP may choose to propagate a route internally or to ignore the announcement, again to implement a technical or administrative policy. Having established mutual route advertisements and acceptance lists, NSPs can then exchange user traffic between each other across an IX.

Attributes of Internet Exchanges

Internet Exchanges have been created in response to a variety of demands and their structure and management policies reflect

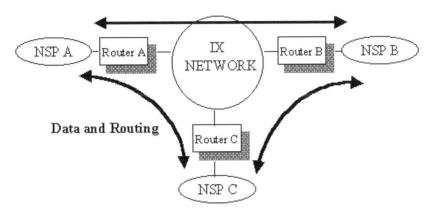

Figure 1 A Typical Internet Exchange.

these diverse requirements. Categorizing Internet Exchanges by both their technology and policy architectures leads us to the following four classes.

- IX Network Structure: collocated and distributed IXes;
- IX Mission Objectives: public and private IXes;
- IX Route Peering Policies: multilateral and bilateral IXes; and
- IX Geographic Scope: national and regional IXes.

We examine each category in detail below.

Network Structure: Collocated and Distributed Internet Exchanges

Most Internet Exchanges have been built with the traditional assumption that IX clients will attach their routers at a common geographical point, called the collocation point. For example, one of the earliest collocated IXes was an Ethernet network at the Pittsburgh Supercomputer Center (PSC), which housed routers from the ARPANET, MILNET, NSFNET, and other wide area networks such as SATNET. The shared Ethernet allowed these networks to communicate routing information, often with protocol translators, and to exchange traffic. Local Area Network (LAN) technologies such as Ethernet and Fiber Distributed Data Interface

(FDDI) continue to provide a reliable and robust substrate upon which interconnection networks can be built.

The advent of wide area link-layer network technologies such as Frame Relay, Switched Multi-Megabit Data Services (SMDS), and Asynchronous Transfer Mode (ATM) makes possible a second form of IX, namely the distributed IX. In this model, rather than NSPs purchasing leased lines from their closest Point of Presence (POP) to the collocated site, the IX network attempts to span a geographic area that includes its client's POPs. A good example of this type of IX is the Ameritech Network Access Point (NAP), which is based on a wide-area ATM network. Here, NSPs in the Chicago area can connect to the NAP simply by connecting to Ameritech's ATM service at their own POP.

For an IX manager, collocated architecture is easier to manage. Upgrading the IX network to keep ahead of traffic and client demand is also easier and cheaper. However, the cost to an NSP of connecting to a collocated IX is higher because the burden of providing a high-speed network to the IX falls upon the NSP. A distributed IX enables an easier and cheaper connection for NSPs. The IX manager, however, is now faced with scaling a Metropolitan Area Network or a Wide Area Network to stay ahead of demand. Local Area Networks are much more cost-effective to scale with both traffic and port access demands.

Mission Objectives: Public and Private Internet Exchanges

Public Internet Exchanges place no restrictions on which NSPs may connect to them. In practice, these IXes do have some basic requirements such as a minimum NSP connection bandwidth (e.g., DS-3 or 45 megabits per second), access to relevant network management information, and, of course, payment of any IX connection fees. The Network Access Points funded by the National Science Foundation (NSF)[3] are examples of public Internet Exchanges.

Private Internet Exchanges allow NSPs that meet some policy criteria established by the IX managers to connect. These criteria could relate to the type of NSP or to its size in terms of traffic carried or clients attached. The Federal Internet Exchange Point (FIX), to which only U.S federal agency networks are allowed to interconnect is a private IX. The FIX-West network located in Ames, California, enabled the Department Of Energy's ESnet, NASA's NSInet, the National Science Foundation's NSFNET, and other agency-sponsored networks to exchange traffic and routing information.

A special case of a private IX is a pairwise IX in which only two NSPs interconnect. A pairwise IX is typically created between two NSPs that exchange a large amount of traffic at topological points in the Internet that are not served well by other IXes. Pairwise private IXes between high-volume NSPs off-load traffic from the public IXes and ensure better service for participants in the private IX. As the Internet connectivity market continues to evolve, a small number of large NSPs has begun to emerge, and pairwise IXes between them is becoming common. For example, SprintLink and InternetMCI have established numerous pairwise IXes.

IX Route Peering Policies: Multilateral and Bilateral Peering

Merely having a presence at an IX does not guarantee an NSP connectivity with other attached NSPs; NSPs can exchange traffic only if they peer with each other. Moreover, IX managers may have a peering policy that affects all attached NSPs, or they may let NSPs decide on peering policies themselves, typically on a bilateral basis.

A few Internet Exchanges have a multilateral peering policy, which implies that a client NSP is expected to carry traffic from all the other NSPs attached to the IX. Conversely, by attaching to such an IX, client networks are assured that they will receive all routes that all the other NSPs carry in their networks. Most IX managers have no peering policies, allowing client NSPs to set up bilateral peering with other NSPs of their choosing.

Internet Exchanges may have clients that are dissimilar in terms of the volume of traffic they exchange with each other. For example, consider the case in which NSP *A* has a small number of customers and NSP *B* has a relatively larger number of customers. *A* thus advertises a small number of reachable destinations to *B*, which typically results in a relatively smaller amount of traffic flow from *B* to *A*. However, NSP *B* advertises a larger number of destinations to A, which results in a larger traffic flow from A to B. Thus, with an enforced multilateral peering arrangement, B would carry more traffic from A than it off-loads to A. This is why most larger, well-established NSPs prefer bilateral peering arrangements with other NSPs that have similar customer bases.

Settlements have been proposed that would charge on the basis of the ratio of traffic sent to a particular NSP to traffic received from that NSP. An NSP with a disproportionate balance of traffic would either pay or receive settlements to compensate for the resources expended in carrying the traffic of its peers.

Geographic Scope: Regional and National Internet Exchanges

Internet Exchanges, which serve to interconnect nationwide and international Network Service Providers, have typically been categorized as national IXes because of the scope of their client NSP backbone networks. However, the increase in the number of NSPs serving local and regional geographic areas has motivated the creation of regional Internet Exchanges. These exchanges typically aggregate traffic to and from a smaller geographic area, such as a metropolis or a state. National NSPs then carry the IX traffic to and from a national IX. The traffic aggregation hierarchy thus created is a very important architectural requirement for scaling the number of Internet Exchanges. Traffic between local and regional NSPs that have different national Network Service Providers does not need to traverse a national IX that may be topologically distant. Rather, local traffic is restricted to the regional IX and network resources are more efficiently utilized.

Policy-Driven Evolution of Internet Exchanges

Policy has affected the evolution of Internet Exchanges, as have technology, competitive forces, and other factors examined above. Internet Exchanges have also affected policy, making the implementation of policy straightforward in some cases and difficult in others. The relationship between Internet Exchanges and policy is perhaps best illustrated by the interaction with commercialization and privatization policies.

During the 1990s, the evolution of the U.S. portion of the Internet has largely been driven by two related policies: commercialization and privatization. Commercialization has broadened the mission of the Internet from its initial focus on supporting research, education, and defense to include commercial (as well as nearly any other imaginable) activity. At the same time, privatization has shifted responsibility for the design, implementation, operation, and funding of the Internet from the federal government to the private sector.

In this section, we examine how Internet Exchanges have evolved hand-in-glove with the commercialization and privatization of the Internet; how exchanges have been driven by a desire to commercialize the Internet, and how interconnects have enabled a smooth transition from a government-funded to a privatized Internet. While policy, and particularly the policy shift toward a commercial, privatized Internet, played a significant role in the development of Internet Exchanges, economic, competitive, and technical factors also played important parts.

For our purposes, we have divided the evolution of the Internet from a federal initiative to a privatized, commercial service into three phases, and we examine the role of Internet Exchanges in each of these phases and relate those roles to changing policies, technologies, economics, and competitive forces.

- *Structured Exchanges in a Federal Internet.* The U.S. federal government played a central role in the Internet from its inception through perhaps early 1995. What we call "structured exchanges" were developed during this phase to support an Internet composed of independently administered networks. These exchanges, for example, allowed the NSFNET backbone to be easily administered and operated independently of the NSFNET regional networks.

- *Alternative Exchanges in an Emerging Commercial Internet.* Starting in about 1990, a number of Internet Exchanges were created primarily to bypass policy restrictions on commercial traffic imposed by the federally funded portions of the Internet. These "alternative exchanges" were crucial to the development of the commercial Internet.

- *Peer Exchanges in a Privatized, Commercial Internet.* The end of the transition from the federally supported Internet to a privatized

Internet was marked by the decommissioning of the NSFNET backbone in 1995. Peer interconnects enabled the creation of a privatized Internet composed of numerous nationwide and regional service providers as well as a smooth transition from the federally sponsored NSFNET to privatized services.

This very brief history is, by necessity, only a terse summary of one facet of a very large project. During this period, a variety of interconnects existed in many forms. We have chosen to focus on interconnects that we consider important either because they enabled a particular policy, because they were created in response to a policy, or because they were critical to the operation of the Internet.

Structured Exchanges in a Federally Supported Internet

The early exchanges within the NSFNET were created primarily to assist the administration and operation of the NSFNET by providing well-defined interfaces between independently administered and operated portions of the NSFNET.

The original NSFNET architecture was a three-tier hierarchy, with the NSFNET backbone at the top. The NSFNET was funded by the National Science Foundation (with considerable cost-sharing by industry), and designed, implemented, and operated by a consortium lead by MERIT Inc. In the second tier were the NSFNET regional networks (also called mid-level networks), which were administered and operated independently of the NSFNET backbone, but heavily depended upon and closely coordinated with it. At the bottom of the hierarchy were the organizations receiving Internet connectivity, which in this era were typically called "campuses."[4]

The NSFNET backbone provided interregional transit services to the regional networks. This considerably simplified the routing challenges faced by the regional networks because the regionals only had to provide routing between the campus networks that they served. Traffic destined for campuses attached to other regional networks was forwarded by the regional networks to the NSFNET backbone, which was responsible for the correct routing of traffic between regions.

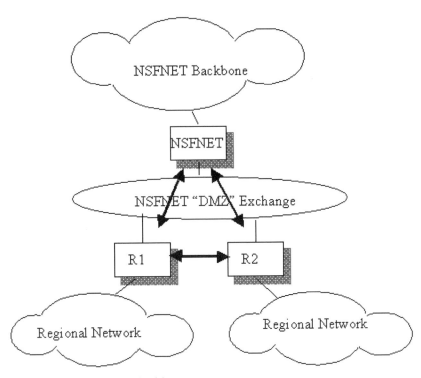

Figure 2 Early NSFNET Architecture.

The NSFNET backbone was implemented as a few dozen nodes interconnected with a partial mesh of point-to-point links. The NSFNET nodes were generally hosted by academic institutions or NSF-funded supercomputer centers. The regional networks connected to the NSFNET backbone by extending their networks to a convenient NSFNET node. A LAN-based exchange, often called a DMZ (referring to the isolation aspect of demilitarization zones), enabled communications between regional networks and the NSFNET backbone, while at the same time providing a degree of isolation between these independently administered networks.

The NSFNET experience demonstrated that well-structured Internet Exchanges contributed to the smooth interaction between independently administered parts of the Internet. A clear demarcation of responsibilities, supported by the Internet Exchange architecture, contributed to the success of the exchanges. The regional network was responsible for transporting its traffic to

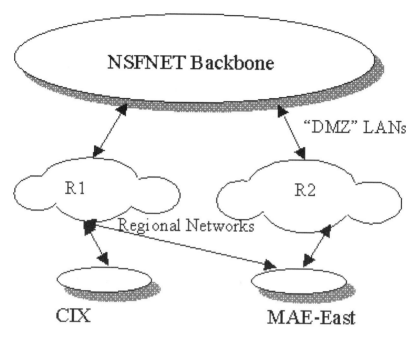

Figure 3 A Typical NSFNET DMZ.

the DMZ LAN, the site hosting the NSFNET node was responsible for ensuring that the DMZ LAN operated smoothly, and the MERIT consortium was responsible for transporting traffic between the DMZ LAN and the rest of the Internet.

In retrospect, the demands placed upon these structured exchanges were simplified by the relatively homogeneous policy environment within which they existed. The attached networks, the NSFNET backbone and the regionals, were completely dependent upon each other and upon the NSF. Without a connection to the NSFNET backbone, which was awarded by the NSF, it was nearly impossible for the regionals to provide Internet connectivity. Conversely, the NSFNET backbone depended on the regional networks to provide Internet connectivity to the campuses. In a similar fashion, both the regionals and the NSFNET backbone were heavily dependent upon the NSF for funding (although some of the regionals' funding came indirectly through grants to connect academic institutions to the regional networks).

Alternative Exchanges in an Emerging Commercial Internet

Undoubtedly the most significant policy of the NSFNET backbone was its acceptable use policy (AUP),[5] which specified that only traffic supporting research and education was permitted on the NSFNET backbone. Inasmuch as the NSFNET backbone was the principal mechanism for interregional transport, it was very difficult for regional networks to exchange traffic that did not conform to the NSFNET AUP (usually called "commercial" traffic). Alternative exchanges were developed to bypass the NSFNET AUP, creating the "commercial" Internet.

Commercial organizations have been connected to the Internet nearly since its inception. Within the NSFNET community, there was a general feeling that commercial organizations should be permitted to connect to the NSFNET, particularly if they communicated primarily with educational and research organizations. The connection of commercial organizations supported the research and education mission of the NSFNET in several ways. It aided and sometimes even enabled educational and research collaboration between industry and academia. Some vendors, particularly those of computer or networking products, used the Internet to provide better service to their research and education customers. Commercial organizations often subsidized academic connections by spreading some of the relatively fixed costs of the regional networks over a larger number of customers, by helping the regional networks attain some economies of scale, and in many cases, through a rate structure which favored academic institutions over commercial organizations.

A number of the regional networks saw commercial organizations as a tremendous potential market segment. Many of them allowed commercial traffic within their own networks, even though commercial traffic was not permitted on the NSFNET backbone. Commercial traffic could be exchanged with "nearby" sites attached to the same regional network, but only research and education traffic could be exchanged with "distant" sites which involved transit across the NSFNET backbone. The complete lack of tools that would enable users to determine whether commercial traffic was allowed between a pair of sites caused no small amount

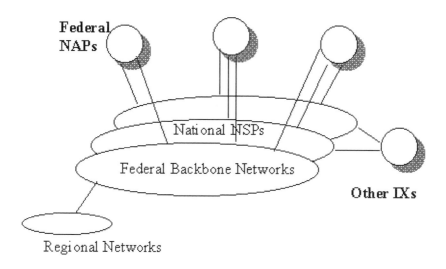

Figure 4 Alternative Exchanges and the NSFNET.

of confusion for users, who simply could not tell when commercial traffic was prohibited and when it was permitted.

In 1990, three network service providers, CERFNET, Alternet, and PSI, formed the Commercial Internet Exchange (CIX)[6] to allow them to exchange commercial traffic among themselves. The CIX created an exchange point in Santa Clara, California, that enabled the three networks to exchange commercial traffic without using the NSFNET backbone. The CIX quickly expanded its membership beyond the three founding members. Approximately a year later, another alternative Internet interconnect, MAE-East, was created in the Washington, DC, area.

The CIX was perhaps the first Internet Exchange created in response to policy concerns, in this case the NSFNET AUP.

The CIX was successful, in a policy sense, in that it achieved its mission of providing an AUP-free method of exchanging commercial traffic between regional networks. Nevertheless, it also gave rise to a number of difficulties. The CIX created a single point of failure and congestion because most commercial traffic between regional networks was transported through it. It also created some very long paths, for example when traffic between two East Coast sites was transported through the CIX on the West Coast.

Perhaps the most serious difficulty which resulted from the creation of the CIX was that in many cases two paths existed between a pair of sites: an AUP path through the NSFNET backbone and a non-AUP path through the CIX. The choice between these two potential paths should have been, in theory, based solely on the content of the traffic, namely whether the traffic conformed to the NSFNET AUP. Unfortunately, there was no mechanism that could mark traffic as AUP or non-AUP. To the network, packets were simply data; there was no difference between AUP and non-AUP traffic. Of course, this situation only compounded the difficulties users faced in trying to determine whether non-AUP traffic was permitted between a pair of sites.

Selecting the appropriate path—the NSFNET or the CIX—was also important because the two paths were very different. The NSFNET backbone had evolved to T3 (45 Mbps) speeds while the CIX remained a T1 (1.5 Mbps) interconnect. Therefore, regional networks wanted to use the CIX only to exchange non-AUP traffic, and the higher-performance NSFNET backbone to exchange AUP traffic. However, because the available routing technology was completely incapable of routing AUP traffic across one path and non-AUP traffic across another path, regional networks used one or more approximations, none of which were particularly good:

- some networks preferred the CIX path over the NSFNET backbone path;
- some networks preferred the NSFNET backbone path;
- some networks refused to use the CIX; and
- many networks used a fair amount of handcrafted routing.

There was an effort to simplify this confusion by classifying end sites as either "research and education" or "commercial." This attempt did not get very far because the path through an IP network is based on the destination of the traffic rather than the source, and not whether the source and destination are in the same class (in this case, whether the source and destination were both commercial sites). This scheme also ignored the fact that some traffic originating from a nominally commercial site would conform to the NSFNET AUP while other traffic would not.

At about the same time, debate arose over the proper architecture for an Internet which could easily support both AUP and non-AUP traffic. One model proposed that a single backbone network transport both AUP and non-AUP traffic, and that mechanisms be developed which would identify non-AUP traffic and charge different rates for transporting AUP and non-AUP traffic. Opponents of this plan viewed it as creating a monopoly for interregional Internet transport. They advocated a number of competing, nationwide networks which exchanged traffic among themselves at Internet Exchanges throughout the country. The success of the CIX and other alternative exchanges largely made this debate moot, because they allowed a monopolistic backbone to be bypassed in the same way that they had allowed the AUP NSFNET backbone to be bypassed.

Peer Exchanges in a Privatized, Commercial Internet

Peer interconnects have made possible the privatization of the Internet, facilitating the relatively smooth transition from federal support. In today's Internet, interregional data transport is provided by a collection of interconnected, nationwide Network Service Providers. A single, centralized core network analogous to the NSFNET backbone no longer exists. Internet interconnects are a fundamental component of this new architecture.

The current Internet architecture is the product of two complementary policy trends. Commercialization was furthered by the alternative exchanges described above. Meanwhile, the NSF found that a substantial portion of its funds available for networking activities was being consumed by the support of operational networks. This operational network funding comprised three components: support for the NSFNET backbone, direct support for regional networks, and grants to educational institutions for connection to the Internet. The heavy demand for funds for operational networking displaced funding for network research projects, a source of some concern on the part of the NSF. The desire to shift funds from operational networking led to a policy of privatization, the migration of responsibility for interregional transport away from the NSF-funded NSFNET backbone to private, nationwide

Network Service Providers. A key part of this strategy was the creation of Internet interconnects that ensured continued universal connectivity.

In 1993, the NSF issued solicitation NSF 93-52 , which specified a new NSFNET architecture in which interregional transport was provided by several nationwide NSPs connected by Internet interconnects. The solicitation called these interconnects "network access points" or "NAPs." A NAP was described as a "conceptual evolution of the FIX and the Commercial Information eXchange (CIX)." NAPs were AUP-free, so the transit of commercial traffic was not to be impeded by policy. Proposals to host and manage NAPs were solicited.

The NSF sponsored four NAPs in response to the solicitation: New York (Sprint), Chicago (Ameritech), California (Pacific Bell), and Washington, DC (MFS). These NAPs enabled the transition from a federally funded NSFNET backbone to an architecture in which interregional transport is provided by interconnected nationwide NSPs. This project enabled the NSF to eliminate the NSFNET backbone and shift funds to other projects.

The peer interconnect-based architecture effectively mitigated other policy-based impediments to traffic. In 1994, the CIX decided that it would not transport data for regional NSPs that were connected to CIX members but were not CIX members themselves. The announcement of this policy generated quite a bit of concern about a balkanized Internet. However, by the time this policy was finally implemented, it affected only a few small NSPs. There were enough Internet interconnects that only those NSPs connected solely to the CIX were potentially affected. Most Internet connectivity either occurred or could occur at other Internet interconnects, so the CIX had only a very limited ability to impose its policy on the Internet as a whole. The parallels between the CIX as a method of circumventing the restrictive effects of the NSFNET AUP and multiple Internet interconnects circumventing the CIX's later efforts to impose policy-based restrictions on traffic flows seem rather ironic.

The CIX's effort at policy-based filtering did, however, highlight a continuing conflict in the privatized Internet. Regional NSPs depend on national NSPs for interregional data transport. The

CIX, by its very nature, allowed both regional and nationwide NSPs to connect, and specified that all networks should exchange traffic with each other. The nationwide NSPs viewed this as requiring them to provide the smaller NSPs attached to the CIX with free transit services. There was also a perception, particularly on the part of the small NSPs attached to the CIX, that the CIX filtering proposal was being used by some of the nationwide NSPs as an unfair competitive tool against the small NSPs.

Scaling the Internet: Interconnect Exchange Issues

As traffic on the Internet continues to grow and connectivity becomes increasingly ubiquitous, designers and policymakers are faced with a number of system scaling

issues. The increasing number of NSPs and the need for globally efficient routing require the establishment of more Internet Exchanges, while increasing traffic requirements force existing IX managers to ensure that IX capacity stays ahead of demand. National Internet Exchanges are typically located at points of high traffic and physical bandwidth (trunk lines) aggregation, which suggests colocating other services such as large Web caches to gain economies of scale. Another key component of Internet system scaling thus far has been the technical evolution of protocols and architecture to accommodate new services. The availability of traffic and performance data has helped researchers suggest protocol improvements. As the number, size, and technical complexity of Internet Exchanges increases, traffic statistics and other sources of data required for network analysis are increasingly difficult to obtain, with potentially severe consequences for scaling the Internet.

Scaling the Number of Interconnect Exchanges

A key advantage of more interconnection points is potentially shorter traffic paths between sources and destinations that are not attached to the same NSP. Routing policy control tools allow NSPs to optimize traffic flows on their backbone networks (albeit with handcrafted configurations). A system architecture in which regional Internet Exchanges use one or more national NSPs for connectivity to the national and international IXes provides a hierarchical means of scaling the number of Internet Exchanges.

However, in order to take advantage of these multiple paths, NSP routers at the interconnect exchanges must carry a complete set of Internet routes. Moreover, every routing fluctuation, or flap, must be processed by these routers. IP routing protocols do not currently have efficient means of damping down the propagation of route flaps, and as the number of Internet Exchanges increase, so does the amount of information that each NSP router must process. This results in a degradation in packet forwarding rates and lost packets. Current research into damping mechanisms shows some promise of alleviating this problem.

Along with the ability to deal gracefully with route flapping, Internet routing protocols are still evolving to best accommodate load balancing and path optimization across multiple IXes. The closest IX exit point for a packet is typically determined by only the destination address and not the combination of the source and destination addresses. The result is an asymmetric path, with traffic in one direction using a different IX than traffic in the opposite direction. While this is usually not a serious operational problem, end-to-end path optimization is still a manual process and fraught with high potential for operator error.

Scaling the Performance of Internet Exchanges

A packet between two end sites, A and B, traverses an interconnection exchange if A and B are customers of two different NSPs. This implies that as the number of NSPs continues to grow and share the marketplace, the volume of interconnection traffic will continue to increase. Currently we see approximately 200–400 megabits per second of sustained traffic across the busiest interconnects (MAE-East and the New York NAP). Additionally, many larger NSPs and some research networks are moving towards OC-3 (155 megabits per second) connections to IXes. Internet Exchanges are high traffic aggregation networks and, if not designed to sustain offered load, they can be choke points in the Internet infrastructure. Thus IX capacity must scale with demand.

Current switching technology dictates the offered capacity at IXes. Some Internet Exchanges use shared and switched FDDI as the switching substrate, which limits inter-NSP bandwidth to 100 megabits per second (or 200 megabits per second with full-duplex router interfaces). Other IXes use ATM switches, which appear to have the potential to scale to higher speeds but have not yet been proven to operate robustly under heavy traffic loads.

System-wide Measurements and Capacity Planning

With new services and applications constantly being prototyped on the Internet, it is crucial that we understand the nature of Internet traffic. Protocol researchers and developers need to adapt existing protocols or create new ones to deal with these new services. Access to traffic statistics of various types and at various time granularities is essential for the effort. In the past, backbone and regional network operators exchanged relevant statistics to optimize traffic flows between their networks. Currently, most commercial NSPs treat their traffic statistics as confidential information.

The challenge for policymakers is to create a forum where traffic information provided by the NSPs is used only for research and analysis, and NSPs can continue to compete on the basis of well-defined service metrics. To this end, the Internet Engineering Task Force (IETF) IP Provider Metrics (IPPM) working group is attempting to define a set of service quality metrics that could be used to objectively characterize NSP service quality. This would effectively remove any advantage (or disadvantage) for NSPs in making available traffic data, while still allowing service distinction on the basis of standard metrics.

Summary: Implications for Policymakers

Oversight

The Internet model of an interconnection of independently administered networks implies that Internet Exchanges will continue to play an important role in the global information infrastructure. The analogy with the U.S. system of airports seems appropriate. Each IX, like each airport, is independently owned and administered. However, because of the interconnectedness of the airline system and because the safety and convenience of passengers are of primary concern, oversight in the form of the Federal Aviation Administration (FAA) exists to protect the integrity of the system. The questions for policymakers are: What, if any, oversight of the system of independently owned and administered Internet Exchanges is necessary to protect Internet end-user service and performance? Who ought to provide that oversight?

Scaling

With the National Science Foundation sponsoring the NSFNET project, the U.S. government was both a Network Service Provider through its cooperative agreement with MERIT, as well as a client for network service through regional network support programs such as the Connections program. As a consequence of this dual role, considerable attention was given to the stability of the system of networks, through applied research in traffic analysis, network management tools, and protocol engineering. While most larger NSPs do have network engineering efforts in house, system-wide research must be continued. Historically, federal funding of Internet-related research has been fundamental to the success of the Internet. Operation of the Internet has been successfully privatized, an evolution in which Internet Exchanges played a key role. However, it is not clear that the funding of research necessary to scale the Internet to meet projected demands has been as successfully assumed by the private sector. In our view, there still remain important roles for the U.S. government to play in supporting critical aspects of Internet research.

This work was supported by national Science Foundation Cooperative Agreement NCR-9321072.

Notes

1. V. Cerf, "The Catenet Model For Internetworking," IEN 48, Information Processing Techniques Office, Defense Advanced Research Projects Agency, July 1978.

2. D. L. Mills and H. Braun, "The NSFNET Backbone Network," *Proceedings Of ACM SIGCOMM 1987.*

3. NSF 93-52, "Network Access Point Manager, Routing Arbiter, Regional Network Providers, and Very High Speed Backbone Network Services Provider for NSFNET and the NREN(SM) PROGRAM," May 1993.

4. B. Chinoy, and H. Braun, "The National Science Foundation Network," SDSC Technical Report GA-A21029, September 1992.

5. "The NSFNET Backbone Acceptable Use Policy," June 1992, available from Merit Inc., at <http://www.merit.edu/nsfnet/acceptable.use.policy>.

6. The Commercial Internet eXchange, <http://www.cix.org>.

Interconnection, Pricing, and Settlements: Some Healthy Jostling in the Growth of the Internet

Richard A. Cawley

Introduction

This chapter examines the issue of settlements and financial transfers within the Internet and between Internet Service Providers (ISPs), and reflects on whether there is a role for public policy or coordination of some kind (presumably at an international level) to support the continued growth and expansion of the Internet. Settlement is treated in a general fashion as well as within a dynamic context, and is not limited to the financial arrangements (or the lack of them) between peering networks at the top of the Internet network hierarchy. The main dynamic aspects that the chapter examines are (1) the transition from cooperative to increasingly competitive network behavior, particularly in the establishment of global backbones and peering groups, and (2) the development of service applications, particularly those requiring priority service quality and/or high bandwidth.

The Internet has a number of virtues, among which are its extremely cost-effective delivery of data packets (via the statistical sharing of network infrastructure) and its ability to encourage usage via (for the most part) flat-rate pricing. However, as it expands and upgrades, the Internet faces a number of challenges. As applications and traffic types become even more diverse (particularly with the growth in real-time applications), and given that bandwidth is not always or everywhere unlimited in capacity, the Internet must find the means to prioritize traffic where necessary and, by implication, to price (implicitly or explicitly) such prioritization. It also faces the challenge of producing the right signals to encourage investment in network capacity and improvements and upgrades in provisioning. This is as much an international issue as it is a national one.

This chapter considers the question of settlement between Internet networks as the Internet continues to develop. It argues that settlement policy must be situated in the context of developments in Internet architecture and protocols and pricing generally. Settlement at a national or international level can be thought of as one aspect of interconnection where interconnection is really about the pricing of access.

Thus the chapter examines the current architecture and pricing of the Internet and the way in which they may evolve as means are found to enable real-time applications or to develop variable levels of service quality beyond the current best effort approach inherent in Transmission Control Protocol/Internet Protocol (TCP/IP). It also looks at current practice for Internet settlements and financial transfers and examines some of the pressures for change or modification, particularly as participants attempt to exercise market power and as the number of interconnecting networks grows and spreads geographically. It then suggests some principles to follow (and pitfalls to avoid), while drawing some lessons both from Internet practice and from the telecommunications arena.

Despite its phenomenal growth and increasing commercial success, the Internet remains in an early evolutionary phase. It is still an interesting mix of academic and commercial networks, cooperative and competitive, despite the withdrawal of the early modest public funding it had received. In addition, the Internet faces a number of key upgrading transitions. One of them is the introduction of possible quality of service choices (in addition to the single best effort service currently available). This may occur via any of a number of routes, such as the deployment of Resource Reservation Protocol (RSVP) or simply through the establishment of variable quality of service levels in inter- and intra-company networks. Another important transition is tackling the current shortage (and inefficient use) of addresses, with Internet Protocol version 6 (IPv6) offering a possible solution (though not to all the routing and addressing problems that characterize a growing Internet) if it can be comprehensively deployed.

Against this background a startling process of growth and innovation centering on the Internet and the World Wide Web is taking place; it is linked to a whole range of developments, including rapid advances in browser software, increasing PC processing power, faster routers, and now the development of IP switches. For at least two reasons, 1996 may well be a landmark year for the Internet. First, a number of more commonly used pieces of software for Internet telephony have emerged – something which RSVP deployment may well further encourage. For example, Netscape has incorporated CoolTalk into Navigator 3.0, VocalTec has made versions of its telephony software available for both Windows95 and PowerPC, and the Intel/Microsoft partnership is also trying to establish a standard with its telephony software. If nothing else, the demand for 16Mb RAM PCs is likely to be stimulated. The other important development is the exploitation, in the United States at least, of the Intel Intercast circuit board which puts broadcast TV alongside Web page interaction on PCs; parallel developments enable wide-screen television sets to put interactive Web pages alongside the traditional image. Compaq and Hauppage Computer Works began shipping Olympic Games-ready interactive PCs in July 1996, and AST and Sony also announced intentions to produce Intercast-ready PCs. Increasing PC processing power and the decreasing price of bandwidth are likely to accelerate the process of voice and video transport over the Internet. It does not really matter if the analysts say that Internet telephony is of inferior quality or that it will bring the Internet down. People will use it and improvements will keep occurring.

Just as significantly, the expansion of the Internet offers three important features for the traditional communications world. First, it presents a means and a justification for the incremental upgrading of local access capacity, a feature that was missing in the traditional telephone-to-broadband vision. Second, it offers the interactivity so sorely missing in the broadcast model. Third, and probably most important, it offers a challenge to the archaic pricing model of the telecommunications world.

Many have called for institutional or coordinated solutions for interconnection and settlement in the Internet. Some, within the context of a range of policy issues including greater geographical development and solutions to addressing and other problems, have appealed for an international governing body like the International Telecommunication Union (ITU) for the Internet. The general message of this chapter on interconnection and settlement is that market solutions are better than institutional ones even if they involve periods of apparent anarchy and chaos.

This is not to say that there are not problems ahead in Internet scaling and that the externalities or transaction costs involved may favor public policy or coordinated solutions. On the content side, the work on the Platform for Internet Content Selection (PICS) being undertaken by the World Wide Web Consortium is a good example. Problems related to addressing also require coordinated action even if it is complemented by market mechanisms. However, one of the aims of this chapter in examining pricing and interconnect issues in the Internet is to warn of the dangers of excessive institutional or managed influences, particularly on settlement. The problems that still plague pricing and settlements in telecommunications (the international context is the prime example) demonstrate how difficult it is to adapt institutional arrangements once they are in place.

The Dynamic Context of Pricing and Settlements in the Internet

Although the Internet continues to be upgraded in many of its component areas (e.g., the parts of the backbone in the United States operated by MCI and Sprint were upgraded to 155 megabits per second in 1996), the growth in users, traffic, and the range of applications (e.g., Web page traffic has now surpassed electronic mail and become the largest category of Internet traffic) means that congestion in certain parts of the network and/or at certain times of the day is problematic. Generally, evidence on congestion tends to be anecdotal. A thorough assessment of congestion by neutral parties is difficult, particularly now that traffic figures on the Internet are not widely available, as they were until 1994 via Merit Network Inc. MFS does make available traffic profiles through the main interconnect points that it manages.[1] In addition, there are attempts under way to assemble a number of pertinent network metrics in a coordinated and consistent fashion.[2] This seems a worthwhile exercise if only to show that the Internet is still managing to grow gracefully despite the occasional hiccup.

One of the difficulties is that perceived Internet congestion can arise for a number of reasons or take a number of forms depending on the application being used. Bottlenecks may be caused by a variety of factors, including the processing power of the PC being employed, the speed of the local connection, the access network and equipment of the ISP, the Internet itself, or the destination server being accessed.

But given that Internet congestion is a problem, a number of proposals have been made to address it, particularly in the context of the current one-class, best-effort service model. It should be noted that congestion pricing (or its absence) is just one element in the overall pricing structure of the Internet, even if it has naturally attracted much attention. One of the earliest proposals for congestion pricing[3] involves a very sophisticated form of taxation, or "smart market", which also serves to extract consumer surplus for future investment in the network. Other proposals have been made and congestion pricing has also been investigated for multiple networks.[4]

At the same time, Selwyn and Townsend[5] have warned of the dangers of moving to usage-based pricing for the Internet, bearing in mind the overhead or transaction costs involved (particularly in the context of packet-switched connectionless networks such as the Internet) and the fact that telecommunications networks (which for so long have exemplified inefficient pricing structures) are beginning to move from usage-based toward more flat-rate pricing formulae.

One added complication is that while the congestion and pricing debate has been under way, moves have also been afoot to develop technical means to prioritize traffic or applications, handle real-time applications, and in general develop variable quality of service.[6] The specification for the RSVP reservation protocol has now been agreed although questions still remain over how reservation attempts will be accounted and priced. Clark[7] has proposed a very practical approach to introducing quality of service (plus a means to signal where there is a need to increase capacity), and has argued the need to get the right mechanisms implemented within the Internet to control bandwidth allocation. Shenker and others[8] have put forward the notion of edge pricing.

In this context, a number of practical difficulties have been highlighted. On the user side, applications might have different requirements with respect to congestion parameters. These could range from a bound on the delay of the last packet arriving to a set of bounds on individual packets. On the network or accounting side, things are complicated by the fact that an application involves a large number of packets traversing a number of routers and networks in contrast, say, to the case of a single letter or package which is assigned a given level of service at the point of sending or the single accounting record associated with a traditional public switched telephone call. Even reducing the accounting load by means of sampling techniques still potentially imposes a large transaction cost on the monitoring and pricing of congestion.

In addition, other special features of the Internet include, in particular, the rather common circumstance in which the receiver rather than the sender requests the transaction (file or Web page download), the greater complexity of signaling willingness to pay for a given level of service quality, plus the case of multicast communications (which is an important and common feature of the Internet and the use of the IP protocol).

Much of the initial debate about quality of service, in particular in regard to real-time applications, has taken place in the context of the development of RSVP. The RSVP specification consists of two service models in addition to the current best effort service model. The highest level of service quality is denominated "guaranteed service" which essentially involves reserving path-specific resources through the network. The second level is denominated "controlled load" and does not involve a bound on delay but is equivalent to the experience of using an unloaded network. The specific way a user (sender or receiver) will make her reservation or quality preference known and how this will be accounted for and charged are still not clear. The current best effort model which involves no usage or congestion charge within the network would continue to exist. This model, with zero incremental charges, does not of course prevent ISPs from offering packages, as they do now, which include usage charges, denominated in terms of log-on or dial-up time. Conversely, ISPs could offer variable quality of service based on (differential) flat-rate charges as opposed to usage-based ones, although they would need to develop incentive-compatible pricing structures with respect to capacity constraints.

The deployment of RSVP may therefore be the backdoor through which incremental or usage or congestion charging will be introduced to the Internet. At the same time, if properly engineered, such a development may permit a wide range of rival pricing schemes to emerge. A key feature will be to ensure that the advent of variable quality of service does not degrade current best effort service with its low or zero incremental charges.

In many ways, however, the lead on this may come from intranets or the equivalent of virtual private internets. It is, after all, the corporate sector that is at the fore in demanding security, service quality assurances, as well as real-time applications such as voice and video conferencing over the Internet.

The Wider Context of Technological Developments Affecting Internet Growth

The proposals for congestion pricing and the likely deployment of quality of service or reservation request possibilities also need to be set against the broader context of technological development in internetworking generally. As of August 1996, there were an estimated 40–50 million users connected to the Internet via about 13 million hosts. Many of these are connected via corporate Local Area Networks (LANs) or university campuses, but increasing numbers are connecting via individual ISP subscriptions. At the moment, these individual subscriptions appear to be split fairly evenly between the "handholding" usage-based charging of companies such as America Online and Compuserve and the "sort-it-out-yourself" flat-rate subscriptions with the many local, regional, and national ISPs. In addition, telephone companies are increasingly signing up Internet users directly.

No one knows exactly where all this is leading though companies and users are increasingly seeing the practical benefits of doing things over the Internet Protocol, despite congestion and other problems. It is also easy to organize private networking over IP within the context of the public Internet; hence the development of intranets, the IP equivalents of virtual private networks with automatic access to the public Internet. At the same time, the strains on routing throughput rise as LAN speeds, desktop processing speeds, and backbone speeds all increase. Many recognize that Asynchronous Transfer Mode (ATM) will play an important role as traffic speeds and types develop, and ATM/IP compatibility therefore becomes an issue. ATM is already being deployed to transport and manage IP traffic in backbone networks, but there is a range of views (often depending on industry background) as to whether pure ATM will become widespread or whether IP will dominate with ATM being exploited in a more simple fashion. One interesting reconciliation of IP and ATM (to achieve fast switching and routing over IP without the complexity of ATM) is Ipsilon's development of an IP switch based on the General Switched Management Protocol (GSMP) and the Ipsilon Flow Management Protocol (IFMP) that the company has developed.

It may not seem particularly important which technological means are used to allow the Internet to grow, become quicker, and handle more types of traffic, but it may well be that they will have an impact on the pricing structures that develop. For example, an IP-dominated route seems more likely to preserve the cost-effective, flat-rate pricing approach that has characterized Internet development to date. However, although ATM tariffs are higher than those of Frame Relay (or Switched Multimegabit Data Services [SMDS] and other "cloud-based" approaches) and are more complex (mainly because of the range of service classes) than both Frame Relay and dedicated circuits, it is fair to say that ATM pricing is in its early stages and it is difficult to predict what the outcome will be.

Current Internet Interconnect and Settlements Practice

Settlements in a general context can be thought of as payments or financial transfers between networks or Internet Service Providers, or for that matter users, in return for interconnection and interoperability. In practice, the supply of interconnection amounts to the ability to deliver or pass on packets from an interconnecting network or user. Only the large networks which peer with each other at the top of the Internet hierarchy are able to guarantee delivery to the full address space; others have to buy transit or interconnect with a network or networks that can guarantee the interconnection. Consequently, networks with a large number of end-users are more sought after. The general tradition in the Internet has been that payments from users at the periphery migrate toward the center but without any systematic settlements policy between the larger networks in the middle. The larger peering networks have therefore admitted and routed packets in return for generating and passing on their own traffic.

However, it is important to emphasize that Internet interconnection and settlements practice has already evolved substantially and the topology and hierarchy of interconnecting networks are now very complex. Initially, when the U.S. backbone was run by the National Science Foundation (NSF), the network hierarchy was relatively simple and flat. Users connected to regional networks which connected in turn to the backbone.

In 1990, the Commercial Internet Exchange (CIX) was formed by CERFnet, PSI, and AlterNet to provide an alternative interconnection mechanism for commercial providers. CIX members agreed to exchange traffic on a no-settlement basis. The disadvantage was that the interconnect point was on the West Coast of the United States, requiring a link to that point. This interconnect exchange remains the only global multilateral exchange point, though only a couple of dozen of the approximately 150 CIX members use it. ISPs now join CIX as much for the trade association benefits as for the interconnection and traffic exchange arrangements. ISPs can in any case interconnect their networks to the spreading Internet backbone or to peer networks at more and more places throughout the world. In 1991, the Metropolitan Area Ethernet-East (MAE-East) interconnect arrangement (provided by MFS) began as an experimental link between AlterNet, PSI, and Sprintlink. MAE-East and MAE-West have now developed into major interconnect points in the United States. The Federal Internet Exchange (FIX) East and West were also established to provide interconnect points for a number of public sector networks.

In 1993, four new Network Access Points (NAPs) were established under the sponsorship of the NSF: the New York NAP managed by Sprint, the Chicago NAP run by Ameritech, the Stockton, California, NAP managed by PACBell, and the Washington, DC, NAP run by MFS. Since the establishment of these four "public" interconnect points (which to some extent marked the retreat of the NFS from its key Internet involvement), a whole series of private exchanges has sprung up both in the United States and around the world.

As the number of networks and interconnect points multiplies, the nature of interconnection and settlements becomes more diverse. At some exchanges, ISPs collocate equipment, at others the interconnection is distributed. Some exchanges are "public," or fully open, others are private. Finally, at some interconnect points, multilateral settlement agreements are in force while at others bilateral arrangements have to be struck.

Moreover, as the number of networks and ISPs has grown and spread geographically, the larger networks have become more discriminating in their choice of peers. Just as large users have an incentive to pose as ISPs in order to peer at higher levels of the network hierarchy, the bigger ISPs have an incentive to weed out smaller members of their peer group and try to make them pay to interconnect. The dynamics of the growing Internet are becoming complex, particularly as a number of large players are trying to establish themselves as global backbone providers. As the competitive model edges out the cooperative one, bilateral interconnection arrangements at new private interconnection points are becoming more common than multilateral interconnection arrangements at public interconnection points.

In any case, the interconnection stakes are rising as the Internet grows. At one time, membership in CIX and a low-speed line to the exchange were sufficient to peer with the major networks. Now some of the large networks require a 45 Mbps presence at a minimum of three exchanges to conclude peering arrangements, thereby raising the entry costs considerably.

In general, however, the value of settlements is relatively small compared to the total amount of capital invested in the Internet just as the overall turnover of ISPs is low relative to the whole communications sector. This is true because (in contrast to the traditional telephone network, for example) a high proportion of overall network costs is borne by the companies and individuals that derive benefit from being connected to the Internet. These costs comprise equipment and labor associated with the terminating equipment and networks. In addition, dedicated links to the Internet Service Provider or beyond are often paid for directly. The parallel for the residential or private user is that the individual pays a fee to an ISP but at the same time purchases a PC, modem, and software and either rents an analog exchange line or an Integrated Services Digital Network (ISDN) line or pays for dedicated access (frequently obtained by the ISP on her behalf).

Typically, monies collected at the periphery by ISPs are passed toward the center to compensate the providers of backbone capacity and routers. To the extent that backbone providers are ISPs with individual customer or company accounts, they may both be payers or forwarders of monies they collect at the edge, or receivers of monies from ISPs using their backbone and routing capacity.

The general principle for settlement between lower and higher network levels has been that the ISP pays (essentially on its customers' behalf) based upon the capacity of the onward link. In some instances, settlement appears to be based on a committed information rate, paralleling a tariff option of Frame Relay. A company or large user interconnecting directly with the backbone or higher level in the network would also in principle pay settlement in the same fashion, based on interconnecting capacity. One question that has already arisen is whether such a payment should reflect not only the capacity of the link but also the traffic load and profile, i.e., be usage- rather than capacity-based. This issue is taken up in the following sections on pricing.

The continued successful growth of the Internet depends on, among other things, both effective interconnection (and, where appropriate, settlement) at the core of the network, and the ability to continue to attract monies via new users at the edge. In this context, several issues arise. The first is whether the more competitive model of interconnection and settlements that is emerging is sustainable by itself despite some of the turbulence involved. The second is whether increased use of real-time applications (via variable service quality or the ability to reserve network resources) will require some additional and coordinated settlements mechanisms. The third is the impact that the growing interrelationship between the Internet and traditional telecommunications networks will have on pricing.

An additional question is the settlement of dues for content as opposed to the settlement of dues for access or transport of packets. So far, much content has been provided free of charge. Where charges are levied, they could be handled quite independently of traffic which might or might not be priced at the margin or on a usage basis. However, content providers for ISPs might have an interest in having monies collected on their behalf. In truth, as secure electronic payments schemes emerge, this facility is just as likely to be handled by specialist third parties or dealt with directly between consumer and content provider. In many respects the issue that is more important, when traffic (and/or content) involves a usage fee, is how this can be billed to the receiver rather than the sender.

The remainder of this chapter examines the three issues raised above. Given that settlements are equivalent to net interconnection charges which in turn are a function of interconnection prices and costs, a number of pricing issues are examined. A strong argument is made in favor of flat-rate or capacity-based pricing as opposed to usage-based pricing. However, in a genuinely competitive model, a whole range of pricing approaches may emerge. The pricing scheme which has been employed to develop the Internet in New Zealand[9] is often cited as an example of a successful traffic-charging or usage-based scheme. In fact, it is closer to a proxy capacity-sharing scheme to enable gradual upgrading of the international link. The fact that payments are linked to expected levels of use (with a feedback mechanism) means that it lies somewhere between a capacity-based, flat-rate scheme and a strictly usage-based scheme.

Some Background on Pricing

As pointed out by MacKie-Mason and Varian,[10] users should in general face prices that reflect the resource costs that they induce so that they can make informed decisions about the use of such resources. This section is a short digression on pricing theory which is aimed at framing the discussion on pricing principles in both the Internet and the adjacent telecommunications sector so as to provide the background to settlement issues in both sectors.

Efficient or optimal pricing and resource allocation involve the calculation of optimal prices for potential investments and then, given the prices that will be charged, undertaking all investments whose benefits exceed costs. The optimal pricing rule involves equating demand prices to marginal costs. A particular problem that arises in telecommunications is that setting demand prices equal to marginal costs leads to deficits. The deficit problem arises in particular because there is no mechanism to induce consumers to reveal their preferences which would thus enable the relevant consumer surplus to be extracted. In fact, such mechanisms are often forbidden. Perfect price discrimination would be efficient (although not necessarily attractive to consumers who like to walk away with some consumer surplus) though in such a case unobtainable. In this situation two-part or multi-part tariffs can provide a practical solution even though they are not fully efficient. Essentially a fixed charge is added to the marginal cost determination. This fixed charge should be distinguished from any fixed charge intended to recover the cost of, say, connecting a particular user to a network. Two-part tariffs are not fully efficient because the added fixed charges may deter some users who at marginal cost prices would be willing to join the network and consume.

Further efficiency and practical problems arise at this general level. To the extent that significant pricing distortions exist in other parts of the economy, efficiency requires the consideration of second best conditions. Moreover, the necessity to balance budgets either at a general or sector-specific level requires the marking up of marginal cost prices to cover any revenue shortfalls. This is examined in the more practical context of interconnection pricing in the next section.

One issue that is pertinent to pricing in both the Internet and the telecommunications sector is the presence of joint or common costs. This becomes more significant as the Internet moves toward a variable quality of service model. In this way it will more closely resemble some aspects of electricity or postal networks. For example, electricity networks accommodate both residential and business users, including companies that require specific guarantees on supply levels and uninterrupted usage. Postal networks provide varying quality levels or delivery delays in exchange for a scale of charges.

Optimal pricing with joint costs (the straightforward example is peak-load pricing) involves charging for each type of output so that the available facilities are optimally used. Such an approach provides the case for not charging off-peak users a full share of the provisioning costs. Depending on demand considerations, optimal pricing may even allow off-peak users to pay only for operating costs and not make any contribution to incremental capacity.

Finally, pricing considerations are further complicated by the existence of externalities. This is a key factor in Internet usage. The price system is only efficient in allocating resources when prices reflect marginal opportunity costs. Yet consumption decisions by one user may adversely affect the consumption possibilities of another. This is the argument in favor of pricing congestion by including social costs as well as private costs. If there is no congestion, then marginal costs are zero and there is no need for usage charges.

Matching Prices to Costs in Interconnecting Networks

This section is a further digression on the question of pricing but it makes a specific link back to underlying costs in interconnecting networks. It addresses traditional telecommunications networks as well as the Internet.[11]

The question of pricing and interconnection in telecommunications has ostensibly been examined in recent years because of increasing facilities-based competition on a national basis and the need for entrants to interconnect with incumbent networks. But pricing and interconnection questions also arise in the context of international interconnection between networks particularly as the traditional interconnection and settlement arrangements between monopoly telecommunications providers begin to be undermined by competition.

Mitchell, Neu, Neumann, and Vogelsang[12] provide a rich theoretical and practical framework for the determination of interconnection prices where there are barriers to the market determination of prices for such services. The context is telecommunications interconnection between incumbents and entrants in the liberalizing European markets. They begin by considering the general theoretical approaches to pricing interconnection services. The first is unconstrained socially optimal interconnection charges. They conclude that interconnection pricing at or below marginal costs of providing such services can be optimal, but point out the difficulty of financing revenue shortfalls from taxes or elsewhere. The second approach considered is Ramsey pricing of interconnection charges, where optimal pricing is constrained by revenue requirements and is a function of elasticity parameters. They conclude that the explicit application of such methods leads to complicated and opaque results although the pricing models are useful in suggesting in what circumstances markups over marginal cost are advisable or not. The third approach is the efficient component pricing rule which has been used in some circumstances to regulate the competitive provision of resale services in telecommunications. Here the rule is basically rejected as inappropriate for the introduction of competition into an imperfectly regulated monopoly market. No explicit consideration is made of a fourth possible approach mentioned, which is revenue sharing between interconnecting operators. They acknowledge that such an arrangement may be advantageous as long as the parties are facing sufficient competition from others. Otherwise there is a danger of collusion.

They then set out arguments in favor of an approach based on costs, in particular average incremental costs, with the possibility of markups to cover legitimate revenue requirements where justified. Note that the context here involves some degree of imperfect competition. Such an approach requires identifying cost elements and determining how they should be priced.

Mitchell et al. identify five types of costs involved in providing interconnection services:

• the cost of conditioning the system generally for interconnection;

• the cost of establishing physical interconnection between any two networks, including numbering/routing arrangements;

• the cost in the case of telecommunications of providing sufficient capacity for switching and transmission in order to accommodate interconnecting traffic at peak times;

• the variable costs of setting up calls, billing and so forth; and

• the fixed and variable overhead costs of management and accounting, including overhead related to other categories.

They point out that the capital costs of the first three categories dwarf the predominantly variable or usage costs of the last two. They also focus attention on the third category and go on to consider capacity-based pricing and its link with peak-load pricing. Capacity-based pricing, according to which users pay the relevant charges at each point in time for that part of capacity reserved for them, is excessively complex when a large number of users is involved. However, for a small number of interconnecting users with predictable load requirements it appears to be feasible. Capacity-based pricing can also be compatible with peak-load pricing; the allocation mechanism would be to price capacity in proportion to peak-capacity utilization.

The general conclusion is that, with the exception of a few cost elements linked to variable costs or traffic-sensitive costs, the bulk of interconnection charges should be linked to identifiable capital costs or capacity charges. This, of course, is some way from typical current practice in telecommunications interconnection, which has frequently been based on minutes of traffic and at price levels that indicate considerable markups on incremental costs. Such practice seems to provide evidence that interconnection pricing is influenced by ease of accounting as well as the market power of the entities involved.

It remains to be seen whether capacity-based interconnection arrangements will emerge in telecommunications. However, it is important to note that the gradual emergence of more competitive market forces between interconnecting operators will mean at least that the traditional revenue-sharing correspondent arrangements for international interconnection and settlement will be replaced by more cost-based interconnection or access charges.

In the case of Internet service and interconnection over communications facilities, the technological model and the pricing issues are different but there are some common features. In dealing with congestion and pricing of the Internet, MacKie-Mason and Varian[13] identify the main cost elements generated by Internet users. In effect there is a hierarchical structure for the Internet, with users or groups of users connecting to local or regional networks which in turn link to the backbone networks. The rule of thumb so far has been that interconnecting backbone networks do not charge each other. That, incidentally, has the major advantage of keeping the lawyers out of the equation.

MacKie-Mason and Varian provide the following list of main cost elements that need to be recovered from users:

• the fixed costs of providing network infrastructure;

• the incremental costs of connecting to the network;

• the cost of expanding network capacity;

• the incremental cost of sending packets; and

• the social cost of delaying other users' packets when the network is congested.

The first cost is recovered by flat-rate access fees. In some ways the problem can be likened to that described above dealing with sharing out capacity charges. The relevant principle is the one established above in the section on pricing: apply the cost-benefit test so as to ensure that the willingness to pay exceeds the cost of provision.

The second should be borne by users or interconnecting parties, and this is essentially the case. Where a connection shares an existing facility and entails no extra cost (e.g., a dial-up connection), this element of cost should be priced at zero, which is frequently the case. The question of the social benefits associated with network externalities implies that there is an argument for subsidizing connection at the margin that is related to the public gain from additional connections, or better still to target those who might abstain without a subsidy—but this raises practical difficulties.

The third element is contributing to overall network capacity and has some link with the question of congestion. If network usage never reaches capacity, then there is no need to expand capacity. MacKie-Mason and Varian argue that their proposal for congestion pricing provides the relevant guidance about when to expand capacity. If the cost of expanding capacity to handle more packets is less than the marginal value assigned to those packets (via the smart market or bidding mechanism), then it makes economic sense to expand capacity. Their optimal congestion pricing scheme ensures that only those who wish to use the network when it is at capacity pay for such an expansion. This has a corollary in using the share in capacity use by interconnectors during peak use to allocate cost in the telecommunications example. An alternative way of looking at it is the mimicking of joint ownership of network capacity in proportion to peak use.

The fourth cost element is essentially zero if the network is not congested. The situation changes in moving away from a single best effort quality of service model. The fifth cost element is the one to which much attention has recently turned. As has been pointed out, this is not directly a resource cost but should be considered as part of the social cost associated with sending extra packets. An optimal price would reflect the marginal cost of delay, if any, induced by additional packets and equal to the demand price of sending additional packets.

With the exception of the fifth element, the costs listed above are reflected in current Internet pricing structures. In the context of interconnection or settlements between different parts of the network, they are based on the effective capacity or speed of access, which serves as a proxy for the requirement for peak capacity in one or both directions.

Having treated the question of efficient pricing in networks, it is important to emphasize that genuine market rivalry may give rise to all forms and shapes of pricing. The period between 1893 and 1910 when the independent American telephone companies successfully took on AT&T in signing up customers should serve as an important reminder.[14] It was during that period that the flat-rate local telephone service model appeared (developed as a key entry strategy, where permitted, by the independents), and one that has fortunately survived until this day.

The Robustness of Current Pricing and Settlements Arrangements

One pertinent question is, how robust are the current pricing and settlement arrangements? Moreover, if they are to be changed, in which direction should they go and what principles should guide the changes?

The preceding section has extolled some of the virtues of flat-rate pricing at the wholesale and retail levels. Flat rates are often efficient, people like them, and they encourage usage. Implicitly it has been argued that settlement or net interconnection fees where they do exist should be linked to peak capacities rather than traffic flows. This does not mean that retail prices at the edge are automatically flat-rate. They could exhibit a range of possibilities as they do to some extent now, which is to be expected in a competitive ISP market.

What is more uncertain is whether the current overall settlement system is sustainable, particularly in the light of pressure from the larger networks to be more discriminatory with respect to their peering arrangements, and whether the development of quality of service (and pricing to match) will raise pressure to have a more formal, usage-based approach to settlements. The remainder of this chapter looks at these issues, but first considers settlements in the telecommunications sector and pressures for change there.

Settlements in Telecommunications

Before considering the sustainability of current settlements or net interconnection schemes in the Internet, it seems worthwhile to consider some of the pitfalls and drawbacks of the settlements process (and, for that matter, pricing) in parts of the telecommunications sector.

The traditional international settlement process in telecommunications has, to put it bluntly, been a disaster. Many of the institutional arrangements were put in place in good faith and served the important goal of finding a convenient, practical way to transfer monies at regular intervals and in agreed currency terms between a large number of administrations or operators. However, these arrangements have not been able to adapt to changing technological and commercial factors. Attempts by consultative committees to reform the original guidelines have met with resistance to change, and in any case have been unable to keep pace with technical and commercial changes in the sector. With its focus on bilateral negotiation on a global basis, the system also contains strong incentives for net recipients to resist and block changes. Furthermore, the accounting basis for settlements has automatically entrenched a system of usage-based charges.

Despite these significant price disincentives, international (public switched) traffic growth has managed a fairly respectable 10–15 percent annual growth rate. But this is considerably lower than the growth in telecommunications traffic over private facilities and is completely dwarfed by the magnitude of Internet traffic growth. Fortunately, increased facilities-based international telecommunications competition is finally beginning to undermine the system, but it remains extraordinarily resistant to change. Another fortunate side effect of increasing facilities-based competition is that the price of international circuits will further decline to reflect underlying costs. Higher effective speeds over fiber plus lower circuit prices translate into more capacity per dollar, although they do not necessarily solve the congestion problem.

Telecommunications settlements in the European context (Telephone relations between countries in Europe and the Mediterranean Basin or the TEUREM system, which exploited the regional provisions of the International Telecommunication Union guidelines) have operated differently than the global (or intercontinental) model. The European arrangement has some advantages, but for a number of reasons the outcome has been almost as disastrous as the intercontinental system. Rather than being based on an overall accounting rate split between the two operators, the European system of late has been defined essentially in terms of termination payments. Operators link (on a permanent basis) to a point of presence in the terminating country (the direction of the call for accounting purposes can of course be separated from the party which originally sets up the communication) by means of leased international half-circuits (as many as are required depending on whether a number of countries are being transited), and then pay termination fees based on measured delivered traffic.

One advantage of this system over the international bilateral negotiated accounting system has been that the multilaterally agreed termination fees were generally lower than the accounting rate equivalent, though still above cost. The drawbacks, however, have been several. First, monopoly telecommunications provision meant that the markups on cost to retail customers were considerable. Second, despite attempts to keep pace with declining cost structures, the cost of leased circuits and termination fees were set above what they should have been. Third, while some fee elements were flat-rate rather than usage-based, the significant minute-based charges automatically constrained the way retail tariffs were levied. In essence, the system has been rather similar to the interexchange access payments system in the United States but without long-distance competition and with very little regulatory oversight of underlying costs.

The systematic liberalization of telecommunications that is now occurring in Europe should ensure that the current system is replaced with something that looks much more like a set of decentralized interconnection arrangements (some negotiated, some regulated, with the prospect of a transition to more genuine market rivalry). Moreover, there will be alternative supply sources for leased circuits and increasing competition at the retail level. In principle, operators will be free to interconnect at whatever points of presence they so desire. However, whether they will be able to secure interconnection arrangements (for switched traffic) on a capacity rather than a usage basis remains to be seen. Until the former occurs, retail tariff structures are likely to be framed in usage terms even if the market is much more competitive. It may well be that variable, two-part tariff packages will begin to emerge in much the same way as has occurred in the more genuinely competitive, wireless cellular market.

The Dynamics of Internet Interconnection and Settlement

Earlier, this chapter described how interconnection, network hierarchy, and settlements in the Internet have already evolved into a complex mix of public and private interconnection, with bilateral and multilateral exchange and settlement arrangements and intense jostling between market participants to establish who has the right to sit at the top of the hierarchy (or even at a particular exchange) and thereby peer or exchange traffic on a no-settlement basis.

Of the thousands of Internet Service Providers around the world, only about 150 are members of the Commercial Internet Exchange (just over half of those are based in the United States, the remainder elsewhere), and only a couple of dozen of these directly exploit the capacity to interconnect at the CIX exchange. Half a dozen or more ISPs provide the bulk of backbone service in the United States over capacity that is owned by the three or four main long-distance infrastructure operators. At a more global level, half a dozen to a dozen entities are candidates for provision of international Internet services. Clearly, to provide a global backbone, as well as managing the network, signing up customers, and interconnecting with the rest of the address space, an operator has to have access to infrastructure. The remainder and vast majority of ISPs operate nationally or even locally and frequently resell service where regulatory restrictions make access to infrastructure problematic. They nevertheless provide an important function in signing up customers (large and small) and bringing in monies at the edge. Inevitably a consolidation phase will occur, much as it did with many local U.S. telephone companies in the early part of this century. At the same time, a more competitive model appears to be emerging at both the regional and global level; at the moment it is primarily aimed at the intranet and business markets.

Already there is substantial evidence that larger ISPs are refusing to deal with smaller providers, and subgroups of mutual interest or size are already being established to exchange traffic on a no-settlement basis. Smaller ISPs, particularly those outside the United States, therefore face a number of trade-offs in their interconnection strategy. For example, they could face the cost of paying for a dedicated connection to a "public" exchange point in the United States (or to a private one and negotiating exchange) or possibly in their home country; they may have to pay to interconnect with the national backbone operator(s) and pay transit; or they may attempt to become larger players more quickly, e.g., by consolidating geographically.

Much of what is observed seems to be chaotic but healthy market jostling and startup strategies in an industry with dramatic potential in an early growth phase. Any policy concerns should focus on issues such as anti-competitive behavior, possible market failure, or any genuine public good or interest questions.

The possibility of freely negotiated interconnection in the telecommunications context (not yet a reality) usually raises two main concerns. The first is that in the transition to competition, entrants may face difficulties in obtaining access to incumbent networks, particularly at reasonable prices. The second is that in a more mature competitive phase, established networks may use interconnection agreements to enforce collusive behavior.

Certainly there may be problems for Internet entrants in certain places, but some of the difficulties are gradually being dealt with through telecommunications deregulation. Potential divergences in the size of the higher-level networks mean that there will be incentives for some to abandon the principle of mutual exchange of traffic on a peer basis. In theory there is nothing wrong with refusing to deal or to peer, providing the entity concerned is not in a dominant market position; the refused party can always go elsewhere. It is less clear whether there will also be incentives for a small number of networks to break away and collude on interconnection pricing. Although this is a possibility, the market is still intensely competitive and users (both large and small) have considerable flexibility in their choice of the ISP(s) that they employ. In that sense, interconnection and settlement are best left to market forces.

The Deployment of Variable Quality of Service and the Approach to Congestion

There still seem to be some questions about how quickly the RSVP reservation protocol will be deployed and how specific the link between the ability to try to reserve network resources and the formal accounting and payment for such functionality will be. It also remains to be seen whether RSVP deployment will delight or disappoint in its ability to allow people to exploit various real-time audio and video applications. It may be that resource reservation or priority will work via direct and specific payments for specific path reservations, and thus there will likely be an impact on settlement processes since paths will need to be reserved across networks. At the same time, the accounting and engineering solutions may leave room for a number of competing pricing approaches to emerge so that low users could, if they wished, choose to pay on a usage basis while larger users could pay on a flat-fee or subscription basis. Once again, interconnection and settlement between networks would have to be negotiated.

More important, other technical means are likely to emerge to satisfy desires for better or variable service quality or the ability to exploit certain applications. This seems most likely in the corporate or intranet context, where certain sectors or companies are already demanding "premium" IP service. Because of the vast demand from the corporate sector for data communications of all types, including intracompany voice or video conferencing over IP, much of the pricing and settlement experimentation is likely to be played out there.

The Interplay between the Internet and the Telecommunications Sector

One of the interesting policy issues is the increasing interplay between the Internet and the traditional telecommunications sector, with signs of a similar interplay developing between the Internet and broadcasting. This stems partly from the increasing involvement of the telecommunications companies, which have realized that something is up; ironically it is the traditional telecommunications companies that have been most vociferous in calling for organized settlement mechanisms for the Internet. But the interplay also results from the promise of more widespread and successful use of Internet telephony and other potential benefits.

The interplay between the Internet and the telecommunications sector is currently observable at two distinct levels, one local, the other more global. At the global level, many of the larger telecommunications players want to establish an international Internet backbone presence for strategic reasons, particularly as large corporate clients increasingly want services over IP. But in this arena they are meeting up with some of the more developed U.S. Internet networks, which are used to doing things cooperatively.

At the local level, there are major access issues related to the pricing of leased circuits (or even to ISDN) and, in particular in the residential segment, related to the use of the local loop for dial-up purposes. So far, and despite the 1996 petition by the America's Carriers Telecommunication Association (ACTA) in the United States concerning internet telephony (which in any case was poorly argued because of the tenuous link that was made between software and common carriage and thereby the need to regulate), American ISPs and users have been able to exploit dial-up access at essentially zero incremental cost. Nevertheless, some have argued that substantial levels of Internet penetration impose costs on local exchange companies. In fact, there seems to be some disagreement as to whether local exchanges are able to handle the load, or are actually under severe pressure from Internet growth, or simply need to undertake small incremental investments to deal with the problem. As the pricing discussion earlier in the chapter indicated, if increasing Internet use does not actually increase required peak-load capacity, there is no requirement for any compensation from users via their ISPs. However, the specific question of peak-load capacity and how it is priced, taking into account a certain amount of geographical and seasonal averaging, is a complex one.

Perhaps a more fundamental question in the United States is whether local exchange companies, which by and large receive little additional compensation when local exchange lines are used for hours rather than minutes per day, will continue to deal favorably with ISPs as enhanced service providers or whether at some stage they will decide to fight back. The access charge issue is likely to figure prominently in the Federal Communications Commission's work on interconnection and universal service in the implementation of the 1996 Telecommunications Act. The correct approach would be to drastically reduce access charges, narrow down the costs attributed to plain old telephone service at the local level, maybe have a bit more rebalancing and let the local companies quickly into the long-distance market, but the final outcome could be much more protracted.

The Congestion Issue

Congestion has already been mentioned as an externality problem (which some have advocated pricing on a dynamic usage basis) in the context of best effort service in the Internet. The likely introduction of variable quality of service has also been addressed although this may take place in such a way that a number of pricing models could emerge.

The preceding section also highlighted the relevance of congestion in the telecommunications context. Here there is clearly an accumulated experience of traffic profiles and queuing problems which is specific to telecommunications networks. But it is important to emphasize that the congestion problem has been dealt with in this context by several means, including, in some parts of the world, rationing. To a large degree peak-load pricing, or variations thereof, has been used. But straightforward engineering or excess capacity solutions have also been employed (e.g., at the local exchange level in North America). And as an earlier section indicated, the Bell system has retained the flat-rate pricing model which emerged during a period of intense operator rivalry some 100 years ago, and which is now a key factor in stimulating Internet adoption and usage in the United States.

Conclusions

This chapter has examined interconnection and settlements in the Internet and has emphasized the dynamic context in which developments are taking place. In particular, it has highlighted the complex mix of interconnection and settlement mechanisms that are appearing and the various market incentives and trade-offs that are influencing behavior as the Internet becomes more commercial and competitive.

The chapter has extolled the virtues (and appropriateness) of capacity-based pricing and flat-rate tariffs, while acknowledging that congestion and quality of service issues in the Internet have yet to be successfully tackled, and that in any case, genuine market rivalry, particularly in an industry in an early growth phase, may give rise to all kinds of pricing models.

Calls for a systematic or coordinated approach to settlement policy appear to be directed at interconnection between peering networks at the top of the Internet hierarchy, where typically networks exchange traffic on a no-settlement basis. However, the dynamics are rapidly changing as the Internet grows and expands geographically. Many networks are actively assessing their traffic flows to determine whether they should modify their peering policies. In addition, many of the calls for systematic settlements seem to be coming from some of the established telecommunications operators, which appear to be trying to leverage their positions with respect to the number of users they can command, or indeed to recoup some of their own investments to provide improved service quality from other market players. In addition, it is not unambiguously clear, for instance, that large networks automatically receive a net imbalance of traffic from smaller ones.

The general conclusion, therefore, is that interconnection and settlement are best left to market forces and that no systematic coordination or intervention is required. Indeed, a range of interconnection, pricing, and settlement models could emerge and even coexist.

The coordinated international settlement system that persists in the telecommunications sector is a disaster, and it is taking a long time to undo it. Fortunately the system is being gradually undermined as international facilities-based competition increases. In this new context, settlement will reflect interconnection costs and prices, much of which can be linked to flat-rate elements. Moreover, liberalization of telecommunications can assist the development of market-based interconnection and settlement models, will further reduce underlying access and infrastructure costs, and will make it easier for ISPs in many countries to develop their networks.

At the same time, a number of prospective developments raise questions about Internet interconnection, pricing, and settlements in the future. One that has already been mentioned is the fact that the Internet is in an early growth phase and still in the transition to a more commercial stage with all the implications that has for start-up strategies and jostling for position. Currently, ISPs value corporate customers much more than private or residential ones. After all, there is little profitability in the latter. However, although much of the current focus is on intranet and corporate development, the growth of electronic commerce will have substantial implications for the value of connecting private consumers.

The development of variable quality of service (via RSVP or other means) and the demand for real-time and higher bandwidth applications raise questions regarding pricing, whether the lowest-quality best effort service will deteriorate as a consequence, and whether network resource reservations have particular implications for interconnection and settlement. It is, however, still possible to price variable service quality levels using flat-rate means, and indeed a number of pricing models could emerge. In addition, there are some questions over technological developments (and related pricing implications) involving IP over ATM or the use of IP switches.

The increasing interplay between the Internet and the traditional telephone network raises another concern. It has been observed that the main pressures on current Internet stability are at the center (i.e., the dynamics between the larger peering networks) and at the periphery. At the center, the number of peer networks is growing, network size is likely to be more variable, and a model of competing backbone operators seems to be emerging. At the edge, there is a risk that turbulence in telecommunications reform will lead to a backlash in some places by local operators which until now have made their local loops available at relatively marginal rates to ISPs that sign up customers. This may raise the price of basic Internet access, although the prospect of local competition for Internet delivery modes will act in the opposite direction and also holds the promise of steady incremental upgrades in access speed and quality.

Although increasing competition in the telecommunications sector raises some tricky issues (such as the pricing of local loops to ISPs or for Internet usage), it heralds the possibility of significant competition in the backbone, lower costs and lower prices of bandwidth, and it should help to generate a range of solutions, such as Frame Relay, SMDS, fast Ethernet, and ATM over which IP can be transported.

It is perhaps appropriate to end by posing the question of whether a systematic settlement system or policy would have al-

Table 1 Internet Development in Major OECD Countries (Hosts per 1,000 Population)

	July 1995	January 1996	July 1996
Belgium	2.4	3.1	4.3
Denmark	7.1	10.0	14.8
Germany	4.3	5.6	6.7
Greece	0.5	0.8	1.2
Spain	1.0	1.4	1.6
France	2.0	2.4	3.3
Ireland	2.8	4.2	6.0
Italy	0.8	1.3	2.0
Luxembourg	4.0	4.6	7.2
Holland	8.9	11.4	14.0
Austria	5.1	6.6	8.9
Portugal	0.9	0.9	1.8
Finland	22.1	41.2	54.5
Sweden	12.2	17.2	21.2
United Kingdom	5.0	7.8	9.9
Australia	11.7	17.5	22.3
Canada	9.1	13.0	14.5
Japan	1.3	2.2	4.0
United States	16.6	23.5	31.6
OECD average	6.3		12.6

Source: Network Wizards, OECD

lowed the Internet to grow more quickly. The answer, I think, is no. Would swifter liberalization of telecommunications have stimulated faster or more even Internet development? Here, I think, the answer is yes, and there is some evidence to support this claim in Table 1, which shows proxy measures of Internet growth with respect to population for the major OECD countries. Can Internet development upset the traditional pricing structures in telecommunications? The answer is yes. Will incumbent telecommunications companies try to resist by attempting to extend the market power they have to the Internet domain? Probably. Is all the jostling that is occurring good for users and Internet growth? Also yes.

The major outstanding question is whether engineering or pricing solutions will prevail in dealing with congestion and real-time applications. There is some evidence that the creation of abundance will prevail over the pricing of scarcity. First, demands for priority service and real-time applications in the business community will be dealt with via intranets. Second, the research community appears likely to receive special treatment via specific initiatives in response to its request for uncongested high-speed bandwidth. Third, the residential user will be able to gradually upgrade service possibilities as new competitive access possibilities emerge. However, to the extent that the telecommunications companies can control local access competition and influence the interconnection and settlement model, alternative access possibilities will be limited and usage-based pricing models will persist.

The author is an official of the European Commission. Nothing in this chapter should be construed as representing the policies of the Commission.

Notes

1. <http://www.mfs.datanet.com/MAE/index.html>.

2. <http://www.tomco.net/~tmonk/cooperation.html>.

3. J. K. MacKie-Mason and H. R. Varian, "Pricing the Internet," in B. Kahin and J. Keller, eds., *Public Access to the Internet* (Cambridge, Mass.: MIT Press, 1995).

4. Lehr and Weiss, "The Political Economy of Congestion Charges and Settlements in Packet Networks," Telecommunications Policy 20(3) (April 1996).

5. Selwyn and Townsend, "Internet Pricing: Lessons to Be Learned from the Public Switched Network," paper presented at the 2nd Annual Conference of the Consortium for Research on Telecommunications Policy, Northwestern University, 1996.

6. D. Clark, S. Shenker, and L. Zhang, "Supporting Real-Time Applications in an Integrated Services Packet Network: Architecture and Mechanism," in Proceedings SigComm '92, 1992; S. Shenker, D. Clark, and L. Zhang, "Service or Infrastructure: Why We Need a Network Service Model," in Proceedings of the 1st International Workshop on Community Networking, San Francisco, 1994; R. Braden, D. Clark, and S. Shenker, "Integrated Services in the Internet Architecture: An Overview," Request for Comment (RFC) 1633 (1994); and S. Shenker, "Service Models and Pricing Policies for an Integrated Services Internet," in B. Kahin and J. Keller, eds., *Public Access to the Internet* (Cambridge, Mass.: MIT Press, 1995).

7. D. Clark, "Adding Service Discrimination to the Internet," *Telecommunications Policy* 20(3) (April 1996).

8. S. Shenker, D. Clark, D. Estrin, and Herzog, "Pricing in Computer Networks: Reshaping the Research Agenda," *Telecommunications Policy* 20(3) (April 1996).

9. N. Brownlee, " New Zealand Experiences with Network Traffic Charging," available at <http://www.press.umich.edu:80/jep/econTOC.html>.

10. MacKie-Mason and Varian, "Pricing the Internet."

11. The first part draws heavily on B. M. Mitchell, W. Neu, K.-H. Neumann, and I. Vogelsang, "The Regulation of Pricing of Interconnection Services," in Gerald Brock, ed., *Toward a Competitive Telecommunication Industry* (Hillsdale, N.J.: Erlbaum, 1995), the second part on MacKie-Mason and Varian, "Pricing the Internet."

12. Mitchell et al., "The Regulation of Pricing of Interconnection Services."

13. MacKie-Mason and Varian, "Pricing the Internet."

14. D. Gabel, "Competition in a Network Industry: The Telephone Industry, 1984–1910," *The Journal of Economic History* 54(3) (September 1994).

Settlement Systems for the Internet

Maria Farnon and Scott Huddle

Introduction

Today, the Internet remains based on a "sender keeps all" (SKA) model of settlements between networks, meaning that no money exchanges hands, regardless of the volume of traffic or level of connectivity exchanged among providers. This is in contrast to the voice telephony business, which provides a well-established system of settlements. Internet Service Providers (ISPs) currently conduct bilateral arrangements to exchange traffic at the public exchange points at zero cost.

The Internet has been doubling in size every 12 months for the past several years, and it is now experiencing an even faster rate of growth outside of the United States. It is increasingly evident that the continued successful growth of the Internet depends on, among other things, the development of an alternative to the SKA model. At the moment, companies that have committed to major infrastructure investments are increasingly reluctant to interconnect with smaller networks because of the inefficiencies of SKA.

In this chapter we examine the growth of the global Internet and examine some of the requirements to sustain this growth. We identify the positive network externalities that exist with the connection of new hosts that increase the value of the network for all connected hosts.[1] The goal, therefore, is to establish an economic model that encourages the socially optimal number of connected hosts to the Internet. We examine a theoretical model that simulates the current pricing and settlement structure of the Internet and show that, under a zero-settlement scheme, the social optimum cannot be reached. We extend the model to examine the requirements of an efficient settlement scheme to achieve a socially optimal outcome and examine several possible technical and policy means to implement the scheme.

Introducing a fee-based settlement system promotes more interconnection among network providers as ISPs are now adequately compensated for network expansion. Settlements allow small providers to grow their networks and reduce their costs, and allow incumbent providers to be fairly compensated for their costs. A properly constructed settlement system also correctly values transit service and encourages providers to interconnect their networks.

A history of the current interconnection architecture will be briefly reviewed. Several potential settlement models will be evaluated including models based on traffic volume, route announcements, network addresses, and network size. The feasibility of implementing a settlement model within the current Internet infrastructure will be analyzed.

The Internet Architecture

Beginning in 1969, the U.S. Advanced Research Projects Agency (ARPA) sponsored research to develop a distributed computer network. This sponsorship resulted in ARPANET—a packet-switched network employing traditional point-to-point links. ARPA thus initiated what developed into a much broader project to create the underlying Internet protocol: Transmission Control Protocol/Internet Protocol (TCP/IP). Multiple U.S. government agencies were involved in the development of TCP/IP, including the National Science Foundation (NSF), the Department of Energy, the Department of Defense, and others.

The success of TCP/IP encouraged the NSF to fund a national backbone network, the NSFNET, beginning in 1985. The NSFNET first linked the five NSF supercomputing centers to the ARPANET. In 1986, the NSF further funded the creation of several regional Internet networks. The Internet then began the trend of explosive growth that continues today. By early 1996, the Internet reached ten million host computers. As the popularity of the Internet soared through the early 1990s, it evolved from a network primarily used by the research and education community to a network that supports mission-critical business applications. This trend was accelerated by the decommissioning of the NSFNET in April 1995, when the functioning of the Internet was transitioned to commercial networks.

As part of this migration to the private sector, the NSF established and funded four Network Access Points (NAPs): the New York NAP (Sprint), the San Francisco NAP (Bellcore with Pacific Bell as the operator), the Chicago NAP (Bellcore with Ameritech as the operator), and the Washington, DC, NAP (Metropolitan Fiber Systems, Inc.).[2] The NSF defined a NAP as "a high speed network or switch to which a number of networks can be connected via routers for the purpose of traffic exchange and interoperation."[3] The NSF foresaw an Internet architecture that hinged on these public interconnection points, which would be available to commercial Internet networks to attach and exchange traffic with other networks, thereby allowing their customers to communicate.

Current Interconnection Architecture

In addition to the NSF-funded NAPs, there are several other major public interconnection points in the United States, including MAE-East and MAE-West (MAE indicates Metropolitan Area Ethernet), operated by MFS, as well as the CIX-SMDS cloud, operated by the Commercial Internet Exchange (CIX). There are also international exchanges, including the London Internet Exchange (LINX), the Global Internet Exchange (GIX), and MAE-Paris.

The exchange of traffic at these public interconnection points occurs based on one of two models: bilateral or multilateral agreements. A bilateral agreement is typically a contract between two providers that specifies the exchange of customer traffic through one or more public interconnection points. A multilateral agreement is typically a contract among several providers to exchange customer traffic through a single interconnection point. The exchange point operated by the Commercial Internet Exchange offers an example of the latter. The CIX router was established in 1991 for the first commercial networks that were prohibited from exchanging traffic with the NSFNET as a result of the acceptable use policy (AUP). The CIX router offered privately funded networks the opportunity to exchange traffic, and the CIX agreement mandated that every member that connected would exchange traffic with all other networks connected to the CIX.

Although no settlements are imposed, every CIX member pays a membership fee. The bilateral model has predominated at all of the other exchange points located in the United States. Under this model, a network pays the facility owner to place a router and connect to the exchange architecture. The network may then conclude bilateral agreements with other networks connected at this point to exchange traffic, but is not obligated to do so. The exchange of traffic allows either network to terminate traffic on the other's network. An important point here is that no "transit" occurs. Transit is defined as the transport of traffic across the backbone and delivered to other networks for termination.

Regardless of whether it follows the bilateral or multilateral arrangement, an Internet interconnection agreement is based on the "bill and keep" financial model. As Simnett, Spacek, and Srinagesh explain, bill and keep is an "extreme" model because the termination of traffic has "a zero price, resulting in zero payments from one carrier to the other," while all other interconnection arrangements in the telecommunications industry typically result in the transfer of revenue from one carrier to another. SKA or bill and keep is also extreme because it "does not envisage any provider charging end users for terminating traffic,"[4] as happens with collect or incoming cellular voice calls.

Why has the exchange of traffic in the Internet environment evolved so differently from that of the voice world? The answer hinges on the characteristics of a packet-switched network. Unlike voice networks, where the flow of traffic is roughly balanced, traffic on the Internet tends to be asymmetric between information providers and entities that request information. Also in contrast to the voice network, Internet traffic is connectionless. On the Internet, a data stream is broken into a series of packets, each of which has the information necessary for routing to the final destination. The individual packets may take different routes to the final location and may even arrive at different times. They are then reassembled into the original stream. Additionally, it is can be difficult to calculate how much traffic is being exchanged, determine who is responsible for originating the traffic, and prevent fraud.

Although the NSF originally intended to fund the NAPs for five years, in August 1996 the agency announced the end of its sponsorship of the four NSF NAPs. The NSF had successfully overseen the transition of the Internet from government sponsorship to a wholly commercial structure. The NAPs provided a critical element by providing an interim, public infrastructure that ensured the continued functioning of the global Internet. However, although the NSF has withdrawn its support of the NAPs, clearly this architecture must again be transformed to a more rational economic model.

Future Evolution of the NAP Architecture

Several developments have prompted the necessity of transforming the current Internet settlement architecture. First, the "neutral" nature of the NAPs has largely been eroded. The NAPs were established by the NSF to serve a public interest: namely, to prevent the balkanization of the Internet by establishing a public interconnection architecture. However, the NAPs are currently operated by third parties who may act opportunistically given that they are both ISPs and NAP operators. As both NAP operators and ISPs, these companies may offer customers the ability to connect to the NAPs (here the term NAP is used generically) as an inexpensive alternative to buying a direct connection to another ISP. Furthermore, the ISP/NAP operator not only can price its Internet access products to align with the NAP connection costs, but also can use the NAP facility to offer other services, including Web site hosting, co-location of servers, and so on.

Second, the exponential growth of Internet traffic[5] has largely overwhelmed the ability of the NAP infrastructure to scale adequately. The congestion occurring at the public exchange points poses a major problem for ISPs whose customers rely on their Internet access for mission-critical applications. This pressure has only increased as the Internet has been transformed from a network used primarily by the research and education community to one that is dominated by for-profit organizations.[6]

Finally, the explosive growth of the Internet access industry has spawned the formation of thousands of new ISPs. Most of these are smaller, regional networks that are not investing in building national infrastructures. Rather, they are relying on the SKA model to ensure that their traffic is transported across the global Internet at no cost other than the coordination costs to arrange interconnection agreements. This is what Spacek and Srinagesh refer to as "cream skimming" by new ISP entrants.[7]

The SKA system is not efficient, and therefore not sustainable. Gerald W. Brock articulates two conditions that are necessary for the viability of a SKA settlement model: (1) traffic flows are roughly balanced between the interconnecting networks; and (2) the cost to a firm for terminating traffic is low in relation to the costs of measuring and charging for traffic, so that even with a traffic imbalance a company will prefer the SKA model to cost-based termination charges.[8]

While the first condition is true for only a small number of Internet backbone networks, increasingly the second is not valid either (the challenges associated with measuring and charging for traffic will be examined later in the chapter). Thus, it seems clear that both the SKA financial model and the NAP architecture model are no longer viable.

Policy changes enacted by some of the major backbone providers provided the first indication that this architecture could no longer continue as it was first conceived. Among other requirements, some carriers demand that peer networks attach to a minimum of three interconnection points and maintain a national 45 Mbps network.

Clearly, the viability of the NAP architecture is under serious question. There seem to be two alternatives which result: the interconnection agreements concluded at the NAPs reflect the relative value of the good (i.e., traffic or routes) that is being exchanged, or the NAPs are replaced by direct, bilateral interconnection arrangements between networks which are priced according to the balance of traffic flows or levels of connectivity.

Of course, a hybrid solution is also possible, whereby the NAPs continue as under the first alternative, but coexist with direct peering arrangements where the mutual traffic load warrants. The hybrid scenario may offer the most attractive solution, because it eliminates the ability of a firm to "cream skim" the market, and also addresses the physical infrastructure challenges of the NAPs.

Survey of Other Settlement Systems

Telecommunications Interconnection Agreements for U.S. Access Charges

Interconnection charges levied by U.S. Local Exchange Carriers (LECs) for transport and termination on the local network constitute a major cost of business for other communications providers. These access charges have several goals, the foremost of which is to cover LEC infrastructure costs.

Interexchange Carriers (IXCs) pay access charges to the LECs for both ends of a long-distance call: origination and termination. Cellular companies pay access charges only if the calls terminated on the LEC network. Typically, LECs do not charge access fees to other LECs for exchanging traffic, relying on a SKA model. However, in cases where LECs act as long-distance carriers, they generally pay the same fees as IXCs.

As Jamison explains, IXCs pay by far the largest proportion of access charges. There are three elements to these fees:

• *Local Switching*: IXC pays LEC for processing calls through the LEC local switch.

• *Local Transport*: IXC pays LEC for carrying calls from the local switch to the IXC network.

• *Common Carrier Line Charge (CCLC)*: IXC pays LEC for allowing the use of lines that connect customers to LEC local switches.[9]

According to Jamison, the access charges levied on IXCs constitute a markup of about 300 percent over LEC costs.

The United States Telecommunications Act of 1996 (S.652) radically changes the terms under which an IXC and LEC interconnect, and the payments associated with interconnection. Passed in February 1996, the Telecommunications Act mandates that each telecommunications carrier has the duty to "interconnect directly or indirectly with the facilities and equipment of other telecommunications carriers."[10] Section 251 is perhaps the most important provision of the act because, by requiring interconnection and unbundling of LEC network elements, it introduces competition into the local communications market.

Interconnection can refer simply to the physical linking of two networks, or to both the linking of facilities and the transport and termination of traffic. Interconnection rights, as defined by the FCC, "[allow] competing carriers to choose the most efficient points at which to exchange traffic with incumbent LECs...."

The 1996 act is silent on the issue of pricing for interconnection, other than to outline general requirements for "just and fair" compensation.[11] The determining factor for a just and fair arrangement is the "mutual and reciprocal recovery" by each party for the costs of transport and termination of calls that originate on the facilities of another carrier.[12]

The LECs proposed that pricing be based on the "efficient component pricing rule" (ECPR). Under this model, an incumbent LEC that sells an essential input element would set the price of that input element equal to incremental costs plus opportunity costs. The LECs argued that pricing for access could only be set at marginal cost under conditions of perfect competition, which do not yet exist. Furthermore, they suggested that if price equals marginal cost—which ignores the historical costs of building a network—this would discourage new entrants from building their own facilities.

However, in August 1996, the FCC determined that the incumbent LEC may only charge interconnection fees based on "total service long-run incremental costs" (TSLRIC), and will not allow interconnection charges to cover other costs such as embedded[13] or accounting costs, opportunity costs, universal service subsidies, and access charges.[14]

Telecommunications Interconnection Agreements and International Settlements

Another example of settlements occurs internationally between carriers. Domestic carriers receive payments from international carriers for calls that terminate on the domestic network. Typically, the originating carrier pays the terminating carrier an amount equal to one half of the negotiated "accounting rate" for each minute or call delivered. (Accounting rates are negotiated between countries.) The carriers then settle based on the net traffic flow.[15]

Why Settle?

Positive Network Externalities

The Internet has been doubling in size every 12 months for the past several years. The exponential growth of the Internet points to the effect of positive network externalities. An externality is defined as an indirect effect of one party's actions on another.[16] Externalities may be either positive or negative: a party may impose costs on other parties without compensation, or confer a benefit on other parties without deriving compensation for doing so. Positive network externalities imply that each additional host connected to the Internet increases the overall social value of the network. The more connected hosts, the more value the Internet represents for all users.

The current economic model of zero settlements, combined with the rapid international expansion of the Internet, presents a challenge to backbone network providers. A foretaste of this problem has already become evident in the United States as more and more regional networks connect to the NAPs. Under the current SKA model, these regional networks interconnect for free with national-level networks that have invested large amounts of capital and other resources to construct a sophisticated infrastructure. The regional networks thus benefit by receiving a large number of routes from the national-level provider, and gaining access to a nationwide infrastructure at no cost.

The problem for the U.S. national-level networks becomes exacerbated as the non-U.S. networks seek the same interconnection rights. Essentially, a non-U.S. network that concludes an interconnection agreement with a major U.S. ISP will gain transport rights for its traffic across the United States and a disproportionate number of routes. The interconnecting U.S. network does not benefit equally because typically the international network will be confined to a single country and carry a very limited number of routes.

The continued successful growth of the Internet depends on developing an alternative to the SKA model. Firms that have committed to major infrastructure investments may be reluctant to interconnect with smaller networks. Furthermore, given that NAP operators have also become competitors, ISPs may be wary of the existing public interconnection architecture. These developments shed significant uncertainty on the continuation of the Internet as a cohesive, cooperative collection of connected networks.

Introducing a fee-based settlement system promotes more interconnection among network providers as ISPs are now properly compensated for network expansion. Settlements allow small providers to grow their networks and reduce their costs, and allow large providers to be fairly compensated for their larger infrastructure costs of handling more customers. An efficient method for settlements encourages the socially optimal outcome, namely, inducing the maximally efficient number of connected hosts to the Internet. Without a settlements system, the Internet will never be as connected as would be possible if interconnection fees were established.

A Theoretical Example

Gerald W. Brock illustrates an efficient interconnection framework that may also be applied to the Internet environment.[17] Imagine a scenario in which there are two companies, A and B, and each values communication with the other at 2. An ISP wishing to connect the two companies will build a circuit to each of their locations to a costless central switch. Each circuit to the companies has a cost of 1. If only one of the companies subscribes, there is no communication or value; but if both connect, there are two paths (A to B and B to A) and a value of 4, while the total cost is 2. In a perfectly competitive market, any pricing plan that produces total revenue in excess of total cost will be eliminated by competition. Thus the "natural" price for each subscriber is 1, a price that charges each subscriber for the cost incurred to connect that

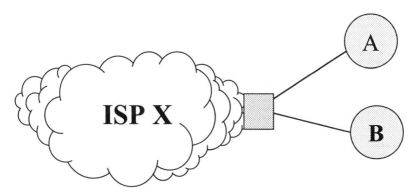

Figure 1 A Competitive Network without Interconnection.

company. However, because of network externalities there is actually a range of pricing schemes that can exist besides the cost-based price, even in a competitive market.

Imagine that the ISP charges 1.5 to A and 0.5 to B. Normally, competition would eliminate this sort of price discrimination (new entrants might serve the customers paying the high prices and leave the low-paying ones to an incumbent), but that is not possible in this case as the competitor must attract both A and B, otherwise there is no communication value.

If the incumbent ISP (ISP X) were required to offer free interconnection, this price discrimination would not be possible. An entrant ISP (ISP Y) to the (1.5, 0.5) price market can compete for A alone by building a circuit from A to the central switch and demanding interconnection from ISP X. Company A prefers ISP Y's price of 1 over ISP X's price of 1.5 and gains connection to B through the interconnection. Because ISP X is left with a system that costs 1 and a revenue of 0.5, it must then raise the price of B to 1 to cover its costs.

In this two-company example, and in general, an ISP can only sustain price discrimination if it retains control over interconnection, and cannot sustain price discrimination against entry if free interconnection is mandated.

Continuing with Brock's example, consider the addition of a third company, C, to the network. The addition of C adds four new communication links to the network: A to C, B to C, C to A, and C

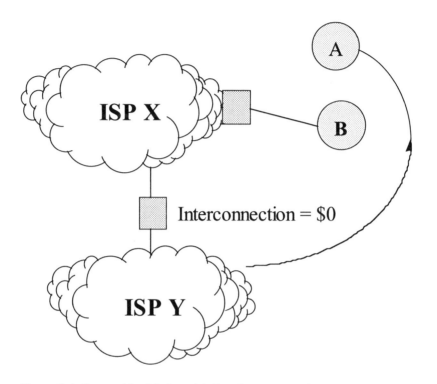

Figure 2 A Competitive Market with Free Interconnection.

to B. Assume that each of these new paths is valued at 0.4. The total network increases in value by 1.6 when C is connected, but the cost increase is only 1. It is therefore socially beneficial to have C on the network. From C's perspective, though, the value of connection is 0.8 (its value of connections to A and B), i.e., the social value of C's connection exceeds C's private value of the connection. Notice that if the ISP charges the nondiscriminatory price of 1, C will not connect to the network, and the optimal social value is not achieved.

In a competitive market with no interconnection requirements, if ISP X maintains a nondiscriminating price structure (i.e., the price is the same for all customers), it will not connect user C. However, if ISP X is able to introduce discriminatory pricing, it will be able to connect all three users. Imagine a price vector of (1.3, 1.3, 0.4). At these prices all three firms will subscribe, the ISP will cover total cost and make all of the users better off than they were in the nondiscriminatory two-user network.[18]

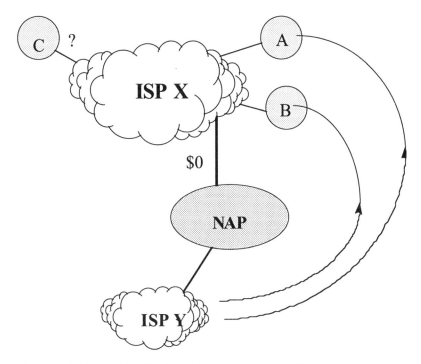

Figure 3 A Competitive Market with Interconnection Fees.

However, that price vector is not sustainable under requirements of free interconnection as outlined above; a new ISP will attempt to serve A and B at a lower price than the 1.3 and will use the free interconnect to reach C. ISP X will be forced to raise its price to 1 to cover costs, which will motivate C to disconnect from the network, lowering the overall social value of the network.

In the three-company example there is no nondiscriminatory price that reaches the socially optimal and efficient state. There is a discriminatory price that reaches this state, but only if free interconnection is not required. If free interconnection exists, it is not possible to reach this optimal state.

Two conclusions result from this discussion. First, because of network externalities, price discrimination is desirable in order to attract the maximum number of connected users. Second, interconnection between Internet networks must also be priced efficiently.

Pricing Interconnection

Further extending the theoretical model, we note the following factors that will result in an efficient price for interconnection:

- in a competitive market, the sum of access prices for A, B, and C will exactly cover costs;
- the maximum that C will pay to reach A and B is 0.8; and
- the maximum that A or B will pay to reach C is 0.4.

We can see that there is a range of discriminatory pricing structures that can exist that will meet these requirements. A subset of possible solutions is shown in the Table 1. Note that while there is a range of transfer prices, the providers are indifferent to the results since their revenue exactly covers costs. Furthermore, each of the companies will agree to the price since the benefits that they receive are greater than their costs. The last case, in which network C pays nothing, is an interesting edge case and will be further explored in later work.

How To Settle?

The theoretical model points out the need for a system to determine an interconnection scheme. The general method of any settlement system is twofold: first determine an agreed accounting rate and then apply it to some unit of measurement of utility. Unfortunately there a number of practical problems that need to be overcome to implement an effective system for the Internet. In this section we describe the technology of routing, identify a number of possible settlement systems, and evaluate their effectiveness and practicality in today's Internet.

Background

Connectivity on the Internet is the result of accepting and using a "route announcement" from other networks. Networks exchange these routing announcements using a routing protocol. Classless Inter-Domain Routing (CIDR) is the current mechanism for describing networks on the Internet. CIDR uses two components—an

Table 1 Ranges of Interconnection Fees

Company	Cost		
A	1.1	1.3	1.5
B	1.1	1.3	1.5
C	0.8	0.4	0.0
Total Cost	3	3	3
Transfer required from ISP Y to ISP X	0.2	0.6	1.0

IP address that describes the start of its address range, and a prefix length that describes the bounds of the announcement. A network with a prefix length of 24 represents 256 addresses, a 23 is 512 addresses, a 16 is 65,536 addresses, and so on.

Determining Costs

ISPs provide both a physical layer interface and a logical connection to the Internet "cloud." The cost of a connection to a particular ISP is a combination of both of these components.

The physical interface will typically include costs for the access circuit, router, terminal servers, and other hardware the ISP uses to connect the customer to its site. The ISP will typically interconnect multiple sites with leased lines to form a backbone in a number of possible topologies. The ISP may also connect the network to Internet exchange points such as the NAPs.

There are a number of other pieces that form the logical connection for IP service, including route announcements, address space, and traffic on the backbone. In the current Internet the costs of all of these are typically zero. The result of a zero-cost allocation of shared resources is well known to result in "the tragedy of the commons." A group within the Internet Engineering Task Force (IETF) has recently started to examine some of the issues surrounding these costs in working groups. Ideally, a cost determination will include both physical costs as well as "soft costs," perhaps expressed as an average marginal cost. The complete determination of a final settlement cost is beyond the scope of this chapter and will be largely determined by bilateral negotiations.

Determining Utility

At first thought, a valuation system based on traffic seems to be a natural mechanism on which to settle since it is directly related to the traffic flows and the cost of infrastructure, i.e., the "size of the pipe." However, byte-based settlements are extremely troublesome. Specifically, in a connectionless environment such as the Internet, a byte-based system suffers if it cannot be implemented end-to-end. It is also difficult to tell the benefactor of a given traffic flow with client/server-based applications—a user can send a small request and receive a large flow in return. Moreover, it is not clear who the benefactor of the traffic would be. Lastly, any byte-based settlement system is open to the possibility of arbitrage by either party, and even from third parties. The development of a settlement scheme based on traffic alone seems unlikely.

A Thought Experiment

Imagine a large computer network of interconnected computer networks. This network is comprised of many groups of varying sized networks, some large and some very small. In this network imagine that traffic flows from network to network roughly based on the size of the network—a small network tends to send and receive a small amount of traffic compared to a very large network.

Further imagine that if we wanted to know precisely the amount of traffic that flows through network to network, obtaining and processing this information would be very costly and difficult and, as pointed out in the section above, might not tell us much anyway. Finally, imagine that a rather simple mechanism exists that can quantify the relative size of the networks in this large network of networks.

In this thought experiment, it would then be possible to construct a settlement system based solely on the sizes of the networks since they would then provide a key to the underlying traffic flows between them.

It is proposed, given relatively large numbers of routes, that this assumption holds roughly true for today's Internet. More precisely, by counting the number of distinct routes that a given network

BigISP   **LilISP**

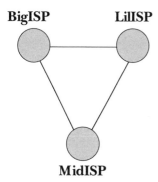

MidISP

Figure 4 A Simple Interconnection Topology.

Table 2 Idealized Settlement Scheme under Sender Keeps All

	Payee		
Payer	BigISP	MidISP	LilISP
BigISP	—	1/2	1/2
MidISP	1/2	—	1/2
LilISP	1/2	1/2	—

announces, we are able to construct a metric that can be used to compare different networks. Routes are a useful metric since they are representative of the connectivity gains (i.e., what each party gains); measurable on a bilateral basis; and less vulnerable to arbitrage by a third party.

A Simple Route-Based Settlement Model

Imagine an internet of three different ISPs, BigISP, MidISP, and LilISP. Each ISP wants to interconnect to the others, resulting in a network topology that looks like the diagram in Figure 4 below. The costs of each connection is 1. Table 2 illustrates how under the present scheme, values are typically thought to be shared.

This situation tends to benefit small providers because it allows them (the LilISPs) to gain access to the bigger providers (BigISPs) at a discount. Connectivity to the bigger providers encourages the smaller ISPs to grow. Yet there is little incentive for the larger

Table 3 Realistic Settlement Scheme under Sender Keeps All

Payer	Payee BigISP	MidISP	LilISP
BigISP	–	0	0
MidISP	1	–	0
LilISP	1	1	–

Table 4 Share of Connectivity

Group	Routes
BigISP	1400
MidISP	500
LilISP	100

provider to buy bandwidth to the smaller providers since they do not receive a gain in connectivity (i.e., routes) that is proportionate to their costs. As a result, smaller providers cannot buy connections to the big ISPs at the half rate, and are thus forced to buy full connections to the larger networks. Additionally, since they now are customers of the larger networks, the smaller providers have little clout to negotiate better deals. Finally, since they fill their pipes, they must purchase additional connections to the larger networks at full price. The resulting matrix is shown in Table 3.

Under the proposed scheme, costs would be shared based on the share of connectivity that the two networks provide each other. "Connectivity" here is used to indicate the number of routes that a network offers. The greater the number of routes, the greater the connectivity value. Presume that the BigISP offers the largest number of routes, whereas LilISP offers the least number.

Using the figures in Table 4, the distribution of settlement fees (costs) are proportionate to the value offered by each network. MidISP pays LilISP for connectivity to 100 of 600 routes (their total connectivity), or one-sixth of the interconnection costs.

In this scenario, the large ISPs get a proportionate gain to their costs, and, in fact, have an incentive to sell connections on a

Table 5 Route-Based Settlement Fees

Payer	Payee		
	BigISP	MidISP	LilISP
BigISP	—	5/19	1/15
MidISP	14/19	—	1/6
LilISP	14/15	5/6	—

BigISP   **LilISP**

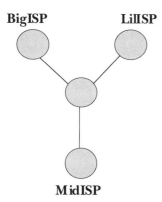

MidISP

Figure 5 Interconnection via a Common Exchange Point.

settlement basis. Small providers can purchase the bandwidth that they desire from the larger networks at a reduced rate and can lower their costs. Additionally, the small networks have a scheme by which as they grow their connectivity costs will decrease.

The route-based scheme of settlement can then be applied to the costs between ISPs to roughly allocate benefits to the two networks. Networks of approximately the same size would split the costs of interconnection. Networks of disproportionate size would be weighted to the traditional customer/provider relationship.

The IXP Case. Further expanding this thought mode, let us examine the case in which an Internet Exchange Point exists where multiple providers can connect and establish logical exchange ("peering") points. The cost of connection to the exchange point is 1.

This results in the same distribution as the simple interconnection scenario outlined in Figure 4. The existence of a common

Table 6

	Payee		
Payer	BigISP	MidISP	LilISP
BigISP	–	5/19	1/15
MidISP	14/19	–	1/6
LilISP	14/15	5/6	–

Table 7

Group	Routes
ISP-A	600
ISP-B	600
ISP-C	600
ISP-D	200

exchange point does not affect the outcome of settlements between the providers, although it does increase their individual costs.

Extended IXP—Congestion. If traffic flows to and from BigISP and the IXP exceed the capacity of a single link, it may be necessary to install a second connection to the IXP. Note that this is an inefficiency inherent in the IXP concept.

Imagine a network of providers that is dominated by several large providers, say ISPs A, B, and C, and one other small provider, network D. Table 7 shows how the number of routes carried by each provider under this scenario might look.

Table 8 shows how traffic flows among the ISPs might look (in megabits per second).

If the link capacity is 45 megabits per second, the links to the IXP will be congested. The large ISPs will have an incentive to drop the peering arrangement with the small ISP since they do not derive as much value from this connection.

This is exactly one of the problems that smaller providers see today; they are unable to obtain peering arrangements with the larger ISPs. The large ISPs are forced to prioritize arrangements

Table 8 Traffic Flows among ISPs

| | Destination | | | |
Source	ISP-A	ISP-B	ISP-C	ISP-D
ISP-A	—	21	21	7
ISP-B	21	—	21	7
ISP-C	21	21	—	7
ISP-D	7	7	7	—
Total	49	49	49	21

```
cpe2.res#show ip bgp
BGP table version is 1218291, local router ID is 166.45.31.1
Status codes: s suppressed, d damped, h history, * valid, > best,
i - internal
Origin codes: i - IGP, e - EGP, ? - incomplete

Network      Next Hop        Metric    LocPrf   Weight   Path
*> 4.0.0.0   204.189.255.1             0 3561   86       1 i
*            204.70.176.97      64     0 3561   86       1 i
*> 6.0.0.0   204.70.176.97     124     0 3561   568      ?
```

Figure 6 Snapshot of the Global Routing Table.

and otherwise artificially limit the number of peer networks because of the bandwidth and cost concerns at the NAPs.

Under the route settlement model, all parties are now fairly compensated for links to the NAPs and the right signals in terms of additional investment are given.

Implementation

A scheme like the one above could be implemented today fairly simply, but it would have to be done carefully so as to avoid introducing negative externalities into the system. A count of routes by their provider can be obtained from a snapshot of the global routing table; this can be extracted from a centrally connected router that is part of the "default-free" area of the Internet. On a Cisco router, this is evident in the following command in Figure 6.

Table 9 MAE-East: Subset of the Global Routing Table

AS	Number of Routes
Alternet	6458
ANS	2360
BBNPlanet	3751
Eunet	1092
Netcom	410
Sprint	13191
TeliaNet	321
Total (1469 ASs seen)	34256

Where multiple routes to a network existed, the preferred route would be selected, and would represent the path to the route at the time of the extract. Data could then be collected from the Internet Routing Registry (IRR) to generate an appropriate name for each Autonomous System (AS), and the data could be summarized by AS. The Routing Arbiter project publishes some of this information today.[19] Table 9 is a subset of the global routing table as seen at MAE-East on August 28, 1996.

Limitations of This Scheme

There are some potential problems that an implementation of this scheme would need to avoid. In particular, networks should not be given incentives to arbitrarily increase the number of routes that they announce by splitting routing announcements.[20] This could be solved by "proxy-aggregating" routing announcements, by accounting for the scope of the routing announcement to its equivalent number of end hosts,[21] or by introducing a separate route-charging model as is being discussed within the IETF.

This method could be further improved if the assumption of homogeneity of a route value could be removed, for example by allowing individual networks to value their announcement.[22] The scheme as described is not a dynamic one, but perhaps does not need to be depending on settlement units. A more dynamic scheme, though, might allow providers to bid on transport services, negotiate backup transit service, or provide better load balancing between providers.

Who Settles?

The Role of Government

Unlike the Internet, carriers in the voice telephony market are required by law to interconnect with other carriers to enhance the competitive environment. The Federal Communications Commission (FCC) had six months after the passage of the Telecommunications Act in which to establish the general requirements on interconnection, but it is the states which maintain the real power to determine and approve specific interconnection plans.

Under the Telecommunications Act of 1996, the state public utility commissions have the right to mediate or arbitrate any dispute between the parties arising as a result of negotiations on interconnection.[23] In fact, at any point during the negotiations, a party may request the involvement of the state commission. Furthermore, the FCC determined that the rules it established via the Telecommunications Act would be national in scope, thus guaranteeing "consistent, minimum" and equivalent standards in every state.

According to the FCC, if carriers can voluntarily agree on interconnection prices, these agreements will be submitted directly to the states for approval under Section 252 of the act. However, if the carriers fail to determine the prices in the course of voluntary negotiations, the state commissions will have to set those prices.

At the moment, it appears very unlikely that the U.S. government will seek to regulate the Internet. The FCC is not only constrained in terms of resources, but is also reluctant in an era of government downsizing to expand its regulatory responsibilities. Finally, the Internet, at least through 1996, appears to be working well as a somewhat anarchic collection of private networks.

However, two issues are significant enough to warrant government intervention. First, if the trends sparked by the SKA settlements model continue and thus discourage networks from interconnecting, then the government might have reason to mandate interconnection among networks. However, this chapter has also determined that is an efficient pricing mechanism can be established for the exchange of traffic, then the right incentives would be created to encourage interconnection, and thus achieve the social optimum in terms of user connectivity.

Second, a universal service requirement might be imposed. While it is certainly desirable to extend network service to company C in the theoretical example above, we do not extend this model to address the question of universal service (i.e., providing connection/access regardless of externalities). At some future point Internet service may come to be regarded as an essential service. At that point, additional interconnection fees will be imposed to subsidize universal service requirements, and government oversight will be likely. A complete analysis of the requirements of universal access to Internet service is beyond the scope of this chapter.

Conclusion

This chapter has demonstrated that the SKA settlement system on which the Internet is based today is flawed. In order for the SKA model to function efficiently, two conditions must be fulfilled: (1) the level of connectivity must be roughly equal between networks; and (2) the costs of transporting and terminating traffic must be less than the costs of developing a payment scheme. Because the first condition holds true only for a limited number of networks, there is little incentive for networks that maintain a large number of routes to connect with networks that possess only a few customer routes. Because the number of routes exchanged is often imbalanced, a structure of zero payments places an unequal burden on networks that have invested in a broad national infrastructure and carry a large number of routes. Thus, the lack of incentives to interconnect—both in terms of money and connectivity value— prevents the Internet from continuing to grow as a collection of networks. The theory of positive network externalities reveals that a network gains in value with every additional user. However, as long as ISPs are reluctant to interconnect their networks, then the social optimum—meaning the maximum number of users that can connect to the Internet—cannot be attained.

Only by establishing an efficient method for settlements between providers can the social optimum be achieved. Efficiency is defined here as a system that is technically workable, that fairly compensates all providers, and promotes interconnection among networks.

Closely tied to the question of the financial model is the challenge of the physical interconnection architecture. As this chapter points out, the NSF created the NAPs in order to seamlessly transfer the Internet from the public to the private sphere. Although the transition has been successfully accomplished, the exchange points are facing two problems: they are no longer considered neutral; and the NAP infrastructure is not scaling adequately to the exponential increase in the volume of traffic. While this chapter does not seek to address this challenge directly, it seems likely that if an efficient pricing mechanism were established for interconnection, then all parties might be properly motivated to create more efficient physical facilities for interconnecting networks, which would in turn promote the overall goal of increased connectivity.

This chapter has evaluated the possibility of implementing a settlement system based on routes. The settlement process depends on a mutually agreed accounting rate, and a mutually agreed valuation or usage rate. A simple implementation of a settlement scheme could employ routing announcements to determine valuation, but might introduce additional problems as well. Further work to examine dynamic, scaleable, end-to-end settlements schemes is necessary.

The views expressed in this chapter are those of the authors and do not necessarily represent the views or policies of MCI. This chapter is dedicated in part to the horrible coffee and fabulous atmosphere at SoHo's Tea and Coffee in Washington, DC, with special thanks to Helene and the boys.

Notes

1. "Host" is defined as any computer that is connected to the Internet.

2. NSF Program Guideline NSF 93-52, issued in May 1993, provided for a new interconnection architecture to replace the NSFnet. This program comprised four components under five-year cooperative agreements, including the establishment of the NSF NAPs.

3. Ibid.

4. Simnet et al. (1995), 3.

5. In 1987, the Internet served more than 10,000 computers. By 1989, the network had grown to more than 100,000, and by mid-1996 reached ten million. Source: Network Wizards.

6. In January 1996, the *.com* domain easily dominated with 46 percent of registered domain names. Source: Network Wizards, January 1996.

7. Simnet et al. (1995).

8. Ibid.

9. Jamison (1995).

10. United States Telecommunications Act of 1996, II, 251(a)(1).

11. Ibid., Sec. 252(d)(2)(A).

12. Ibid., Sec. 252(d)(2)(A)(i).

13. Embedded costs reflect historical purchase prices.

14. United States Telecommunications Act of 1996.

15. Simnet et al. (1995).

16. Stiglitz (1988).

17. Brock (1994).

18. A range of price vectors are, of course, possible; for example (1.2, 1.2, .6), (1.4, 1.4, .2), and even (1.5, 1.5, 0.5) would all be possible price sets.

19. Available at <http://compute.merit.edu/routes.html>.

20. For example, instead of announcing a single route with a prefix length of 25, an ISP could choose to announce two routes, each with a prefix length of 24.

21. A route announcement with a prefix length of 25 would then be equal to 512 hosts, as would two announcements with a prefix length of 24. It should be noted that, in a separate analysis, both the order and the relative weights of Autonomous Systems remain the same whether counting by routes or by address space until the number of routes is very small (less than five percent of the global pool). This is consistent with the "large number of routes" in the thought experiment.

22. Sean Doran (1996) has written within the PIARA group of just such a scheme that would use an additional transitive property within BGP4 which he calls "Bag-of-\$." His proposal primarily focuses on the control and pricing of route "flaps," but its use as a cross-provider settlement scheme is also possible.

23. United States Telecommunications Act of 1996, Sec. 252.

Bibliography

Bar, Francois, Michael Borrus, and Richard Steinberg. 1995. Islands in the Bit-Stream: Charting the NII Interoperability Debate. Paper presented at a conference on Interoperability and the Economics of Information Infrastructure,

Rosslyn, Va., July 6–7, 1995. Available at <http://www-leland.stanford.edu/~fbar/islands.pdf>.

Bailey, Joseph P. 1995. Economics and Internet Interconnection Agreements. Paper presented at MIT Workshop on Internet Economics, Cambridge, MA, March 1995.

Brock, Gerald W. 1994. *Telecommunications Policy for the Information Age*. Cambridge, Mass.: Harvard University Press.

Brock, Gerald W, ed. 1995. *Toward a Competitive Telecommunications Industry*. Mahwah, N.J.: Lawrence Erlbaum Associates.

Comer, Douglas E. 1995. *Internetworking with TCP/IP*, Vol. 1. Englewood Cliffs, N.J.: Prentice-Hall.

Doran, Sean. 1996. Re: What is an Internet Number. PIARA mailing list (August 19).

Huber, Peter W., Michael K. Kellogg, and John Thorne. 1996. *The Telecommunications Act of 1996*. Boston: Little, Brown and Company.

Jamison, Mark A. 1995. A Competitive Framework for Pricing Interconnection in a Global Telecommunications Market. *Denver Journal of International Law and Policy* 23(3) (Summer): 513–533.

National Science Foundation. 1993. NSF 93-52: Network Access Point Manager, Routing Arbiter, Regional Networks Providers, and Very High Speed Backbone Network Services Provider for NSFnet and the NREN (SM) Program.

National Science Foundation. 1996. The Next Generation Internet: Another Step in the Successful Transition to the Commercial Internet. Press Release 96-45 (August 15).

Matrix Information and Directory Services. 1996. Global Domain Names Grow Rapidly Worldwide. Press release (June 24).

Simnett, Richard, Thomas R. Spacek, and Padmanabhan Srinagesh. 1995. An Economic Analysis of the Claimed Applicability of the Bill and Keep Interconnection Arrangement to Local Telecommunication Competition. Bellcore research paper.

Stiglitz, Joseph E. 1988. *Economics of the Public Sector*. Second edition. New York: W.W. Norton & Company.

The Hong Kong Internet Exchange: The Economics, Evolution, and Connectivity of Asian Internet Infrastructure

Milton Mueller, Joseph Y. Hui, and Che-hoo Cheng

This chapter discusses some of the issues in institutional develop-ment, policy, and economics raised by the development of regional Internet exchanges. It focuses in particular on the Hong Kong Internet Exchange (HKIX), a local exchange that has developed under the auspices of the Chinese University of Hong Kong (CUHK). Since April 1995, HKIX has served as a neutral, noncom-mercial exchange point for Hong Kong's burgeoning Internet Service Provider (ISP) market. Unique routing, pricing, and con-nection policies for this infrastructure were developed through academic and commercial collaboration. Continued growth and intensified competition, however, are forcing HKIX to enter a new phase of development. It must reassess its sources of funding, its policies toward ISPs, and its potential role as a standard-setter and value-added service provider. It must also face the prospect of the formation of an alternative exchange.

We start by describing the origin and policies of HKIX and identifying the issues that have arisen in its development. We then analyze the economics of Internet exchanges in more conceptual terms. The chapter is particularly concerned with the factors that affect the incentives of ISPs to join a single Internet exchange or to break apart and form a new one. We focus on the tension between market pressures for service differentiation and competition, on the one hand, and widespread connectivity and resource sharing, on the other. We believe that the issues facing HKIX are or will be typical of those that will face other regional Internet exchanges.

HKIX

Origins

Many ISPs outside the United States connect to the Internet by leasing circuits to the United States. With this star topology, local traffic within a country or a large city may have to be routed through the United States. This is highly undesirable because international private leased circuits are expensive, and the flow of information will be slower. Setting up an Internet exchange for exchange of local traffic can therefore have great benefit s. But interconnecting local ISPs is not easy when there are many ISPs involved. Politics and commercial competition make cooperation difficult. Hong Kong managed to overcome this problem because a neutral third party, the Chinese University of Hong Kong (CUHK), took the initiative to set up an exchange point.

CUHK set up the first 64 Kbps Internet link in Hong Kong in September 1991. With the formation of the Hong Kong Academic and Research Network (HARNET) in 1992, this link was shared with all other institutions of higher education in Hong Kong.[1]

In late 1993, two small commercial Internet Service Providers were set up with their own 64 Kbps links to the United States. As one of them, HK Supernet, was a spin-off of a university (the Hong Kong University of Science and Technology), it had a direct connection to HARNET from the very beginning. The other, HKIGS, was a small independent ISP with no connections to the other two networks. At that time local connectivity was unimportant because the vast majority of Internet content and connectivity was in the United States.

In September 1994, HKIGS set up a local T1 circuit to CUHK, allowing its customers, including those of downstream ISPs, to have faster and more direct communications with HARNET. HKIGS was in charge of the rental of the local T1 circuit (around US$1,200 per month), and CUHK provided the router port for the connection. Although all parties involved gained benefits, HK Supernet and HKIGS still were not connected locally because HARNET, as a purely academic network, could not do transit for them.

Hong Kong's Internet development exploded in 1995. ISP companies were established by former bulletin board operators, paging companies, and even listed companies and large multinationals. At the end of 1995, more than 40 ISPs had been licensed by Hong Kong's Office of the Telecommunications Authority (OFTA), and the estimated number of users had grown to 100,000. Most ISPs had direct links overseas. Others were just "piggyback" ISPs relying on ISPs with a local presence to do transit for them.

With more and more local content and information exchanges, intra-Hong Kong communications became more important. Commercial ISPs could not afford to route intra-Hong Kong traffic overseas because their overseas links were expensive and relatively slow. Although all of them wanted to establish local interconnection, they could not easily cooperate with their competitors, and full-mesh interconnection among all 40 was out of the question.

In view of these problems, and having the precedent of connecting to HKIGS, CUHK set up the framework of HKIX. The proposed arrangement was that participating ISPs would pay for leased circuits to CUHK and the routers would be placed there. CUHK was responsible for providing space, electricity, air conditioning, and a simple Ethernet network to connect the routers of all the participants. The first two HKIX connections (LinkAGE Online and Global Link) were set up in April 1995. By mid-May 1996, 27 commercial ISPs were connected, including some regional and global ISPs such as Global IP, IBM Global Network, AT&T, and Hong Kong Telecom.[2]

Policies

HKIX's success is an outgrowth of a number of policies.

- *Neutrality.* CUHK is perceived as a neutral party by the commercial ISPs. To maintain this status it must carefully avoid any activities that compete with the participants. It must also be perceived as a nonprofit setup, as the ISPs would like to retain profitable business opportunities for themselves.
- *Peering and Settlements.* HKIX requires that all participants engage in mandatory multilateral peering. Unlike London's LINX, HKIX does not allow ISPs to refuse to accept traffic from other ISPs; everyone on HKIX is equal. Such an arrangement ensures that intra-Hong Kong traffic is routed through the fastest possible

path.[3] Also, HKIX imposes no usage charges or settlements on the exchange of local traffic. These policies maximize connectivity among Hong Kong's ISPs and encourage new ISPs to join.

- *Membership Requirements.* To join HKIX, ISPs must (1) offer access services to their customers; (2) have global Internet connectivity independent of HKIX facilities; (3) have the licenses required by the Hong Kong government—specifically the Public Non-Exclusive Telecommunication Service (PNETS) license; be self-sufficient, including having their own primary domain name, electronic mail, World Wide Web, and news servers; and (5) run BGP4 to peer with the HKIX route server and their upstream, peer, and downstream providers if those providers are also on HKIX (this is for better management of routing).

Issues and Controversies

Organizational Issues. HKIX began as an informal extension of certain activities and interests of CUHK's Computer Services Center (CSC) staff. After seven months, traffic demand strained the capacity of the simple Ethernet hub. HKIX also found itself in the center of several public policy and business controversies that arose in conjunction with Internet growth. It was evident that continued growth would require dedicated human resources, significant investment in capital equipment, and a more formal organization for administration and policymaking.

The university's Information Engineering Department responded to these challenges by winning a HK$8 million grant from the Industrial Support Fund of the Hong Kong government's Industry Department. The project plans to work with the Computer Services Center to upgrade HKIX into a high-capacity Regional Internet Infrastructure (RII).[4] The RII wants to upgrade the hardware infrastructure to Ethernet switches and Asynchronous Transfer Mode (ATM). Equally important, the project proposes to leverage the capabilities of the upgraded HKIX to provide services well beyond simple connectivity. The RII hopes to:

- provide alternative routing through the hub and other ISPs for ISPs whose international link goes down or becomes congested;

- support "type of service" traffic management so that services with different bandwidth and latency requirements can be provided reliably;
- hold discussion forums among users, carriers, ISPs, and content providers about issues of management, economics, and policy; and
- develop user interfaces for audio and video conferencing via the Internet.

The government grant will support the RII for two years (June 1996 to June 1998). However, the potential for growth of HKIX is limited by divisions of bureaucratic turf. HKIX is run by the university's Computer Services Center, whereas RII is based in the Information Engineering Department, an academic department. Operating HKIX brings CSC prestige and perhaps a greater claim on university resources, but as a nonprofit service department it has no direct interest in expanding its capabilities, making it self-sustaining, or developing new technological capabilities. Although it recognizes the value of the RII initiative, the CSC does not want to relinquish operational control of HKIX. Thus the RII's ability to upgrade the capabilities of HKIX may be restricted.

The Business-Government Boundary Issue. HKIX's success in winning government support for two years does not eliminate the question of whether, over the long term, it is running a business or providing a public service. The most logical way to obtain funding is to implement charges for the services HKIX provides. The commercial value of expanding Internet capabilities is evident to all. As the Internet matures, commercial ISPs and local telecommunications firms may view a subsidized RII as an obstacle to their own development of commercial services and capabilities. Some ISPs, particularly some of the larger ones, already regard HKIX warily for fear that it will eventually become a competing ISP.

Cooperation-Competition Problem. The most fundamental problem HKIX faces is the tension between Internet Service Providers' need to compete for commercial advantage and HKIX's mission of providing a site for nondiscriminatory cooperation and connectivity. This tension emerged most explicitly when HKIX modified its rules regarding "piggyback" ISPs in December 1995. Initially, HKIX served only first-tier ISPs (those with their own dedicated international bandwidth). Small, newly established ISPs and some large transit providers pressured HKIX to open up the exchange to piggyback ISPs. The first-tier ISPs strongly opposed this because it eliminated or reduced the competitive advantage they had obtained by investing in their own international bandwidth. HKIX dismissed these fears and relaxed its entry requirements. This incident created some friction between HKIX and certain first-tier ISPs. Partly as a result of this, a small group of larger Hong Kong ISPs began discussions to form a new, commercial Internet exchange in August 1996 (see below).

Internet Exchange Economics

ISP Economics

Because Internet exchanges play an intermediary role in the ISP market, we begin with some observations about the economics of ISPs. Although they engage in a variety of ancillary services, ISPs basically produce two things: Internet connectivity and Internet content. Their production of connectivity has two dimensions: bandwidth and access. That is, ISPs can increase their output of connectivity by increasing their bandwidth (which reduces delay and enables a wider variety of services to be delivered), or by increasing the number of other ISPs, content providers, or end-users to which they are connected. The value of ISP service increases as both dimensions of connectivity are increased.

ISPs can connect with other ISPs and users in a variety of ways. To use the framework presented by Bailey and McKnight,[5] ISPs can enter into: (1) peer-to-peer bilateral interconnection agreements, (2) hierarchical bilateral agreements, (3) third-party administrator agreements, or (4) cooperative agreements. HKIX can be categorized as a third-party administrator for local interconnection. But many smaller Hong Kong ISPs rely on hierarchical bilateral agreements with larger Hong Kong ISPs for both local and international connectivity.

An ISP's investment in connectivity creates external benefits. Adding more bandwidth, users, and content increases the value not only of its own product, but also the value of other ISPs' service if they are connected. The ISP does not directly profit from the latter. The external benefits, however, are usually thought to be reciprocal.

Over the past two years of growth it has become evident that one aspect of the production of connectivity, dial-up access, suffers from diseconomies of scale. The burden of customer support, accounting and billing, and hardware maintenance appear to increase disproportionately as the number of dial-up customers increases. Another notable trend in ISP development is the growing importance of content production. The need for investment in indigenous content production is much greater in non-English-language countries such as Hong Kong than it is in the United States. ISPs with English-reading customers can merely provide hyperlinks to the wealth of information resources already developed in the West. ISPs in Hong Kong and the rest of Asia, however, must produce new content to differentiate themselves from the others and to sustain growing demand for their services. In Hong Kong, the entry of Hong Kong Telecom's "Netvigator" into the Internet market in April 1996 marked an important change in the character of the market. With its huge capital resources, Hong Kong Telecom is able to make major investments in quality content and generally raise the standard of service expected from ISPs.

Establishing Internet Exchanges

For ISPs based outside the United States, the economic benefits of a local Internet exchange are fairly straightforward. A local exchange provides: (1) more efficient connectivity and reduced delay through the substitution of local for international bandwidth; and (2) reduced transaction costs associated with negotiating and coordinating interconnection arrangements.

Bandwidth Substitution. A local Internet exchange will reduce bandwidth costs by the proportion:

$$\frac{[P_l(a) + P_i(1 - a)]}{P_i}$$

where P_i is the price of international bandwidth, P_l is the price of local bandwidth, and (a) is the proportion of total traffic that can

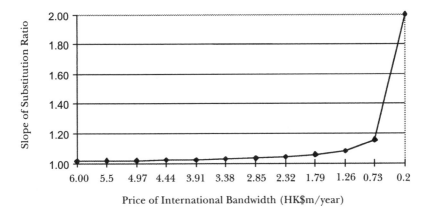

Figure 1 Bandwidth Substitution.

be routed through the exchange. In the case of Hong Kong, the price of an international leased T1 circuit to the United States (HK$6 million per year) is 62.5 times the cost of a local T1 circuit (HK$96,000 per year). If these values for P_l and P_i are plugged into the formula above and (a) is allowed to vary, the resulting line has a slope of 1.02; i.e., each percentage point increase in the proportion of traffic that can be handled locally results in a roughly equal percentage point decrease in total bandwidth costs. This represents substantial savings, as HKIX estimates that one-third to one-half of the traffic of its ISPs is now local in origin and destination.

This model is not very sensitive to changes in relative prices. P_i must decline by a factor of nearly 10 to make a noticeable difference in the slope (from 1.02 to 1.2). The slope does not reach 2.0 until P_i declines by a factor of 30; i.e., until international bandwidth is only about twice as expensive as local bandwidth (see Figure 1).

Reductions of this magnitude in the price of international bandwidth could occur; certainly they are justified on a cost basis. On the U.S.-Asian routes bandwidth prices are becoming increasingly competitive. But local bandwidth is also becoming less expensive in Hong Kong because of competition among four local telecom providers. In all likelihood, the combination of bandwidth substitution and delay reduction will continue to sustain demand for the local connectivity of an Internet exchange for the foreseeable future.

Coordination Economies. The issue of coordinating connectivity is more complicated. It is obvious that as the number of ISPs grows, the number of transactions required to establish full connectivity among them increases approximately as the square.[6] A local Internet exchange might emerge organically from bilateral transactions among individual participants in the ISP market. But this outcome faces a variety of obstacles.

Assume, first, that there is one ISP with market dominance of local users and traffic. Such a dominant ISP would be the natural convergence point for local interconnection negotiations. Its very dominance, however, might make it believe that it had little to gain from local interconnection; the positive externalities it provided to other ISPs would exceed those it would obtain from them. Even if the large ISP was willing to go along with such a negotiation, the smaller ISPs might be unwilling to trust it to manage and control the Internet exchange facility. Whoever controlled such a facility would gain commercially sensitive information about the traffic patterns and users of other ISPs.

If control of the ISP market is widely dispersed, different obstacles emerge. The problem of who will host the facility, and whether this entity can be trusted with commercially sensitive information, still exists. But the cost of negotiation and coordination increases. A critical mass problem also exists. For any individual ISP, the added value (in terms of bandwidth substitution) of interconnecting with one or two others is minimal. Not until a certain threshold is reached do the costs and risks of cooperating with one's competitors seem to be worthwhile. In a competitive and fragmented market, how can this threshold be attained?

A private solution to the local interconnection problem seems likely only if there is an oligopoly with more or less equal shares of the market. This allows a smaller, more manageable number of parties to exceed the critical mass threshold. This result is significant, and will be applied later to the formation of an alternative exchange in Hong Kong.

Given the preceding analysis, the success of CUHK in setting up HKIX is easily explained. CUHK offered facilities already in place, a noncommercial, neutral meeting ground for competing ISPs, subsidized operations, and technical competence.

Competing Exchanges?

Once a local Internet exchange is established, a new set of economic forces comes into play. On one hand, agglomeration economies enhance the value of the Internet exchange and give it an increasingly important role in the expansion of Internet service capabilities. On the other hand, competition among ISPs creates strong pressure to differentiate their service. That and competition for traffic among telecommunications carriers may lead to the formation of alternative Internet exchanges.

Agglomeration and Inertia. Like any product with strong network externalities, Internet exchanges exhibit inertia. It is difficult for members to sacrifice the reciprocal benefits of interconnection after they have joined. A successful Internet exchange also starts to develop agglomeration economies. It attracts the points of presence of international carriers, for example, further enhancing its value as an exchange point. HKIX is already encouraging ISPs in Thailand, Australia, and Shanghai to enter into bilateral peering or hierarchical interconnection agreements with HKIX members. This allows the cost of international bandwidth within the region to be shared. Existing examples include agreements between Singapore's SingNet and Hong Kong Telecom, and between NIS/Japan and Hong Kong's LinkAge.

Bandwidth substitution economies can be enhanced by content caches. Caching stores information downloaded from the World Wide Web in the local memory of the server; thus there is no need to retrieve documents, images, etc., from overseas sites. The amount of content available locally increases dramatically. Caching not only magnifies bandwidth substitution economies, but also reinforces the exchange's agglomeration economies. The larger the proportion of local users who coalesce on a single exchange, the more likely it is that the cache will contain the most frequently retrieved content.

Centrifugal Forces. Recently Star Internet, Hong Kong Telecom-IMS, LinkAge, AsiaOnline, and HKNet attempted to form a new, commercial Internet exchange in Hong Kong. The first two commercial ISPs probably have the largest number of users (Star has 22,000–24,000; HKT-IMS 17,000–20,000). It is evident that a new

Internet exchange will represent an additional expense for participating ISPs, not a cost saving. Forming an alternative Internet exchange incurs additional transactions costs (negotiating, contracting, etc.). Bandwidth substitution economies will be slightly reduced, because each participating ISP plans to maintain a connection to HKIX. The new Internet exchange will not be supported with tax funds, so the cost of operating it must be paid fully. How, then, to explain this phenomenon in economic terms?

The new group claims that its main concern is a backup capability—that local traffic volume has increased to the point where international routing is no longer feasible—hence an exchange outage at HKIX would cripple local Internet usage. There is some validity to this argument. HKIX has had some outages, although recent upgrades have greatly improved its reliability. Outages and congestion, however, could be remedied by additional investments in HKIX. The real issue, we believe, is the commercial ISPs' need for market differentiation and to assert more control over their own destiny.

The key consideration is the network externality, and specifically any imbalance that might exist between the network benefits an ISP gives and the network benefits it gets by participating in a local exchange. A large ISP or group of large ISPs aspiring toward greater dominance of the market could attempt to form a new exchange (while retaining membership in the old one) in order to differentiate their service quality and marketing efforts from all others. Or, they might attempt to leverage the imbalance in external benefits by withdrawing from one local exchange and forming another, more exclusive one. Another possibility is that a larger ISP could address an imbalance in network benefits by making smaller ISPs pay for interconnection with them; that is, it would move from a peer relationship to a hierarchical relationship. In this section we analyze this prospect.

Picture an ISP universe with n providers visualized as a matrix. Rows represent incoming traffic; columns represent outgoing traffic (see Figure 2). If each ISP has a comparable number of users, and each ISP's users are equally interested in accessing the content of every other ISP, then traffic is evenly distributed. The value in each cell will be the same. In this case, the benefits from participat-

		From ISP				
		a	b	c	d	e–n
	a					
To	b					
ISP	c					
	d					
	e–n					

Figure 2 Internet Exchange as Matrix.

		From ISP					
		a	b	c	d	e–n	
	a	6	6	6	6	6	30%
To	b	5	5	5	5	5	25%
ISP	c	4	4	4	4	4	20%
	d	3	3	3	3	3	15%
	e–n	2	2	2	2	2	10%

Figure 3 Uneven Distribution of Traffic.

		From ISP				
		a	b	c	d	e–n
	a	6	6	6	6	6
To	b	5	5	5	5	5
ISP	c	4	4	4	4	4
	d	3	3	3	3	3
	e–n	2	2	2	2	2

Controlled
Contested$_{in}$
Contested$_{out}$
Conceded

Figure 4 Segments Created by Competition.

ing in the exchange are perfectly reciprocal and the alliance is stable.

Suppose that traffic is unevenly distributed. An uneven distribution could be produced by some ISPs having more users, more desirable content, or a combination of both. If ISP a's server contains the most popular content, then the row representing traffic from its own subscribers and those of other ISPs will contain higher than average values. Obviously, this scenario is more realistic than a perfectly even distribution. ISPs will likely fall into some kind of hierarchy ranging from the biggest/most popular to the smallest/least popular (see Figure 3).

Given the scenario in Figure 3, suppose that the top three ISPs—a, b, and c—decided to form their own local Internet exchange. They may or may not decide to withdraw from the other one. Either way, it would not mean total disconnection from d–n. If the Internet exchanges were exclusive, sites on the competing exchanges would be accessed through slower and more expensive international bandwidth. If the new coalition maintained dual membership, there would be no difference in connectivity unless one of the exchanges went down, or one of them developed special service capabilities (e.g., content caching or prioritized routing of packets).

Such a scenario divides the matrix into four distinct segments (Figure 4) which can be labelled *controlled, contested$_{in}$, contested$_{out}$,* and *conceded.* The controlled segment, (a, a) through (c, c), represents traffic internal to the new exchange on both ends. The new coalition does not lose any of the benefits of interconnection here. The conceded segment, (d, n) to (n, n), represents traffic that is both generated by and directed to the excluded ISPs. This segment also does not represent a sacrifice because it was and is external to the coalition members.

The interesting issues revolve around the two contested segments. This can be divided into two parts: traffic that used to flow *from* the excluded ISPs *to* the new coalition members, and traffic that used to flow *from* the new coalition members *to* the excluded ISPs. We call them contested$_{in}$ and contested$_{out}$. The distinction is important, because users of ISPs a, b, and c will directly perceive changes in the quality or capability of traffic in the contested$_{out}$

segment when they attempt to access servers of excluded ISPs. But users of a, b, and c will be oblivious to changes in the quality or capability of traffic in the contested$_{in}$ segment. Any deterioration or limitations will be felt only by the users of ISPs d through n.

The interesting question here is, how many customers of ISPs d through n can be influenced to switch to ISPs a, b, or c because of any differentiation of service quality or capability in the contested segments created by the division between the two exchanges? Suppose, for example, that the universal exchange has an outage while the new, more exclusive exchange does not. A user of ISP d will have to access *all* local sites through international bandwidth, and will probably experience irritating delays. A user of ISP a, in contrast, will only experience this inconvenience in that portion of traffic in the contested$_{out}$ cell.

In short, by forming an additional exchange, ISPs a, b, and c can differentiate their service quality from the other ISPs. Will the new exchange remain exclusive in order to maintain differentiation between members and nonmembers? Or will it attempt to attract as many additional members as possible? Several different outcomes are possible. If a new exchange does succeed in establishing a premium reputation, it may be able to charge profitable entry fees to allow users to join. Or, the larger participants in the more exclusive exchange will be able to leverage the network externality to substitute hierarchical bilateral agreements for third-party peering relationships with the excluded exchanges. In other words, the excluded ISPs will have to pay them for connectivity instead of receiving it for free. In this case the commercially sustained Internet exchange starts to become a direct competitor of the government-funded Internet exchange. In an environment like Hong Kong's this is likely to cause political problems for the noncommercial Internet exchange, and it may be forced to privatize.

The analysis indicates that the distribution and balance of traffic is important. Traffic distribution is a reasonable proxy for the relative value users attach to access to various sites. Major concentrations of traffic would indicate that there are significant imbalances in the network benefits realized by the different players. How evenly distributed is Hong Kong's Internet exchange traffic in reality? Figure 5, using empirical data from August 1996, plots the

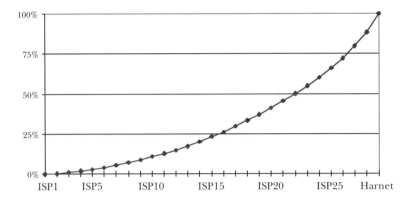

Figure 5 Cumulative Traffic of ISPs in HKIX.

cumulative traffic share of all 27 HKIX ISPs, plus the Chinese University and Harnet. A perfectly even distribution would produce a straight line from zero percent to 100 percent. The more concave the line, the greater the concentration of traffic share in the top ISP's hands.

The plot shows some concavity, but not much. Hong Kong's five or six top universities (CUHK and Harnet) only control slightly more than 20 percent of the traffic. The top four commercial ISPs (ISP23–ISP27) control the next 25 percent. The next six commercial ISPs control about 25 percent. The bottom 16 ISPs account for the remaining 25 percent. The distribution could become more concentrated in the future if and when smaller ISPs fail—one already has—but for now, an alternative Internet exchange coalition faces a difficult task attracting a critical mass. A new, commercial Internet exchange also faces daunting problems regarding who or what will host it.

Conclusion

HKIX will remain a central player in Hong Kong's Internet market for some time. And its role in the early development of Hong Kong's Internet market shows that impartial, noncommercial organizations can be crucial in getting local Internet exchanges off the ground. It seems likely, however, that the provision of local Internet exchange service will become more competitive and commercial.

This is part of a global trend toward less concentration and more variety in Internet interconnection arrangements. Despite significant agglomeration economies and scale economies in Internet exchange operation, the need for product differentiation, attempts by ISPs to avoid commodity pricing, and attempts to exert strategic leverage will motivate ISPs to form subset Internet exchanges, or to substitute bilateral hierarchical relationships for multilateral peering relationships. This is most likely to occur when a small number of ISPs gain a significant market share, making it easier for them to coalesce and increasing the gains they might achieve by differentiating themselves from the broad mass of smaller ISPs. In addition, the need for capital investment and technological innovation in Internet exchanges to progress to more advanced services makes it unlikely that a nonprofit, governmental administration can to continue to play a central role indefinitely. If Internet exchanges do not invest and innovate, the market will pass them by. If they do, they will move closer and closer to the commercial sector.

Notes

1. In September 1993, the link was upgraded to 128 Kilobits per second, and in Fall 1995 to T1.

2. For a current list and aggregated traffic statistics, see <http://www.cuhk.edu.hk/hkix/ connected.html>.

3. A router server (Cisco 2501) is used to provide a single view of routing for all participants. Each router on HKIX belongs to the same autonomous system (AS) as the corresponding ISP. It must peer with the route server (using BGP4 via the HKIX Ethernet and announce all routes of the internal networks and downstream ISPs. It must also accept all routes distributed by the route server.

4. Joseph Y.N. Hui, Kwok-wai Cheung, and Chehoo Cheng, "High Capacity Network Infrastructures for Internet Service Providers and Multimedia Applications." Application for Industrial Support Fund, the Chinese University of Hong Kong, December 1995.

5. Joseph Bailey and Lee McKnight, "Scalable Internet Interconnection Agreements and Integrated Services," in this volume.

6. If N is the number of ISPs, establishing full-mesh interconnection would require $[N(N-1)]/2$ transactions and the same number of local leased circuits.

Service Quality

IP Performance Metrics

Guy T. Almes

Background and IP[1] Performance Metrics[2] Objectives

Since the NSFNET program was initiated in the mid-1980s, the Internet has become an increasingly important enabling technology for the research and education missions of U.S. higher education. During this period, however, the Internet has grown in complexity to the point where even well-informed Internet users and engineers have a somewhat fuzzy understanding of the topology of the Internet, of the paths taken by their data from one Internet site to another, and of the reliability and performance of those paths.

Thus, while the Internet has improved in performance and reliability, the user's understanding of these features has declined.

Growth in Complexity of Internet Topology

One cause of this lack of understanding stems from the increasing complexity of Internet topology. During the late 1980s, for example, early users of the NSFNET often understood the path from their university to the university of a key colleague, at least at the level of the sequence of "IP clouds" passed on the way. This sequence was simple, there were usually no alternative paths available, and the path (again at this level of detail) was symmetric.

As the Internet evolved during the early 1990s, several competing national backbones emerged, the number of exchange points (including private exchanges between pairs of networks) among

them grew, and, for a variety of reasons relating to routing protocols and policy, routing (even at the IP cloud level) between pairs
of sites on the Internet grew more asymmetric. There are a number
of consequences of this new architecture, of which the following
are only a few:

• Even well-informed Internet users and Internet engineers at the
campus and regional level may have a hard time keeping up with
the cloud-level paths that packets may take from campuses on one
regional network[3] to campuses on another.

• Due to asymmetric routing, the path taken from one site to
another may differ from that taken from the second site back to the
first. Such circular paths are becoming common in the Internet,
and tend to produce routes subject to the performance and
reliability problems of *both* backbones and *both* exchange points.

• These asymmetric routes may also be highly suboptimal. The
resulting asymmetric path, even absent any performance or reliability problem in either backbone, could exhibit greater round-
trip delay than would a well-selected symmetric path in both
directions.

Thus, whenever the Internet succeeds in providing its users with
the illusion of a single TCP/IP fabric, users are happy. Whenever
a performance and reliability problem emerges, however, the user
faces a complex situation in trying to understand which IP cloud
along the path to the desired destination (and back!) is the source
of the problem.

Growth in Internet Traffic

A second cause of concern is that many portions of the Internet,
even those with strong engineering and provisioning, are facing
long-term difficulties in keeping up with the growth in Internet
traffic.

During the classic NSFNET era of 1985 to 1995, for example,
traffic on the backbone doubled every 12 months, and a concerted
effort by a number of participants in the NSFNET project was
required to keep up with this growth. Thus, over a ten-year period,

the key wide-area links of the NSFNET grew from 56 kilobits per second to 45 megabits per second. This required major advances in technology, provisioning, and operations, but growth in capacity did more or less keep up with growth in traffic.

During spring 1995, the university networking community moved from a single NSFNET backbone service to multiple competing commercial backbones. Following this transition, traffic on at least one key national backbone has doubled every six months, and this seems to be a typical situation faced by the engineers and managers of the national backbones.[4] Keeping up with this level of traffic growth will be a major challenge to the technology and provisioning of these engineers and managers.

Thus, the Internet user community can expect that many IP clouds, even those with relatively strong engineering and provisioning, are likely to experience congestion for the foreseeable future.[5]

The Changing Nature of Inter-Provider Relationships

A third cause of concern is the natural change in the business relationships among IP providers.

During the classic NSFNET era, the relationship between the different IP providers was primarily cooperative. Thus, for example, different NSFNET regional networks generally served disjoint markets, and the primary interactions between regionals, or between any given regional and the backbone, was in cooperating to serve users from these disjoint markets. Each provider (both regional and backbone) benefited when other providers were strong (since this enhanced the quality of the service each was able to deliver to its users), and providers were generally very willing to share information about the problems they were encountering. Providers might even brag about the problems they were having, since that would improve their chances for receiving government funding for solving those problems!

Gradually, however, multiple national backbones emerged and multiple regional providers emerged within many markets. This development had, of course, many advantages for users. One disadvantage, however, was that providers gradually became less willing to disclose information about the operational, engineering, or provisioning problems within their networks. Rather than being justification for funding, those problems might become fodder for the sales force of competing providers!

IP Performance Metrics Objectives

Taking these trends together, we see that:

• growth in the complexity of Internet topology makes it hard for users to know which IP clouds their packets cross;

• growth in Internet traffic makes it hard for providers to engineer and provision their IP clouds to keep up with traffic; and

• the increasingly competitive Internet business environment makes it problematic for providers to share information on the operational, engineering, or provisioning problems they are having.

Thus, the shift from the classic NSFNET to the current Internet architecture has brought a mixture of good and bad, and much of the bad results from the complexity of the current architecture and the confusion it causes for even well-informed users and engineers.

These trends motivate users and providers from many parts of the Internet to work together to create technology and infrastructure *to enable users and service providers (at all levels) to have an accurate common understanding of the performance and reliability of given Internet paths and to have an accurate common understanding of what segment of a given Internet path limits that performance and reliability.*

These objectives are being addressed by several different groups within the Internet community. The balance of this chapter reports on the Internet Engineering Task Force (IETF) effort in this area, surveys some of the relevant technologies, and articulates some policy issues that could help these objectives to be met.

The IETF IP Performance Metrics Effort

The Nature of the IETF Effort

At the spring 1995 meeting of the IETF, held in Danvers, Massachusetts, an IP Provider Metrics (IPPM) Birds of a Feather (BOF) session explored ways that the IETF might work on metrics for the performance and reliability of operational IP clouds. As with several operational requirements issues, it was important to be sensitive to the concerns of both users and providers.

The session resulted in a decision to form an IPPM effort within the IETF's existing Benchmarking Methodology Working Group (BMWG), part of the Operational Requirements Area. The effort has been organized within the BMWG because IPPM is trying to do the same thing for operational IP clouds that the BMWG has been doing for single devices for quite a while. Under this structure, the first IPPM session was held at the summer 1995 IETF meeting in Stockholm, and there has been an IPPM session at every IETF meeting since.

It is important to stress that, as with many Internet engineering issues, the proper division of labor must be achieved between work done within the IETF and work done by harmonious efforts outside the IETF. In the case of IPPM, several concerns were and are at stake:

• The crafting of well-considered metrics for measuring the performance and reliability delivered by portions of the operational Internet is very much within the scope of the IETF's work.

• The design and implementation of tools to measure the resulting metrics are best accomplished by people acting outside the scope of the IETF, but making effective use of the metrics and reporting their experiences and technical insights at IETF IPPM sessions.

• The application of the resulting metrics and tools to solving specific problems in understanding Internet performance and reliability will similarly be done by Internet users and providers (including IETF members) acting outside the scope of the IETF, but reporting their experiences and technical insights at IETF IPPM sessions.

• The application of these metrics and tools to making business decisions between and among Internet users and providers might be fruitful, but is definitely outside the scope of the IETF effort.

As the work of the effort progresses, this division of labor will likely become better understood.

Accomplishments to Date

At the summer 1996 IETF meeting in Montreal, a draft technical framework document was presented and discussed. A number of insights into the nature of effective metrics were shared, and a set of specific metrics for work to be done by the next IETF meeting was enumerated. Among the key ideas that the framework document presented were the following:

• a set of criteria for metrics, including criteria to ensure that metrics are well defined and avoid inducing artificial performance goals;

• a set of terms for Internet paths and clouds;

• a careful delineation of the notions of metrics, measurement methodologies, and an understanding of measurement errors and uncertainties;

• a distinction between metrics specified with respect to the "analytical framework" of the Internet and those specified with respect to empirical tools; and

• a distinction among "singleton" metrics (e.g., a measurement of delay at a given time), "samples" of such singletons (e.g., a sequence of delay measurements between the same two points but at different times), and "statistics" of such samples (e.g., the median of the delay values from such a sample).

Work in Progress

Between the IETF's summer 1996 meeting and its fall meeting in San Jose, California, several work items were in progress, including specific metrics for connectivity, for one-way delay, for flow capacity, and for packet loss and revisions to the framework document that reflect issues that arise in the specific metrics. Among the key ideas that have emerged in this work are an improved understanding of issues involving time, the sampling of singleton metrics and statistics on them, and the calibration of measurement tools.

As in many IETF efforts, the real value of this work on defining metrics will be the extent to which it both enables and benefits from work done by IETF members outside the scope of the IETF itself.

A Survey of Measurement Technologies

This section briefly surveys several measurement technologies relevant to IPPM work, with emphasis on their motivation and policy implications. The focus is on tests to measure delay, packet loss, and flow capacity since these are among the chief metrics of interest to users. Distinction is made between active tests, in which the performance experienced by test traffic is measured, and passive tests, in which ordinary user traffic is observed and its performance measured.

From a policy viewpoint, the primary message is that the success of the IPPM effort depends on the community having access to a variety of high-quality tools. Investment in such tools is thus well motivated.

Active Tests for Delay and Packet Loss

The primary tool still used for measuring delay and packet loss is ping, a simple application built around the ICMP echo-request and echo-reply protocol.[6] The simplicity and general usefulness of this tool are wonderful, but there are several problems with it in the context of IPPM work:

• Ping only measures round-trip delay, and we need to accurately track the one-way delay, as well as the variations in delay with variations in load, between pairs of hosts in each direction.

• When we try to measure delay to an exchange point, it is common to ping a router at that exchange point. Due to the low priority attached within a router to responding to pings, these measurements are pessimistic by an uncertain amount.

• Similarly, ping tests can give an exaggerated report of packet loss.

Another tool in common use, traceroute, suffers from the same flaws.

If computers used in testing can be placed at both the source and the destination of paths to be tested, then other alternatives present themselves. For example, suppose that computers were placed at key Internet locations both at campus networks and at the exchange points between IP clouds. Suppose further that these computers were synchronized so that their clocks agreed very closely. Then one-way delay could be measured along the one-way paths from one computer to another. Given fast work stations and modern GPS-based clocks, such techniques are practical.[7] By using dedicated computers as both the source and the destination of test packets, several of the problems with ping and traceroute can be avoided.

Active Tests for Flow Capacity

The primary tool for measuring flow capacity is simply to stream a large amount of traffic across a path of interest, typically using an ordinary TCP-based application, and to observe what can be achieved. There are several problem with this approach for IPPM applications:

• Although such an observation might relate well to the performance expectations of the particular platforms and application software, it will be influenced heavily by the efficiency of the IP stacks, the CPU capabilities, and the application implementations at either end.

• Any such measurement congests the network. In fact, a good, modern TCP-based application with a large stream to transmit *will* congest the bottleneck link or router along the path. In some cases, this link will be the user's own access circuit, but in other cases, some shared trunk of a backbone or regional network will become congested. Thus, any widespread use of such a technique by users must be actively discouraged.

• While ping does allow rough measures of delay to the routers along the path and thus sheds some light on which router or link along the path is responsible for increasing delay or packet loss, the situation is even worse for flow capacity measurements since most routers are not configured to support a large stream directed at it (e.g., most routers are configured *not* to support the TCP stream discard service). Even if they were configured to support it, the results would be inaccurate due to the lower-priority scheduling of this service in contrast to other demands on the router.

One technique that addresses some of these shortcomings is Mathis's treno tool. Treno attempts to use services that are predictably supported by routers to mimic the flow control present in TCP. Even with treno, however, the following issues must be considered:

• As with other current tools for measuring flow capacity, treno congests (at least) the bottleneck link or router along the path.

• When used in diagnostic mode, treno relies on the rapid generation by routers of ICMP TTL-expired messages.[8] Due to the low priority attached by a router to the generation of these messages, measurement inaccuracies can result. The CPU of routers will also be heavily burdened.

Despite these shortcomings, treno is currently the state-of-the-art in active tests of flow capacity, and is the basis of current IETF work in flow capacity metrics.

There is some hope, though opinions differ on this point, that a combination of very occasional, direct active tests of flow capacity (using treno or a similar tool), together with frequent active tests of delay and packet loss, can yield data that could then be used to indirectly estimate flow capacity. This would have the advantage of allowing estimates of flow capacity without the heavy overhead of frequent direct flow capacity measurements.

In summary, active tests can be used to measure delay, packet loss, and flow capacity, and they have the following advantages:

• They can be used both on campus networks (near host computers) and at or near exchange points.

• They do not "eavesdrop" on ordinary user traffic.[9]

Their key disadvantage is that they do generate extra traffic on the Internet. Their placement both at campus networks and at or near exchange points enables active tests to help identify which IP cloud along a given IP path is the primary source of delay or packet loss, or the primary constraint on flow capacity.

Passive Tests for Flow Capacity

An alternative means of measuring flow capacity is to passively observe user traffic near the edges of the Internet to measure the actual throughput (and in some cases delay and packet loss) being experienced by user traffic. The idea is to observe the headers of all the TCP packets of a given application, then record the timestamp and byte sequence number of each packet. As the TCP flow progresses, the byte sequence number will increase with time, and the rate of increase indicates the flow capacity actually experienced by the flow.

These passive tests have several key advantages:

• They impose no artificial loading on operational IP clouds.

• They observe the actual throughputs being experienced by users, with applications and flow sizes actually being used.

• They observe true end-to-end throughput, including the effect of heavily loaded servers and the implementations of TCP present in the source and destination machines.

• When kept on local databases, they can be used to compare currently observed performance with performance observed in the past.

These passive tests also have several disadvantages:

• They use source and destination computers and networking software that cannot be standardized or controlled. Thus, in some cases, apparently bad network performance will be caused by an inadequately configured server or one running obsolete TCP software.

• They measure only end-to-end performance and can shed no light on which IP cloud along the path is the cause of bad performance.

• The data from them must be treated as very sensitive, since they could be used to indicate the usage of the network by particular individuals. In practice, this requires systematic and nondiscretionary aggregation of the data.

These disadvantages can be addressed in several ways. By using active and passive tests of flow capacity together, we can adjust for the lack of standardization of the hosts involved in the passive tests. By using passive tests to indicate where a flow capacity problem exists and then using active tests to analyze the specific IP cloud that causes the problem, we can make up for the pure end-to-end nature of the passive tests. And, by ensuring the aggregation of data about specific user traffic before the data get to any off-campus databases, we can address the potential privacy issues.

In addition, it is sometimes possible to use passive tests to measure delay and packet loss. This can be done, for example, by observing when a file server issues IP-level retransmissions in recovering from a lost packet, or by observing the time delay between a file server's transmission of a data packet and the file server's receipt of the corresponding acknowledgment. As a general rule, however, passive tests are most applicable to tests of flow capacity.

In summary, passive tests can be used to measure flow capacity, and they have the following advantages:

• They do not generate extra traffic on the Internet.

• They measure performance *as seen by real users.*

Their key disadvantages are the following:

• Since they eavesdrop on user traffic, they must *only* be used in ways that do not impinge on user privacy. For example, passive tests must never be performed at exchange points.

• Since they are pure end-to-end tests, they do not shed light on which IP cloud along the path is the bottleneck.

Finally, passive tests can also be used to measure things outside the normal scope of IP performance metrics, such as the nature of use of the Internet at a given site.

Development of an IPPM Infrastructure

Once the tools are available to enable the active and passive tests surveyed above, infrastructure must be planned, deployed, and managed to permit an effective program of ongoing tests. In some cases such infrastructure will consist simply of passive tests and simple active tests made from campuses. Several attributes of the more advanced active tests, however, motivate a more complex infrastructure:

- They can safely be deployed both on campus networks (near user hosts) and at or near exchange points.

- When deployed in both locations, they can be used to measure delay, packet loss, and flow capacity on both an end-to-end basis and also a cloud-to-cloud basis along paths.

- Active tests, particularly active tests of one-way delay, benefit greatly from have access to closely synchronized clocks.

These attributes motivate deploying an infrastructure (or perhaps several competing infrastructures) that will include closely synchronized clocks and well-managed measurement computers at both campuses and exchange points.

Also, due to the possibility that some of the measurements may be embarrassing to some providers, it is probably unrealistic to rely on the providers themselves to provide such an infrastructure. There thus appears to be a need for the user community to take initiatives to plan, deploy, and manage such an infrastructure. Among the policy issues that should be addressed are the following:

- Exchange point managers must be open to the placement of active measurement computers at their exchange points. (In the case of private exchanges, this means that providers must be open to the placement of active measurement computers at private exchange points.)

- Managers of these measurement computers must be accountable for the security of the measurement computers and for the technical quality and lack of bias of their testing procedures.

- Very accurate time services are needed at the exchange points where measurement computers might be placed.

Policy Implications

Given the needs addressed by the IPPM effort, the level of activity in the IETF and elsewhere, and the need for high-quality tools and infrastructure, several policy implications can be noted:

- Reducing the problems that motivate the IPPM effort would help Internet users and providers. For example, when and as the provider community learns how to improve the engineering of inter-IP-cloud exchange points and inter-domain routing, problems associated with the complexity of Internet topology will be ameliorated.

• Any improvements in the technology and provisioning of the national (and international!) backbones will ameliorate problems associated with congestion.

• When and as providers learn how to exchange relevant engineering measurements with the user community and with each other, problems associated with the withholding of information will decrease.

• The work of the IETF, and specifically of the Operational Requirements Area, needs to be supported as one key way to encourage the evolution of commonly accepted and well-designed metrics.

• Funding agencies should act favorably on proposals for investigators to contribute to the IETF IPPM work on metrics and the sharing of the best IPPM-related measurement technology.

• Similarly, funding agencies should act favorably on proposals to improve IPPM-related measurement technology and tools, particularly when the resulting technology and tools would become widely available.

• Exchange point managers and agencies with Internet oversight responsibilities should encourage the deployment of high-quality time services at exchange points.

• Similarly, exchange point managers and agencies with Internet oversight responsibilities should encourage the deployment of IPPM-related measurement infrastructure at exchange points.

• Providers should welcome the deployment of IPPM-related measurement infrastructure at exchange points, while demanding accuracy and lack of bias in those performing the measurements.

• Members of the user community should take the initiative in designing, deploying, and operating the measurement infrastructure needed, while being sensitive to the needs of providers for accuracy and lack of bias.

• Members of the user community should use the results of IPPM measurements both to hold their providers accountable and to better understand the nature of the performance and reliability of the Internet they use. The result will be increased accountability and less finger-pointing.

If these recommendations are adopted, the IPPM efforts will contribute to a healthier Internet for both users and providers.

Acknowledgment

The author is solely responsible for the policy opinions expressed here. Several others, however, deserve acknowledgment for their contributions to the IPPM effort. Matt Mathis led the spring 1995 IPPM BOF; he has also provided leadership within the IPPM effort in a number of ways, including his technical work in the development of the treno and earlier wping tools. Vern Paxson provided many of the key technical ideas present in the Framework document of the IETF IPPM effort. David Wasley deserves credit for encouraging and contributing to the understanding of IPPM as valuable to higher education. Finally, I would also like to thank Scott Bradner for his helpful comments on this chapter.

Notes

1. Throughout this chapter, IP denotes the Internet Protocol, and TCP denotes the Transmission Control Protocol, two key components of the TCP/IP protocol suite.

2. This chapter was originally presented at the Harvard workshop as a paper titled "IP Provider Metrics," due to the name originally introduced in the 1995 IETF Birds of a Feather session and used for much of the time since. With the guidance of the Operational Requirements Area directors, we are now using the term "IP performance metrics" (IPPM) to stress that it is the performance of IP clouds, whether engineered by providers or users, that we aim to measure.

3. Throughout this chapter, the term "regional" denotes an IP cloud that directly connects a given campus to the Internet.

4. The primary cause of this shift from doubling every 12 months to doubling every six months is beyond the scope of this chapter, but seems to relate to growth in traffic related to the World Wide Web. Web traffic had been growing very rapidly even well before the spring 1995 transition, but it was only then that it became the dominant source of Internet traffic.

5. Though it might be regarded as outside the scope of an Internet-related IPPM effort, we note that many of the same engineering and provisioning issues are also confronted by engineers of corporate intranets.

6. ICMP denotes the Internet Control Message Protocol of the TCP/IP protocol suite. ICMP echo-reply packets are generated in response to ICMP echo-request packets.

7. GPS denotes the Global Positioning System in which a set of satellites is used to provide positioning and timing information to sites around the world.

8. An ICMP TTL-expired message is generated by a router when a packet is discarded because it has been forwarded over more hops than specified in the TTL field of the packet's IP header.

9. It should be noted that measurement machines used for active tests must be carefully designed to ensure that they cannot be reconfigured to listen to user traffic.

Cooperation in Internet Data Acquisition and Analysis

Tracie Monk and K Claffy

Introduction

The Internet is emerging from a sheltered adolescence, full of potential and growing exponentially, but still relatively ignorant of the real world. It now faces a crossroads. Citizens, corporations, and governments are waking to the opportunities presented by a truly connected global economy, and reexamining fundamental principles of intellectual property law and communications in light of the realities of cyberspace. Organizational behavior and boundaries, business practices and financial systems are also adapting to the new medium. Society is on the verge of the information revolution.

The number of North American Internet Service Providers pioneering this revolution stands at over 3,000, approximately a dozen of which qualify as national backbone providers. Internationally, the number of Internet hosts almost doubled over the year ending July 1996, reaching 12,881,000. Domains quadrupled over this period to 488,000.[1] Competition is fierce among the builders and operators of this nascent infrastructure, driven by demands for additional capacity and new customers. However, neither the industry nor the research community that developed and nurtured the early Internet are devoting significant attention to assessing the Internet's current robustness or future capacity needs.

This chapter has three parts. The first provides background on the current Internet architecture and describes why measurements are a key element in the development of a robust and financially successful commercial Internet. The second discusses the current state of Internet metrics analysis and steps under way within the Internet Engineering Task Force (IETF) and other arenas to encourage the development and deployment of Internet performance monitoring and workload characterization tools. Finally, the chapter offers a model for a cooperative association for Internet data analysis among Internet competitors.

The Current Internet: Requirements for Cooperation

No centralized authority oversees the development of the current commercial architecture of the Internet. Providers, including traditional telephone companies, Regional Bell Operating Companies (RBOCs), cable companies, and utilities, view one another as competitors and are therefore reluctant to coordinate their efforts. Yakov Rekhter, Internet researcher at Cisco Systems, notes that:

Despite all the diversity among the providers, the Internet-wide IP connectivity is realized via Internet-wide distributed routing, which involves multiple providers, and thus implies a certain degree of cooperation and coordination. Therefore, we need to balance the provider goals and objectives against the public interest of Internet-wide connectivity and subscriber choices. Further work is needed to understand how to reach the balance.[2]

Most large providers currently collect basic statistics on the performance of their own infrastructure, typically including measurements of utilization, availability, and possibly rudimentary assessments of delay and throughput. In the era of the post-NSFNET backbone service, the only baseline against which these networks can evaluate performance is their own past performance metrics. No data or even standard formats are available against which to compare performance with other networks or any other baseline. Increasingly, both users and providers need information on end-to-end performance, which is beyond the realm of what is controllable by individual networks.

The Transition

From 1986 to 1995 the National Science Foundation's NSFNET backbone served as the core of the Internet. Its decommissioning in April 1995 ushered in a new era in which commercial providers have assumed responsibility for extending Internet services to millions of existing and new users. At the same time, this change left the Internet community with no dependable public source of statistics on Internet traffic flows.[3]

The post-April 1995 architecture involved four new projects sponsored by the National Science Foundation (NSF):

1. General purpose Network Access Points (NAPs) to which commercial backbone networks would connect to avert network partitioning as the NSFNET went away.[4]

2. A routing arbiter, charged with the task of providing routing coordination in the new NSFNET architecture and promoting stability of Internet routing in a significantly fluctuating environment—including: maintaining routing policy databases and servers at the four priority NAPs (and later at the FIX West/MAE-West facility); developing advanced routing technologies, strategies, and management tools; and working with National Service Providers (NSP), ISPs, and NAP providers to resolve routing problems at the NAPs.

3. Financial support for interconnecting regional networks, with declining NSF funding to support the transition and commercialization of providers serving the U.S. higher education community.

4. Continued leading edge network research, development, and services through a cooperative agreement between NSF and MCI for the very high speed Backbone Network Services (vBNS).

In August 1996, NSF announced the next step toward full commercialization of the existing Internet, declaring the NAPs and operational services of the Routing Arbiter (RA) successful and commercially viable. NSF will phase out its support for what they distinguished as priority NAPs and the Routing Arbiter service, and remove its stipulation that regional providers procure transit from NSPs that peer at each priority NAP.

This announcement comes at a time when the number of metropolitan and regional peering points are increasing, as are the number of networks that peer or want to peer. NSPs have also begun to favor direct peering arrangements with one another outside of the NAP architecture as a more economical and technically efficient means of sharing traffic between large networks. The higher education and research sectors are also shifting their attention toward a second-generation architecture supported by high-performance connections, and expanded use of the NSF/MCI vBNS and other federally sponsored research and education networks.

The transition to the new commercial environment, with its privately operated services and cross-service provider NAP switching points, has significantly complicated statistics collection and left the Internet community without a dependable public source of statistics on Internet workloads. This most recent step in the transition, however, removes most of the government's remaining influence and increases the community's dependence on commercial providers to cooperatively manage this still fragile infrastructure. Empirical investigations of the nature of current workloads and their resource requirements, as well as how they change over time, remain a vital element in supporting the continued evolution of the Internet.

Importance of Workload Profiles for Internet Pricing and Service Qualities

The Internet still strongly needs realistic pricing models and other mechanisms to allocate and prioritize its scarce resources, particularly bandwidth. Existing pricing practices center around leased line tariffs. As providers begin to employ multiple business models (various usage-based and fixed-price schemes), they face questions about which aspects of their service to charge and how to measure them. For example, one can measure bandwidth and traffic volumes in several ways, including average port utilization, router throughput, Simple Network Management Protocol (SNMP) counters, and quotas of certain levels of priority traffic.[5]

For example, Australia's Telstra imposes tariffs only on incoming traffic in order to encourage Australia's content provision to a global market.[6] Such usage-based tariffs are less common in the U.S. market, where many believe that they would stifle the utility of a growing, thriving Internet. However, this view receives increasing scrutiny, and usage-based pricing is already the norm for Integrated Services Digital Network (ISDN) and other phone-based Internet services. Even some backbone ISPs now offer usage-based charging (albeit at a rough granularity), which often can decrease customers' bills if they typically under utilize their prescribed bandwidth. By the end of the decade, pricing models in the U.S. will likely have evolved into more refined and coherent methods. These models may include sample-based billing and measurement of traffic at the network provider boundaries, where individual providers apply alternative accounting techniques, e.g., measuring the source vs. destination of flows.[7]

U.S. providers are among the first to acknowledge the need for mechanisms to support more rational cost recovery, e.g., accurate accountability for resources consumed. The absence of these economic measures is troublesome given the ill-preparedness of the U.S. Internet architecture and providers to deal with a large aggregation of flows, particularly if a significant number of those flows are several orders of magnitude higher volume than the rest (e.g., video conferencing).

This disparity in size between most current Internet flows/ transactions and newer multimedia applications with much higher volume and duration necessitates revised metrics of network behavior. Analysis of traffic flows at the federally sponsored FIX-West facility, for example, have demonstrated averages of 15 packets per flow. As illustrated in the table and graphics below, typical cuseeme and mbone flows are exponentially higher.

It is also important to note that average or mean flow statistics may be misleading since some flows are orders of magnitude larger than the mean (a "heavy-tailed distribution"). Given this caveat, we note that the smaller mean volume of the cuseeme flows relative to that of the mbone flows is consistent with the characteristic usage of the applications. Cuseeme end-users typically connect to each other for brief point-to-point conversations (often several times trying to get it working), resulting in many flows that are short by multimedia standards. Mbone flows, in contrast, tend to represent meetings,

Table 1 Illustrative Sample Flows from FIX-West (Source: NLANR, August 30, 1996)

Application	Flows	Packets	Bytes	Seconds	Type
Web	96,482	1,443,763	821,696,977	1,091,907	Absolute
	0.302	0.330	0.595	0.193	Fraction of total
	569	14	8,516	11	Average packet size, packets/ flow, bytes/flow, du/flow
ftp-data	850	124,586	73,647,232	28,717	Absolute
	0.003	0.028	0.053	0.005	Fraction
	591	146	86,643	33	Average packet size, packets/ flow, bytes/flow, du/flow
Mbone	35	202,636	51,292,766	9,226	Absolute
[tunnel	0.000	0.046	0.037	0.002	Fraction of total
traffic]	253	5,789	1,465,507	263	Average packet size, packets/ flow, bytes/flow, du/flow
cuseeme	15	16,288	6,385,996	3,812	Absolute
	0.000	0.004	0.005	0.001	Fraction
	392	1,085	425,733	254	Average packet size, packets/ flow, bytes/ flow, du/flow

workshops, conferences, and concerts that last for hours if not days at a time. In addition, current tools only measure mbone tunnel traffic, resulting in multiple mbone sessions appearing as a single flow.

Simple mean or peak utilization figures are therefore ineffective in addressing ISP engineering needs, without also knowing the transaction profile constituting and perhaps dominating those figures. Tracking workload profiles requires measuring flow data at relevant network locations. Currently, the only significant public source of multipoint workload characterization is from the FIX-West facility and at several NSF supercomputing sites.

Figures 1–3 provide graphical depictions of three types of traffic across FIX-West. Note that the average (mean) of general Internet traffic fluctuates at around 50–80 packets per flow. Cuseeme and mbone traffic, however, show significant unpredictability and variability in their averages, ranging around 500 packets per flow and 10,000 packets per flow, respectively. (Readers can take their own samplings using available tools at: http://www.nlanr.net/NA).

Demands by Internet users for providers to implement multiple service levels are increasing. From an ISP standpoint, such offerings will allow increased revenue through alternative business quality services. From the user's perspective, the ability to contract for higher-priority service will enable many industries to switch from intranets and private networks to a lower-cost, ubiquitous Internet-based infrastructure. The ability to specify or reserve these services, however, requires development and implementation of mechanisms for accounting and pricing, which inevitably depend on reliable traffic flow data. Factors inhibiting such financial measures in the United States include the unclear dynamics of inter-ISP business mechanics. While some suggest that telecommunications sector settlements models may have relevance to ISP settlements, most industry analysts agree that the connectionless nature of the Internet Protocol (IP) demands entirely new pricing and settlement models.

Rational pricing of multiple service qualities will also provide clear feedback to providers and users on the value of Internet resources. As equipment vendors develop, and ISPs deploy, technologies that support quality signals, services should evolve to permit users to designate a service quality for which they are willing to pay, with higher demand services such as video-conferencing priced according to their value to the user.

Threat of Government Intervention

With the simultaneous diversification and usage explosion of the infrastructure, Internet Service Providers have not been in a position to provide accurate statistical models. Given the narrow profit

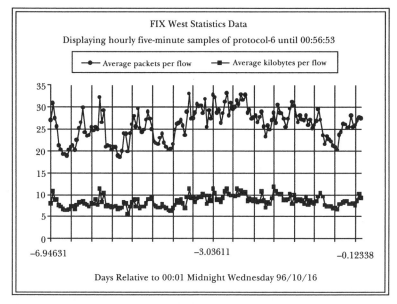

Figure 1 General Traffic Flows at FIX-West.

margins and dearth of qualified manpower in the industry, providers are reluctant to dedicate manpower or other resources to statistics collection and analysis, allocating them instead to the monumental tasks associated with accommodating service demand. Eventually, larger telecommunications companies will devote attention to this area. Unfortunately, there may not be sufficient pressure upon the NSPs until problems such as congestion and outages worsen, and either billed customers demand (and are willing to pay for) better guarantees and data integrity, or the government intercedes to dictate acceptable policies and practices for the Internet.

The telecommunications industry's experience offers a classic example of the government inserting itself and dictating cooperation among competing companies. In 1992 the Federal Communications Commission (FCC) mandated the formation of the Network Reliability Council (now the Network Reliability and Interoperability Council)[8] following a major communications outage on the East Coast. Since the Internet has only recently received attention as a critical element of the national infrastructure, it has escaped such

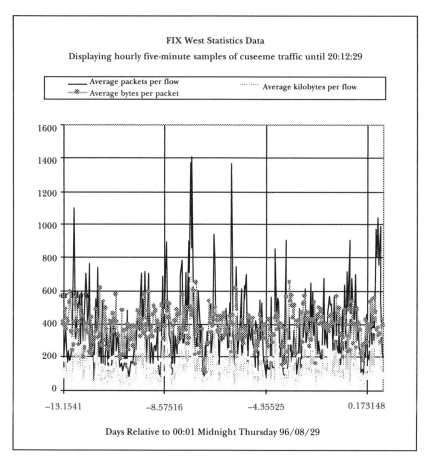

Figure 2 Cuseeme Traffic Flows at FIX-West.

intense regulatory scrutiny. As the emerging backbone of the national and global information infrastructures (NII/GII) however, this relative obscurity may be a passing luxury.

In Executive Order 13010 dated July 15, 1996, President Clinton established a Commission on Critical Infrastructure Protection, to develop "a strategy for protecting and assuring the continued operation of this nation's critical infrastructures" including telecommunications, electrical power systems, gas and oil transportation, banking and finance, transportation, water supply systems, emergency services, and continuity of government. Its mission

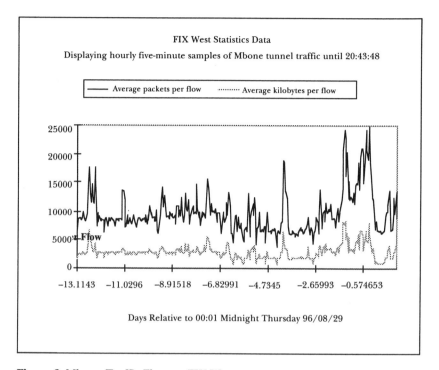

Figure 3 Mbone Traffic Flows at FIX-West.

objectives refer directly to the importance of "cyber threats," its output (due July 1997) includes proposals for "statutory or regulatory changes necessary to effect its recommendations."

Most recently, attention has focused on RBOC claims that the Internet has detrimental effects on their telephony infrastructure. While many Internet analysts contest these allegations, the FCC and the Network Reliability and Interoperability Council (NRIC) are reviewing a study sponsored by the baby Bell companies on the impacts of the Internet's growth during spring 1996 period.[9] The FCC's interest in this subject is closely tied to its review of the America's Carrier Telecommunication Association (ACTA) petition, requesting that Internet telephony be banned, and to renewed discussions surrounding the so-called modem tax.[10]

While the FCC, National Telecommunications Information Agency (NTIA), and Congress have thus far been relatively silent on regulation of the Internet, it is idealistic to assume that they will remain so. Failure of industry participants to respond to requirements for more formal mechanisms of cooperation will slow the current pace of the Internet's evolution, particularly for electronic commerce and higher-grade services. It will also increase the pressure upon governments, both U.S. and foreign, to intercede to protect these critical information resources.

Steps toward Improving Internet Measurements

"The new commercial Internet is characterized by hundreds of ISPs, many on shoestring budgets in low margin competition. They generally view statistics collection as a luxury that has never proven its operational utility. The last publicly available source of Internet workload and performance data, for the NSFNet backbone, was basically a gift from the NSF—an investment of U.S. tax dollars with the hope that tools, methodologies, theories of traffic, refinements and feedback would emerge from groups like the Internet Engineering Task Force. But there was never any fiscal pressure to justify allocating the resources required to collect statistics."—K Claffy[11]

Implications of the Transition for Data Acquisition and Analysis

The Internet architecture remains in a state of transition. The large number of commercial providers and the proliferation of cross-service provider exchange points render statistics collection a much more difficult task. In addition, the challenges inherent in Internet operation, particularly given its still best effort underlying protocol technology, fully consume the attention of ISPs. Given their absence from the list of their top priorities, data collection and analysis continue to languish.

Yet it is detailed traffic and performance measurement that has heretofore been essential to identifying the causes of network problems and ameliorating them. Trend analysis and accurate network/systems monitoring permit network managers to identify hot spots (overloaded paths), predict problems before they occur, and avoid them by efficient deployment of resources and optimization of network configurations. As the nation and world become increasingly dependent on the NII/GII, mechanisms to enable infrastructure-wide planning and analysis will be critical.

Efforts Stimulating Action by Providers

Since the advent of the World Wide Web, the proliferation of users and the lack of cooperation among commercial ISPs have resulted in significant degradation of service quality for some of the higher-end user communities. The higher education and research communities were among the first groups to depend on the Internet, and also among the most vocal in publicly acknowledging its recent inability to meet their growing expectations. Since the Educom-sponsored Monterey Conference in October 1995 focusing on academia's networking requirements, representatives of the higher education community have met repeatedly, in forums sponsored by the Federation of American Research Networks (FARNET), Educom's National Telecommunications Task Force (NTTF) and others, to assess their internetworking needs and develop plans to address them.

At an August 1996 meeting in Colorado Springs, Colorado, a post-Monterey White Paper concluded that "the commodity Internet may not evolve rapidly enough to meet higher education's imminent and foreseeable high performance enterprise networking and internetworking capacity and service needs." Participants at the meeting set goals for a second-generation Internet to support the higher education and research communities, aimed at interconnecting enterprise networks in various stages of migration to higher-performance technologies, and at controlling cost and pricing/allocation models from within the enterprise. General requirements for this Internet II include:[12]

• improved information security;

• authorization and authentication capabilities; and

• network management capabilities including performance audits.

Internet II would also have definable and measurable qualities of service, including:

• latency and jitter specifications;

• bandwidth interrogation and reservation capabilities; and

• packet delivery guarantees.

The business community is also reassessing its goals for the Internet. In October 1996, the industry-driven Cross Industry Working Team (XIWT) held two invitational workshops on Internet evolution. The first meeting focused on defining the near term requirements of major Internet user groups;[13] the second addressed implications of these and other requirements for Internet Service Providers and vendors. The latter event concentrated on developing mechanisms for Internet industry cooperation, including those related to facilitating the technical and business practices and procedures needed to improve the performance of Internet applications and services by enhancing cooperation among providers of Internet services, equipment and applications.

Other user groups that view the Internet as mission critical are moving independently to address their industries' service requirements. Most notable is the Automotive Industry Action Group (AIAG), who have selected an "overseer" to support the major automobile manufacturers and their thousands of suppliers, by:

• certifying a small number of highly competent Internet Service Providers to interconnect automotive trading partner's private networks;

• monitoring providers' ongoing compliance with performance standards;

• enforcing strict security mechanisms to authenticate users and protect data, thereby creating a virtual private network for the auto industry.

The AIAG has identified several metrics it views as critical to this initiative and future monitoring efforts. These include performance metrics such as latency, packet/cell loss, link utilization, throughput, and Border Gateway Protocol version 4 (BGP4) configuration and peering arrangements; as well as reliability metrics such as physical route diversity; routing protocol convergence times; disaster recovery plans; backbone, exchange point and access circuit availability; and replacement speed of failed customer premise equipment.[14]

Within the federal community, the National Science Foundation has been the most proactive in supporting Internet measurement research and traffic analyses.[15] However, other federal agencies are increasingly active in this critical arena. The Department of Energy, for example, has established a measurement working group and has tasked teams of high energy physics community researchers with monitoring global Internet traffic patterns and performance metrics for ESnet.[16] The Department of Defense (through the Defense Advanced Research Projects Agency and the High Performance Computing Modernization Office) hosted an ATM performance measurement workshop in June and is currently developing and deploying measurement tools such as NetSpec across its ATM networks.[17] The Federal Networking Council (FNC) is also forming a statistics/metrics cross-agency working group and has expressed support for the creation of a North American Coordinating Committee for Intercontinental Research Networking (CCIRN) statistics/metrics working group.[18]

Technical Challenges

The sections below describe some of the current and future technical challenges associated with Internet metrics and collection of statistics.

Lack of Common Definitions. There are several modest efforts under way to collect statistics across specific networks or at select peering points.[19] Unfortunately, these efforts lack a common framework and common definitions of Internet metrics, limiting the comparability of results. The IETF's Internet Provider Performance Metrics (IPPM) working group is addressing this situation via development of an IP performance metrics framework.[20] IPPM members are also developing draft Requests for Comment (RFCs) defining metrics for roundtrip and one-way delay; flow capacity; packet loss, modulus of elasticity, and connectivity/availability; and route persistence and route prevalence. Such steps toward a more strongly specified common framework will facilitate future metrics discussions.

Lack of Consensus on Traffic Modeling. There is as yet no consensus on how statistics can support research in IP traffic modeling. There is also skepticism within the Internet community regarding the utility of empirical studies: critics claim that because the environment changes so quickly, within weeks any collected data is only of historical interest. They argue that research is better served by working on mathematical models rather than by empirical surveys that capture, at most, only one stage in network traffic evolution.

However, prediction of performance metrics, e.g., queue lengths or network delays, using traditional closed-end mathematical modeling techniques such as queuing theory, have met with little success in today's Internet environment. Although the assumption of Poisson arrivals was acceptable years ago for characterizing small Local Area Networks (LANs), as a theory of wide area internetworking behavior, Poisson arrivals—in terms of packet arrivals within a connection, connection arrivals within an aggregated stream of traffic, and packet arrivals across multiple connections—have demonstrated significant inconsistency with collected data.[21]

A further contributing factor to the lag of Internet traffic modeling is the early financial structure of the Internet. A few U.S. government agencies assumed the financial burden of building and maintaining the early transit network infrastructure, leaving little need to trace network usage for the purposes of cost recovery. As a result, since the transition, Internet customers have had little leverage with their service providers regarding service quality.

Lack of Adequate Tools. Many applications in the current Internet architecture inherently depend on the availability of the infrastructure on a fairly pervasive scale. Yet Wide Area Networking (WAN) technologies and applications have advanced much faster than has the analytical and theoretical understanding of Internet traffic behavior. Devices connected to WANs are increasing at 30 to 50 percent per year, networking traffic doubling every ten to 18 months by some estimates, and vendors such as Netscape aim to release new products every six months. Overall, Internet-related companies continue to pour money into hardware, pipes, and multimedia-capable tools, with little attention to the technical limitations of the underlying infrastructure or tools to monitor this increasingly complex system.

Even the basic application level protocols of the Transmission Control Protocol/Internet Protocol (TCP/IP) suite, e.g., File Transfer Protocol (FTP) and telnet, are becoming less reliable in the face of network congestion and related infrastructure problems. Yet network managers, including both ISPs and end-users, have few tools available to effectively monitor networks (end-to-end) so as to avoid potential problems. Performance of such applications depends on many interrelated factors, including: packet loss, network end-to-end response time, number and quality of intermediate hops and the route used, link bandwidth and utilization, and end node capability. There is no suite of tools available for remotely monitoring, assessing or directly intervening to affect these conditions, particularly if the problem arises beyond an individual network's border.[22]

As traditional phone companies enter the Internet marketplace, armed with years of experience with analytic tools for modeling telephony workloads and performance, it is tempting to assume imminent remedy of the shortage of measurement tools. Unfortunately, models of telephony traffic developed by Bell Labs and others are not readily replicable for the Internet industry. Internet traffic is not only fundamentally inconsistent with traditional queuing theory since it is framed with best effort rather than deterministic service protocols, but it also exists on an infrastructural mesh of competing service providers with slim profit margins. As a result, telephony tables of acceptable blocking probability (e.g., inability to get a dial tone when you pick up the phone) suggest standards that far exceed those achievable in today's marketplace.

Emerging Technologies. Currently available tools for monitoring IP traffic (layer-three) focus on metrics such as response time and packet loss (ping), reachability (traceroute), throughput (e.g., FTP transfer rates), and some workload profiling tools (e.g., OC3mon and Cisco routers' flow statistics). These metrics are significantly more complex when applied to IP "clouds." For example, there is still no standard methodology for aggregating metrics such as loss measurement over various paths through a cloud and communicating it as a single metric for the provider.

With the transition to ATM and high-speed switches, IP layer analysis may no longer be technically feasible. Most commercial ATM equipment, for example, is not capable of accessing IP headers. In addition, the primary network access and exchange points in the United States are chartered as layer-two entities, providing services at the physical or link layer without regard for the higher layers. Because most of the NSFNET statistics reflected information at and above layer-three, the exchange points cannot use the NSFNET statistics collection architecture as a model upon which to base their own operational collection. Many newer layer-two switches, e.g., DEC gigaswitch and ATM switches, have little if any capability to perform layer-three statistics collection, or even look at traffic in the manner allowed on a broadcast medium (e.g., Fiber Distributed Data Interface (FDDI) and Ethernet), where a dedicated machine can collect statistics without interfering with packet forwarding. Statistics collection functionality in newer switches takes resources directly away from forwarding, driving customers toward switches of competing vendors who sacrifice such functionality in exchange for speed.

Table 2 identifies key uses for Internet statistics and metrics, both within individual networks and throughout the infrastructure. The characteristics of requisite tools, their likely deployment options, and the status/problems associated with their use are also identified.

In viewing this table and similar Internet measurement materials, it is helpful to distinguish between tools designed for Internet performance and reliability measurement and those meant for traffic flow characterization. While there is a dearth of tools in both areas, equipment and software designed to measure performance and network reliability are generally more readily available and easier to deploy by users and providers alike. Many of these tools treat the Internet as a black box, measuring end-to-end features such as packet loss, latency, and jitter from points originating and terminating outside individual networks. These performance and reliability tools are fundamental to evaluating and comparing alternative providers and to monitoring service qualities.

Traffic flow characterization tools, however, can yield a wealth of data on the internal dynamics of individual networks and cross-provider traffic flows. They enable network architects to better engineer and operate their networks and to better understand global traffic trends and behavior, particularly as new technologies and protocols are introduced into the global Internet infrastructure. Deployment of this type of tool must be within the networks, particularly at border routers and at peering points. Traffic flow characterization tools therefore require a much higher degree of cooperation and involvement by service providers than do performance-oriented tools.

Both types of measurement tools are critical to enhancing the overall quality and robustness of the Internet. They also contribute to our ability to ensure the continued evolution of the Internet infrastructure, both in strengthening its ability to meet the needs of its diverse user communities and maintaining its flexibility to accommodate opportunities presented by future technologies and applications.

Cooperative Association for Internet Data Analysis

The authors believe that the best means for addressing the cooperation requirements outlined in this chapter would be the formation of a provider consortium. Market pressures on ISPs to participate in such a forum include the increasing dependence of users (customers of providers) on the Internet for mission critical applications, resulting in demands for higher qualities of service and evidence of performance compliance by providers. Economic models of the Internet are also evolving and will soon include settlements based on authenticated, and likely confidential provider statistics. Finally, the meshed nature of the global Internet dictates that no single company can do it alone. Systemic improvements to the Internet infrastructure and to the operational practices of its providers will necessitate collaboration and cooperation among the competitive telecommunications firms.

An industry-driven consortium could spearhead efforts to develop cross-network outage and trouble ticket tracking; monitor congestion and relevant traffic patterns, including routing; promote studies of peering relationships and testbeds for examining emerging Internet technologies and protocols such as IP version 6, dynamic caching, bandwidth reservation protocols and QoS routing; and provide a forum for discussion and eventual implementation of charging policies.[23]

From the standpoint of statistics collection and analysis, such a forum could:

• Facilitate the identification, development and deployment of measurement tools across the Internet;

• Provide commercial providers with a neutral, confidential vehicle for data sharing and analysis;

Table 2 Internet Metrics and Tools: Illustrative Requirements, Uses and Current Status

Requirements	Description	Tool(s) Characteristics	Deployment	Status/ Problems
Internet-wide Planning (end-to-end)	•dynamic Web cache management •optimize queuing •congestion & scaling dynamics •aggregate transport behavior •capacity and topology planning	•trace-driven experiments (full headers) •flow characterization •Autonomous System (AS) traffic matrices (measures of aggregated traffic flow, route leakage, etc.)* •visualization tools	•few high aggregation exchange points •core backbone routers and multihomed networks	•tools not generally available •ISPs reluctant to report •routers do not support •complicated by trend toward private peering •switches cannot "sniff" data; requires tools on every port
Network Planning (ISP-specific)	•dynamic Web cache management •optimize queuing •congestion & scaling dynamics •aggregate transport behavior •capacity and topology planning	•trace-driven experiments (full headers) •flow characterization •Autonomous System (AS) traffic matrices (measures of aggregated traffic flow, route leakage, etc.)* •visualization tools	•beacons strategically located throughout backbone	•requires availability of better tools, education as to their importance and use, and standard interpretation of their use
Internet-wide Management (end-to-end)	•outage reporting (host unreachable) •trouble ticket tracking	•various database implementations and automated probe measurement and reporting	•individual networks reporting to centralized authority	•low economic incentives •ISPs reluctant to report
Testing New Applications/ Protocols	•IP version 6, bandwidth reservation, Quality of Service (QoS), caching, multicast, directory services	•interoperability tracking across ISPs	•few high aggregation peering points •internal/ border routers	•low economic incentives

Cooperation in Internet Data Acquisition

Benchmarking Routers and Switches	•performance, reliability and interoperability	•traffic generators, monitors, analyzers	•peering points •internal and backbone routers	•no current mechanisms for standardized field testing
Performance Monitoring: reliability, availability, serviceability	•evaluating ISP performance, e.g., latency, loss, throughput •route stability/ flapping/ reachability	•Mathis's treno; Paxson's probe daemon; ping •route (BGP) tables	•exchange points •connection of multi-homed networks •border routers •uncongested customer sites •network beacons •Routing Arbiter (RA) servers	•no validated standard metrics •no comparability among provider statistics •current tools too invasive •limited statistics on capabilities in routers: none in switches; most ISPs not using RA Database
Database Performance Monitoring: Quality of Service and Settlements	•required for billing user/ customers	•required for transit and related agreements	•measures of usage, i.e., router or access server statistics, header sampling, flow meters •exchange points and routers	•no validated standard metrics or agreements •no auditing capabilities for users

*Router vendors are in no position to support the collection of traffic matrices despite the general perception that aggregate traffic matrices are crucial to backbone topology engineering. In addition to allowing the discovery of mistraffic, e.g, route leakage or a customer accidentally sending huge amounts of unintended traffic into the core, traffic matrices combined with route flap data are essential to an ISP's ability to communicate problems to peer ISPs when necessary. Backbone engineers consider traffic matrix data significantly more important than flow data for short- to medium-term engineering, and they may be essential to the investigation of major Internet issues (e.g., routing, addressing) as well.

While telephone companies have long measured traffic matrices for phone network engineering, ISPs have had technical, legal, and resource limitations as obstacles to collecting, not to mention sharing, such measurements. Collecting packet headers, though essential for researchers to develop realistic models and analysis techniques, is even more technically and logistically problematic.

• Provide networking researchers and the general Internet community with reliable data on Internet traffic flow patterns; and

• Enhance communications among commercial Internet Service Providers, exchange/peering point providers, and the broader Internet community.

Business Constraints on Cooperation

The business constraints hindering such cooperation relate to the competitive nature of the Internet business environment, and the appearance of industry collusion by major providers. However, a charter with principles of openness and inclusion can readily address these concerns, as well as constraints arising from the lack of adequate pricing models and other mechanisms for economic rationality in Internet business practices.

Probably the most relevant constraint to cooperation is data privacy, which has always been a serious issue in network traffic analysis. Many ISPs have service agreements prohibiting them from revealing information about individual customer traffic. Collecting and using more than aggregate traffic counts often requires customer cooperation regarding what to collect and how to use it. However, provisions of the Omnibus Crime Control and Safe Streets Act of 1968, Section 2511(2)(a)(i) accord communications providers considerable protection from litigation:

It shall not be unlawful under this chapter for an operator of a switchboard, or an officer, employee, or agent of a provider of wire or electronic communication service, whose facilities are used in the transmission of a wire communication, to intercept, disclose, or use that communication in the normal course of his employment while engaged in any activity which is a necessary incident to the rendition of his service or to the protection of the rights of property of the provider of that service, except that a provider of wire communication service to the public shall not utilize service observing or random monitoring except for mechanical or service quality control checks.

Responsible providers could go further than the law and anonymize monitored traffic with tools such as tcpdpriv, virtually eliminating any accusations of breach of privacy.[24]

Technical Constraints on Cooperation

Technology constraints hindering the collection and analysis of data on Internet metrics center on the nascent development stage of IP and ATM measurement tools and supporting analysis technologies, and on complications arising from adoption of new and emerging technologies, e.g., gigaswitches and ATM. Generally, we view these and other technical constraints as solvable given sufficient technical attention and market pressure.

Next Steps

Despite the business and technical challenges, requirements for cooperation among Internet providers will continue to grow, as will demands for enhanced data collection, analysis, and dissemination. The development of an effective provider consortium to address these needs would require, minimally:

• participation by three or more of the major service providers, e.g., ANS, AT&T, BBN Planet, MCI, Netcom, PSI, Sprint, or UUNet;

• participation by a neutral third party with sufficient technical skills to provide the core data collection and analysis capabilities required by the consortium;

• appropriate privacy agreements to protect the interests of members;

• agreement on which basic metrics to collect, collate, analyze, and present (assuming differences in the granualarities of data available to consortium members vs. approved researchers vs. the general public); and

• agreement on the tools to develop, particularly those related to emerging infrastructures using new technologies.

A consortium organization could also make available a solid, consistent library of tools that would appeal to both users and providers. Data collection by the consortium should strictly focus on engineering and evolution of the overall Internet environment, e.g., accurate data on traffic patterns that could enhance engineers' ability to design efficient architectures, conserving staff and other resources currently devoted to this task. The right statistics collection and cross-ISP dissemination mechanisms would also facilitate faster problem resolution, saving the time and money now devoted to tracking problems (e.g., route leakage, link saturation and route flapping). Finally, experience with data will foster the development of more effective usage-based economic models, which in turn will allow ISPs to upgrade their infrastructure in accordance with evolving customer demands.

Developing the appropriate metrics and tools to measure traffic phenomena, as well as end-to-end performance and workflow characteristics, remains a daunting task. Other areas where resources are needed to improve the Internet infrastructure include:

• development of more powerful routers for core Internet components, a prohibitively expensive endeavor with too small a potential market and thus too little return to motivate vendors to pursue independently;

• sponsorship of short-term research into basic traffic engineering methodologies given limited data, and longer term research into the implications of realistic theoretical and empirical traffic characterization; and

• development of a public measurement infrastructure.[25]

The opinions in this chapter are those of the authors and do not necessarily reflect the views of any organizations with which the authors are affiliated.

Notes

1. Information on Network Wizard's Internet Domain Name Survey, July 1996 is available at <http://www.nw.com/zone/WWW/report.html>.

2. From Yakov Rekhter, Routing in a Multi-Provider Internet, Internet Request for Comment Series, RFC 1787, April 1995.

3. "The NSFnet Backbone Service: Chronicling the End of an Era" by Susan R. Harris, Ph.D., and Elise Gerich, in ConneXions, 10 (4) (April 1996), provides a good overview of the NSFNET 1989–1995; see <http://www.merit.edu/nsfnet/.retire.html>. During this period, Merit collected statistics on the Internet's traffic. These statistics are available at: <http://www.merit.net/nsfnet/statistics/>.

4. See CerfNet's map of key Network Service Provider Interconnections and Exchange Points at <http://www.cerf.net/cerfnet/about/interconnects.html>.

5. "Mitigating the Coming Internet Crunch: Multiple Service Levels via Precedence" by R. Bohn, H.-W. Braun, K. Claffy, and S. Wolff (1994) proposes three components of a short-term solution. First, network routers would queue incoming packets by IP precedence value instead of the customary single-threaded First-In-First-Out (FIFO). Second, users and their applications would use different and appropriate precedence values in their outgoing transmissions according to some defined criteria. Third, Network Service Providers could monitor the precedence levels of traffic entering their networks, and use some mechanism such as a quota system to discourage users from setting high precedence values on all their traffic. All three elements can be implemented gradually and selectively across the Internet infrastructure, providing a smooth transition path from the present system. The experience we gain from implementation will furthermore provide a valuable knowledge base from which to develop sound accounting and billing mechanisms and policies in the future. The paper is available at <http://www.nlanr.net/Papers/mcic.html>.

6. An excellent summary of pricing practices and policies in OECD countries is in the OECD report: *Information Infrastructure Convergence and Pricing: The Internet* (January 1996) at <http://www.oecd.org/dsti/gd_docs/s96_xx e.html>. Hal Varian's Web site at <http://www.sims.berkeley.edu/resources/infoecon> provides a useful introduction to Internet economics.

7. In his recent Internet draft RFC, on metrics for Internet settlements, Brian Carpenter of CERN asserts that financial settlements are a "critical mechanism for exerting pressure on providers to strengthen their infrastructures." He suggests that metrics used in Internet settlements should not rely on expensive instrumentation such as detailed flow analysis, but on simple measurements, estimated, if necessary, by statistical sampling. See the Internet draft at <ftp://ds.internic.net/internet-drafts/draft-carpenter-metrics-00.txt>.

8. Additional information on the Network Reliability and Interoperability Council is available at <http://www.fcc.gov/oet/nric and http://www.fcc.gov/oet/info/standards/nrc/fg1/>. The electric industry's power grid network has many similarities to that of the connectionless IP network. For information on the North American Electric Reliability Council (NERC), see <http://galaxy.tradewave.com/galaxy/Business-and-Commerce/General-Products-and-Services/Energy/Electric-and-Gas-Utilities/North-American-Electric-Reliability-Council–NERC.html>.

9. See <http://ba.com/ea/fcc>.

10. See <http://www.fcc.gov/ccb.html>.

11. From K. Claffy, "Closing the Internet Statistics Gap," in *TeleGeography 1996/97: Global Telecommunications Traffic Statistics & Commentary*.

12. On August 8–9, 1996, FARNET, with support from the Resource Allocation Committee, Educom's NTTF, the Coalition for Networked Information,

NYSERNet, Advanced Network and Services (ANS) and NSF, convened a workshop at Cheyenne Mountain in Colorado Springs, Colorado. Workshop attendees included leaders in networking from the higher education community, industry and government. The workshop sought to continue previous steps to articulate higher education's networking needs and requirements for the rest of this century and beyond. Details on this meeting are available at: <http://www.farnet.org/cheyenne/>. For additional information on FARNET and Educom's National Telecommunications Task Force, see their Web sites at <http://www.farnet.org> and <http://www.educom.edu>.

13. On October 8–9, 1996, the Cross-Industry Working Team (XIWT) sponsored an invitational meeting on Internet Performance and Service Quality for representatives of the higher education/research community; government; and the manufacturing, publishing, finance, and content provision sectors. The goal of the meeting was to identify key Internet metrics and services that a broad cross-section of users would like addressed by Internet service providers (ISPs) and the user community. The participants concluded that the ISP industry should work cooperatively, both with other ISPs in an industry-driven forum and with independent user-driven initiatives, to develop, measure, and share metrics and related information in order to continue the growth and maturation of the Internet and to improve its performance. The results of this meeting were communicated at a follow-on invitational meeting with Internet Service Providers on October 10, 1996. For more information on this meeting, see <http://WWW.CNRI.Reston.VA.US:3000/XIWT/documents/Workshop_Notes/IperfUserReqs.html>.

14. Information on the automotive industry's telecommunications initiatives is available at the Automotive Industry Action Group's (AIAG) Telecommunications working group page: <http://www.aiag.org/summaries/telecomm.html>. Robert Moskowitz of Chrysler also described some of these activities at NLANR's ISMA workshop in February 1996. His remarks can be found at <http://www.nlanr.net/ISMA/Positions/moskowitz.html>.

15. NSF has supported several recent projects and events related to Internet traffic analysis. NLANR efforts include:

- the Internet Statistics and Metrics Analysis (ISMA) workshop (February 1996): <http://www.nlanr.net/ISMA>;

- traffic measurements at the FIX West facility and across the vBNS: <http://www.nlanr.net/NA>;

- visualizations of caching traffic and mbone topologies, as well as BGP peering relationships among autonomous systems: <http://www.nlanr.net/INFO>;

- development of software using modified pings to assess end-to-end performance: <http://www.nlanr.net/Viz/End2end>; and

- summaries of available provider and NAP statistics: <http://www.nlanr.net/INFO> and other sources of relevant statistics/metrics information.

The NSF-supported Routing Arbiter project collects network statistics at the Ameritech, MAE-East, MAE-West, PacBell, and Sprint interconnection points. The Merit/ISI RA Web page <http://www.ra.net/statistics/> is a launching point from which to view both graphical and text representations of routing instabilities, NAP statistics, trends, etc. Merit also maintains links to several ISP- and user-oriented measurement tools at: <http://www.ra.net/tools/>.

16. The Department of Energy's ESnet established a "State of the Internet" working group in May 1996. The working group and ESnet's Network Monitoring Task Force (NMTF) are working with other organizations to implement enhanced Wide Area Networking (WAN) statistics collection/analysis throughout its network and the global high energy physics community.

17. In June 1996, the University of Kansas hosted an ATM performance workshop. The workshop sought to exchange ideas on ATM WAN measurement tools and techniques, discuss ATM WAN experiments to establish today's performance limits, identify the factors that affect performance, and to identify first-order opportunities for improving network performance. Its focus was on "solid engineering techniques for measurements, concise analysis of measurements that have been taken, improvements made, and proposals for what should be done in the near future to further enhance performance." Papers presented at this meeting are available at <http://www.tisl.ukans.edu/Workshops/ATM_Performance/>.

18. The Coordinating Committee for Intercontinental Research Networking (CCIRN) is setting up a working group on Internet statistics and metrics. Europe's TERENA, Asia's Asia-Pacific Networking Group (APNG), and the US Federal Networking Council (see <http://www.fnc.gov>) have the responsibility to establish similar working groups for their continents. CCIRN anticipates that participation in these groups will include representatives from commercial, research, and government sectors.

19. See <http://www.nlanr.net/INFO>.

20. See this Internet draft RFC and other IP Performance Metrics materials at <http://www.advanced.org/IPPM>.

21. Although Internet traffic does not exhibit Poisson arrivals, the cornerstones of telephony modeling, a number of researchers have measured a consistent thread of self-similarity in Internet traffic. Several metrics of network traffic have heavy-tailed distributions, including: call holding times (CCSN/SS7) (telephone call holding times); telnet packet interarrivals; FTP burst size upper tail; and transmission times of World Wide Web (WWW) files.

Recent theorems have shown that aggregating traffic sources with heavy-tailed distributions leads directly to (asymptotic) self-similarity. In an article for *Statistical Science* (1994), W. Willinger identified three minimal parameters for a self-similar model: (1) the Hurst (H) parameter, which reflects how the time correlations scale with the measurement interval; (2) variance of the arrival process; and (3) mean of the arrival process.

Although self-similarity is a parsimonious concept, it comes in many different colors, and we only now are beginning to understand what causes it. Self-similarity implies that a given correlational structure is retained over a wide range of time scales. It can derive from the aggregation of many individual, albeit highly variable, on/off components. The bad news about self-similarity is that it is a significantly different paradigm that requires new tools for dealing with traffic measurement and management. Load service curves (e.g., delay vs. utilization) of classical queuing theory are inadequate; for self-similar traffic, even metrics of means and variances indicate little unless accompanied by details of the correlational structure of the traffic. In particular, self-similarity typically predicts queue lengths much higher than do classical Poisson models. Researchers have analyzed samples and found fractal components of behavior in a wide variety of network traffic (SS7, ISDN, Ethernet and FDDI LANs, backbone access points, and ATM).

Still unexplored is the underlying physics that could give rise to self-similarity at different time scales. That is, at millisecond time scales, link layer characteristics (i.e., transmission time on media) would dominate the arrival process profile, while at the 1–10 second time scales the effects of the transport layer would likely dominate. Queueing characteristics might dominate a range of time scales in between, but in any case the implication that several different physical networking phenomena manifest themselves with self-similar characteristics merits further investigations into these components.

22. See Les Cottrell and Connie Logg, "Network Monitoring for the LAN and WAN," paper presented at Oak Ridge National Lab (ORNL), June 24, 1996, available at <http://www.slac.stanford.edu/~cottrell/tcom/ornl.htm>.

23. The number of forums representing the Internet industry's service providers, vendors, content developers and others is growing rapidly. Several of the established groups are listed below. We do not imply that any of these organizations possess the mandate or capacity to facilitate the types of technical and engineering collaborations we describe in this chapter.

- Canadian Association of Internet Providers (CAIP): <http://www.caip.ca>
- Commercial Internet eXchange (CIX): <http://www.cix.org>
- CommerceNet: <http://www.commerce.net>
- Cross Industry Working Team (XIWT): <http://www.xiwt.org>
- Internet Society (ISOC): <http://www.isoc.org>
- ISP Consortium: <http://www.ispc.org>
- North American Network Operators Group (NANOG): <http://www.merit.edu/routing.arbiter/NANOG/NANOG.html>
- Reseaux IP Europens (RIPE): <http://www.ripe.net/>
- World Internet Alliance (WIA): <http://www.wia.org/>

24. Developed by Greg Minshall of Ipsilon, tcpdpriv takes packets captured by tcpdump and removes or scrambles data—e.g., source and destination hosts and ports—within the packet to protect privacy.

25. For additional information on the topics presented in this chapter, see: "A Survey of Internet Statistics / Metrics Activities," T. Monk and K. Claffy at: <http://www.nlanr.net/metricsurvey.html> and K. Claffy, "Closing the Internet Statistics Gap," in *TeleGeography 1996/97: Global Telecommunications Traffic Statistics & Commentary* and it's Web version entitled "but some data is worse than others: measurement of the global Internet," K. Claffy at <http://www.nlanr.net/zachary.html>.

Contributors

Guy T. Almes (almes@advanced.org) is Vice President for Network Development at Advanced Network & Services. His work there includes developing technology and infrastructure for the IPPM project and leading the engineering effort of the Internet2 project. He has served on the Computer Science faculty of the University of Washington and Rice University.

Ashley Andeen (aandeen@ics.uci.edu) is a graduate student at the University of California at Irvine in the Information and Computer Science department.

Joseph P. Bailey (bailey@rpcp.mit.edu) is a doctoral candidate in the MIT Technology, Management and Policy Program and a research assistant with the MIT Research Program on Communications Policy (http://rpcp.mit.edu), Center for Technology, Policy, and Industrial Development.

Steven M. Bellovin (smb@research.att.com), one of the originators of netnews, is a researcher on network security issues at AT&T Labs and a member of the Internet Architecture Board.

Scott Bradner (sob@harvard.edu) is a Senior Technical Consultant at the Harvard University Office of the Provost. He has been involved in the design, operation, and use of data networks at Harvard since the early days of the ARPANET. He is also the codirector of the Operational Requirements Area in the IETF, an IESG member, and an elected trustee of the Internet Society, where he serves as the Vice President for Standards.

Richard A. Cawley (rca@dg13.cec.be) is Principal Official at the General Directorate for Telecommunications and the Information Market (http://www.ispo.cec.be) of the European Commission.

Che-hoo Cheng (chcheng@cuhk.edu.hk) is Head of the Data Communications and Networking Section of the Computer Services Center at the Chinese University of Hong Kong (http://www.cuhk.edu.hk/). He is in charge of the university's campus network and also the Hong Kong Internet eXchange (http://www.hkix.net/).

Bilal Chinoy (bac@sdsc.edu) is a Staff Scientist at the San Diego Supercomputer Center (SDSC), where he directs and conducts research in high-speed, multimedia and collaborative computer networking. He is the co-Principal Investigator for the NSF-sponsored Network Access Point (NAP), operated by Sprint Inc.

K Claffy (kc@nlanr.net) is an Associate Research Scientist at the University of California, San Diego, and co-Principal Investigator for NSF's National Laboratory for Applied Network Research (NLANR: http://www.nlanr.net). She is active in the development of new traffic measurement and visualization tools and is instrumental in the creation of the new Cooperative Association for Internet Data and Analysis (CAIDA: http://www.nlanr.net/Caida).

Maria Farnon (mfarnon@ALPHA1.RESTON.MCI.NET) works in Internet Marketing at MCI Telecommunications <http://www.mci.com>. She holds a Master's Degree in Law and Diplomacy from the Fletcher School, where she focused on international communications and business.

William A. Foster (wfoster@BPA.arizona.edu) tracks governance issues for the Commercial Internet Exchange Association (CIX), a worldwide trade association of Internet Service Providers (ISPs). He is also a Graduate Research Assistant with the Mosaic Group at the University of Arizona, where he is pursuing a degree in international information systems.

Alexander Gigante (75061.3624@compuserve.com) is an attorney practicing in New York City. A former general counsel of Simon & Schuster, he specializes in intellectual property matters, representing major publishers and Internet-related companies.

Sharon Eisner Gillett (sharoneg@victory-research.com) is a Research Affiliate with the Center for Coordination Science at MIT's Sloan School of Management (http://ccs.mit.edu) and the principal of Victory Research, a consultancy focusing on the telecommunications underpinnings of the Internet. She is the author of "Connecting Homes to the Internet: An Engineering Cost Model of Cable vs. ISDN" (http://www.tns.lcs.mit.edu/publications/mitlcstr654.html).

Mark Gould (Mark.Gould@bris.ac.uk) is a Lecturer in the Law Department at the University of Bristol (http://www.bris.ac.uk/Depts/Law/). He also chairs the Internet Group of the British and Irish Legal Education Technology Association (http://www.law.warwick.ac.uk/html/bileta_home_page.html).

Eric Hoffman (hoffman@caida.org) is a network researcher who focuses on IP and ATM network architecture. He is currently working at the Cooperative Association for Internet Data Analysis (CAIDA) on network measurement and visualization.

Scott Huddle (huddle@mci.net) is a network engineer at MCI's Internet Engineering department.

Joseph Y. Hui (jhui@ie.cuhk.edu.hk) is Professor of Electrical and Computer Engineering at Rutgers and Professor of Information Engineering at the Chinese University of Hong Kong. His current research interests include multimedia networks, coding and information theory, wireless information networks, and switching, protocol, traffic, and security issues for integrated broadband networks.

David R. Johnson (david.johnson@counsel.com) is Chairman of Counsel Connect, the online meetingplace for the legal profession, and a Co-Director of the Cyberspace Law Institute. He previously practiced computer law as a partner of Wilmer, Cutler and Pickering.

Brian Kahin (kahin@harvard.edu) is an Adjunct Lecturer in Public Policy, and Director of the Information Infrastructure Project in the Science, Technology, and Public Policy Program at the John. F. Kennedy School of Government, Harvard University (http://ksgwww.harvard.edu/iip). He is also General Counsel for the Annapolis-based Interactive Multimedia Association.

Mitchell Kapor (mkapor@kei.com) founded Lotus Development Corporation and co-founded the Electronic Frontier Foundation. He is currently Adjunct Professor in the Media Arts and Sciences program at the Massachusetts Institute of Technology.

James Keller (jkeller@harvard.edu) is Associate Director of the Information Infrastructure Project at Harvard University.

John Leslie King (king@dixie.ics.uci.edu) is Professor of Information and Computer Science at the University of California at Irvine.

Lee W. McKnight (mcknight@rpcp.mit.edu) is Lecturer in Technology and Policy, Principal Research Associate with the Research Program on Communications Policy (http://rpcp.mit.edu), and Principal Investigator of the Internet Telephony Interoperability Consortium at the MIT Center for Technology, Policy, and Industrial Development.

Don Mitchell (dmitchel@nsf.gov) has been in the NSF's Division for Networking and Communications Research and Infrastructure (NCRI) since 1987 (http://www.cise.nsf.gov/ncri/Donhome.html). His involvement with Internet registration issues began in 1990, when he became the NSF liaison when NCRI was funding "internet" (nonmilitary) registration through DoD awards and is the NSF program official for the InterNIC project.

Tracie Monk (tmonk@nlanr.net) is Director, External Affairs—CAIDA (http://www.nlanr.net/Caida), and program coordinator for NSF's National Laboratory for Applied Network Research (NLANR: http://www.nlanr.net) at the University of California, San Diego. Prior to joining UCSD, she was a senior manager at DynCorp, supporting the Federal Networking Council.

Milton Mueller (milton@scils.rutgers.edu) is Assistant Professor of Communication at the Rutgers School of Communication, Information, and Library Studies and Visiting Scholar at the Hong Kong University of Science and Technology. He has written three monographs on telecommunications policy in Hong Kong and China.

Carl Oppedahl (carl@oppedahl.com) is a partner in the intellectual property firm of Oppedahl & Larson (http://www.patents.com).

David G. Post (postd@erols.com) is Visiting Associate Professor of Law at Georgetown University Law Center and Co-Director of the Cyberspace Law Institute (http://www.cli.org).

Yakov Rekhter (yakov@cisco.com) is a Technical Leader at Cisco Systems. He was one of the architects, and a major software developer, for the Phase II NSFNET Backbone. He is also one of the leading designers of the Border Gateway Protocol.

Paul Resnick (presnick@research.att.com) leads the Public Policy Research group at AT&T Labs. The group's mission is to make it safe, fun, and profitable for people to interact with strangers.

A. M. Rutkowski (amr@netmagic.com) is Vice-President for Internet Business Development at General Magic, Inc., a mobile agent and personal communicator software developer. He is responsible for developing the company's Internet-related business strategies, opportunities, product positioning, and Federal Systems division (http://www.chaos.com/rutkowski.html).

Timothy J. Salo (salo@msc.edu) is Director of Networks at the Minnesota Supercomputer Center, Inc. He is the Principal Investigator for MSCI's portion of the ARPA-funded MAGIC Gigabit Testbed (http://www.msci.magic.net) and an Additional Principal Investigator for the NSF-funded Sprint Network Access Point (NAP) project. His major area of interest is the integration of wide-area ATM networks into large, public IP internets.

Philip L. Sbarbaro (phils@netsol.com) is Outside General Counsel of Network Solutions, Inc., and a partner in the Washington, D.C., firm of Hanson and Molloy. He has overseen and been involved with 18 of the 20 suits brought against NSI by various trademark owners and Internet domain name holders around the world.

Robert Shaw (shaw@itu.int) is an Advisor on Global Information Infrastructure (GII) issues at the International Telecommunications Union (ITU) in Geneva, Switzerland, an international treaty organization specializing in global telecommunications coordination and development.

Index